CERTIFICATE.

I certify that this Edition of the Book of Common Prayer has been compared with a certified copy of the Standard Book, as the Canon directs, and that it conforms thereto.

SAMUEL HART,
Custodian of the Standard Book of Common Prayer.

December 8, 1892.

THE

BOOK OF COMMON PRAYER

And Administration of the Sacraments and other Rites and Ceremonies of the Church

ACCORDING TO THE USE OF

THE PROTESTANT EPISCOPAL CHURCH
IN THE UNITED STATES OF AMERICA

TOGETHER WITH

The Psalter or Psalms of David

Oxford
PRINTED AT THE UNIVERSITY PRESS
NEW YORK: HENRY FROWDE
91 & 93, FIFTH AVENUE

TABLE OF CONTENTS.

THE RATIFICATION

OF THE

BOOK OF COMMON PRAYER.

❦

By the Bishops, the Clergy, and the Laity of the Protestant Episcopal Church in the United States of America, in Convention, this Sixteenth Day of October, in the Year of our Lord one thousand seven hundred and eighty-nine.

This Convention having, in their present session, set forth *A Book of Common Prayer, and Administration of the Sacraments, and other Rites and Ceremonies of the Church,* do hereby establish the said Book: And they declare it to be the Liturgy of this Church: And require that it be received as such by all the members of the same: And this Book shall be in use from and after the First Day of October, in the Year of our Lord one thousand seven hundred and ninety.

PREFACE.

✦

IT is a most invaluable part of that blessed *liberty where-with* CHRIST *hath made us free*, that in his worship different forms and usages may without offence be allowed, provided the substance of the Faith be kept entire; and that, in every Church, what cannot be clearly determined to belong to Doctrine must be referred to Discipline; and therefore, by common consent and authority, may be altered, abridged, enlarged, amended, or otherwise disposed of, as may seem most convenient for the edification of the people, "according to the various exigencies of times and occasions."

The *Church of England*, to which the Protestant Episcopal Church in these States is indebted, under GOD, for her first foundation and a long continuance of nursing care and protection, hath, in the Preface of her Book of Common Prayer, laid it down as a rule, that "The particular forms of Divine Worship, and the Rites and Ceremonies appointed to be used therein, being things in their own nature indifferent and alterable, and so acknowledged, it is but reasonable that upon weighty and important considerations, according to the various exigencies of times and occasions, such changes and alterations should be made therein, as to those who are in place of authority should, from time to time, seem either necessary or expedient."

The same Church hath not only in her Preface, but likewise in her Articles and Homilies, declared the necessity and expediency of occasional alterations and amendments in her Forms of Public Worship; and we find accordingly, that, seeking to "keep the happy mean between too much stiffness in refusing, and too much easiness in admitting variations in things once advisedly established, she hath, in the reign of several Princes, since the first compiling of her Liturgy in the time of Edward the Sixth, upon just and weighty considerations her thereunto moving, yielded to make such alterations in some particulars, as in their respective times were thought convenient; yet so as that the main body and essential parts of the same (as well in the chiefest materials, as in the frame and order thereof) have still been continued firm and unshaken."

Her general aim in these different reviews and alterations hath been, as she further declares in her said Preface, "to do that which, according to her best understanding, might most tend to the preservation of peace and unity in the Church; the procuring of reverence, and the exciting of piety and devotion in the worship of GOD; and, finally, the cutting off occasion, from them that seek occasion, of cavil or quarrel against her Liturgy." And although, according to her judgment, there be not "anything in it contrary to the Word of GOD, or to sound doctrine, or which a godly man may not with a good conscience use and submit unto, or which is not fairly defensible, if allowed such just and favourable construction as in common equity ought to be allowed to all human writings"; yet upon the principles already laid down, it cannot but be supposed that further alterations would in time be found expedient. Accordingly, a commission for a review was issued in the year 1689: but this great and good work miscarried at that time; and the Civil Authority has not since thought proper to revive it by any new commission.

But when in the course of Divine Providence, these American States became independent with respect to civil government, their ecclesiastical independence was necessarily included; and the different religious denominations of Christians in these States were left at full and equal liberty to model and organize their respective Churches, and forms of worship, and discipline, in such manner as they might judge most convenient for their future prosperity; consistently with the constitution and laws of their country.

The attention of this Church was in the first place drawn to those alterations in the Liturgy which became necessary in the prayers for our Civil Rulers, in consequence of the Revolution. And the principal care herein was to make them conformable to what ought to be the proper end of all such prayers, namely, that "Rulers may have grace, wisdom, and understanding to execute justice, and to maintain truth": and that the people "may lead quiet and peaceable lives, in all godliness and honesty."

PREFACE.

But while these alterations were in review before the *Convention*, they could not but, with gratitude to GOD, embrace the happy occasion which was offered to them (uninfluenced and unrestrained by any worldly authority whatsoever) to take a further review of the Public Service, and to establish such other alterations and amendments therein as might be deemed expedient.

It seems unnecessary to enumerate all the different alterations and amendments. They will appear, and it is to be hoped, the reasons of them also, upon a comparison of this with the Book of Common Prayer of the Church of England. In which it will also appear that this Church is far from intending to depart from the Church of England in any essential point of doctrine, discipline, or worship; or further than local circumstances require.

And now, this important work being brought to a conclusion, it is hoped the whole will be received and examined by every true member of our Church, and every sincere Christian, with a meek, candid, and charitable frame of mind; without prejudice or prepossessions; seriously considering what Christianity is, and what the truths of the Gospel are; and earnestly beseeching Almighty GOD to accompany with his blessing every endeavour for promulgating them to mankind in the clearest, plainest, most affecting and majestic manner, for the sake of JESUS CHRIST, our blessed Lord and Saviour.

CONCERNING THE SERVICE OF THE CHURCH.

THE Order for Morning Prayer, the Litany, and the Order for the Administration of the Lord's Supper or Holy Communion, are distinct Services, and may be used either separately or together; *Provided*, that no one of these Services be habitually disused.

The Litany may be used either in place of the Prayers that follow the *Prayer for The President of the United States* in the Order for Morning Prayer, or in place of the Prayers that follow the *Collect for Aid against Perils* in the Order for Evening Prayer.

On any day when Morning and Evening Prayer shall have been said or are to be said in Church, the Minister may, at any other Service for which no form is provided, use such devotions as he shall at his discretion select from this Book, subject to the direction of the Ordinary.

For Days of Fasting and Thanksgiving, appointed by the Civil or by the Ecclesiastical Authority, and for other special occasions for which no Service or Prayer hath been provided in this Book, the Bishop may set forth such Form or Forms as he shall think fit, in which case none other shall be used.

THE ORDER
HOW THE PSALTER IS APPOINTED TO BE READ.

THE Psalter shall be read through once every month, as it is there appointed, both for Morning and for Evening Prayer. And when a month hath one-and-thirty days, it is ordered that the same Psalms shall be read on the last day of the said month which are appointed for the day before.

The Minister shall, on the days for which they are appointed, use the Proper Psalms, as set forth in the Table of Proper Psalms. But *Note*, That, on other days, instead of reading from the Psalter as divided for Daily Morning and Evening Prayer, he may read one of the Selections set out by this Church.

TABLE OF PROPER PSALMS ON CERTAIN DAYS.

First Sunday in Advent.	Morning. 8, 50	Evening. 96, 97	Easter-even.	Morning. 4, 16, 17	Evening. 30, 31
Christmas-day.	19,45, 85	89, 110, 132	Easter-day.	2, 57,111	113,114,118
Circumcision.	40, 90	65, 103	Ascension-day.	8, 15, 21	24, 47, 108
Epiphany.	46, 47, 48	72, 117, 135	Whitsunday.	48, 68	104, 145
Purification.	20, 86,87	84, 113, 101	Trinity-Sunday.	29, 33	93, 97, 150
Ash-Wednesday.	6, 32, 38	102,130,143	Transfiguration.	27, 61,93	84, 99, 133
Annunciation.	89	131,132,138	St. Michael's.	91, 103	34, 148
Good Friday.	22, 40,54	69, 88	All Saints' Day.	1, 15,146	112,121,149

TABLE OF SELECTIONS OF PSALMS.

First.	Psalms. 1, 15, 91	Eleventh.	Psalms. 80, 81
Second.	4, 31 to v. 7, 91, 134	Twelfth.	84, 122, 131
Third.	19, 24, 103	Thirteenth.	85, 93, 97
Fourth.	23, 34, 65	Fourteenth.	102
Fifth.	26, 43, 141	Fifteenth.	107
Sixth.	32, 130, 121	Sixteenth.	118
Seventh.	37	Seventeenth.	123, 124, 125
Eighth.	51, 42	Eighteenth.	139, 145
Ninth.	72, 93	Nineteenth.	147
Tenth.	77	Twentieth.	148, 149, 150

THE ORDER
HOW THE REST OF THE HOLY SCRIPTURE
IS APPOINTED TO BE READ.

THE Old Testament is appointed for the First Lessons, and the New Testament for the Second Lessons, at Morning and Evening Prayer throughout the Year.

And to know what Lessons shall be read every day, look for the day of the month in the Calendar following, and there ye shall find the Chapters that shall be read for the Lessons both at Morning and at Evening Prayer; except only the Movable Holy-days, which are not in the Calendar; and the Immovable, where there is a blank left in the column of Lessons; the Proper Lessons for all which days are to be found in the Table of Proper Lessons.

If in any Church, upon a Sunday or Holy-day, both Morning and Evening Prayer be not said, the Minister may read the Lessons appointed either for Morning or for Evening Prayer.

At Evening Prayer on Sunday, the Minister may read the Lesson from the Gospels appointed for that day of the month, in place of the Second Lesson for the Sunday.

Upon any day for which no Proper Lessons are provided, the Lessons appointed in the Calendar for any day in the same week may be read in place of the Lessons for the day.

On Days of Fasting and Thanksgiving, especially appointed, and on occasions of Ecclesiastical Conventions and of Charitable Collections, the Minister may appoint such Lessons as he shall think fit in his discretion.

HYMNS AND ANTHEMS.

HYMNS set forth and allowed by the authority of this Church, and Anthems in the words of Holy Scripture or of the Book of Common Prayer, may be sung before and after any Office in this Book, and also before and after Sermons.

TABLES OF LESSONS OF HOLY SCRIPTURE,

TO BE READ AT MORNING AND EVENING PRAYER THROUGHOUT THE YEAR.

A TABLE OF PROPER LESSONS FOR SUNDAYS.

SUNDAYS.	MORNING.		EVENING.	
	FIRST LESSON.	SECOND LESSON.	FIRST LESSON.	SECOND LESSON.
In Advent.				
—— 1	Isaiah— 1 to v. 28	Luke —1 to v. 26	Isaiah —— 2	Revelation —— 1
—— 2	—— 5 to v. 26	—— 1 v. 26 to 57	—— 24	—— 2
—— 3	—— 25	—— 1 v. 57	—— 28 to v. 23	—— 3
—— 4	—— 30 to v. 22	—— 3 to v. 23	—— 32	—— 22
After Christmas.				
—— 1	—— 35	—— 2 v. 25	—— 40	Hebrews —— 2
—— 2	—— 41 to v. 22	Mark —1 to v. 16	—— 42 to v. 22	1 Corinthians — 1
After Epiphany.				
—— 1	—— 44 v. 6	Matthew —2 v. 13	—— 45	Romans —— 10
—— 2	—— 51	John — 1 v. 29	—— 52 to v. 13	1 Corinthians — 3
—— 3	—— 54	Matthew — 4 v. 12	—— 55	2 Corinthians — 4
—— 4	—— 56 to v. 9	Luke —4 v. 14 to 33	—— 59	—— 5
—— 5	—— 61	—— 7 v. 19	—— 62	Galatians —— 2
—— 6	—— 65 v. 8	Mark — 6 to v. 30	—— 66	—— 2
Septuagesima.	Jeremiah —5 v. 10	Matthew —— 5	Jeremiah —22 v. 13	Ephesians —— 1
Sexagesima.	—— 35	—— 6	—— 36	—— 2
Quinquagesima.	Lam.— 1 to v. 17	—— 7	Lam.— 3 to v. 37	—— 3
In Lent.				
—— 1	Jeremiah 7 to v. 21	—— 10	Jeremiah 9 to v. 25	—— 4
—— 2	Ezekiel —— 14	Luke —10 to v. 25	Daniel —— 3	—5 v. 15 & 6 to v. 10

A TABLE OF PROPER LESSONS FOR SUNDAYS.

SUNDAYS.	MORNING.		EVENING.	
	FIRST LESSON.	SECOND LESSON.	FIRST LESSON.	SECOND LESSON.
In Lent.				
——3	Ezekiel ——18 v. 20	Mark ——9 to v. 30	Daniel ————5	Romans ————14
——4	Micah ————6	John ———5 v. 24		Philippians ——1
——5	Zechariah ——13	Luke ———21	——7 to v. 19	————3
——6	————9 v. 9	Matthew ——26	————9	John——11 v. 47 & 12 to v. 20
Easter-day.	Exodus 12 to v. 29*	————28	Exodus 15 to v. 22*	Acts ——2 v. 22
After Easter.				
——1	Isaiah——43 to v. 22	Acts ————1	Isaiah——48 to v. 20	1 Cor.——15 to v. 23
——2	Hosea 13 to v. 15	————3	Hosea——14	Colossians ————1
——3	Joel ——3 v. 9	4 to v. 36	Mic. 3 v. 9 & 4 to v. 8	————3
——4	Micah ————5	————5	Nahum ————1	1 Thessalonians ——3
——5	Zechariah ————8	————6	Zechariah ——10	————4
After Ascension.	Joel ——2 v. 21	John ———17	Zephaniah ——3	Heb. 4 v. 14 & 5 to v. 11
Whitsunday.	Deuteronomy——5	Hebrews——12 v. 14	Isaiah 10 v. 33 & 11	Acts——19 to v. 11
Trinity.	Gen.——1 & 2 to v. 4	Matthew ————3	Genesis ——2 v. 4	1 John————5
After Trinity.				
——1	————3	Acts ——8 v. 2	————6	1 Timothy ————6
——2	——3 v. 20 & 9 to v. 20	——9 to v. 32	15 to v. 19	2 Timothy ————2
——3	————37	————10	————42	——3 & 4 to v. 9
——4	————41	————11	————45	Titus 2 & 3 to v. 10
——5	————49	————14	————50	Hebrews ————10

*Note, That the Old Testament Lessons appointed for Easter-day may be interchanged, the one for the other, at the discretion of the Minister.

A TABLE OF PROPER LESSONS FOR SUNDAYS.

SUNDAYS.	MORNING.		EVENING.	
	FIRST LESSON.	SECOND LESSON.	FIRST LESSON.	SECOND LESSON.
After Trinity.				
—— 6	Exodus ——— 3	Acts —15 to v. 31	Ex. 5 v. 5 & 6 to v. 9	Hebrews —— 11
—— 7	—— 9 v. 13	—— 17	—— 10 v. 21 & 11	—— 12
—— 8	—— 14	—— 20 v. 7	Numbers —— 22	—— 13
—— 9	Num.— 16 to v. 41	—— 24	—— 23	James —— 1
—— 10	—23 & 24 to v. 2	—— 26	—— 2	—— 2
—— 11	Deut.—4 to v. 25	Matthew —— 18	Deut.—4 v. 25 to 41	—— 3
—— 12	—— 6	—19 v. 27 & 20 to v. 17	—— 7	—— 4
—— 13	—— 9 v. 9	—— 23	—— 32 to v. 44	—— 5
—— 14	—— 33	—— 25	—— 34	1 Peter —— 1
—— 15	Joshua —— 23	Mark —— 4	Joshua —— 24	—— 2
—— 16	Judges —— 4	—— 13	Judges —— 5	—— 3
—— 17	1 Samuel —— 12	Luke —— 12	1 Samuel —— 17	—— 4
—— 18	1 Chronicles—17	—— 15	2 Sam.—12 to v. 24	—— 5
—— 19	1 Kings —3 to v. 16	—— 19 to v. 28	2 Chronicles—— 6	2 Peter —— 1
—— 20	—— 17	John —3 to v. 23	1 Kings —— 18	—— 2
—— 21	—— 19	—— 5	2 Kings —— 5	—— 3
—— 22	2 Kings —— 19	—8 to v. 48	2 Chronicles—35	1 John —— 1
—— 23	Proverbs —— 1	—— 9	Proverbs —— 2	—— 2
—— 24	—— 3	—10 to v. 31	—— 8	—— 3
—— 25	—— 9	—11 to v. 47	—— 11	—— 4
—— 26	—— 15	—— 15	—— 16	2 John
Next before Advent.	**Malachi** —— 3 & 4	—— 16	Eccles. —— 11 & 12	Jude

A TABLE OF PROPER LESSONS FOR HOLY-DAYS.

HOLY-DAYS.	MORNING.		EVENING.	
	FIRST LESSON.	SECOND LESSON.	FIRST LESSON.	SECOND LESSON.
St. Andrew.	Numbers—10 v. 29	John—1 v. 29 to 43	Isaiah——55	John 12 v. 20 to 42
St. Thomas.	2 Kings 6, 8 to 24	Mark——16 v. 9	2 Kings——7	——14 to v. 15
Nativity.	Isaiah—9 to v. 8	Luke——2 to v. 15	Isaiah 7 v. 10 to 17	Titus 2 v. 11 & 3 to v. 9
St. Stephen.	Genesis 4 to v. 17	Acts 6 & 7 to v. 17	2 Chr. 24 v. 15 to 26	Acts——7 v. 17 to 55
St. John.	Exodus——33 v. 7	John 13 v. 21 to 36	Isaiah——6	2 John——
Holy Innocents.	Jer.——31 to v. 18	Matt.——18 to v. 15	Jer.——49 v. 13	Mark 10 v. 13 to 28
Circumcision.	Genesis 17 to v. 15	Romans——2 v. 17	Deut.——10 v. 12	Colossians——2
Epiphany.	Isaiah——60	——11	Isaiah——49 to v. 14	Luke——3 v. 15 to 23
Conversion of St. Paul.	Wisdom——5	Acts——22 to v. 22	Jer.——1 to v. 11	Acts——26
Purification of the Virgin Mary.	1 Samuel——3	Gal. 3 v. 15 & 4 to v. 8	Haggai——2 to v. 10	1 John——3 to v. 9
St. Matthias.	——2 v. 27	John——6 v. 47	Isaiah——22 v. 15	——2 v. 15
Annunciation of the Virgin Mary.	Genesis——3 to v. 16	Luke—1 v. 39 to 57	1 Samuel 2 to v. 11	——1 to v. 19
Ash-Wednesday.	Isaiah——58	——15	Jonah——3	Heb.——12 to v. 18
Monday before Easter.	Gen.—3 v. 20 & to 4 10 [v. 17]	John——14	Num.——20 to v. 14	1 Cor.——10 to v. 12

A TABLE OF PROPER LESSONS FOR HOLY-DAYS.

HOLY-DAYS.	MORNING.		EVENING.	
	FIRST LESSON.	SECOND LESSON.	FIRST LESSON.	SECOND LESSON.
Tuesday before Easter.	Num.—21 to v. 10	John —————— 15	Lev.—16 v. 6 to 25	Hebrews 9 to v. 16
Wednesday before Easter.	Zechariah——11	John —————— 13	Gen.—37 v. 3 to 29	1 Peter—1 to v. 22
Thursday before Easter.	Exod. 16 v. 4 to 16	—————— 6 v. 27	—————— 14 v. 14	Hebrews—7
Good Friday.	Genesis 22 to v. 19	—————— 18	Isaiah 52 v. 13 & 53	1 Peter—2
Easter-even.	Isaiah 28 v. 9 to 21	Luke —— 23 v. 50	Exodus —————— 13	Hebrews—4
Monday in Easter-week.	Exodus—15 v. 22	—————— 24 to v. 13	Job —————— 19	Mark —————— 16
Tuesday in Easter-week.	Isaiah—28 to v. 20	John — 21 to v. 16	2 Kin. 13 v. 14 to 22	John —————— 21 v. 15
St. Mark.	—————— 62	Mark—1 to v. 21	Ezekiel—1 to v. 15	Acts—12 v. 24 & 13 to v. 14
St. Philip and St. James.	—————— 61	John—6 v. 22 to 59	Zechariah —————— 4	—————— 15 to v. 32
Ascension-day.	2 Kings—2 to v. 23	Luke —— 24 v. 44	Daniel 7 v. 9 to 15	Eph.—4 to v. 17
Monday in Whitsun-week.	Genesis—11 to v. 10	1 Cor. —————— 14 v. 20	Num. 11 v. 16 to 31	1 Corinthians — 12

XV

A TABLE OF PROPER LESSONS FOR HOLY-DAYS.

HOLY-DAYS.	MORNING.		EVENING.	
	FIRST LESSON.	SECOND LESSON.	FIRST LESSON.	SECOND LESSON.
Tuesday in Whitsun-week.	Ezekiel ——33 v. 25	Acts — 2 v. 12 to 22	1 Samuel —19 v. 18	Galatians ——— 5
St. Barnabas.	Malachi —2 to v. 11	——— 4 v. 23	Isaiah —40 to v. 12	Acts — 13 v. 43 & 14 to v. 19
St. John Baptist.	———3 to v. 13	Matthew —— 3	Malachi 3 v. 13 & 4	Matt.— 14 to v. 13
St. Peter.	Ezekiel ——— 34	John ——— 21	Zechariah —— 3	Acts — 4 v. 8 to 23
St. James.	2 Kings —1 to v. 17	Luke —— 9 v. 46	Jer. — 26 to v. 16	Mark 1 v. 14 to 40
Transfiguration.	Exodus — 34 v. 29	2 Corinthians — 3	Malachi — 4 v. 2	Matthew 17 to v. 14
St. Bartholomew.	Genesis — 28 v. 10	John —— 1 v. 43	Deut.—18 v. 15	1 Peter 1 v. 22 & 2 to v. 13
St. Matthew.	1 Kings —— 19	Luke —— 5 v. 27	1 Chr. —29 to v. 20	Mark —— 2 v. 13
St. Michael.	Genesis —— 32	Acts —12 to v. 24	Daniel — 10 v. 4	Rev. — 14 v. 6 & 15
St. Luke.	Ecclus. 38 to v. 15	Luke — 1 to v. 24	Isaiah ———38	Acts — 1 to v. 15
St. Simon and St. Jude.	Isaiah 28 v. 9 to 19	John —14 v. 15	Jeremiah — 3 v. 12	Jude ————
All Saints.	Wisdom —3 to v. 10	Heb.—11 v. 32 & 12 to v. 7	Wisdom 5 to v. 17	Rev. —19 to v. 17

PROPER LESSONS FOR THE FORTY DAYS
OF LENT.

A TABLE OF PROPER LESSONS

FOR THE

FORTY DAYS OF LENT,

And for the Rogation and Ember-days,

WHICH MAY BE USED IN PLACE OF THOSE APPOINTED IN
THE CALENDAR.

DAYS.	MORNING.		EVENING.	
	FIRST LESSON.	SECOND LESSON.	FIRST LESSON.	SECOND LESSON.
LENT.				
1. *Ash-Wednesday.*	Isaiah .. 58	Luke.... 15	Jonah .. 3	Heb. 12 to v. 18
2. Thursday.	.. 50 to v. 17	Mark 11 v. 12	Jer. 3 v. 12 & 4 to v. 8	Romans ... 1
3. Friday.	Micah 7	Matt. 12 to v. 22	Zeph. 3	 3
4. Saturday.	Amos .. 3	.. 12 v. 22	Amos .. 5	 4
FIRST SUNDAY IN LENT.				
5. Monday.	Zechariah 1	.. 13 to v. 24	Zechariah 2	1 Timothy 1
6. Tuesday.	Ezekiel.. 8	13 v. 24 to 44	Ezekiel... 9	 2
7. Wednesday. *Ember-day.*	2 & 3 to v. 10	.. 13 v. 44	.... 3 v. 10	 3
8. Thursday.	.. 20 to v. 27	.. 14 v. 22	.. 20 v. 27	 4
9. Friday. *Ember-day.*	.. 33 to v. 21	.. 15 to v. 18	.. 34 to v. 17	 5
10. Saturday. *Ember-day.*	.. 34 v. 17	.. v. 14	.. 37 to v. 15	Titus ... 1
SECOND SUNDAY IN LENT.				
11. Monday.	Job 1	.. 19 to v. 16	Genesis .. 7	Romans.. 5
12. Tuesday.	 2	.. 19 v. 16	 8	.. 8 to v. 22
13. Wednesday.	 3	.. 21 v. 28	 13	.. v. 22
14. Thursday.	 4	.. 24 to v. 29	 18	.. 9 to v. 18
15. Friday.	 14	.. 24 v. 29	19 v. 12 to 30	.. 9 v. 18
16. Saturday.	 19	Mark 1 v. 21	21 v. 9 to 22	.. 13 to v. 22

xvii

PROPER LESSONS FOR THE FORTY DAYS OF LENT,

AND FOR THE ROGATION AND EMBER-DAYS.

DAYS.	MORNING.		EVENING.	
	FIRST LESSON.	SECOND LESSON.	FIRST LESSON.	SECOND LESSON.
THIRD SUNDAY IN LENT.				
17. Monday.	Job 27	Mark 2 to v. 18	Exodus...17 [19	1 Cor. ... 4
18. Tuesday.	 28	.. 5 to v. 21	Lev. 19 to v.	 5
19. Wednesday.	 29	... 5 v. 21	Num.13v.17	 6
20. Thursday.	 30	... 6 v. 45	...14 to v. 26	9 to v. 24
21. Friday.	...... 31 v. 4	7 v. 14 to 31	......15 v. 17	10 v. 12
22. Saturday.	 32	... 8 v. 22	Joshua... 7	...14 v. 26
FOURTH SUNDAY IN LENT.				
23. Monday.	...38 to v. 19	... 9 v. 33	1 Samuel 3	2 Cor. ... 2
24. Tuesday.	...38 v. 19	...10 to v. 17	 4	 3
25. Wednesday.	 39	10 v. 17 to 35	 16	 7
26. Thursday.	 40	...10 v. 35	...28 to v. 21	...12 to v. 16
27. Friday.	 41	...12 to v. 18	2 Sam. 24 to v. 15	Galatians 2
28. Saturday.	 42	...12 v. 18	...24 v. 15	1 Thess... 2
FIFTH SUNDAY IN LENT.				
29. Monday.	Deut. 28 to v. 15	Luke 11v.29	1 Kings 9 to v. 10	2 Thess... 2
30. Tuesday.	28 v.15 to 47	...12 to v. 22	...10 to v. 14	Hebrews 3
31. Wednesday.	...28 v. 58	...12 v. 22 to 41	2 Kings 6 to v. 24	 5
32. Thursday.	 30	...12 v. 41	 22	 6
33. Friday.	Jer. 13 to v. 15	John 5 to v. 24	Ezra 9	 8
34. Saturday.	...13 v. 15	...12 v. 20	Jer. 18 to v. 18	...10 v. 28
SUNDAY NEXT BEFORE EASTER.				
35. Monday before Easter.	Gen.3 v.20 & 4 to v. 17	 14	Num. 20 to v. 14	1 Cor. 10 to v. 12
36. Tuesday before Easter.	Num. 21 to [v. 10	 15	Lev. 16 to v. 25	Heb. 9 to v. 22
37. Wednesday before Easter.	Zechariah 11	 13	Gen. 37 v. 3	1 Peter...1 to

PROPER LESSONS FOR THE FORTY DAYS OF LENT,

And for the Rogation and Ember-days.

DAYS.	MORNING.		EVENING.	
	FIRST LESSON.	SECOND LESSON.	FIRST LESSON.	SECOND LESSON.
38. *Thursday before Easter.*	Ex...16 v.4 to 16	John 6 v.27	Gen. 14 v.14	Hebrews ..7
39. *Good Friday.*	Gen.22 to v. 19	 18	Is...52 v.13 & 53	1 Peter ..2
40. *Easter-even.*	Is. 38 v.9 to 21	Luke 23 v. 50	Exodus ..13	Hebrews..4
THE ROGATION-DAYS.				
Monday.	Deut..... 8	Matt. 6 v.24	Deut. 28 to v. 15	James ..1 to v. 18
Tuesday.	1 Kings 8 v. 22 to 41	Luke..11 to v. 14	Isaiah .. 64	 4
Wednesday.	Jer. 14	John 6 v.24 to 41	Hab. 3	 5
THE EMBER-DAYS IN WHITSUN-WEEK.				
Wednesday.	Is...6 to v.9	Luke 6 v.12 to 24	Jer. 31 v. 27	1 Cor. 1 v.18
Friday.	 61	.. 10 to v.25	..42 to v.13	 2
Saturday.	Ezek. 13 to v. 17	.. 12 to v.13	Ezek. 14 to v. 12	..... 9 v. 7
THE EMBER-DAYS IN SEPTEMBER.				
Wednesday.	Deut.18 v.15	Acts 1 to v. 10	1 Kings 19 v. 27	2 Cor.... 4
Friday.	2 Kings 2 to v. 23	.. 4 to v.13	Jer. 6 v.9 to 30	 5
Saturday.	Hosea .4 to v.10	.. 4 v.13 to 24	Micah 3 v.5	Heb. 13 v.7 to 22
THE EMBER-DAYS IN DECEMBER.				
Wednesday.	Jer. ... 23 to v. 16	John 1 v.29	Jer. 23 v. 16	Ephes. 4 to v. 17
Friday.	..26 to v.20	... 5 v. 33	Malachi ..2	1 Thess...5
Saturday.	Malachi 3 to v. 13	Luke 12 v.35 to 40	..3 v. 13 & 4	2 Timothy 1

A TABLE OF LESSONS

FOR

JANUARY.

CALENDAR.			MORNING PRAYER.		EVENING PRAYER.	
			FIRST LESSON.	SECOND LESSON.	FIRST LESSON.	SECOND LESSON.
1	A	*Circumcision.*				
2	b		Gen...1 & 2 to v. 4	Matthew 1	Gen...2 v. 4	Acts.....1
3	c		 3	 2	 4	..2 to v. 22
4	d		 5	 3	 6	..2 v. 22
5	e		 7	 4	 8	 3
6	f	*Epiphany.*				
7	g		 9	..5 to v. 27	10 v. 21 & 11 to v. 10	..4 to v. 32
8	A		11 v. 27 & 12	..5 v. 27	 13	4 v. 32 & 5 to v. 17
9	b		 14	..6 to v. 19	 15	..5 v. 17
10	c		 16	..6 v. 19 & 7 to v. 7	..17 to v. 23	 6
11	d		..18 to v. 17	..7 v. 7	..18 v. 17	..7 to v. 30
12	e		19 v.12 to 30	..8 to v. 18	 20	..7 v. 30
13	f		 21	..8 v. 18	..22 to v. 20	..8 to v. 26
14	g		 23	..9 to v. 18	..24 to v. 29	..8 v. 26
15	A		24 v. 29 to 52	..9 v. 18	..24 v. 52	..9 to v. 23
16	b		25 v. 5 to 27	..10 to v. 24	25 v. 27 & 26 to v. 7	..9 v. 23
17	c		..26 v. 12	..10 v. 24	..27 to v. 30	10 to v. 24
18	d		27 v. 30 to 46	 11	27 v. 46 & 28	..10 v. 24
19	e		..29 to v. 21	12 to v. 22	31 to v. 25	 11
20	f		..31 v. 25	..12 v. 22	32 to v. 22	 12
21	g		..32 v. 22	13 to v. 24	 33	..13 to v. 26
22	A		..35 to v. 21	13 v. 24 to 44	 34	..13 v. 26
23	b		35 v. 20 & 40	..13 v. 44	..37 to v. 17	 14
24	c		41 v. 17 to 38	..14 to v. 22	..41 v. 38	..15 to v. 30
25	d					
26	e	*Converion of St. Paul.*	..42 to v. 25	..14 v. 22	..42 v. 25	15 v. 30 & 16 to v. 16
27	f		..43 to v. 15	..15 to v. 21	..43 v. 15	..16 to v. 16
28	g		..44 to v. 14	..15 v. 21	..44 v. 14	..17 to v. 16
29	A		..45 to v. 16	 16	..45 v. 16 & 46 to v. 8	..17 v. 16
30	b		..46 v. 26 & 47 to v. 12	 17	..47 v. 13	..18 to v. 24
31	c		 48	..18 to v. 21	 49	..18 v. 24 & 19 to v. 21

A TABLE OF LESSONS
FOR
FEBRUARY.*

		CALENDAR.	MORNING PRAYER.		EVENING PRAYER.	
			FIRST LESSON.	SECOND LESSON.	FIRST LESSON.	SECOND LESSON.
1	d		Gen. 50 to v. 15	Matt. 18 v. 21	Gen. 50 v. 15	Acts 19 v. 21
2	e	Purification of Virgin Mary.				
3	f		Exodus .. 1	..19 to v. 27	Exodus .. 2	..20 to v. 17
4	g		... 3	19. 27 & 20 to v. 17	.. 4 to v. 24	..20 v. 17
5	A		. 4 v. 27 & 5 to v. 19	..20 v. 17	.5 v. 19 & 6 to v. 14	..21 to v. 27
6	b		. 6 v. 28 & 7 to v. 14	..21 to v. 23	... 7 v. 14	21 v. 27 & 22 v. 22
7	c		. 8 to v. 16	..21 v. 23	.. 8 v. 16	..22 v. 22 & 23 to v. 12
8	d		. 9 to v. 13	..22 to v. 15	.. 9 v. 13	..23 v. 12
9	e		... 10	..22 v. 15	... 11	...24
10	f		..12 to v. 29	... 23	..12 v. 29	...25
11	g		... 13	..24 to v. 29	... 14	...26
12	A		...15	..24 v. 29	...16	..27 to v. 18
13	b		... 17	..25 to v. 31	... 18	..27 v. 18
14	c		... 19	..25 v. 31	...20 to v. 25	..28 to v. 17
15	d		22 v. 21 & 23 to v. 20	..26 to v. 30	..23 v. 20	..28 v. 17
16	e		...24	26 v. 30 to 57	..25 to v. 24	Romans.. 1
17	f		..28 to v. 13	..26 v. 57	28 v. 13 to 39	...2
18	g		29. 38 & 30 to v. 17	..27 to v. 27	31 v. 12 & 32 to v. 15	...3
19	A		..32 v. 15	..27 v. 27	...33	...4
20	b		..34 to v. 18	... 28	..34 v. 18	...5
21	c		35 v. 20 & 36 to v. 8	Mark 1 to v. 21	..40 v. 17	...6
22	d		Lev. to v. 22 & 10 to v. 12	.. 1 v. 21	Lev. 16 to v. 25	...7
23	e		..19 to v. 19	.. 2 to v. 23	19 v. 30 & 20 to v. 9	...8
24	f	St. Matthias.		.. 2 v. 23 & 3 to v. 13	...25 v. 9	
25	g		..25 to v. 35	.. 3 v. 13	..25 v. 35	...9
26	A		..26 to v. 21	.. 3 v. 13	..26 v. 21	...10
27	b		Numbers 11	.. 4 to v. 35	Num. 9 v. 15 & 10 to v. 11	...11
28	c		10 v. 29 & 11 to v. 16	. 4 v. 35 & 5 to v. 21	..11 v. 16	...12
29	d		... 12	Matthew 7	..13 to v. 25	Hebrews 12

Note, That except in every Leap-year, February hath 28 days only.

A TABLE OF LESSONS

FOR

MARCH.

CALENDAR.			MORNING PRAYER.		EVENING PRAYER.	
			FIRST LESSON.	SECOND LESSON.	FIRST LESSON.	SECOND LESSON.
	1	d	Num. 13 v. 25&14 to v. 5	Mark 5 v. 21	Num. 14 v. 5 to 26	Romans 13
	2	e	.. 14 v. 26	..6 to v. 14	..16 to v. 23	.. 14
	3	f	.. 16 v. 23	6 v. 14 to 30	.. 17	.. 15
	4	g	.. 20	.. 6 v. 30	.. 21	.. 16
	5	A	..22 to v. 21	..7 to v. 24	..22 v. 21	1 Cor... 1
	6	b	.. 23	..7 v. 24	.. 24	.. 2
	7	c	.. 25	.. 8	27 v. 12	.. 3
	8	d	.. 32	..9 to v. 30	..35 v. 9	.. 4
	9	e	Deut. 1 to v. 19	9 v. 30	Deut. 1 v.19	.. 5
	10	f	..2 to v. 26	..10 to v. 32	2 v. 26 & 3 to v. 18	.. 6
	11	g	.. 3 v. 18	10 v. 32	..4 to v. 25	.. 7
	12	A	.. 4 v. 25	..11 to v. 27	..5 to v. 22	.. 8
	13	b	.. 5 v. 22	11 v. 27 & 12 to v. 13	.. 6	.. 9
	14	c	.. 7	12 v. 13 to 28	.. 8	.. 10
	15	d	.. 9	12 v. 28	.. 10	.. 11
	16	e	.. 11	.. 13	..15 to v. 19	.. 12
	17	f	.. 16	..14 to v. 26	..17 v. 8	.. 13
	18	g	.. 18	14 v. 26 to v. 53	.. 19	.. 14
	19	A	.. 24 v. 5	14 v. 53	.. 26	..15 to v. 35
	20	b	.. 27	..15 to v. 42	..28 to v. 15	15 v. 35
14	21	c	.. 28 v. 15 to 47	15 v. 42 & 16	..28 v. 47	.. 16
3	22	d	.. 29	Luke 1 to v. 26	.. 30	2 Cor... 1
	23	e	..31 to v. 30	1 v. 26 to 57	31 v. 30 & 32 to v. 44	.. 2
11	24	f	32 v. 44 & 33	1 v. 57	.. 34	.. 3
	25	g	Annunciation of Virgin Mary.			
19	26	A	Joshua.. 1	..2 to v. 21	Joshua.. 2	.. 4
8	27	b	.. 3	2 v. 21	.. 4	.. 5
	28	c	.. 5	.. 3	..6 to v. 20	.. 6
16	29	d	.. 7	..4 v. 16	.. 9	.. 7
5	30	e	8 v. 30	..4 v. 16	.. 10	.. 8
	31	f	10 to v. 15	5 to v. 17	.. 14	.. 9

A TABLE OF LESSONS

FOR

APRIL.

CALENDAR.			MORNING PRAYER.		EVENING PRAYER.	
			FIRST LESSON.	SECOND LESSON.	FIRST LESSON.	SECOND LESSON.
13	1	g	Josh.17v.14 & 18 to v.11	Luke 5 v. 17	Josh. 19 v. 49 & 20	2 Cor... 10
2	2	A	...21 v. 43 & 22 to v.10	..6 to v. 20	22 v. 10	 11
	3	b	 23	.... 6 v. 20	 24	12
10	4	c	Judges... 1	..7 to v. 19	Judges... 2	13
	5	d	 3	7 v. 19 to 36	4	Gal.... 1
18	6	e	 5	.... 7 v. 36	.6 to v. 25	 2
7	7	f	.... 6 v. 25	..8 to v. 22	 7	 3
	8	g	.. 8 v. 32 & 9 to v.25	8 v. 22 to 40	9 v. 48 & 10 to v. 10	 4
15	9	A	..10 v. 10 & 11 to v.12	.... 8 v. 40	11 v. 12	 5
4	10	b	 13	..9 to v. 18	 14	 6
	11	c	 15	9 v. 18 to 43	 16	Eph. ... 1
12	12	d	..17 & 18 to v. 11	..9 v. 43	.. 18 v. 11	 2
1	13	e	Ruth ... 1	..10 to v.25	Ruth .. 2	 3
	14	f	 3	..10 v. 25	 4	 4
9	15	g	1 Sam... 1	..11 to v. 29	1 Sam. 2 to v. 22	 5
	16	A	.. 2 v. 22	..11 v. 29	 3	 6
17	17	b	 4	..12 to v. 22	 5	Phil. .. 1
6	18	c	 6	12v.22 to 41	 7	 2
	19	d	 8	.. 12 v. 41	.. 9 to v. 25	 3
	20	e	..9 v. 25 & 10 to v. 17	..13 to v. 18	..10 v. 17 & 11 to v. 14	 4
	21	f	11v.14 & 12	.. 13 v. 18	14v.24 to 47	Col..... 1
	22	g	..14 to v.24	..14 to v. 25	..16	 2
	23	A	 15	14 v. 25 & 15 to v. 11	 16	 3
	24	b	..17 to v. 31	.. 15 v. 11	17 v. 31 to 55	 4
	25	c	St. Mark.			
	26	d	17 v. 55 & 18	..16 to v. 19	 19	1 Thess. 1
	27	e	..20 to v.18	.. 16 v. 19	.. 20 v. 18	 2
28	28	f	 21	..17 to v. 20	 22	 3
29	29	g	 23	.. 17 v. 20	..24 & 25 to v. 2	 4
	30	A	 26	..18 to v.18	.. 28 v. 3	 5

A TABLE OF LESSONS
FOR
MAY.

CALENDAR.			MORNING PRAYER.		EVENING PRAYER.	
			FIRST LESSON.	SECOND LESSON.	FIRST LESSON.	SECOND LESSON.
1	b	St. Philip & St James.				
2	c		1 Sam. 30 to v. 26	Luke ..18 v. 18	1 Sam .. 31	2 Thess. 1
3	d		2 Sam.. 1	19 to v. 28	2 Sam. 2 to v. 18	 2
4	e		.. 2 v. 18	..19 v. 28	.. 3 v. 17	 3
5	f		 4	..20 to v. 27	 5	1 Tim. 1
6	g		 6	..20 v. 27	7 to v. 18	 2
7	A		7 v. 18	..21	 9	 3
8	b		 11	..22 to v. 31	..12 to v. 24	 4
9	c		13 v. 37 & 14 to v. 26	22 v. 31 to 54	..15 to v. 16	 5
10	d		..15 v. 16	..22 v. 54	..16 to v. 16	 6
11	e		16 v. 16 & 17 to v. 24	23 to v. 26	17 v. 24 & 18 to v. 18	2 Tim.. 1
12	f		..18 v. 18	23 v. 26 to 50	..19 to v. 24	 2
13	g		..19 v. 24	23 v. 50 & 24 to v. 13	..22 to v. 31	 3
14	A		..22 v. 31	..24 v. 13	..23 to v. 24	 4
15	b			John 1 to v. 29	1 Kin. 1 to v. 29	Titus 1
16	c		1 Kin. 1 v. 23	..1 v. 29	1 Chr. 28 to v. 21	....
17	d		1 Chr. 28 v. 20 & 29 to v. 20	 2	..29 v. 10	 3
18	e		1 Kings 3	3 to v. 22	1 Kin. 4 v. 20	Philemon
19	f		 5	3 v. 22	6 to v. 15	Hebrews 1
20	g		7 to v. 22	4 v. 31	7 v. 27	 2
21	A		8 to v. 22	..4 v. 31	8 v. 22 to 54	 3
22	b		8 v. 54	5 to v. 24	9 to v. 10	 4
23	c		10 to v. 14	5 v. 24	10 v. 14	 5
24	d		11 to v. 26	6 to v. 22	11 v. 26	 6
25	e		12 to v. 25	6 v. 22 to 41	12 v. 25 & 13 to v. 11	 7
26	f		..13 v. 11	6 v. 41	..14 to v. 21	 8
27	g		2 Chron. 12	7 to v. 25	2 Chron. 13	 9
28	A		 14	7 v. 25	 15	 10
29	b		16 & 17 to v. 14	8 to v. 21	1 Kin. 16 v. 25 & 16 to v. 8	 11
30	c		1 Kin. 16 v. 8	8 v. 21	 17	 12
31	d		..18 to v. 21	 9	..13 v. 21	 13

A TABLE OF LESSONS
FOR
JUNE.

CALENDAR.			MORNING PRAYER.		EVENING PRAYER.	
			FIRST LESSON.	SECOND LESSON.	FIRST LESSON.	SECOND LESSON.
1	e	....	1 Kings 19	John 10 to v. 22	1 Kin. 20 to v. 22	James.. 1
2	f	....	....20 v. 22	....10 v. 22	 21	 2
3	g	....	.. 22 to v. 41	..11 to v. 21	2 Chron. 19	 3
4	A	....	2 Chr. 20 to v. 20	11 v. 21 to 47	....20 v. 20	 4
5	b	....	1 Kin. 22 v. 7.1 & 2 Kin.1	11 v. 47 & 12 to v. 20	2 Kings 2	 5
6	c	....	2 Kings 2	....12 v. 20	 4	1 Peter 1
7	d	....	 5	..13 to v. 21	.. 6 to v. 24	 2
8	e	....	.. 6 v. 24	..13 v. 21	 7	 3
9	f	....	.. 8 to v. 16	 14	2 Chron. 21	 4
10	g	....	2 Chron. 22	 15	2 Kings 9	 5
11	A	St. Barnabas.				
12	c	....	2 Kin. 10 to v. 18	..16 to v. 16	....10 v. 18	2 Peter 1
13	d	....	2 Chron. 23	..16 v. 16	2 Chron. 24	 2
14	e	....	2 Kings 13	 17	.. 25 to v. 17	 3
15	f	....	.. 14 v. 8	..18 to v. 28	 26	1 John 1
16	g	....	15 v. 8 to 32	..18 v. 28	..27 & 28 to v. 16	 2
17	g	....	.. 16 v. 5	..19 to v. 25	2 Kin. 17 to v. 24	 3
18	A	....	....17 v. 24	..19 v. 25	....18 to v. 13	 4
19	b	....	2 Chron. 29 to v. 21	- 20 to v. 19	2 Chron. 30 & 31 to v. 2	 5
20	c	....	.. 32 to v. 20	....20 v. 19	2 Kings 19	2 John..
21	d	....	Isaiah .. 38	..21 to v. 15	....20 v. 12	3 John..
22	e	....	2 Chron. 33	..21 v. 15	 22	Jude ..
23	f	....	2 Kings 23 to v. 21	Acts.... 1	..23 v. 21 & 24 to v. 8	Matt... 1
24	g	Nativity of St. John Baptist.				
25	A	....	24 v. 8 & 25 to v. 8	- 2 to v. 22	.. 25 v. 8	 2
26	b	....	Ezra .. 1	2 v. 22	Ezra 2 v. 68 & 3	 3
27	c	....	 4	 3	 5	 4
28	d	....	 6	.. 4 to v. 32	 7	5 to v. 27
29	e	St. Peter.				
30	f	....	.. 8 v. 21	4 v. 32 & 5 to v. 17	 9	.. 5 v. 27

CALENDAR.		MORNING PRAYER.		EVENING PRAYER.	
		FIRST LESSON.	SECOND LESSON.	FIRST LESSON.	SECOND LESSON.
1	g	Ezra 10 to v. 20	Acts 5 v. 17	Neh. ... 1	Matt. 6 to v. 19
2	A	Neh. ... 2	6	4	6 v. 19 & 7 to v. 7
3	b	5	7 to v. 30	6 & 7 to v. 5	7 v. 7
4	c	7 v. 73 & 8	7 v. 30	12 v. 43 & 13 to v. 15	8 to v. 18
5	d	13 v. 15	8 to v. 26	Esth. 1 & 2	8 v. 18
6	e	Esth. 2 v. 15 & 3	8 v. 26	4	9 to v. 18
7	f	5	9 to v. 23	6	9 v. 18
8	g	7 & 8 to v. 3	9 v. 23	Job ... 1	10 to v. 24
9	A	Job ... 2	10 to v. 24	3	10 v. 24
10	b	4	10 v. 24	5	11
11	c	6	11	7	12 to v. 22
12	d	8	12	9	12 v. 22
13	e	10	13 to v. 26	11	13 to v. 24
14	f	12	13 v. 26	13	13 v. 24 to v. 53
15	g	14	14	15 to v. 17	13 v. 44
16	A	16	15 to v. 30	17	14
17	b	19	15 v. 30 & 16 to v. 16	21	15 to v. 21
18	c	22	16 v. 16	23	15 v. 21
19	d	24	17 to v. 16	25 & 26	16
20	e	27	17 v. 16	28	17
21	f	29	18 to v. 24	30	18 to v. 21
22	g	31	18 v. 24 & 19 to v. 21	32	18 v. 21
23	A	33	19 v. 21	34	19 to v. 27
24	b	35	20 v. 17	36	19 v. 27 & 20 to v. 17
25	c	*St. James.*			
26	d	37	20 v. 17	38	20 v. 17
27	e	39	21 to v. 27	40	21 to v. 22
28	f	41	21 v. 27 & 22 to v. 23	42	21 v. 22
29	g	Prov. 1 to v. 20	22 v. 23 & 23 to v. 12	Prov. 1 v. 20	22 to v. 15
30	A	2	23 v. 12	10	22 v. 15
31	b	12	24	13	23

A TABLE OF LESSONS

FOR

AUGUST.

CALENDAR			MORNING PRAYER		EVENING PRAYER	
			FIRST LESSON	SECOND LESSON	FIRST LESSON	SECOND LESSON
1	c		Prov ... 14	Acts .. 25	Prov ... 15	Matt. 24 to v. 29
2	d		16	26	20	24 v. 29
3	e		23 v. 16	27 to v. 18	24	25 to v. 31
4	f		25	27 v. 18	26	25 v. 31
5	g		27	28	28	26 to v. 30
6	A	Transfiguration.				
7	b		30 to v. 18	Romans 1	31 v. 10	26 v. 30 to 57
8	c		Eccles. 1	2	Eccles. 2	26 v. 57
9	d		3	3	4	27 to v. 27
10	e		5	4	6	27 v. 27
11	f		7	5	8	28
12	g		9	6	10	Mark 1 to v. 21
13	A		11	7	12	1 v. 21
14	b		Jeremiah 1	8	Jer. 2 to v. 20	2 to v. 28
15	c		2 v. 20	9	3 v. 12	2 v. 28 & 3 to v. 13
16	d		4 to v. 19	10	5	3 v. 13
17	e		6 to v. 22	11	7 to v. 21	4 to v. 35
18	f		7 v. 21	12	8	4 v. 35 & 5 to v. 21
19	g		9	13	10	5 v. 21
20	A		11	14	13 to v. 24	6 to v. 14
21	b		15	15	16	6 v. 14 to 30
22	c		17	16	18 to v. 18	6 v. 30
23	d		19	1 Cor. 1	21	7 to v. 24
24	e	St. Bartholomew.				
25	f		22	2	23 to v. 33	7 v. 24
26	g		23 to v. 17	3	26	8
27	A		28	4	29 to v. 20	9 to v. 30
28	b		30	5	31 v. 15 to 35	9 v. 30
29	c		33	6	34	10 to v. 32
30	d		35	7	36	10 v. 32
31	e		37	8	38	11 to v. 27

A TABLE OF LESSONS

FOR

SEPTEMBER.

CALENDAR.		MORNING PRAYER.		EVENING PRAYER.	
		FIRST LESSON.	SECOND LESSON.	FIRST LESSON.	SECOND LESSON.
1	f	Jer. 39	1 Cor. .. 9	Jer. 40	Mark 11 v.27 & 12 to v. 13
2	g	 41	10	 42	12 v.13 to 28
3	A	 43	11	.44 to v. 15	.. 12 v. 28
4	b	..44 v. 15	12	 45	 13
5	c	 46	13	.50 to v. 21	.14 to v. 26
6	d	..50 v. 21	14	.51 v. 54	14 v.26 to 53
7	e	.52 to v. 15	.15 to v. 35	..52 v. 15	..14 v. 53
8	f	Lam. .. 1	.15 v. 35	Lam. 2 to v. 20	.15 to v. 42
9	g	.. 3 to v. 37	16	.. 3 v. 37	15 v. 42 & 16
10	A	Ezek. .. 1	2 Cor. .. 1	Ezekiel 2	Luke 1 to v. 26
11	b	 3	2	 7	1 v. 26 to 57
12	c	 8	3	 9	.. 1 v. 57
13	d	..11 v. 14	4	.12 v. 17	2 to v. 21
14	e	.13 to v. 17	5	 14	.. 2 v. 21
15	f	.18 to v. 19	6	.18 v. 19	 3
16	g	.20 to v. 27	7	.20 v. 27	.4 to v. 16
17	A	..24 v. 15	8	.23 to v. 21	.4 v. 16
18	b	..23 v. 21	9	 34	.5 to v. 17
19	c	..36 v. 21	10	 35	.5 v. 17
20	d	Daniel.. 1	11	Dan. 2 to v. 24	.6 to v. 20
21	e	St. Matthew.			
22	f	.. 2 v. 24	12	 3	6 v. 20
23	g	.. 4 to v. 19	13	.. 4 v. 19	.7 to v. 19
24	A	 5	Gal. .. 1	 6	7 v. 19 to 36
25	b	 7	2	 8	.7 v. 36
26	c	 9	3	 10	.8 to v. 22
27	d	.11 to v. 30	4	.11 v. 30	8 v. 22 to 40
28	e	 12	5	Hos. 2 v. 14	8 v. 40
29	f	St. Michael and All Angels.			
30	g	Hosea 4 to v. 13	6	5 v. 8 & 6 to v. 7	.9 to v. 18

A TABLE OF LESSONS

FOR

OCTOBER.

	CALENDAR.		MORNING PRAYER.		EVENING PRAYER.	
			FIRST LESSON.	SECOND LESSON.	FIRST LESSON.	SECOND LESSON.
1	A	....	Hosea ... 3	Ephes. ... 1	Hosea ... 10	Luke 9 v. 18 to 43
2	b	e	....	 2	13 to v. 15	... 9 v. 43
3	c	d	11 & 12 to v.7	 14	Joel ... 1	10 to v. 25
4	d	e	Joel 2 to v. 15	 2	2 v. 15 to 28	...10 v. 25
5	e	....	2 v. 28 & 3 to v. 9	 5	3 v. 9	11 to v. 29
6	f	....	Amos 1 & 2 to v. 6	 6	Amos ... 3	...11 v. 29
7	g	a	 4	Phil. ... 1	 5	12 to v. 22
8	A	....	 7	 2	 8	12 v. 22 to 41
9	b	....	 9	 3	Obadiah	12 v. 41
10	c	d	Jonah ... 1	 4	Jonah ... 2	13 to v. 18
11	d	e	 3	Col. ... 1	 4	...13 v. 18
12	e	....	Micah 1 to v. 10	 2	Micah... 2	14 to v. 25
13	f	....	 3	 3	 4	14 v. 25 & 15 to v. 11
14	g	....	 5	 4	 6	15 v. 11
15	A	b	 7	1 Thess. ... 1	Nahum ... 1	16 to v. 19
16	b	c	Nahum ... 2	 2	 3	16 v. 19
17	c	d	Hab. ... 1	 3	Hab. ... 2	17 to v. 20
18	d	St. Luke.	 3	 4	....	17 v. 20
19	e	....	Zeph. ... 1	 5	Zeph. ... 1	...17 v. 20
20	f	g	Zeph. ... 2	 5	 3	18 to v. 18
21	g	a	Haggai ... 1	2 Thess. ... 1	Haggai ... 2	...18 v. 18
22	A	b	Zech. ... 1	 2	Zech. ... 2	19 to v. 28
23	b	c	 3	 3	 4	...19 v. 28
24	c	d	 5	1 Tim. ... 1	 6	20 to v. 27
25	d	e	 7	 2	 8	...20 v. 27
26	e	....	 9	 3	 10	21 to v. 5
27	f	....	 11	 4	 12	21 v. 5 to 31
28	g	St. Simon and St. Jude.	....	....	....	....
29	A	....	 13	 5	 14	22 v. 31 to 54
30	b	....	Malachi ... 1	 6	Malachi ... 2	22 v. 54
31	c	....	3 to v. 13	2 Tim. ... 1	3 v. 13 & 4	23 to v. 26

A TABLE OF LESSONS
FOR
NOVEMBER.

CALENDAR.			MORNING PRAYER.		EVENING PRAYER.	
			FIRST LESSON.	SECOND LESSON.	FIRST LESSON.	SECOND LESSON.
1	d	*All Saints.*				
2	e		*Tobit* .. 13	2 Tim.. 2	*Wisdom* 1	Luke 23 v. 26 to 50
3	f		*Wisdom* 4 v. 7	3	..6 to v. 22	23 v. 50 & 24 to v. 13
4	g		..7 v. 15	4	..8 to v. 19	..24 v. 13
5	A		..9	Titus.. 1	..13	John 1 to v. 29
6	b		..16 to v. 14	2	..19	..1 v. 29
7	c		*Ecclus..* 1	3	*Ecclus..* 2	..2
8	d		..3 to v. 24	Philem.	..4	..3 to v. 22
9	e		..5	Hebrews 1	..6 v. 18 & 7 to v. 11	..3 v. 22
10	f		..9 v. 15 & 10 to v. 18	2	..10 v. 18	..4 to v. 31
11	g		..15	3	16 v. 26 & 17 to v. 20	..4 v. 31
12	A		..18 to v. 15	4	..18 v. 15	..5 to v. 24
13	b		..21 to v. 14	5	22 v. 23 & 23 to v. 15	..5 v. 24
14	c		..24 to v. 19	6	..24 v. 19	..6 to v. 22
15	d		30 v. 11 & 31 to v. 12	7	..34 v. 13	6 v. 22 to 41
16	e		..35	8	38 v. 24 & 39 to v. 12	..6 v. 41
17	f		..39 v. 13	9	..41 to v. 14	..7 to v. 25
18	g		42 v. 17 & 43 to v. 11	10	..44	..7 v. 25
19	A		..47 to v. 12	11	..50 to v. 25	..8 to v. 21
20	b		..51	12	*Baruch* 4 v. 19 & 5	..8 v. 21
21	c		*Isaiah* .. 1	13	*Isaiah..* 2	..9
22	d		..3 to v. 16	James.. 1	..5 to v. 18	..10 to v. 22
23	e		..5 to v. 18	2	..5 v. 18	..10 v. 22
24	f		..6	3	..7	..11 to v. 21
25	g		..8 to v. 18	4	..8 v. 18 & 9 to v. 8	..11 v. 21 to 47
26	A		..9 v. 8	5	..10 to v. 20	11 v. 47 & 12 to v. 20
27	b		..10 v. 20	1 Peter 1	..11	..12 v. 20
28	c		..12	2	..13	..13 to v. 21
29	d		..14 to v. 24	3	..17	..13 v. 21
30	e	*St. Andrew.*				

A TABLE OF LESSONS

FOR

DECEMBER.

CALENDAR.			MORNING PRAYER.		EVENING PRAYER.	
			FIRST LESSON.	SECOND LESSON.	FIRST LESSON.	SECOND LESSON.
1	f	....	Isaiah .. 18	1 Peter 4	Is. 19 to v. 18	John 14
2	g	....	19 v. 18 & 20	5	..21 to v. 13	.. 15
3	A	....	..22 to v. 15	2 Peter 1	..22 v. 15	..16 to v. 16
4	b	....	..23	2	..24	..16 v. 16
5	c	....	..25	3	..26	.. 17
6	d	....	..27	1 John.. 1	..28 to v. 14	..18 to v. 28
7	e	....	..28 v. 14	2	..29	..18 v. 28
8	f	....	..30 to v. 18	3	..30 v. 18	.19 to v. 25
9	g	....	..31	4	..32	.19 v. 25
10	A	....	..33	5	..34	20 to v. 19
11	b	....	..35	2 John..	..40	20 v. 19
12	c	....	..41 to v. 17	3 John..	..41 v. 17	.21 to v.15
13	d	....	..42 to v. 17	Jude ..	42 v. 17 & 43 to v. 8	.21 v. 15
14	o	....	..43 v. 8	Rev... 1	..44 to v. 21	Rev ... 2 to v. 18
15	f	....	44 v. 21 & 45 to v. 8	..2 v. 18 & 3 to v. 8	..45 v. 8	..3 v. 7
16	g	....	..46	4	..47	5
17	A	....	..48	6	.49 to v. 13	7
18	b	....	.49 v. 13	8	..50	9
19	c	....	.51	10	.52 to v. 13	11
20	d	....	52 v. 13 & 53	12	..54	13
21	e	St. Thomas.				
22	f	....	..55	14	..56	15
23	g	....	..57	16	..58	17
24	A	....	..59	18	..60	.19 to v. 11
25	b	Christmas-day.				
26	c	St. Stephen.				
27	d	St. John Evangelist.				
28	e	Innocents.				
29	f	....	..61	.19 v. 11	..62	..20
30	g	....	..63	.21 to v. 15	..64	.21 v. 15
31	A	....	..65	22 to v. 5	..66	.. 22 v. 8

TABLES AND RULES
FOR THE
MOVABLE AND IMMOVABLE FEASTS,
TOGETHER WITH THE
DAYS OF FASTING AND ABSTINENCE,
THROUGH THE WHOLE YEAR.

❧ RULES
TO KNOW WHEN THE MOVABLE FEASTS AND HOLY-DAYS BEGIN.

EASTER-DAY, on which the rest depend, is always the First *Sunday* after the Full Moon, which happens upon or next after the Twenty-first Day of *March*; and if the Full Moon happen upon a Sunday, *Easter-day* is the Sunday after.

But *Note*, That the Full Moon, for the purposes of these Rules and Tables, is the Fourteenth Day of a Lunar Month, reckoned according to an ancient Ecclesiastical computation, and not the real or Astronomical Full Moon.

Advent-Sunday is always the nearest Sunday to the Feast of St. Andrew, whether before or after.

Septuagesima		Nine	
Sexagesima		Eight	Weeks before
Quinquagesima	Sunday is	Seven	*Easter.*
Quadragesima		Six	
Rogation-Sunday		Five Weeks	
Ascension-day	is	Forty Days	after *Easter.*
Whitsunday		Seven Weeks	
Trinity-Sunday		Eight Weeks	

❧ A TABLE OF FEASTS,
TO BE OBSERVED IN THIS CHURCH THROUGHOUT THE YEAR.

All Sundays in the Year.	The Annunciation of the Blessed Virgin.
The Circumcision of our Lord JESUS CHRIST.	St. Mark the Evangelist.
The Epiphany.	St. Philip and St. James the Apostles.
The Conversion of St. Paul.	The Ascension of our Lord JESUS CHRIST.
The Purification of the Blessed Virgin.	
St. Matthias the Apostle	St. Barnabas the Apostle.

A TABLE OF FEASTS (cont.)

The Nativity of St. John Baptist.	All Saints.
St. Peter the Apostle.	St. Andrew the Apostle.
St. James the Apostle.	St. Thomas the Apostle.
The Transfiguration of our Lord JESUS CHRIST.	The Nativity of our Lord JESUS CHRIST.
St. Bartholomew the Apostle.	St. Stephen the Martyr.
St. Matthew the Apostle.	St. John the Evangelist.
St. Michael and all Angels.	The Holy Innocents.
St. Luke the Evangelist.	Monday and Tuesday in Easter-week.
St. Simon and St. Jude the Apostles.	Monday and Tuesday in Whitsun-week.

A TABLE OF FASTS.

Ash-Wednesday.   Good Friday.

OTHER DAYS OF FASTING,

ON WHICH THE CHURCH REQUIRES SUCH A MEASURE OF ABSTINENCE AS IS MORE ESPECIALLY SUITED TO EXTRAORDINARY ACTS AND EXERCISES OF DEVOTION.

I. The Forty Days of *Lent*.
II. The *Ember-days* at the Four Seasons, being the *Wednesday, Friday,* and *Saturday* after { The First *Sunday* in Lent, The Feast of *Pentecost, September* 14, and *December* 13.
III. The three *Rogation-days*, being the *Monday, Tuesday,* and *Wednesday* before *Holy Thursday,* or the *Ascension* of our Lord.
IV. All the *Fridays* in the Year, except *Christmas-day*.

In addition to the above, the first *Thursday* in *November* (or, if any other day be appointed by the Civil Authority, then such day) shall be observed as a Day of *Thanksgiving* to Almighty God, for the Fruits of the Earth, and all other Blessings of his merciful Providence.

THE Numbers prefixed to the several Days, in the foregoing Calendar, between the twenty-first Day of March and the eighteenth Day of April, both inclusive, denote the Days upon which those Full Moons do fall, which happen upon or next after the twenty-first Day of March, in those Years of which they are respectively the Golden Numbers; and the Sunday Letter next following any such Full Moon points out Easter-day for that Year. All which holds until the Year of our Lord 1899 inclusive; after which Year, the places of these Golden Numbers will be to be changed, as is hereafter expressed.

To find Easter-day, look in the first column of the Calendar, between the twentieth Day of March and the nineteenth Day of April, for the Golden Number of the Year, against which stands the Day of the Paschal Full Moon. Then look in the third column for the Sunday Letter next after the Day of the Full Moon; and the Day of the Month standing against that Sunday Letter is Easter-day. If the Full Moon happen upon a Sunday, then (according to the first rule) the next Sunday after is Easter-day.

To find the Golden Number, or Prime, add 1 to the Year of our Lord, and then divide by 19; the remainder, if any, is the Golden Number: but if nothing remain, then 19 is the Golden Number.

To find the Dominical or Sunday Letter, and the places of the Golden Numbers in the Calendar, see the General Tables which follow.

A TABLE

TO FIND THE DOMINICAL OR

SUNDAY LETTER.

To find the Dominical or Sunday Letter, according to the Calendar, for any given Year of our Lord, look for the next preceding Hundredth Year in the lower part of this Table, and for the Remainder of the number of the Year in the upper part; and against the Hundredth Year, under the Remainder, you have the Sunday Letter.

Note, That in all Biasextile or Leap-years, the Letter under the number marked with an asterisk is the Sunday Letter for the Months of January and February; and the Letter under the number not so marked is the Sunday Letter for the Remainder of the Year.

YEARS IN EXCESS OF HUNDREDS OF YEARS.							
0*	0	1	2	3	4*	4	5
	6	7	8*	8	9	10	11
12*	12	13	14	15	16*	16	
	17	18	19	20*	20	21	22
23	24*	24	25	26	27	28*	
	28	29	30	31	32*	32	33
34	35	36*	36	37	38	39	
40*	40	41	42	43	44*	44	
	45	46	47	48*	48	49	50
51	52*	52	53	54	55	56*	
	56	57	58	59	60*	60	61
62	63	64*	64	65	66	67	
68*	68	69	70	71	72*	72	
	73	74	75	76*	76	77	78
79	80*	80	81	82	83	84*	
	84	85	86	87	88*	88	89
90	91	92*	92	93	94	95	
96*	96	97	98	99			

HUNDREDS OF YEARS.												
1600	2000	2400	2800	3200	B	A	G	F	E	D	C	B
1700	2100	2500	2900	3300		C	B	A	G	F	E	D
1800	2200	2600	3000	3400		E	D	C	B	A	G	F
1900	2300	2700	3100	etc.		G	F	E	D	C	B	A

A TABLE TO FIND EASTER-DAY,

FROM THE YEAR OF OUR LORD 1786, TO THE YEAR OF OUR LORD, 2013.

BOTH INCLUSIVE, BEING THE TIME OF TWELVE CYCLES OF THE MOON.

Golden Number.	Year of our Lord.	Easter-day.	Year of our Lord.	Easter-day.	Year of our Lord.	Easter-day.
1	1786	April 16	1824*	April 18	1862	April 20
2	1787	 8	1825	 3	1863	 5
3	1788*	March 23	1826	March 26	1864*	March 27
4	1789	April 12	1827	April 15	1865	April 16
5	1790	 4	1828*	 6	1866	 1
6	1791	 24	1829	 19	1867	 21
7	1792*	 8	1830	 11	1868*	 12
8	1793	March 31	1831	 3	1869	March 28
9	1794	April 20	1832*	April 22	1870	April 17
10	1795	 5	1833	 7	1871	 9
11	1796*	March 27	1834	March 30	1872*	March 31
12	1797	April 16	1835	April 19	1873	April 13
13	1798	 8	1836*	 3	1874	 5
14	1799	March 24	1837	March 26	1875	March 28
15	1800	April 13	1838	April 15	1876*	April 16
16	1801	 5	1839	March 31	1877	 1
17	1802	 18	1840*	April 19	1878	 21
18	1803	 10	1841	 11	1879	 13
19	1804*	 1	1842	March 27	1880*	March 28
1	1805	 14	1843	April 16	1881	April 17
2	1806	 6	1844*	 7	1882	 9
3	1807	March 29	1845	March 23	1883	March 25
4	1808*	April 17	1846	April 12	1884*	April 13
5	1809	 2	1847	 4	1885	 5
6	1810	 22	1848*	 23	1886	 25
7	1811	 14	1849	 8	1887	 10
8	1812*	March 29	1850	March 31	1888*	 1
9	1813	April 18	1851	April 20	1889	 21
10	1814	 10	1852*	 11	1890	 6
11	1815	March 26	1853	March 27	1891	March 29
12	1816*	April 14	1854	April 16	1892*	April 17
13	1817	 6	1855	 8	1893	 2
14	1818	March 22	1856*	March 23	1894	March 25
15	1819	April 11	1857	April 12	1895	April 14
16	1820*	 2	1858	 4	1896*	 5
17	1821	 22	1859	 24	1897	 18
18	1822	 7	1860*	 8	1898	 10
19	1823	March 30	1861	March 31	1899	 2

TABLE TO FIND EASTER-DAY—(cont.).

Golden Number.	Year of our Lord.	Easter-day.	Year of our Lord.	Easter-day.	Year of our Lord.	Easter-day.
1	1900	April 15	1938	April 17	1976*	April 18
2	1901	 7	1939	 9	1977	 10
3	1902	March 30	1940*	March 24	1978	March 26
4	1903	April 12	1941	April 13	1979	April 15
5	1904*	 3	1942	 5	1980*	 6
6	1905	 23	1943	 25	1981	 19
7	1906	 15	1944*	 9	1982	 11
8	1907	March 31	1945	 1	1983	 3
9	1908*	April 19	1946	 21	1984*	 22
10	1909	 11	1947	 6	1985	 7
11	1910	March 27	1948*	March 28	1986	March 30
12	1911	April 16	1949	April 17	1987	April 19
13	1912*	 7	1950	 9	1988*	 3
14	1913	March 23	1951	March 25	1989	March 26
15	1914	April 12	1952*	April 13	1990	April 15
16	1915	 4	1953	 5	1991	March 31
17	1916*	 23	1954	 18	1992*	April 19
18	1917	 8	1955	 10	1993	 11
19	1918	March 31	1956*	 1	1994	 3
1	1919	April 20	1957	 21	1995	 16
2	1920*	 4	1958	 6	1996*	 7
3	1921	March 27	1959	March 29	1997	March 30
4	1922	April 16	1960*	April 17	1998	April 12
5	1923	 1	1961	 2	1999	 4
6	1924*	 20	1962	 22	2000*	 23
7	1925	 12	1963	 14	2001	 15
8	1926	 4	1964*	March 29	2002	March 31
9	1927	 17	1965	April 18	2003	April 20
10	1928*	 8	1966	 10	2004*	 11
11	1929	March 31	1967	March 26	2005	March 27
12	1930	April 20	1968*	April 14	2006	April 16
13	1931	 5	1969	 6	2007	 8
14	1932*	March 27	1970	March 29	2008*	March 23
15	1933	April 16	1971	April 11	2009	April 12
16	1934	 1	1972*	 2	2010	 4
17	1935	 21	1973	 22	2011	 24
18	1936*	 12	1974	 14	2012*	 8
19	1937	March 28	1975	March 30	2013	March 31

Note, That the Years marked with an asterisk are Bissextile or Leap-years.

A TABLE OF THE MOVABLE FEASTS,

ACCORDING TO THE SEVERAL DAYS THAT EASTER CAN POSSIBLY FALL UPON.

Easter-day.	Sundays after Epiphany.	Septua-gesima Sunday.	First Day of Lent.	Ascension-day.	Whit-sunday.	Sundays after Trinity.	Advent-Sunday.
Mar. 22	1	Jan. 18	Feb. 4	Apr. 30	May 10	27	Nov. 29
.... 23	1	 19	 5	May 1	 11	27	 30
.... 24	1	 20	 6	 2	 12	27	Dec. 1
.... 25	2	 21	 7	 3	 13	27	 2
.... 26	2	 22	 8	 4	 14	27	 3
.... 27	2	 23	 9	 5	 15	26	Nov. 27
.... 28	2	 24	 10	 6	 16	26	 28
.... 29	2	 25	 11	 7	 17	26	 29
.... 30	2	 26	 12	 8	 18	26	 30
.... 31	2	 27	 13	 9	 19	26	Dec. 1
Apr. 1	3	 28	 14	 10	 20	26	 2
.... 2	3	 29	 15	 11	 21	26	 3
.... 3	3	 30	 16	 12	 22	25	Nov. 27
.... 4	3	 31	 17	 13	 23	25	 28
.... 5	3	Feb. 1	 18	 14	 24	25	 29
.... 6	3	 2	 19	 15	 25	25	 30
.... 7	3	 3	 20	 16	 26	25	Dec. 1
.... 8	4	 4	 21	 17	 27	25	 2
.... 9	4	 5	 22	 18	 28	25	 3
.... 10	4	 6	 23	 19	 29	24	Nov. 27
.... 11	4	 7	 24	 20	 30	24	 28
.... 12	4	 8	 25	 21	 31	24	 29
.... 13	4	 9	 26	 22	June 1	24	 30
.... 14	4	 10	 27	 23	 2	24	Dec. 1
.... 15	5	 11	 28	 24	 3	24	 2
.... 16	5	 12	Mar. 1	 25	 4	24	 3
.... 17	5	 13	 2	 26	 5	23	Nov. 27
.... 18	5	 14	 3	 27	 6	23	 28
.... 19	5	 15	 4	 28	 7	23	 29
.... 20	5	 16	 5	 29	 8	23	 30
.... 21	5	 17	 6	 30	 9	23	Dec. 1
.... 22	6	 18	 7	 31	 10	23	 2
.... 23	6	 19	 8	June 1	 11	22	 3
.... 24	6	 20	 9	 2	 12	22	Nov. 27
.... 25	6	 21	 10	 3	 13	22	 28

Note, That in a Bissextile or Leap-year, the number of Sundays after *Epiphany* will be the same as if *Easter-day* had fallen on Day later than it really does. And, for the same reason, one Day must, in every Leap-year, be added to the Day of the Month given by the Table for *Septuagesima* Sunday, and for the First Day of Lent: unless the Table gives some Day in the Month of *March* for it; for in that case, the Day given by the Table is the right Day.

GENERAL TABLES

FOR

FINDING THE DOMINICAL OR SUNDAY LETTER,

AND THE PLACES OF THE GOLDEN NUMBERS
IN THE CALENDAR.

TABLE I.

6	5	4	3	2	1	0
B	**C**	**D**	**E**	**F**	**G**	**A**
				1600	1700	1800
1900 2000	2100	2200	2300 2400	2500	2600	2700 2800
2900	3000	3100 3200	3300	3400	3500 3600	3700
3800	3900 4000	4100	4200	4300 4400	4500	4600
4700 4800	4900	5000	etc.			

TO find the Dominical or Sunday Letter for any given Year of our Lord, add to the Year its fourth part, omitting fractions, and also the Number, which, in Table I., standeth at the top of the column wherein the number of Hundreds contained in that given Year is found; divide the sum by 7, and if there be no remainder, then A is the Sunday Letter; but if any number remain, then the Letter which standeth under that Number at the top of the Table, is the Sunday Letter.

Note, That in all Bissextile or Leap-years, the Letter found as above will be the Sunday Letter from the first Day of March inclusive, to the End of the Year.

TABLE II.

TO find the Days to which the Golden Numbers ought to be prefixed in the Calendar in any given Year of our Lord, consisting of entire Hundred Years, and in all the intermediate Years betwixt that and the next Hundredth Year following, look in the first column of this Table for the given Year, consisting of entire Hundreds, and against it, under each Golden Number, you will find the Day of the Month to which that Golden Number ought to be prefixed in the Calendar, during that period of One Hundred Years; and if the number of the Day be greater than 20, it is a Day of March; but if it be less than 20, it is a Day of April.

The asterisk, affixed to certain Hundredth Years, denotes those Years which are still to be accounted Bissextile or Leap-years in the new Calendar; whereas all the other Hundredth Years are to be accounted only common Years.

YEARS OF OUR LORD	THE GOLDEN NUMBERS																		
	1	2	3	4	5	6	7	8	9	10	11	12	13	14	15	16	17	18	19
1600*	12	1	21	9	29	17	6	23	14	3	23	11	31	18	8	28	16	5	25
1700, 1800	13	2	22	10	30	18	7	27	15	4	24	12	1	21	9	29	17	6	26
1900, 2000*, 2100	14	3	23	11	31	18	8	28	16	5	25	13	2	22	10	30	17	7	27
2200, 2400*	15	4	24	12	1	21	9	29	17	6	23	14	3	23	11	31	18	8	28
2300, 2500	16	5	25	13	2	22	10	30	18	7	27	15	4	24	12	1	21	9	29
2600, 2700, 2800*	17	6	26	14	3	23	11	31	18	8	28	16	5	25	13	2	22	10	30
2900, 3000	18	7	27	15	4	24	12	1	21	9	29	17	6	23	14	3	23	11	31
3100, 3200*, 3300	18	8	28	16	5	25	13	2	22	10	30	17	7	27	15	4	24	12	1
3400, 3500, 3600*	21	9	29	17	6	26	14	3	23	11	31	18	8	28	16	5	25	13	2
3500, 3700	22	10	30	18	7	27	15	4	24	12	1	21	9	29	17	6	26	14	3
3800, 3900, 4000*	23	11	31	18	8	28	16	5	25	13	2	22	10	30	17	7	27	15	4
4100	24	12	1	21	9	29	17	6	23	14	3	23	11	31	18	8	28	16	5
4200, 4300, 4400*	25	13	2	22	10	30	18	7	27	15	4	24	12	1	21	9	29	17	6
4500, 4600	26	14	3	23	11	31	18	8	28	16	5	25	13	2	22	10	30	17	7
4700, 4800*, 4900	27	15	4	24	12	1	21	9	29	17	6	26	14	3	23	11	31	18	8
5000, 5200*	28	16	5	25	13	2	22	10	30	18	7	27	15	4	24	12	1	21	9
5100, 5300	29	17	6	26	14	3	23	11	31	18	8	28	16	5	25	13	2	22	10
5400, 5500, 5600*	30	18	7	27	15	4	24	12	1	21	9	29	17	6	26	14	3	23	11
5700, 5800	31	18	8	28	16	5	25	13	2	22	10	30	17	7	27	15	4	24	12
5900, 6000*, 6100	1	19	9	29	17	6	26	14	3	23	11	31	18	8	28	16	5	25	13
6200, 6400*	2	22	10	30	18	7	27	15	4	24	12	1	21	9	29	17	6	26	14
6300, 6500	3	23	11	31	18	8	28	16	5	25	13	2	22	10	30	17	7	27	15
6600, 6800*	4	24	12	1	21	9	29	17	6	26	14	3	23	11	31	18	8	28	16
6700, 6900	5	25	13	2	22	10	30	18	7	27	15	4	24	12	1	21	9	29	17
7000, 7100, 7200*	6	26	14	3	23	11	31	18	8	28	16	5	25	13	2	22	10	30	17
7300, 7400	7	27	15	4	24	12	1	21	9	29	17	6	26	14	3	23	11	31	18
7500, 7600*, 7700	8	28	16	5	25	13	2	22	10	30	18	7	27	15	4	24	12	1	21
7800, 8000*	9	29	17	6	26	14	3	23	11	31	18	8	28	16	5	25	13	2	22
7900, 8100	10	30	18	7	27	15	4	24	12	1	21	9	29	17	6	26	14	3	23
8200, 8300, 8400*	11	31	18	8	28	16	5	25	13	2	22	10	30	17	7	27	15	4	24

THE ORDER FOR
DAILY MORNING PRAYER.
❊

¶ *The Minister shall always begin the Morning Prayer by reading one or more of the following Sentences of Scripture.*

¶ *On any day not a Sunday, he may omit the Exhortation following, saying instead thereof, Let us humbly confess our sins unto Almighty God, and may end the Morning Prayer with the Collect for Grace and 2 Cor. xiii. 14.*

¶ *On any day when the Holy Communion is immediately to follow, the Minister may, at his discretion, pass at once from the Sentences to the Lord's Prayer, first pronouncing, The Lord be with you. Answer. And with thy spirit. Minister. Let us pray.*

THE LORD is in his holy temple: let all the earth keep silence before him. *Hab.* ii. 20.

I was glad when they said unto me, We will go into the house of the LORD. *Psalm* cxxii. 1.

Let the words of my mouth, and the meditation of my heart, be alway acceptable in thy sight, O LORD, my strength and my redeemer. *Psalm* xix. 14, 15.

Grace be unto you, and peace, from God our Father, and from the Lord Jesus Christ. *Phil.* i. 2.

Repent ye, for the Kingdom of heaven is at hand. *Advent. St. Matt.* iii. 2.

Prepare ye the way of the LORD, make straight in the desert a highway for our God. *Isaiah* xl. 3.

Behold, I bring you good tidings of great joy, which shall be to all people. For unto you is born *Christmas.* this day in the city of David a Saviour, which is Christ the Lord. *St. Luke* ii. 10, 11.

From the rising of the sun even unto the going down of the same my Name shall be great *Epiphany.* among the Gentiles; and in every place incense shall be offered unto my Name, and a pure offering: for my Name shall be great among the heathen, saith the LORD of hosts. *Mal.* i. 11.

Awake, awake; put on thy strength, O Zion; put on thy beautiful garments, O Jerusalem. *Isaiah* lii. 1.

Is it nothing to you, all ye that pass by? behold, and see if there be *Good Friday.* any sorrow like unto my sorrow which is done unto me, wherewith the LORD hath afflicted me. *Lam.* i. 12.

He is risen. The Lord is risen *Easter.* indeed. *St. Mark* xvi. 6. *St. Luke* xxiv. 34.

This is the day which the LORD hath made; we will rejoice and be glad in it. *Psalm* cxviii. 24.

Seeing that we have a great High Priest, that is passed into the *Ascension-* heavens, Jesus the Son of God, let us come boldly unto the throne of grace, that we may obtain mercy, and find grace to help in time of need. *Heb.* iv. 14, 16.

Because ye are sons, God hath *Whitsunday.* sent forth the Spirit of his Son into your hearts, crying, Abba, Father. *Gal.* iv. 6.

There is a river, the streams whereof shall make glad the city of God, the holy place of the tabernacles of the Most High. *Psalm* xlvi. 4.

The hour cometh, and now is, when the true worshippers shall worship the Father in spirit and in truth. *St. John* iv. 23.

Holy, holy, holy, Lord God Almighty, *Trinity-Sunday.* which was, and is, and is to come. *Rev.* iv. 8.

When the wicked man turneth away from his wickedness that he hath committed, and doeth that which is lawful and right, he shall save his soul alive. *Ezek.* xviii. 27.

I acknowledge my transgressions: and my sin is ever before me. *Psalm* li. 3.

Hide thy face from my sins, and blot out all mine iniquities. *Psalm* li. 9.

The sacrifices of God are a broken spirit: a broken and a contrite heart, O God, thou wilt not despise. *Psalm* li. 17.

Rend your heart, and not your garments, and turn unto the LORD your God: for he is gracious and merciful, slow to anger, and of great kindness, and repenteth him of the evil. *Joel* ii. 13.

To the Lord our God belong mercies and forgivenesses, though we have rebelled against him; neither have we obeyed the voice of the LORD our God, to walk in his laws which he set before us. *Dan.* ix. 9, 10.

O LORD, correct me, but with judgment; not in thine anger, lest thou bring me to nothing. *Jer.* x. 24. *Psalm* vi. 1.

I will arise and go to my father, and will say unto him, Father, I have sinned against heaven, and before thee, and am no more worthy to be called thy son. *St. Luke* xv. 18, 19.

Enter not into judgment with thy servant, O LORD; for in thy sight shall no man living be justified. *Psalm* cxliii. 2.

If we say that we have no sin, we deceive ourselves, and the truth is not in us; but if we confess our sins, God is faithful and just to forgive us our sins, and to cleanse us from all unrighteousness. 1 *St. John* i. 8, 9.

¶ *Then the Minister shall say,*

DEARLY beloved brethren, the Scripture moveth us, in sundry places, to acknowledge and confess our manifold sins and wickedness; and that we should not dissemble nor cloak them before the face of Almighty God our heavenly Father; but confess them with an humble, lowly, penitent, and obedient heart; to the end that we may obtain forgiveness of the same, by his infinite goodness and mercy. And although we ought, at all times, humbly to acknowledge our sins before God; yet ought we chiefly so to do, when we assemble and meet together to render thanks for the great benefits that we have received at his hands, to set forth his most worthy praise, to hear his most holy Word, and to ask those things which are requisite and necessary, as well for the body as the soul. Wherefore I pray and beseech you, as many as are here present, to accompany me with a pure heart, and humble voice, unto the throne of the heavenly grace, saying—

A General Confession.

¶ *To be said by the whole Congregation, after the Minister, all kneeling.*

ALMIGHTY and most merciful Father; We have erred, and strayed from thy ways like lost sheep. We have followed too much the devices and desires of our own hearts. We have offended against thy holy laws. We have left undone those things which we ought to have done; And we have done those things which we ought not to have done; And there is no health in us. But thou, O Lord, have mercy upon us, miserable offenders. Spare thou those, O God, who confess their faults. Restore thou those who are penitent; According to thy promises declared unto mankind in Christ Jesus our Lord. And grant, O most merciful Father, for his sake; That we may hereafter live a godly, righteous, and sober life, To the glory of thy holy Name. Amen.

The Declaration of Absolution, or Remission of Sins.

¶ *To be made by the Priest alone, standing; the People still kneeling.*

ALMIGHTY God, the Father of our Lord Jesus Christ, who desireth not the death of a sinner, but rather that he may turn from his wickedness and live, hath given power, and commandment, to his Ministers, to declare and pronounce to his people, being penitent, the Absolution and Remission of their sins. He pardoneth and absolveth all those

who truly repent, and unfeignedly believe his holy Gospel. Wherefore let us beseech him to grant us true repentance, and his Holy Spirit, that those things may please him which we do at this present; and that the rest of our life hereafter may be pure and holy; so that at the last we may come to his eternal joy; through Jesus Christ our Lord.

¶ *The People shall answer here, and at the end of every Prayer,* Amen.

¶ *Or this.*

ALMIGHTY God, our heavenly Father, who of his great mercy hath promised forgiveness of sins to all those who, with hearty repentance and true faith, turn unto him; Have mercy upon you; pardon and deliver you from all your sins; confirm and strengthen you in all goodness; and bring you to everlasting life; through Jesus Christ our Lord. *Amen.*

¶ *Then the Minister shall kneel, and say the Lord's Prayer; the People still kneeling, and repeating it with him, both here, and wheresoever else it is used in Divine Service.*

OUR Father, who art in heaven, Hallowed be thy Name. Thy kingdom come. Thy will be done on earth, As it is in heaven. Give us this day our daily bread. And forgive us our trespasses, As we forgive those who trespass against us. And lead us not into temptation; But deliver us from evil: For thine is the kingdom, and the power, and the glory, for ever and ever. *Amen.*

¶ *Then likewise he shall say,*

O Lord, open thou our lips.

Answer. And our mouth shall show forth thy praise.

¶ *Here, all standing up, the Minister shall say,*

Glory be to the Father, and to the Son, and to the Holy Ghost;

Answer. As it was in the beginning, is now, and ever shall be, world without end. Amen.

Minister. Praise ye the Lord.

Answer. The Lord's Name be praised.

¶ *Then shall be said or sung the following Anthem; except on those days for which other Anthems are appointed; and except also, when it is used in the course of the Psalms, on the nineteenth day of the month.*

Venite, exultemus Domino.

O COME, let us sing unto the Lord:

let us heartily rejoice in the strength of our salvation.

Let us come before his presence with thanksgiving : and show ourselves glad in him with psalms.

For the LORD is a great God : and a great King above all gods.

In his hand are all the corners of the earth : and the strength of the hills is his also.

The sea is his, and he made it : and his hands prepared the dry land.

O come, let us worship and fall down : and kneel before the LORD our Maker.

For he is the Lord our God : and we are the people of his pasture, and the sheep of his hand.

O worship the LORD in the beauty of holi-ness : let the whole earth stand in awe of him.

For he cometh, for he cometh to judge the earth : and with righteousness to judge the world, and the people with his truth.

¶ *Then shall follow a Por-tion of the* PSALMS, *as they are appointed, or one of the Selections of Psalms. And at the end of every Psalm, and likewise at the end of the* Venite, Bene-dicite, Benedictus, Jubi-late, *may be, and at the end of the whole Portion, or Selection from the Psal-ter, shall be sung or said the* Gloria Patri :

GLORY be to the Father, and to the Son : and to the Holy Ghost ;

As it was in the be-ginning, is now, and ever shall be : world without end. Amen.

¶ *At the end of the whole Portion of the Psalms or Selection from the Psalter, the Gloria in excelsis may be sung or said instead of the Gloria Patri.*

¶ *Then shall be read the* FIRST LESSON, *according to the Table or Calendar. After which shall be said or sung the following Hymn.*

¶ *Note, That before every Lesson, the Minister shall say,* Here beginneth such a Chapter [*or Verse of such a Chapter*] of such a Book; *and after every Lesson,* Here endeth the First [*or the Second*] Lesson.

Te Deum laudamus.

WE praise thee, O God: we acknowledge thee to be the Lord.

All the earth doth worship thee: the Father everlasting.

To thee all Angels cry aloud: the Heavens, and all the Powers therein;

To thee Cherubim and Seraphim: continually do cry,

Holy, Holy, Holy: Lord God of Sabaoth;

Heaven and earth are full of the Majesty: of thy glory.

The glorious company of the Apostles: praise thee.

The goodly fellowship of the Prophets: praise thee.

The noble army of Martyrs: praise thee.

The holy Church throughout all the world: doth acknowledge thee;

The Father: of an infinite Majesty;

Thine adorable, true: and only Son;

Also the Holy Ghost: the Comforter.

Thou art the King of Glory: O Christ.

Thou art the everlasting Son: of the Father.

When thou tookest upon thee to deliver man: thou didst humble thyself to be born of a Virgin.

When thou hadst overcome the sharpness of death : thou didst open the Kingdom of Heaven to all believers.

Thou sittest at the right hand of God : in the glory of the Father.

We believe that thou shalt come : to be our Judge.

We therefore pray thee, help thy servants : whom thou hast redeemed with thy precious blood.

Make them to be numbered with thy Saints : in glory everlasting.

O Lord, save thy people : and bless thine heritage.

Govern them : and lift them up for ever.

Day by day : we magnify thee;

And we worship thy Name : ever, world without end.

Vouchsafe, O Lord : to keep us this day without sin.

O Lord, have mercy upon us : have mercy upon us.

O Lord, let thy mercy be upon us : as our trust is in thee.

O Lord, in thee have I trusted : let me never be confounded.

¶ Or this Canticle.

Benedicite, omnia opera Domini.

O ALL ye Works of the Lord, bless ye the Lord : praise him, and magnify him for ever.

O ye Angels of the Lord, bless ye the Lord : praise him, and magnify him for ever.

O ye Heavens, bless ye the Lord : praise him, and magnify him for ever.

O ye Waters that be above the firmament, bless ye the Lord :

praise him, and magnify him for ever.

O all ye Powers of the Lord, bless ye the Lord: praise him, and magnify him for ever.

O ye Sun and Moon, bless ye the Lord: praise him, and magnify him for ever.

O ye Stars of heaven, bless ye the Lord: praise him, and magnify him for ever.

O ye Showers and Dew, bless ye the Lord: praise him, and magnify him for ever.

O ye Winds of God, bless ye the Lord: praise him, and magnify him for ever.

O ye Fire and Heat, bless ye the Lord: praise him, and magnify him for ever.

O ye Winter and Summer, bless ye the Lord: praise him, and magnify him for ever.

O ye Dews and Frosts, bless ye the Lord: praise him, and magnify him for ever.

O ye Frost and Cold, bless ye the Lord: praise him, and magnify him for ever.

O ye Ice and Snow, bless ye the Lord: praise him, and magnify him for ever.

O ye Nights and Days, bless ye the Lord: praise him, and magnify him for ever.

O ye Light and Darkness, bless ye the Lord: praise him, and magnify him for ever.

O ye Lightnings and Clouds, bless ye the Lord: praise him, and magnify him for ever.

O let the Earth bless the Lord: yea, let it praise him, and magnify him for ever.

O ye Mountains and Hills, bless ye the Lord: praise him, and magnify him for ever.

O all ye Green Things upon the earth, bless ye the Lord : praise him, and magnify him for ever.

O ye Wells, bless ye the Lord : praise him, and magnify him for ever.

O ye Seas and Floods, bless ye the Lord : praise him, and magnify him for ever.

O ye Whales, and all that move in the waters, bless ye the Lord : praise him, and magnify him for ever.

O all ye Fowls of the air, bless ye the Lord : praise him, and magnify him for ever.

O all ye Beasts and Cattle, bless ye the Lord : praise him, and magnify him for ever.

O ye Children of Men, bless ye the Lord : praise him, and magnify him for ever.

O let Israel bless the Lord : praise him, and magnify him for ever.

O ye Priests of the Lord, bless ye the Lord : praise him, and magnify him for ever.

O ye Servants of the Lord, bless ye the Lord : praise him, and magnify him for ever.

O ye Spirits and Souls of the Righteous, bless ye the Lord : praise him, and magnify him for ever.

O ye holy and humble Men of heart, bless ye the Lord : praise him, and magnify him for ever.

¶ *Then shall be read, in like manner, the* SECOND LESSON, *taken out of the New Testament, according to the Table or Calendar.*

¶ *And after that shall be sung or said the Hymn following: but* Note, That, *save on the Sundays in Advent, the latter portion thereof may be omitted.*

Benedictus. St. Luke i. 68.

BLESSED be the Lord God of Israel: for he hath visited and redeemed his people;

And hath raised up a mighty salvation for us: in the house of his servant David;

As he spake by the mouth of his holy Prophets: which have been since the world began;

That we should be saved from our enemies: and from the hand of all that hate us.

To perform the mercy promised to our forefathers: and to remember his holy covenant;

To perform the oath which he sware to our forefather Abraham: that he would give us;

That we being delivered out of the hand of our enemies: might serve him without fear;

In holiness and righteousness before him: all the days of our life.

And thou, child, shalt be called the prophet of the Highest: for thou shalt go before the face of the Lord to prepare his ways;

To give knowledge of salvation unto his people: for the remission of their sins,

Through the tender mercy of our God: whereby the day-spring from on high hath visited us;

To give light to them that sit in darkness, and in the shadow of death: and to guide our feet into the way of peace.

¶ *Or this Psalm.*

Jubilate Deo. Psalm c.

O BE joyful in the LORD, all ye lands: serve the LORD with gladness, and come before his presence with a song.

Be ye sure that the LORD he is God; it is he that hath made us, and not we ourselves: we are his people, and the sheep of his pasture.

O go your way into his gates with thanksgiving, and into his courts with praise: be thankful unto him, and speak good of his Name.

For the LORD is gracious, his mercy is everlasting: and his truth endureth from generation to generation.

¶ *Then shall be said the Apostles' Creed by the Minister and the People, stand-*ing. *And any Churches may, instead of the words,* He descended into hell, *use the words,* He went into the place of departed spirits, *which are considered as words of the same meaning in the Creed.*

I BELIEVE in God the Father Almighty, Maker of heaven and earth:

And in Jesus Christ his only Son our Lord: Who was conceived by the Holy Ghost, Born of the Virgin Mary: Suffered under Pontius Pilate, Was crucified, dead, and buried: He descended into hell; The third day he rose again from the dead: He ascended into heaven, And sitteth on the right hand of God the Father Almighty: From thence he shall come to judge the quick and the dead.

I believe in the Holy

Ghost: The holy Catholic Church; The Communion of Saints: The Forgiveness of sins: The Resurrection of the body: And the Life everlasting. Amen.

¶ *Or this.*

I BELIEVE in one God the Father Almighty, Maker of heaven and earth, And of all things visible and invisible:

And in one Lord Jesus Christ, the only-begotten Son of God; Begotten of his Father before all worlds, God of God, Light of Light, Very God of very God; Begotten, not made; Being of one substance with the Father; By whom all things were made: Who for us men and for our salvation came down from heaven, And was incarnate by the Holy Ghost of the Virgin Mary, And was made man: And was crucified also for us under Pontius Pilate; He suffered and was buried: And the third day he rose again according to the Scriptures: And ascended into heaven, And sitteth on the right hand of the Father: And he shall come again, with glory, to judge both the quick and the dead; Whose kingdom shall have no end.

And I believe in the Holy Ghost, The Lord, and Giver of Life, Who proceedeth from the Father and the Son; Who with the Father and the Son together is worshipped and glorified; Who spake by the Prophets: And I believe one Catholic and Apostolic Church: I acknowledge one

Baptism for the remission of sins: And I look for the Resurrection of the dead: And the Life of the world to come. Amen.

¶ *And after that, these Prayers following, all devoutly kneeling; the Minister first pronouncing,*

The Lord be with you.

Answer. And with thy spirit.

Minister.

Let us pray.

O Lord, show thy mercy upon us.

Answer. And grant us thy salvation.

Minister. O God, make clean our hearts within us.

Answer. And take not thy Holy Spirit from us.

¶ *Then shall follow the* COLLECT FOR THE DAY, *except when the Communion Service is read; and then the Collect for the day shall be omitted here.*

A Collect for Peace.

O GOD, who art the author of peace and lover of concord, in knowledge of whom standeth our eternal life, whose service is perfect freedom; Defend us thy humble servants in all assaults of our enemies; that we, surely trusting in thy defence, may not fear the power of any adversaries, through the might of Jesus Christ our Lord. Amen.

A Collect for Grace.

O LORD, our heavenly Father, Almighty and everlasting God, who hast safely brought us to the beginning of this day; Defend us in the same with thy mighty power; and grant that this day we fall into no sin, neither run into any kind of danger; but that all our doings, being ordered by thy governance, may be righteous in thy sight; through Jesus Christ our Lord. *Amen.*

A Prayer for The President of the United States, *and all in Civil Authority.*

O LORD, our heavenly Father, the high and mighty Ruler of the universe, who dost from thy throne behold all the dwellers upon earth; Most heartily we beseech thee, with thy favour to behold and bless thy servant THE PRESIDENT OF THE UNITED STATES, and all others in authority; and so replenish them with the grace of thy Holy Spirit, that they may always incline to thy will, and walk in thy way. Endue them plenteously with heavenly gifts; grant them in health and prosperity long to live; and finally, after this life, to attain everlasting joy and felicity; through Jesus Christ our Lord. *Amen.*

¶ *The following Prayers shall be omitted here when the* LITANY *is said, and may be omitted when the Holy Communion is immediately to follow.*

A Prayer for the Clergy and People.

ALMIGHTY and everlasting God, from whom cometh every good and perfect gift; Send down upon our Bishops, and other Clergy, and upon the Congregations committed to their charge, the healthful Spirit of thy grace; and, that they may truly please thee, pour upon them the continual dew of thy blessing. Grant this, O Lord, for the honour of our Advocate and Mediator, Jesus Christ. *Amen.*

A Prayer for all Conditions of Men.

O GOD, the Creator and Preserver of all mankind, we humbly beseech thee for all sorts and conditions of men; that thou wouldest be pleased to make thy ways known unto them, thy saving health unto all nations. More especially we pray for thy holy Church universal; that it may be so guided and governed by thy good Spirit, that all who profess and call themselves Christians may be led into the way of truth, and hold the faith in unity of spirit, in the bond of peace, and in righteousness of life. Finally, we commend to thy fatherly goodness all those who are any ways afflicted, or distressed, in mind, body, or estate [*especially those for whom our prayers are desired;*] that it may please thee to comfort and relieve them, according to their several necessities; giving them patience under their sufferings, and a happy issue out of all their afflictions. And this we beg for Jesus Christ's sake. *Amen.*

This may be said when any desire the prayers of the Congregation.

A General Thanksgiving.

ALMIGHTY God, Father of all mercies, we, thine unworthy servants, do give thee most humble and hearty thanks for all thy goodness and loving-kindness to us, and to all men; [* *particularly to those who desire now to offer up their praises and thanksgivings for thy late mercies vouchsafed unto them.*] We bless thee for our creation, preservation, and all the blessings of this life; but above all, for thine inestimable love in the redemption of the world by our Lord Jesus Christ; for the means of grace, and for the hope of glory. And, we beseech thee, give us that due sense of all thy mercies, that our hearts may be unfeignedly thankful;

* *This may be said when any desire to return thanks for mercies vouchsafed to them.*

and that we show forth thy praise, not only with our lips, but in our lives, by giving up our selves to thy service, and by walking before thee in holiness and righteousness all our days; through Jesus Christ our Lord, to whom, with thee and the Holy Ghost, be all honour and glory, world without end. *Amen.*

A Prayer of St. Chrysostom.

ALMIGHTY God, who hast given us grace at this time with one accord to make our common supplications unto thee; and dost promise that when two or three are gathered together in thy Name thou wilt grant their requests; Fulfil now, O Lord, the desires and petitions of thy servants, as may be most expedient for them; granting us in this world knowledge of thy truth, and in the world to come life everlasting. *Amen.*

2 Cor. xiii. 14.

THE grace of our Lord Jesus Christ, and the love of God, and the fellowship of the Holy Ghost, be with us all evermore. *Amen.*

Here endeth the Order of Morning Prayer.

THE ORDER FOR
DAILY EVENING PRAYER.

✿

¶ The Minister shall begin the Evening Prayer by reading one or more of the following Sentences of Scripture; and then he shall say that which is written after them. But on days other than the Lord's Day, he may, at his discretion, pass at once from the Sentences to the Lord's Prayer.

THE LORD is in his holy temple : let all the earth keep silence before him. *Hab.* ii. 20.

LORD, I have loved the habitation of thy house, and the place where thine honour dwelleth. *Psalm* xxvi. 8.

Let my prayer be set forth in thy sight as the incense ; and let the lifting up of my hands be an evening sacrifice. *Psalm* cxli. 2.

O worship the LORD in the beauty of holiness ; let the whole earth stand in awe of him. *Psalm* xcvi. 9.

Let the words of my mouth, and the meditation of my heart, be alway acceptable in thy sight, O LORD, my strength and my redeemer. *Psalm* xix. 14, 15.

Watch ye, for ye know not when the master of the house cometh, at *Advent.* even, or at midnight, or at the cock-crowing, or in the morning : lest coming suddenly he find you sleeping. *St. Mark* xiii. 35, 36.

Repent ye; for the Kingdom of heaven is at hand. *St. Matt.* iii. 2.

Behold, the tabernacle of God is with men, and he will dwell *Christmas.* with them, and they shall be his people, and God himself shall be with them, and be their God. *Rev.* xxi. 3.

From the rising of the sun even unto the going down of the same my Name shall be great *Epiphany.* among the Gentiles; and in every place incense shall be offered unto my Name, and a pure offering : for my Name shall be great among the heathen, saith the LORD of hosts. *Mal.* i. 11.

Come ye, and let us walk in the light of the LORD. And he will teach us of his ways, and we will walk in his paths. *Isaiah* ii. 5, 3.

He hath made him to be sin *Good Friday.* for us, who knew no sin; that we might be made the righteousness of God in him. 2 *Cor.* v. 21.

In whom we have redemption through his blood, the forgiveness of sins, according to the riches of his grace. *Eph.* i. 7.

If ye then be risen with Christ, *Easter.* seek those things which are above, where Christ sitteth on the right hand of God. *Col.* iii. 1.

Christ is not entered into the holy places

made with hands, which are the figures of the true; but into heaven itself, now *Ascension.* to appear in the presence of God for us. *Heb.* ix. 24.

The Spirit and the bride say, Come. And let him *Whitsunday.* that heareth say, Come. And let him that is athirst come. And whosoever will, let him take the water of life freely. *Rev.* xxii. 17.

O send out thy light and thy truth, that they may lead me, and bring me unto thy holy hill, and to thy dwelling. *Psalm* xliii. 3.

Holy, holy, holy, is the LORD of *Trinity-* hosts: the *Sunday.* whole earth is full of his glory. *Isaiah* vi. 3.

When the wicked man turneth away from his wickedness that he hath committed, and doeth that which is lawful and right, he shall save his soul alive. *Ezek.* xviii. 27.

I acknowledge my transgressions: and my sin is ever before me. *Psalm* li. 3.

Hide thy face from my sins, and blot out all mine iniquities. *Psalm* li. 9.

The sacrifices of God are a broken spirit: a broken and a contrite heart, O God, thou wilt not despise. *Psalm* li. 17.

Rend your heart, and not your garments, and turn unto the LORD your God: for he is gracious and merciful, slow to anger, and of great kindness, and repenteth him of the evil. *Joel* ii. 13.

To the Lord our God belong mercies and forgivenesses, though we have rebelled against him; neither have we obeyed the voice of the Lord our God, to walk in his laws which he set before us. *Dan.* ix. 9, 10.

O Lord, correct me, but with judgment; not in thine anger, lest thou bring me to nothing. *Jer.* x. 24. *Psalm* vi. 1.

I will arise and go to my father, and will say unto him, Father, I have sinned against heaven, and before thee, and am no more worthy to be called thy son. *St. Luke* xv. 18, 19.

Enter not into judgment with thy servant, O Lord; for in thy sight shall no man living be justified. *Psalm* cxliii. 2.

If we say that we have no sin, we deceive ourselves, and the truth is not in us; but if we confess our sins, God is faithful and just to forgive us our sins, and to cleanse us from all unrighteousness. 1 *St. John* i. 8, 9.

LET us humbly confess our sins unto Almighty God.

¶ *Or else he shall say as followeth.*

DEARLY beloved brethren, the Scripture moveth us, in sundry places, to acknowledge and confess our manifold sins and wickedness; and that we should not dissemble nor cloak them before the face of Almighty God our heavenly Father; but confess them with an humble, lowly, penitent, and obedient heart; to the end that we may obtain forgiveness of the same, by his infinite goodness and mercy. And although we ought, at all times, humbly to acknowledge our sins before God; yet ought we chiefly so to do, when we assemble and meet together to render thanks for the great benefits that we have received at his hands, to set forth his most worthy praise, to hear his most holy Word, and to ask those things which are requisite and necessary, as well for the body as the soul. Wherefore I pray and beseech you, as many as are here present, to accompany me with a pure heart, and humble voice, unto the throne of the heavenly grace, saying—

A General Confession.

¶ *To be said by the whole Congregation, after the Minister, all kneeling.*

ALMIGHTY and most merciful Father; We have erred, and strayed from thy ways like lost sheep. We have followed too much the devices and desires of our own hearts. We have offended against thy holy laws. We have left undone those things which we ought to have done; And we have done those things which we ought not to have done; And there is no health in us. But thou, O Lord, have mercy upon us, miserable offenders. Spare thou those, O God, who confess their faults. Restore thou those who are penitent; According to thy promises declared unto mankind in Christ Jesus our Lord. And grant, O most merciful Father, for his sake; That we may hereafter live a godly, righteous, and sober life, To the glory of thy holy Name. Amen.

The Declaration of Absolution, or Remission of Sins.

¶ *To be made by the Priest alone, standing; the People still kneeling.*

ALMIGHTY God, the Father of our Lord Jesus Christ, who desireth not the death of a sinner, but rather that he may turn from his wickedness and live, hath given power, and commandment, to his Ministers, to declare and pronounce to his people, being penitent, the Absolution and Remission of their sins. He pardoneth and absolveth all those who truly repent, and unfeignedly believe his holy Gospel. Wherefore let us beseech him to grant us true repentance, and his Holy Spirit, that those things may please him which we do at this present; and that the rest of our life hereafter may be pure and holy; so that at the last we may come to his eternal joy; through Jesus Christ our Lord. *Amen.*

¶ *Or this.*

ALMIGHTY God, our heavenly Father, who of his great mercy hath promised forgiveness of sins to all those who, with hearty repentance and true faith, turn unto him; Have mercy upon you; pardon and deliver you from all your sins; confirm and strengthen you in all goodness; and bring you to everlasting life; through Jesus Christ our Lord. *Amen.*

¶ *Then the Minister shall kneel, and say the Lord's Prayer; the People still kneeling, and repeating it with him.*

OUR Father, who art in heaven, Hallowed be thy Name. Thy kingdom come. Thy will be done on earth, As it is in heaven. Give us this day our daily bread. And forgive us our trespasses, As we forgive those who trespass against us. And lead us not into temptation; But deliver us from evil: For thine is the kingdom, and the power, and the glory, for ever and ever. Amen.

¶ *Then likewise he shall say,*

O Lord, open thou our lips.

Answer. And our mouth shall show forth thy praise.

¶ *Here, all standing up, the Minister shall say,*

Glory be to the Father, and to the Son, and to the Holy Ghost;

Answer. As it was in the beginning, is now, and ever shall be, world without end. Amen.

Minister. Praise ye the Lord.

Answer. The Lord's Name be praised.

¶ *Then shall follow a Portion of the* PSALMS, *as they are appointed, or one of the Selections, as they are set forth by this Church. And at the end of every Psalm, and likewise at the end of the Magnificat, Cantate Domino, Bonum est confiteri, Nunc dimittis, Deus misereatur, Benedic anima mea, may be sung or said the Gloria*

Patri; *and at the end of the whole Portion or Selection of Psalms for the day, shall be sung or said the Gloria Patri, or else the Gloria in excelsis, as followeth.*

Gloria in excelsis.

GLORY be to God on high, and on earth peace, good will towards men. We praise thee, we bless thee, we worship thee, we glorify thee, we give thanks to thee for thy great glory, O Lord God, heavenly King, God the Father Almighty.

O Lord, the only-begotten Son, Jesus Christ; O Lord God, Lamb of God, Son of the Father, that takest away the sins of the world, have mercy upon us. Thou that takest away the sins of the world, have mercy upon us. Thou that takest away the sins of the world, receive our prayer. Thou that sittest at the right hand of God the Father, have mercy upon us.

For thou only art holy; thou only art the Lord; thou only, O Christ, with the Holy Ghost, art most high in the glory of God the Father. Amen.

¶ *Then shall be read the* FIRST LESSON, *according to the Table or Calendar.*

¶ *After which shall be sung or said the Hymn called* Magnificat, *as followeth.*

Magnificat. St. Luke i. 46.

MY soul doth magnify the Lord: and my spirit hath rejoiced in God my Saviour.

For he hath regarded: the lowliness of his hand-maiden.

For behold, from

henceforth : all generations shall call me blessed.

For he that is mighty hath magnified me : and holy is his Name.

And his mercy is on them that fear him : throughout all generations.

He hath showed strength with his arm : he hath scattered the proud in the imagination of their hearts.

He hath put down the mighty from their seat : and hath exalted the humble and meek.

He hath filled the hungry with good things : and the rich he hath sent empty away.

He remembering his mercy hath holpen his servant Israel : as he promised to our forefathers, Abraham and his seed, for ever.

¶ *Or this Psalm, except when it is read in the ordinary course of the Psalms, on the nineteenth day of the month,*

Cantate Domino.

Psalm xcviii

O SING unto the LORD a new song : for he hath done marvellous things.

With his own right hand, and with his holy arm : hath he gotten himself the victory.

The LORD declared his salvation : his righteousness hath he openly showed in the sight of the heathen.

He hath remembered his mercy and truth toward the house of Israel : and all the ends of the world have seen the salvation of our God.

Show yourselves joyful unto the LORD, all

ye lands: sing, rejoice, and give thanks.

Praise the LORD upon the harp: sing to the harp with a psalm of thanksgiving.

With trumpets also and shawms: O show yourselves joyful before the LORD, the King.

Let the sea make a noise, and all that therein is: the round world, and they that dwell therein.

Let the floods clap their hands, and let the hills be joyful together before the LORD: for he cometh to judge the earth.

With righteousness shall he judge the world: and the people with equity.

¶ *Or this.*

Bonum est confiteri.

Psalm xcii.

IT is a good thing to give thanks unto the LORD: and to sing praises unto thy Name, O Most Highest;

To tell of thy loving-kindness early in the morning: and of thy truth in the night season;

Upon an instrument of ten strings, and upon the lute: upon a loud instrument, and upon the harp.

For thou, LORD, hast made me glad through thy works: and I will rejoice in giving praise for the operations of thy hands.

¶ *Then a* LESSON OF THE NEW TESTAMENT, *as it is appointed.*

¶ *And after that shall be sung or said the Hymn called* Nunc dimittis, *as followeth.*

Nunc dimittis.

St. Luke ii. 29.

LORD, now lettest thou thy servant depart in peace: according to thy word.

For mine eyes have seen : thy salvation,

Which thou hast prepared : before the face of all people ;

To be a light to lighten the Gentiles : and to be the glory of thy people Israel.

¶ *Or else this Psalm ; except it be on the twelfth day of the month.*

Deus misereatur.

Psalm lxvii.

GOD be merciful unto us, and bless us : and show us the light of his countenance, and be merciful unto us ;

That thy way may be known upon earth : thy saving health among all nations.

Let the people praise thee, O God : yea, let all the people praise thee.

O let the nations rejoice and be glad : for thou shalt judge the folk righteously, and govern the nations upon earth.

Let the people praise thee, O God : yea, let all the people praise thee.

Then shall the earth bring forth her increase : and God, even our own God, shall give us his blessing.

God shall bless us : and all the ends of the world shall fear him.

¶ *Or this.*

Benedic, anima mea.

Psalm ciii.

PRAISE the LORD, O my soul : and all that is within me, praise his holy Name.

Praise the LORD, O my soul : and forget not all his benefits :

Who forgiveth all thy sin : and healeth all thine infirmities ;

Who saveth thy life from destruction : and crowneth thee with mercy and loving-kindness.

O praise the LORD, ye angels of his, ye that excel in strength: ye that fulfil his commandment, and hearken unto the voice of his word.

O praise the LORD, all ye his hosts: ye servants of his that do his pleasure.

O speak good of the LORD, all ye works of his, in all places of his dominion: praise thou the LORD, O my soul.

¶ *Then shall be said the Apostles' Creed by the Minister and the People, standing. And any Churches may, instead of the words,* He descended into hell, *use the words,* He went into the place of departed spirits, *which are considered as words of the same meaning in the Creed.*

I BELIEVE in God the Father Almighty, Maker of heaven and earth:

And in Jesus Christ his only Son our Lord: Who was conceived by the Holy Ghost, Born of the Virgin Mary: Suffered under Pontius Pilate, Was crucified, dead, and buried: He descended into hell; The third day he rose again from the dead: He ascended into heaven, And sitteth on the right hand of God the Father Almighty: From thence he shall come to judge the quick and the dead.

I believe in the Holy Ghost: The holy Catholic Church; The Communion of Saints: The Forgiveness of sins: The Resurrection of the body: And the Life everlasting. Amen.

¶ *Or this.*

I BELIEVE in one God the Father

Almighty, Maker of heaven and earth, And of all things visible and invisible:

And in one Lord Jesus Christ, the only-begotten Son of God; Begotten of his Father before all worlds, God of God, Light of Light, Very God of very God; Begotten, not made; Being of one substance with the Father; By whom all things were made: Who for us men and for our salvation came down from heaven, And was incarnate by the Holy Ghost of the Virgin Mary, And was made man; And was crucified also for us under Pontius Pilate; He suffered and was buried: And the third day he rose again according to the Scriptures: And ascended into heaven, And sitteth on the right hand of the Father: And he shall come again, with glory, to judge both the quick and the dead; Whose kingdom shall have no end.

And I believe in the Holy Ghost, The Lord, and Giver of Life, Who proceedeth from the Father and the Son; Who with the Father and the Son together is worshipped and glorified; Who spake by the Prophets: And I believe one Catholic and Apostolic Church: I acknowledge one Baptism for the remission of sins: And I look for the Resurrection of the dead: And the Life of the world to come. Amen.

¶ *And after that, these Prayers following, all devoutly kneeling; the*

Minister first pronouncing,

The Lord be with you.

Answer. And with thy spirit.

Minister.

Let us pray.

O Lord, show thy mercy upon us.

Answer. And grant us thy salvation.

Minister. O Lord, save the State.

Answer. And mercifully hear us when we call upon thee.

Minister. Endue thy Ministers with righteousness.

Answer. And make thy chosen people joyful.

Minister. O Lord, save thy people.

Answer. And bless thine inheritance.

Minister. Give peace in our time, O Lord.

Answer. For it is thou, Lord, only, that makest us dwell in safety.

Minister. O God, make clean our hearts within us.

Answer. And take not thy Holy Spirit from us.

¶ *Then shall be said the* COLLECT FOR THE DAY, *and after that the Collects and Prayers following.*

A Collect for Peace.

O GOD, from whom all holy desires, all good counsels, and all just works do proceed; Give unto thy servants that peace which the world cannot give; that our hearts may be set to obey thy commandments, and also that by thee, we being defended from the fear of our enemies, may pass our time in rest and quietness; through the merits of Jesus Christ our Saviour. *Amen.*

A Collect for Aid against Perils.

LIGHTEN our darkness, we beseech thee, O Lord; and by thy great mercy defend us from all perils and dangers of this night; for the love of thy only Son, our Saviour, Jesus Christ. *Amen.*

¶ *In places where it may be convenient, here followeth the Anthem.*

¶ *The Minister may here end the Evening Prayer with such Prayer, or Prayers, taken out of this Book, as he shall think fit.*

A Prayer for The President of the United States, *and all in Civil Authority.*

ALMIGHTY God, whose kingdom is everlasting and power infinite; Have mercy upon this whole land; and so rule the hearts of thy servants THE PRESIDENT OF THE UNITED STATES, *The Governor of this State,* and all others in authority, that they, knowing whose ministers they are, may above all things seek thy honour and glory; and that we and all the People, duly considering whose authority they bear, may faithfully and obediently honour them, in thee, and for thee, according to thy blessed Word and ordinance; through Jesus Christ our Lord, who with thee and the Holy Ghost liveth and reigneth ever, one God, world without end. *Amen.*

A Prayer for the Clergy and People.

ALMIGHTY and everlasting God,

from whom cometh every good and perfect gift; Send down upon our Bishops, and other Clergy, and upon the Congregations committed to their charge, the healthful Spirit of thy grace; and, that they may truly please thee, pour upon them the continual dew of thy blessing. Grant this, O Lord, for the honour of our Advocate and Mediator, Jesus Christ. *Amen.*

A Prayer for all Conditions of Men.

O GOD, the Creator and Preserver of all mankind, we humbly beseech thee for all sorts and conditions of men; that thou wouldest be pleased to make thy ways known unto them, thy saving health unto all nations. More especially we pray for thy holy Church universal; that it may be so guided and governed by thy good Spirit, that all who profess and call themselves Christians may be led into the way of truth, and hold the faith in unity of spirit, in the bond of peace, and in righteousness of life. Finally, we commend to thy fatherly goodness all those who are any ways afflicted, or distressed, in mind, body, or estate; [*especially those for whom our prayers are desired;] that it may please thee to comfort and relieve them, according to their several

* This may be said when any desire the prayers of the Congregation.

necessities; giving them patience under their sufferings, and a happy issue out of all their afflictions. And this we beg for Jesus Christ's sake. *Amen.*

A General Thanksgiving.

ALMIGHTY God, Father of all mercies, we, thine unworthy servants, do give thee most humble and hearty thanks for all thy goodness and loving-kindness to us, and to all men; [*particularly to those who desire now to offer up their praises and thanksgivings for thy late mercies vouchsafed unto them.*] We bless thee for our creation, preservation, and all the blessings of this life; but above all, for thine inestimable love in the redemption of the world by our Lord Jesus Christ; for the means of grace, and for the hope of glory. And, we beseech thee, give us that due sense of all thy mercies, that our hearts may be unfeignedly thankful; and that we show forth thy praise, not only with our lips, but in our lives, by giving up our selves to thy service, and by walking before thee in holiness and righteousness all our days; through Jesus Christ our Lord, to whom, with thee and the Holy Ghost, be all honour and glory, world without end. *Amen.*

* *This may be said when any desire to return thanks for mercies vouchsafed to them.*

A Prayer of St. Chrysostom.

ALMIGHTY God, who hast given us grace at this time with one accord to make our common supplications unto thee; and dost promise that when two or three are gathered together in thy Name thou wilt grant their requests; Fulfil now, O Lord, the desires and petitions of thy servants, as may be most expedient for them; granting us in this world knowledge of thy truth, and in the world to come life everlasting. *Amen.*

2 Cor. xiii. 14.

THE grace of our Lord Jesus Christ, and the love of God, and the fellowship of the Holy Ghost, be with us all evermore. *Amen.*

Here endeth the Order of Evening Prayer.

THE LITANY,

OR GENERAL SUPPLICATION.

¶ *To be used after Morning Service, on Sundays, Wednesdays, and Fridays.*

O GOD the Father of Heaven; have mercy upon us miserable sinners.

O God the Father of Heaven; *have mercy upon us miserable sinners.*

O God the Son, Redeemer of the world;

have mercy upon us miserable sinners.

O God the Son, Redeemer of the world; have mercy upon us miserable sinners.

O God the Holy Ghost, proceeding from the Father and the Son; have mercy upon us miserable sinners.

O God the Holy Ghost, proceeding from the Father and the Son; have mercy upon us miserable sinners.

O holy, blessed, and glorious Trinity, three Persons and one God; have mercy upon us miserable sinners.

O holy, blessed, and glorious Trinity, three Persons and one God; have mercy upon us miserable sinners.

Remember not, Lord, our offences, nor the offences of our forefathers; neither take thou vengeance of our sins: Spare us, good Lord, spare thy people, whom thou hast redeemed with thy most precious blood, and be not angry with us for ever.

Spare us, good Lord.

From all evil and mischief; from sin; from the crafts and assaults of the devil; from thy wrath, and from everlasting damnation,

Good Lord, deliver us.

From all blindness of heart; from pride, vain-glory, and hypocrisy; from envy, hatred, and malice, and all uncharitableness,

Good Lord, deliver us.

From all inordinate and sinful affections; and from all the deceits of the world, the flesh, and the devil,

Good Lord, deliver us.

From lightning and tempest; from plague, pestilence, and famine; from battle and murder, and from sudden death,

Good Lord, deliver us.

From all sedition, privy conspiracy, and rebellion; from all false doctrine, heresy, and schism; from hardness of heart, and contempt of thy Word and Commandment,

Good Lord, deliver us.

By the mystery of thy holy Incarnation; by thy holy Nativity and Circumcision; by thy Baptism, Fasting, and Temptation,

Good Lord, deliver us.

By thine Agony and Bloody Sweat; by thy Cross and Passion; by thy precious Death and Burial; by thy glorious Resurrection and Ascension; and by the Coming of the Holy Ghost,

Good Lord, deliver us.

In all time of our tribulation; in all time of our prosperity; in the hour of death, and in the day of judgment,

Good Lord, deliver us.

We sinners do beseech thee to hear us, O Lord God; and that it may please thee to rule and govern thy holy Church universal in the right way:

We beseech thee to hear us, good Lord.

That it may please thee to bless and preserve all Christian Rulers and Magistrates, giving them grace to execute justice, and to maintain truth;

We beseech thee to hear us, good Lord.

That it may please thee to illuminate all Bishops, Priests, and Deacons, with true knowledge and understanding of thy Word; and that both by their preaching and living they may set it forth, and show it accordingly;

We beseech thee to hear us, good Lord.

That it may please thee to send forth labourers into thy harvest;

We beseech thee to hear us, good Lord.

That it may please thee to bless and keep all thy people;

We beseech thee to hear us, good Lord.

That it may please thee to give to all nations unity, peace, and concord;

We beseech thee to hear us, good Lord.

That it may please thee to give us an heart to love and fear thee, and diligently to live after thy commandments;

We beseech thee to hear us, good Lord.

That it may please thee to give to all thy people increase of grace to hear meekly thy Word, and to receive it with pure affection, and to bring forth the fruits of the Spirit;

We beseech thee to hear us, good Lord.

That it may please thee to bring into the way of truth all such as have erred, and are deceived;

We beseech thee to hear us, good Lord.

That it may please

thee to strengthen such as do stand; and to comfort and help the weak-hearted; and to raise up those who fall; and finally to beat down Satan under our feet;

We beseech thee to hear us, good Lord.

That it may please thee to succour, help, and comfort, all who are in danger, necessity, and tribulation;

We beseech thee to hear us, good Lord.

That it may please thee to preserve all who travel by land or by water, all women in the perils of childbirth, all sick persons, and young children; and to show thy pity upon all prisoners and captives;

We beseech thee to hear us, good Lord.

That it may please thee to defend, and provide for, the fatherless children, and widows, and all who are desolate and oppressed;

We beseech thee to hear us, good Lord.

That it may please thee to have mercy upon all men;

We beseech thee to hear us, good Lord.

That it may please thee to forgive our enemies, persecutors, and slanderers, and to turn their hearts;

We beseech thee to hear us, good Lord.

That it may please thee to give and preserve to our use the kindly fruits of the earth, so that in due time we may enjoy them;

We beseech thee to hear us, good Lord.

That it may please thee to give us true repentance; to forgive us all our sins, negligences, and ignorances ; and to endue us with the grace of thy Holy Spirit to amend our lives according to thy holy Word ;

We beseech thee to hear us, good Lord.

Son of God, we beseech thee to hear us.

Son of God, we beseech thee to hear us.

O Lamb of God, who takest away the sins of the world ;

Grant us thy peace.

O Lamb of God, who takest away the sins of the world ;

Have mercy upon us.

¶ *The Minister may, at his discretion, omit all that followeth, to the Prayer,* We humbly beseech thee, O Father, *etc.*

O Christ, hear us.

O Christ, hear us.

Lord, have mercy upon us.

Lord, have mercy upon us.

Christ, have mercy upon us.

Christ, have mercy upon us.

Lord, have mercy upon us.

Lord, have mercy upon us.

¶ *Then shall the Minister, and the People with him, say the Lord's Prayer.*

OUR Father, who art in heaven, Hallowed be thy Name. Thy kingdom come. Thy will be done on earth, As it is in heaven. Give us this day our daily bread. And forgive us our trespasses, As we forgive those who trespass against us. And lead us not into temptation ; But deliver us from evil. Amen.

Minister. O Lord,

deal not with us according to our sins.

Answer. Neither reward us according to our iniquities.

Let us pray.

O GOD, merciful Father, who despisest not the sighing of a contrite heart, nor the desire of such as are sorrowful; Mercifully assist our prayers which we make before thee in all our troubles and adversities, whensoever they oppress us; and graciously hear us, that those evils which the craft and subtilty of the devil or man worketh against us, may, by thy good providence, be brought to nought; that we thy servants, being hurt by no persecutions, may evermore give thanks unto thee in thy holy Church; through Jesus Christ our Lord.

O Lord, arise, help us, and deliver us for thy Name's sake.

O GOD, we have heard with our ears, and our fathers have declared unto us, the noble works that thou didst in their days, and in the old time before them.

O Lord, arise, help us, and deliver us for thine honour.

Glory be to the Father, and to the Son, and to the Holy Ghost;

Answer. As it was in the beginning, is now, and ever shall be, world without end. Amen.

From our enemies defend us, O Christ.

Graciously look upon our afflictions.

With pity behold the sorrows of our hearts.

Mercifully forgive the sins of thy people.

Favourably with mercy hear our prayers.

O Son of David, have mercy upon us.

Both now and ever vouchsafe to hear us, O Christ.

Graciously hear us, O Christ; graciously hear us, O Lord Christ.

Minister. O Lord, let thy mercy be showed upon us;

Answer. As we do put our trust in thee.

Let us pray.

WE humbly beseech thee, O Father, mercifully to look upon our infirmities; and, for the glory of thy Name, turn from us all those evils that we most justly have deserved; and grant, that in all our troubles we may put our whole trust and confidence in thy mercy, and evermore serve thee in holiness and pureness of living, to thy honour and glory; through our only Mediator and Advocate, Jesus Christ our Lord. *Amen.*

A General Thanksgiving.

ALMIGHTY God, Father of all mercies, we, thine unworthy servants, do give thee most humble and hearty thanks for all thy goodness and loving-kindness to us, and to all men; [*particularly to those who desire now to offer up their praises and thanksgivings for thy late mercies vouchsafed unto them.*] We

* This may be said when any desire to return thanks for mercies vouchsafed to them.

bless thee for our creation, preservation, and all the blessings of this life; but above all, for thine inestimable love in the redemption of the world by our Lord Jesus Christ; for the means of grace, and for the hope of glory. And, we beseech thee, give us that due sense of all thy mercies, that our hearts may be unfeignedly thankful; and that we show forth thy praise, not only with our lips, but in our lives, by giving up our selves to thy service, and by walking before thee in holiness and righteousness all our days; through Jesus Christ our Lord, to whom, with thee and the Holy Ghost, be all honour and glory, world without end. *Amen.*

A Prayer of St. Chrysostom.

ALMIGHTY God, who hast given us grace at this time with one accord to make our common supplications unto thee; and dost promise that when two or three are gathered together in thy Name thou wilt grant their requests; Fulfil now, O Lord, the desires and petitions of thy servants, as may be most expedient for them; granting us in this world knowledge of thy truth, and in the world to come life everlasting. *Amen.*

2 Cor. xiii. 14.

THE grace of our Lord Jesus Christ, and the love of God, and the fellowship of the Holy Ghost, be with us all evermore. *Amen.*

PRAYERS AND THANKSGIVINGS

UPON SEVERAL OCCASIONS.

✠

PRAYERS.

¶ *To be used before the General Thanksgiving, or, when that is not said, before the final Prayer of Blessing or the Benediction.*

✠

A Prayer for Congress.

¶ *To be used during their Session.*

MOST gracious God, we humbly beseech thee, as for the people of these United States in general, so especially for their Senate and Representatives in Congress assembled; that thou wouldest be pleased to direct and prosper all their consultations, to the advancement of thy glory, the good of thy Church, the safety, honour, and welfare of thy people; that all things may be so ordered and settled by their endeavours, upon the best and surest foundations, that peace and happiness, truth and justice, religion and piety, may be established among us for all generations. These and all other necessaries, for them, for us, and thy whole Church, we humbly beg in the Name and mediation of Jesus Christ, our most blessed Lord and Saviour. *Amen.*

A Prayer to be used at the Meetings of Convention.

ALMIGHTY and everlasting God, who by thy Holy Spirit didst preside in the Council of the blessed Apostles, and hast promised, through thy Son Jesus Christ, to be with thy Church to the end of the world; We beseech thee to be with the Council of thy Church *here* assembled in thy Name and Presence. Save *us* from all error, ignorance, pride, and prejudice; and of thy great mercy vouchsafe, we beseech thee, so to direct, sanctify, and govern *us* in *our* work, by the mighty power of the Holy Ghost, that the comfortable Gospel of Christ may be truly preached, truly received, and truly followed, in all places, to the breaking down the kingdom of sin, Satan, and death; till at length the whole of thy dispersed sheep, being gathered into one fold, shall become partakers of everlasting life; through the merits and death of Jesus Christ our Saviour. *Amen.*

¶ *During, or before, the session of any General or Diocesan Convention, the above Prayer may be used by all Congregations of this Church, or of the Diocese concerned; the clause,* here assembled in thy Name, *being changed to* now assembled [or about to assemble] in thy Name and Presence; *and the clause,* govern us in our work, *to* govern them in their work.

For the Unity of God's People.

O GOD, the Father of our Lord Jesus Christ, our only Saviour, the Prince of Peace; Give us grace seriously to lay to heart the great dangers we are in by our unhappy divisions. Take away all hatred and prejudice, and whatsoever else may hinder us from godly union and concord: that as there is but one Body and one Spirit, and one hope of our calling, one Lord, one Faith, one Baptism, one God and Father of us all, so we may be all of one heart and of one soul, united in one holy bond of truth and peace, of faith and charity, and may with one mind and one mouth glorify thee; through Jesus Christ our Lord. Amen.

For Missions.

O GOD, who hast made of one blood all nations of men for to dwell on the face of the whole earth, and didst send thy blessed Son to preach peace to them that are far off and to them that are nigh; Grant that all men everywhere may seek after thee and find thee. Bring the nations into thy fold, and add the heathen to thine inheritance. And we pray thee shortly to accomplish the number of thine elect, and to hasten thy kingdom; through the same Jesus Christ our Lord. Amen

For Rain.

O GOD, heavenly Father, who by

thy Son Jesus Christ hast promised to all those who seek thy kingdom, and the righteousness thereof, all things necessary to their bodily sustenance; Send us, we beseech thee, in this our necessity, such moderate rain and showers, that we may receive the fruits of the earth to our comfort, and to thy honour; through Jesus Christ our Lord. Amen.

For Fair Weather.

ALMIGHTY and most merciful Father, we humbly beseech thee, of thy great goodness, to restrain those immoderate rains, wherewith, for our sins, thou hast afflicted us. And we pray thee to send us such seasonable weather, that the earth may, in due time, yield her increase for our use and benefit. And give us grace, that we may learn by thy punishments to amend our lives, and for thy clemency to give thee thanks and praise; through Jesus Christ our Lord. Amen.

In Time of Dearth and Famine.

O GOD, heavenly Father, whose gift it is that the rain doth fall, and the earth bring forth her increase; Behold, we beseech thee, the afflictions of thy people; increase the fruits of the earth by thy heavenly benediction; and grant that the scarcity and dearth, which we now most justly suffer for our sins, may, through thy goodness, be mercifully turned into plenty; for the love of Jesus Christ our Lord, to whom, with thee and the Holy Ghost, be all honour and glory, now and for ever. *Amen.*

In Time of War and Tumults.

O ALMIGHTY God, the supreme Governor of all things, whose power no creature is able to resist, to whom it belongeth justly to punish sinners, and to be merciful to those who truly repent; Save and deliver us, we humbly beseech thee, that, from the hands of our enemies; that we, being armed with thy defence, may be preserved evermore from all perils, to glorify

thee, who art the only giver of all victory; through the merits of thy Son, Jesus Christ our Lord. *Amen.*

For those who are to be admitted into Holy Orders.

¶ *To be used in the Weeks preceding the stated Times of Ordination.*

A LMIGHTY God, our heavenly Father, who hast purchased to thyself an universal Church by the precious blood of thy dear Son; Mercifully look upon the same, and at this time so guide and govern the minds of thy servants the Bishops and Pastors of thy flock, that they may lay hands suddenly on no man, but faithfully and wisely make choice of fit persons, to serve in the sacred Ministry of thy Church. And to those who shall be ordained to any holy function, give thy grace and heavenly benediction; that both by their life and doctrine they may show forth thy glory, and set forward the salvation of all men; through Jesus Christ our Lord. *Amen.*

¶ *Or this.*

ALMIGHTY God, the giver of all good gifts, who of thy divine providence hast appointed divers Orders in thy Church; Give thy grace, we humbly beseech thee, to all those who are to be called to any office and administration in the same; and so replenish them with the truth of thy doctrine, and endue them with innocency of life, that they may faithfully serve before thee, to the glory of thy great Name, and the benefit of thy holy Church; through Jesus Christ our Lord. *Amen.*

For Fruitful Seasons.

¶ *To be used on Rogation-Sunday and the Rogation-days.*

ALMIGHTY God, who hast blessed the earth that it should be fruitful and bring forth whatsoever is needful for the life of man, and hast commanded us to work with quietness, and eat our own bread; Bless the labours of the husbandman, and grant such seasonable weather that we may gather in the fruits of the earth, and ever rejoice in thy goodness, to the praise of thy holy Name;

through Jesus Christ our Lord. *Amen.*

¶ *Or this.*

O GRACIOUS Father, who openest thine hand and fillest all things living with plenteousness; We beseech thee of thine infinite goodness to hear us, who now make our prayers and supplications unto thee. Remember not our sins, but thy promises of mercy. Vouchsafe to bless the lands and multiply the harvests of the world. Let thy breath go forth that it may renew the face of the earth. Show thy loving-kindness, that our land may give her increase; and so fill us with good things that the poor and needy may give thanks unto thy Name; through Christ our Lord. *Amen.*

In Time of great Sickness and Mortality.

O ALMIGHTY God, the Lord of life and death, of sickness and health; Regard our supplications, we humbly beseech thee; and, as thou hast thought fit to visit us for our sins with great sickness and mortality, in the midst of thy judgment, O Lord, remember mercy. Have pity upon us miserable sinners, and withdraw from us the grievous sickness with which we are afflicted. May this thy fatherly correction have its due influence upon us, by leading us to consider how frail and uncertain our life is; that we may apply our hearts unto that heavenly wisdom which in the end will bring us to everlasting life; through Jesus Christ our Lord. *Amen.*

For a Sick Person.

O FATHER of mercies and God of all comfort, our only help in time of need; Look down from heaven, we humbly beseech thee, behold, visit, and relieve thy sick *servant*, for whom our prayers are desired. Look upon *him* with the eyes of thy mercy; comfort *him* with a sense of thy goodness; preserve *him* from the temptations of the enemy; give *him* patience under *his* affliction; and, in thy good time, restore *him* to health, and enable *him* to lead the residue of *his* life in thy fear, and to thy glory. Or else give *him* grace so to take thy visitation, that, after this painful life ended, *he* may dwell with thee in life everlasting; through Jesus Christ our Lord. *Amen.*

For a Sick Child.

A LMIGHTY God, and merciful Father, to whom alone belong the issues of life and death; Look down from heaven, we humbly beseech thee, with the eyes of mercy, upon the sick *child* for whom our prayers are desired. Deliver *him*, O Lord, in thy good appointed time, from *his* bodily pain, and visit *him* with thy salvation; that if it should be thy good pleasure to prolong *his* days here on earth, *he* may live to thee, and be an instrument of thy glory, by serving thee faithfully, and doing good in *his* generation. Or else receive *him* into those heavenly habitations, where the souls of those who sleep in the Lord Jesus enjoy perpetual rest and felicity. Grant this, O Lord, for the love of thy Son, our Saviour, Jesus Christ. *Amen.*

For a Person, or Persons, going to Sea.

O ETERNAL God, who alone spreadest out the heavens, and rulest the raging of the sea; We commend to thy almighty protection, thy *servant,* for whose preservation on the great deep our prayers are desired. Guard *him,* we beseech thee, from the dangers of the sea, from sickness, from the violence of enemies, and from every evil to which *he* may be exposed. Conduct *him* in safety to the haven where *he* would be, with a grateful sense of thy mercies; through Jesus Christ our Lord. *Amen.*

For a Person under Affliction.

O MERCIFUL God, and heavenly Father, who hast taught us in thy holy Word that thou dost not willingly afflict or grieve the children of men; Look with pity, we beseech thee, upon the sorrows of thy *servant,* for whom our prayers are desired. In thy wisdom thou hast seen fit to visit *him* with trouble, and to bring distress upon *him.* Remember *him,* O Lord, in mercy;

sanctify thy fatherly correction to *him;* endue *his* soul with patience under *his* affliction, and with resignation to thy blessed will; comfort *him* with a sense of thy goodness; lift up thy countenance upon *him,* and give *him* peace; through Jesus Christ our Lord. *Amen.*

For Malefactors, after Condemnation.

¶ *Or else the Prayer in the Visitation of Prisoners, beginning,* O Father of mercies, *etc., may be used.*

O MOST gracious and merciful God, we earnestly beseech thee to have pity and compassion upon *those persons* recommended to our prayers, who now *lie* under the sentence of the law, and *are* appointed to die. Visit *them,* O Lord, with thy mercy and salvation; convince *them* of the miserable condition *they are* in, by *their* sins and wickedness; and let the powerful grace produce in *them* such a godly sorrow, and sincere repentance, as thou wilt be pleased to accept. Give *them* a strong and lively faith in thy Son, our blessed Saviour, and make it effectual to the salvation of *their souls.* O Lord, in judgment remember mercy; and whatever sufferings *they are* to endure in this world, yet deliver *them,* O God, from the bitter pains of eternal death. Pardon *their* sins, and save *their souls,* for the sake and merits of thy dear Son, our blessed Saviour and Redeemer. *Amen.*

THANKSGIVINGS.

¶ *To be used after the General Thanksgiving, or, when that is not said, before the final Prayer of Blessing or the Benediction.*

The Thanksgiving of Women after Childbirth.

¶ *To be said when any Woman, being present in Church, shall have desired to return thanks to Almighty God for her safe deliverance.*

O ALMIGHTY God, we give thee humble thanks for that thou hast been graciously pleased to preserve, through the great pain and peril of child-birth, *this woman*, thy *servant*, who *desireth* now to offer *her* praises and thanksgivings unto thee. Grant, we beseech thee, most merciful Father, that *she*, through thy help, may both faithfully live and walk according to thy will in this life present, and also may be *partaker* of everlasting glory in the life to come ; through Jesus Christ our Lord. Amen.

For Rain.

O GOD, our heavenly Father, who by thy gracious providence dost cause the former and the latter rain to descend upon the earth, that it may bring forth fruit for the use of man; We give thee humble thanks that it hath pleased thee, in our great necessity, to send us at the last a joyful rain upon thine inheritance, and to refresh it when it was dry, to the great comfort of us thy unworthy servants, and to the glory of thy holy Name; through thy mercies in Jesus Christ our Lord. Amen.

For Fair Weather.

O LORD God, who hast justly humbled us by thy late visitation of us with immoderate rain and waters, and in thy mercy hast relieved and comforted our souls by this seasonable and blessed change of weather; We praise and glorify thy holy Name for this thy mercy, and will always declare thy loving-kindness from generation to generation; through Jesus Christ our Lord. Amen.

For Plenty.

O MOST merciful Father, who of thy gracious goodness hast heard the devout prayers of thy Church, and turned our dearth and scarcity into plenty; We give thee humble thanks for this thy special bounty; beseeching thee to continue thy loving-kindness unto us, that our land may yield us her fruits of increase, to thy glory and our comfort; through Jesus Christ our Lord. Amen.

For Peace, and Deliverance from our Enemies.

O ALMIGHTY God, who art a strong tower of defence unto thy servants against the face of their enemies; We yield thee praise and thanksgiving for our deliverance from those great and apparent dangers wherewith we were compassed. We acknowledge it thy goodness that we were not delivered over as a prey unto them; beseeching thee still to continue such thy mercies towards us, that all the world may know that thou art our Saviour and mighty Deliverer; through Jesus Christ our Lord. *Amen.*

For *Restoring Public Peace at Home.*

O ETERNAL God, our heavenly Father, who alone makest men to be of one mind in a house, and stillest the outrage of a violent and unruly people; We bless thy holy Name, that it hath pleased thee to appease the seditious tumults which have been lately raised up amongst us; most humbly beseeching thee to grant to all of us grace, that we may henceforth obediently walk in thy holy commandments; and, leading a quiet and peaceable life in all godliness and honesty, may continually offer unto thee our sacrifice of praise and thanksgiving for these thy mercies towards us; through Jesus Christ our Lord. *Amen.*

For *Deliverance from great Sickness and Mortality.*

O LORD God, who hast wounded us for our sins, and consumed us for our transgressions, by thy late heavy and dreadful visitation; and now, in the midst of judgment remembering mercy, hast redeemed our souls from the jaws of death; We offer unto thy fatherly goodness ourselves, our souls and bodies which thou hast delivered, to be a living sacrifice unto thee, always praising and magnifying thy mercies in the midst of thy Church; through Jesus Christ our Lord. *Amen.*

For a Recovery from Sickness.

O GOD, who art the giver of life, of health, and of safety; We bless thy Name, that thou hast been pleased to deliver from *his* bodily sickness *this* thy *servant,* who now *desireth* to return

thanks unto thee, in the presence of all thy people. Gracious art thou, O Lord, and full of compassion to the children of men. May *his heart* be duly impressed with a sense of thy merciful goodness, and may *he* devote the residue of *his* days to an humble, holy, and obedient walking before thee; through Jesus Christ our Lord. *Amen.*

For a Child's Recovery from Sickness.

A LMIGHTY God and heavenly Father, we give thee humble thanks for that thou hast been graciously pleased to deliver from *his* bodily sickness the *child* in whose behalf we bless and praise thy Name, in the presence of all thy people. Grant, we beseech thee, O gracious Father, that *he*, through thy help, may both faithfully live in this world according to thy will, and also may be *partaker* of everlasting glory in the life to come; through Jesus Christ our Lord. *Amen.*

For a Safe Return from Sea.

MOST gracious Lord, whose mercy is over all thy works; We praise thy holy Name that thou hast been pleased to conduct in safety, through the perils of the great deep, *this thy servant*, who now *desireth* to return *his* thanks unto thee in thy holy Church. May *he* be duly sensible of thy merciful providence towards *him*, and ever express *his* thankfulness by a holy trust in thee, and obedience to thy laws; through Jesus Christ our Lord. *Amen.*

A PENITENTIAL OFFICE

FOR ASH-WEDNESDAY.

¶ *On the First Day of Lent, at Morning Prayer, the Office ensuing shall be read immediately after the Prayer,* We humbly beseech thee, O Father, *in the Litany, and in place of what there followeth.*

¶ *The same Office may be read at other times, at the discretion of the Minister.*

¶ *The Minister and the People kneeling, then shall be said by them this Psalm following.*

PSALM 51. *Miserere mei, Deus.*

HAVE mercy upon me, O God, after thy great goodness : according to the multitude of thy mercies do away mine offences.

Wash me throughly from my wickedness : and cleanse me from my sin.

For I acknowledge my faults : and my sin is ever before me.

Against thee only have I sinned, and done this evil in thy sight : that thou mightest be justified in thy saying, and clear when thou art judged.

Behold, I was shapen in wickedness : and in sin hath my mother conceived me.

But lo, thou requirest truth in the inward parts : and shalt make me to understand wisdom secretly.

Thou shalt purge me with hyssop, and I shall be clean : thou shalt wash me, and I shall be whiter than snow.

Thou shalt make me hear of joy and gladness : that the bones which thou hast broken may rejoice.

Turn thy face from my sins : and put out all my misdeeds.

Make me a clean heart, O God : and renew a right spirit within me.

Cast me not away from thy presence : and take not thy holy Spirit from me.

O give me the comfort of thy help again : and stablish me with *thy free Spirit.*

Then shall I teach thy ways unto the wicked : and sinners shall be converted unto thee.

Deliver me from blood-guiltiness, O God, thou that art the God of my health : and my tongue shall sing of thy righteousness.

Thou shalt open my lips, O Lord : and my mouth shall show thy praise.

For thou desirest no sacrifice, else would I give it thee : but thou delightest not in burnt-offerings.

The sacrifice of God is a troubled spirit : a broken and contrite heart, O God, shalt thou not despise.

O be favourable and gracious unto Sion : build thou the walls of Jerusalem.

Then shalt thou be pleased with the sacrifice of righteousness, with the burnt-offerings and oblations : then shall they offer young bullocks upon thine altar.

Glory be to the Father, and to the Son : and to the Holy Ghost;

As it was in the beginning, is now, and ever shall be : world without end. Amen.

¶ *If the Litany hath been already said in full, the Minister may omit all that followeth, to the Prayer, O Lord, we beseech thee, etc.*

Lord, have mercy upon us.

Christ, have mercy upon us.

Lord, have mercy upon us.

OUR Father, who art in heaven, Hallowed be thy Name. Thy kingdom come. Thy will be done on earth, As it is in heaven. Give us this day our daily bread. And forgive us our trespasses, As we forgive those who trespass against us. And lead us not into temptation; But deliver us from evil. Amen.

Minister. O Lord, save thy servants;

Answer. That put their trust in thee.

Minister. Send unto them help from above.

Answer. And evermore mightily defend them.

Minister. Help us, O God our Saviour.

Answer. And for the glory of thy Name deliver us; be merciful to us sinners, for thy Name's sake.

Minister. O Lord, hear our prayer.

Answer. And let our cry come unto thee.

Minister.

Let us pray.

O LORD, we beseech thee, mercifully hear our prayers, and spare all those who confess their sins unto thee; that they, whose consciences by sin are accused, by thy merciful pardon may be absolved; through Christ our Lord. *Amen.*

O MOST mighty God, and merciful Father, who hast compassion upon all men, and who wouldest not the death of a sinner, but rather that he should turn from his sin, and be saved; Mercifully forgive us our trespasses; receive and comfort us, who are grieved and wearied with the burden of our sins. Thy property is always to have mercy; to thee only it appertaineth to forgive sins. Spare us therefore, good Lord, spare thy people, whom thou hast redeemed; enter not into judgment with thy servants, who are vile earth, and miser-

able sinners; but so turn thine anger from us, who meekly acknowledge our vileness, and truly repent us of our faults, and so make haste to help us in this world, that we may ever live with thee in the world to come; through Jesus Christ our Lord. *Amen.*

¶ *Then shall the People say this that followeth, after the Minister.*

TURN thou us, O good Lord, and so shall we be turned. Be favourable, O Lord, Be favourable to thy people, Who turn to thee in weeping, fasting, and praying. For thou art a merciful God, Full of compassion, Long-suffering, and of great pity. Thou sparest when we deserve punishment, And in thy wrath thinkest upon mercy. Spare thy people, good Lord, spare them, And let not thine heritage be brought to confusion. Hear us, O Lord, for thy mercy is great, And after the multitude of thy mercies look upon us; Through the merits and mediation of thy blessed Son, Jesus Christ our Lord. Amen.

¶ *Then the Minister shall say,*

O GOD, whose nature and property is ever to have mercy and to forgive; Receive our humble petitions; and though we be tied and bound with the chain of our sins, yet let the pitifulness of thy great mercy loose us; for the honour of Jesus Christ, our Mediator and Advocate. *Amen.*

THE LORD bless us, and keep us. The LORD make his face to shine upon us, and be gracious unto us. The LORD lift up his countenance upon us, and give us peace, both now and evermore. *Amen.*

THE
COLLECTS, EPISTLES,
AND
GOSPELS,
TO BE USED THROUGHOUT THE YEAR.

¶ *The Collect, Epistle, and Gospel, appointed for the Sunday, shall serve all the Week after, where it is not in this Book otherwise appointed.*

¶ *The Collect appointed for any Sunday or other Feast may be used at the Evening Service of the day before.*

The First Sunday in Advent.

The Collect.

ALMIGHTY God, give us grace that we may cast away the works of darkness, and put upon us the armour of light, now in the time of this mortal life, in which thy Son Jesus Christ came to visit us in great humility; that in the last day, when he shall come again in his glorious majesty to judge both the quick and the dead, we may rise to the life immortal, through him who liveth and reigneth with thee and the Holy Ghost, now and ever. *Amen.*

¶ *This Collect is to be repeated every day, with the other Collects in Advent, unto Christmas-day.*

The Epistle. Rom. xiii. 8.

OWE no man any thing, but to love one another: for he that loveth another hath fulfilled the law. For this, Thou shalt not commit adultery, Thou shalt not kill, Thou shalt not steal, Thou shalt not bear false witness, Thou shalt not covet; and if there be any other commandment, it is briefly comprehended in this saying, namely, Thou shalt love thy neighbour as thyself. Love worketh no ill to his neighbour: therefore love is the fulfilling of the law. And that, knowing the time, that now it is high time to awake out of sleep: for now is our salvation nearer than when we believed. The night is far spent, the day is at hand: let us therefore cast off the works of darkness, and let us put on the armour of light. Let us walk honestly, as in the day; not in rioting and drunkenness, not in chambering and wantonness, not in strife and envying. But put ye on the Lord Jesus Christ, and make not provision for the flesh, to fulfil the lusts thereof.

The Gospel. St. Matt. xxi. 1.

WHEN they drew nigh unto Jerusalem, and were come to Bethphage, unto the mount of Olives, then sent Jesus two disciples, saying unto them, Go into the village over against you, and straightway ye shall find an ass tied, and a colt with her: loose them, and bring them unto me. And if any man say ought unto you, ye shall say, The Lord hath need of them; and straightway he will send them. All this was done, that it might be fulfilled which was spoken by the prophet, saying, Tell ye the daughter of Sion, Behold, thy King cometh unto thee, meek, and sitting upon an ass, and a colt the foal of an ass. And the disciples went, and did as Jesus commanded them, and brought the ass, and the colt, and put on them their clothes, and they set him thereon. And a very great multitude spread their garments in the way; others cut down branches from the trees, and strawed them in the way. And the multitudes that went before, and that followed, cried, saying, Hosanna to the son of David: Blessed is he that cometh in the name of the Lord; Hosanna in the highest. And when he was come into Jerusalem, all the city was moved, saying, Who is this? And the multitude said, This is Jesus the prophet of Nazareth of Galilee. And Jesus went into the temple of God, and cast out all them that sold and bought in the temple, and overthrew the tables of the moneychangers, and the seats of them that sold doves, and said unto them, It is written, My house shall be called the house of prayer; but ye have made it a den of thieves.

The Second Sunday in Advent.

The Collect.

BLESSED Lord, who hast caused all holy Scriptures to be written for our learning; Grant that we may in such wise hear them, read, mark, learn, and inwardly digest them, that by patience and comfort of thy holy Word, we may embrace, and ever hold fast, the blessed hope of everlasting life, which thou hast

given us in our Saviour Jesus Christ. *Amen.*

The Epistle. Rom. xv. 4.

WHATSOEVER things were written aforetime were written for our learning, that we through patience and comfort of the scriptures might have hope. Now the God of patience and consolation grant you to be likeminded one toward another according to Christ Jesus: that ye may with one mind and one mouth glorify God, even the Father of our Lord Jesus Christ. Wherefore receive ye one another, as Christ also received us to the glory of God. Now I say that Jesus Christ was a minister of the circumcision for the truth of God, to confirm the promises made unto the fathers: and that the Gentiles might glorify God for his mercy; as it is written, For this cause I will confess to thee among the Gentiles, and sing unto thy name. And again he saith, Rejoice, ye Gentiles, with his people. And again, Praise the Lord, all ye Gentiles; and laud him, all ye people. And again, Esaias saith, There shall be a root of Jesse, and he that shall rise to reign over the Gentiles; in him shall the Gentiles trust. Now the God of hope fill you with all joy and peace in believing, that ye may abound in hope, through the power of the Holy Ghost.

The Gospel. St. Luke xxi. 25.

AND there shall be signs in the sun, and in the moon, and in the stars; and upon the earth distress of nations, with perplexity; the sea and the waves roaring; men's hearts failing them for fear, and for looking after those things which are coming on the earth: for the powers of heaven shall be shaken. And then shall they see the Son of man coming in a cloud with power and great glory. And when these things begin to come to pass, then look up, and lift up your heads; for your redemption draweth nigh. And he spake to them a parable; Behold the fig tree, and all the trees; when they now shoot forth, ye see and know of your own selves that summer is now nigh at hand. So likewise ye, when ye see these things come to pass, know ye that the kingdom of God is nigh at hand. Verily I say unto you, This generation shall not pass away, till all be fulfilled. Heaven and earth shall pass away: but my words shall not pass away.

The Third Sunday in Advent.

The Collect.

O LORD Jesus Christ, who at thy first coming didst send thy messenger to prepare thy way before thee; Grant that the ministers and stewards of thy mysteries may likewise so prepare and make ready thy way, by turning the hearts of the disobedient to the wisdom of the just, that at thy second coming to judge the world we may be found an acceptable people in thy sight, who livest and reignest with the Father and the Holy Spirit ever, one God, world without end. *Amen.*

The Epistle. 1 Cor. iv. 1.

LET a man so account of us, as of the ministers

of Christ, and stewards of the mysteries of God. Moreover it is required in stewards, that a man be found faithful. But with me it is a very small thing that I should be judged of you, or of man's judgment: yea, I judge not mine own self. For I know nothing by myself; yet am I not hereby justified: but he that judgeth me is the Lord. Therefore judge nothing before the time, until the Lord come, who both will bring to light the hidden things of darkness, and will make manifest the counsels of the hearts: and then shall every man have praise of God.

The Gospel. St. Matt. xi. 2.

NOW when John had heard in the prison the works of Christ, he sent two of his disciples, and said unto him, Art thou he that should come, or do we look for another? Jesus answered and said unto them, Go and shew John again those things which ye do hear and see: the blind receive their sight, and the lame walk, the lepers are cleansed, and the deaf hear, the dead are raised up, and the poor have the gospel preached to them. And blessed is he, whosoever shall not be offended in me. And as they departed, Jesus began to say unto the multitudes concerning John, What went ye out into the wilderness to see? A reed shaken with the wind? But what went ye out for to see? A man clothed in soft raiment? behold, they that wear soft clothing are in kings' houses. But what went ye out for to see? A prophet? yea, I say unto you, and more than a prophet. For this is he, of whom it is written, Behold, I send my messenger before thy face, which shall prepare thy way before thee.

❀

The Fourth Sunday in Advent.

The Collect.

O LORD, raise up, we pray thee, thy power, and come among us, and with great might succour us; that whereas, through our sins and wickedness, we are sore let and hindered in running the race that is set before us, thy bountiful grace and mercy may speedily help and deliver us; through the satisfaction of thy Son our Lord, to whom, with thee and the Holy Ghost, be honour and glory, world without end. *Amen.*

The Epistle. Phil. iv. 4.

REJOICE in the Lord alway: and again I say, Rejoice. Let your moderation be known unto all men. The Lord is at hand. Be careful for nothing; but in every thing by prayer and supplication with thanksgiving let your requests be made known unto God. And the peace of God, which passeth all understanding, shall keep your hearts and minds through Christ Jesus.

The Gospel. St. John i. 19.

THIS is the record of John, when the Jews sent priests and Levites from Jerusalem to ask him, Who art thou? And he confessed, and denied not; but confessed, I am not the Christ. And they asked him, What then? Art thou Elias? And he saith, I am not. Art thou that prophet? And he

answered, No. Then said they unto him, Who art thou? that we may give an answer to them that sent us. What sayest thou of thyself? He said, I am the voice of one crying in the wilderness, Make straight the way of the Lord, as said the prophet Esaias. And they which were sent were of the Pharisees. And they asked him, and said unto him, Why baptizest thou then, if thou be not that Christ, nor Elias, neither that prophet? John answered them, saying, I baptize with water: but there standeth one among you, whom ye know not; he it is, who coming after me is preferred before me, whose shoe's latchet I am not worthy to unloose. These things were done in Bethabara beyond Jordan, where John was baptizing.

✧

The Nativity of our Lord, or the Birthday of Christ, commonly called Christmas-day.

The Collect.

ALMIGHTY God, who hast given us thy

only-begotten Son to take our nature upon him, and as at this time to be born of a pure virgin ; Grant that we being regenerate, and made thy children by adoption and grace, may daily be renewed by thy Holy Spirit ; through the same our Lord Jesus Christ, who liveth and reigneth with thee and the same Spirit ever, one God, world without end. *Amen.*

The Epistle. Heb. i. 1.

GOD, who at sundry times and in divers manners spake in time past unto the fathers by the prophets, hath in these last days spoken unto us by his Son, whom he hath appointed heir of all things, by whom also he made the worlds ; who being the brightness of his glory, and the express image of his person, and upholding all things by the word of his power, when he had by himself purged our sins, sat down on the right hand of the Majesty on high ; being made so much better than the angels, as he hath by inheritance obtained a more excellent name than

they. For unto which of the angels said he at any time, Thou art my Son, this day have I begotten thee ? And again, I will be to him a Father, and he shall be to me a Son ? And again, when he bringeth in the firstbegotten into the world, he saith, And let all the angels of God worship him. And of the angels he saith, Who maketh his angels spirits, and his ministers a flame of fire. But unto the Son he saith, Thy throne, O God, is for ever and ever : a sceptre of righteousness is the sceptre of thy kingdom. Thou hast loved righteousness, and hated iniquity ; therefore God, even thy God, hath anointed thee with the oil of gladness above thy fellows. And, Thou, Lord, in the beginning hast laid the foundation of the earth ; and the heavens are the works of thine hands : they shall perish ; but thou remainest ; and they all shall wax old as doth a garment ; and as a vesture shalt thou fold them up, and they shall be changed : but thou art the same, and thy years shall not fail.

The Gospel. St. John i. 1.

IN the beginning was the Word, and the Word was with God, and the Word was God. The same was in the beginning with God. All things were made by him; and without him was not any thing made that was made. In him was life; and the life was the light of men. And the light shineth in darkness; and the darkness comprehended it not. There was a man sent from God, whose name was John. The same came for a witness, to bear witness of the Light, that all men through him might believe. He was not that Light, but was sent to bear witness of that Light. That was the true Light, which lighteth every man that cometh into the world. He was in the world, and the world was made by him, and the world knew him not. He came unto his own, and his own received him not. But as many as received him, to them gave he power to become the sons of God, even to them that believe on his name: which were born, not of blood, nor of the will of the flesh, nor of the will of man, but of God. And the Word was made flesh, and dwelt among us, (and we beheld his glory, the glory as of the only begotten of the Father,) full of grace and truth.

¶ *If in any Church the Holy Communion be twice celebrated on Christmas-day, the following Collect, Epistle, and Gospel may be used at the first Communion.*

The Collect.

O GOD, who makest us glad with the yearly remembrance of the birth of thine only Son Jesus Christ; Grant that as we joyfully receive him for our Redeemer, so we may with sure confidence behold him when he shall come to be our Judge, who liveth and reigneth with thee and the Holy Ghost, one God, world without end. *Amen.*

The Epistle. Titus ii. 11.

THE grace of God that bringeth salvation hath appeared to all men, teaching us that, denying ungodliness and worldly lusts, we should live soberly, righteously, and godly, in this present world ; looking for that blessed hope, and the glorious appearing of the great God and our Saviour Jesus Christ ; who gave himself for us, that he might redeem us from all iniquity, and purify unto himself a peculiar people, zealous of good works. These things speak, and exhort, and rebuke with all authority. Let no man despise thee.

The Gospel. St. Luke ii. 1.

AND it came to pass in those days, that there went out a decree from Cæsar Augustus, that all the world should be taxed. (And this taxing was first made when Cyrenius was governor of Syria.) And all went to be taxed, every one into his own city. And Joseph also went up from Galilee, out of the city of Nazareth, into Judæa, unto the city of David, which is called Bethlehem ; (because he was of the house and lineage of David :) to be taxed with Mary his espoused wife, being great with child. And so it was, that, while they were there, the days were accomplished that she should be delivered. And she brought forth her firstborn son, and wrapped him in swaddling clothes, and laid him in a manger ; because there was no room for them in the inn. And there were in the same country shepherds abiding in the field, keeping watch over their flock by night. And, lo, the angel of the Lord came upon them, and the glory of the Lord shone round about them : and they were sore afraid. And the angel said unto them, Fear not : for, behold, I bring you good tidings of great joy, which shall be to all people. For unto you is born this day in the city of David a Saviour, which is Christ the Lord. And this shall be a sign unto you ; Ye shall find the babe wrapped in swaddling clothes, lying in a manger. And suddenly there was with the angel a multitude of the heavenly host praising God, and saying, Glory to God in the highest, and on earth peace, good will toward men.

Saint Stephen's Day.

The Collect.

GRANT, O Lord, that, in all our sufferings here upon earth for the testimony of thy truth, we may stedfastly look up to heaven, and by faith behold the glory that shall be revealed; and, being filled with the Holy Ghost, may learn to love and bless our persecutors by the example of thy first Martyr Saint Stephen, who prayed for his murderers to thee, O blessed Jesus, who standest at the right hand of God to succour all those who suffer for thee, our only Mediator and Advocate. *Amen.*

¶ *Then shall follow the Collect of the Nativity, which shall be said continually unto New-Year's Eve.*

For the Epistle. Acts vii. 55.

STEPHEN, being full of the Holy Ghost, looked up stedfastly into heaven, and saw the glory of God, and Jesus standing on the right hand of God, and said, Behold, I see the heavens opened, and the Son of man standing on the right hand of God. Then they cried out with a loud voice, and stopped their ears, and ran upon him with one accord, and cast him out of the city, and stoned him: and the witnesses laid down their clothes at a young man's feet, whose name was Saul. And they stoned Stephen, calling upon God, and saying, Lord Jesus, receive my spirit. And he kneeled down, and cried with a loud voice, Lord, lay not this sin to their charge. And when he had said this, he fell asleep.

The Gospel. St. Matt. xxiii. 34.

BEHOLD, I send unto you prophets, and wise men, and scribes: and some of them ye shall kill and crucify; and some of them shall ye scourge in your synagogues, and persecute them from city to city: that upon you may come all the righteous blood shed upon the earth, from the blood of righteous Abel unto the blood of Zacharias son of Barachias, whom ye slew between the temple and the altar. Verily I say unto you, All these things shall come upon this generation. O Jerusalem, Jerusalem, thou that killest the prophets, and stonest them which are sent unto thee, how often would I have gathered thy children together, even as a hen gathereth her chickens under her wings, and ye would not! Behold, your house is left unto you desolate. For I say unto you, Ye shall not see me henceforth, till ye shall say, Blessed is he that cometh in the name of the Lord.

Saint John the Evangelist's Day.

The Collect.

MERCIFUL Lord, we beseech thee to cast thy bright beams of light upon thy Church, that it, being instructed by the doctrine of thy blessed Apostle and Evangelist Saint John, may so walk in the light of thy truth, that it may at length attain to everlasting life; through Jesus Christ our Lord. *Amen.*

The Epistle. 1 St. John i. 1.

THAT which was from the beginning, which we have heard, which we have seen with our eyes, which we have looked upon, and our hands have handled, of the Word of life; (for the life was manifested, and we have seen it, and bear witness, and shew unto you that eternal life, which was with the Father, and was manifested unto us;) that which we have seen and heard declare we unto you, that ye also may have fellowship with us: and truly our fellowship is with the Father, and with his Son Jesus Christ. And these things write we unto you, that your joy may be full. This then is the message which we have heard of him, and declare unto you, that God is light, and in him is no darkness at all. If we say that we have fellowship with him, and walk in darkness, we lie, and do not the truth: but if we walk in the light, as he is in the light, we have fellowship one with another, and the blood of Jesus Christ his Son cleanseth us from all sin. If we say that we have no sin, we deceive ourselves, and the truth is not in us. If we confess our sins, he is faithful and just to forgive us our sins, and to cleanse us from all unrighteousness. If we say that we have not sinned, we make him a liar, and his word is not in us.

The Gospel. St. John xxi.19.

JESUS saith unto Peter, Follow me. Then Peter, turning about, seeth the disciple whom Jesus loved following; which also leaned on his breast at supper, and said, Lord, which is he that betrayeth thee? Peter seeing him saith to Jesus, Lord, and what shall this man do? Jesus saith unto him, If I will that he tarry till I come, what is that to thee? follow thou me. Then went this saying abroad among the brethren, that that disciple should not die: yet Jesus said not unto him, He shall not die; but, If I will that he tarry till I come, what is that to thee? This is the disciple which testifieth of these things, and wrote *these things: and we know* that his testimony is true. And there are also many other things which Jesus did, the which, if they should be written every one, I suppose that even the world itself could not contain the books that should be written.

The Innocents' Day.

The Collect.

O ALMIGHTY God, who out of the mouths of babes and sucklings hast ordained strength, and madest infants to glorify thee by their deaths; Mortify and kill all vices in us, and so strengthen us by thy grace, that by the innocency of our lives, and constancy of our faith even unto death, we may glorify thy holy Name; through Jesus Christ our Lord. *Amen.*

For the Epistle. Rev. xiv.1.

I LOOKED, and, lo, a Lamb stood on the mount Sion, and with him an hundred forty and four thousand, having his Father's name written in their foreheads. And I heard a voice from heaven, as the voice of many waters, and as the voice of a great thunder: and I heard the voice of harpers harping with their harps: and they sung as it were a new song before the throne, and before the four beasts, and the elders: and no man could learn that song but the hundred and forty and four thousand, which were redeemed from the earth. These are they which were not defiled with women ; for they are virgins. These are they which follow the Lamb whithersoever he goeth. These were redeemed from among men, being the firstfruits unto God and to the Lamb. And in their mouth was found no guile : for they are without fault before the throne of God.

The Gospel. St. Matt. ii. 13.

THE angel of the Lord appeareth to Joseph in a dream, saying, Arise, and take the young child and his mother, and flee into Egypt, and be thou there until I bring thee word : for Herod will seek the young child to destroy him. When he arose, he took the young child and his mother by night, and departed into Egypt : and was there until the death of Herod : that it might be fulfilled which was spoken of the Lord by the prophet, saying, Out of Egypt have I called my son. Then Herod, when he saw that he was mocked of the wise men, was exceeding wroth, and sent forth, and slew all the children that were in Bethlehem, and in all the coasts thereof, from two years old and under, according to the time which he had diligently inquired of the wise men. Then was fulfilled that which was spoken by Jeremy the prophet, saying, In Rama was there a voice heard, lamentation, and weeping, and great mourning, Rachel weeping for her children, and would not be comforted, because they are not.

¶ *If there be any more days before the Sunday after Christmas-day, the Collect, Epistle, and Gospel for Christmas-day shall serve for them.*

✠

The Sunday after Christmas-day.

The Collect.

ALMIGHTY God, who hast given us thy only-begotten Son to take our nature upon him, and as at this time to be born of a pure virgin ; Grant that we being regenerate, and made thy children by adoption and grace, may daily be renewed by thy Holy Spirit ; through the same our Lord Jesus Christ, who liveth and reigneth with thee and the same Spirit ever, one God, world without end. *Amen.*

The Epistle. Gal. iv. 1.

NOW I say, That the heir, as long as he is a child, differeth nothing from a servant, though he be lord of all; but is under tutors and governors until the time appointed of the father. Even so we, when we were children, were in bondage under the elements of the world: but when the fulness of the time was come, God sent forth his Son, made of a woman, made under the law, to redeem them that were under the law, that we might receive the adoption of sons. And because ye are sons, God hath sent forth the Spirit of his Son into your hearts, crying, Abba, Father. Wherefore thou art no more a servant, but a son; and if a son, then an heir of God through Christ.

The Gospel. St. Matt. i. 18.

THE birth of Jesus Christ was on this wise: When as his mother Mary was espoused to Joseph, before they came together, she was found with child of the Holy Ghost. Then Joseph her husband, being a just man, and not willing to make her a publick example, was minded to put her away privily. But while he thought on these things, behold, the angel of the Lord appeared unto him in a dream, saying, Joseph, thou son of David, fear not to take unto thee Mary thy wife: for that which is conceived in her is of the Holy Ghost. And she shall bring forth a son, and thou shalt call his name JESUS: for he shall save his people from their sins. Now all this was done, that it might be fulfilled which was spoken of the Lord by the prophet, saying, Behold, a virgin shall be with child, and shall bring forth a son, and they shall call his name Emmanuel, which being interpreted is, God with us. Then Joseph being raised from sleep did as the angel of the Lord had bidden him, and took unto him his wife: and knew her not till she had brought forth her firstborn son: and he called his name JESUS.

The Circumcision of Christ.

The Collect.

ALMIGHTY God, who madest thy blessed Son to be circumcised, and obedient to the law for man; Grant us the true circumcision of the Spirit; that, our hearts, and all our members, being mortified from all worldly and carnal lusts, we may in all things obey thy blessed will; through the same thy Son Jesus Christ our Lord. *Amen.*

The Epistle. Rom. iv. 8.

BLESSED is the man to whom the Lord will not impute sin. Cometh this blessedness then upon the circumcision only, or upon the uncircumcision also? for we say that faith was reckoned to Abraham for righteousness. How was it then reckoned? when he was in circumcision, or in uncircumcision? Not in circumcision, but in uncircumcision. And he received the sign of circumcision, a seal of the righteousness of the faith which he had yet being uncircumcised: that he might be the father of all them that believe, though they be not circumcised; that righteousness might be imputed unto them also: and the father of circumcision to them who are not of the circumcision only, but who also walk in the steps of that faith of our father Abraham, which he had being yet uncircumcised. For the promise, that he should be the heir of the world, was not to Abraham, or to his seed, through the law, but through the righteousness of faith. For if they which are of the law be heirs, faith is made void, and the promise made of none effect.

The Gospel. St. Luke ii. 15.

AND it came to pass, as the angels were gone away from them into heaven, the shepherds said one to another, Let us now go even unto Bethlehem, and see this thing which is come to pass, which the Lord hath made known unto us. And they came with haste, and found Mary, and Joseph, and the babe lying in a manger. And when they had seen it, they made known abroad the saying which was told them concerning this child. And all they that heard it wondered at those things which were told them by the shepherds. But Mary kept all these things, and pondered them in her heart. And the shepherds returned, glorifying and praising God for all the things that they had heard and seen, as it was told unto them. And when eight days were accomplished for the circumcising of the child, his name was called JESUS, which was so named of the angel before he was conceived in the womb.

¶ *The same Collect, Epistle, and Gospel shall serve for every day after, unto the Epiphany.*

The Epiphany, or the Manifestation of Christ to the Gentiles.

The Collect.

O GOD, who by the leading of a star didst manifest thy only-begotten Son to the Gentiles; Mercifully grant that we, who know thee now by faith, may after this life have the fruition of thy glorious Godhead; through Jesus Christ our Lord. Amen.

The Epistle. Eph. iii. 1.

FOR this cause I Paul, the prisoner of Jesus Christ for you Gentiles, if ye have heard of the dispensation of the grace of God, which is given me to you-ward: how that by revelation he made known unto me the mystery; (as I wrote afore in few words, whereby, when ye read, ye may understand my knowledge in the mystery of Christ) which in other ages was not made known unto the sons of men, as it is now revealed unto his holy apostles and prophets by the Spirit; that the Gentiles should be fellowheirs, and of the same body, and partakers of his promise in Christ by the gospel: whereof I was made a minister, according to the gift of the grace of God given unto me by the effectual working of his power. Unto me, who am less than the least of all saints, is this grace given, that I should preach among the Gentiles the unsearchable riches of Christ; and to make all men see what is the fellowship of the mystery, which from the beginning of the world hath been hid in God, who created all things by Jesus Christ: to the intent that now unto the principalities and powers in heavenly places might be known by the church the manifold wisdom of God, according to the eternal purpose which he purposed in Christ Jesus our Lord: in whom we have boldness and access with confidence by the faith of him.

The Gospel. St. Matt. ii. 1.

WHEN Jesus was born in Bethlehem of Judæa, in the days of Herod the king, behold, there came wise men from the *east to Jerusalem, saying,* Where is he that is born King of the Jews? for we have seen his star in the east, and are come to worship him. When Herod the king had heard these things, he was troubled, and all Jerusalem with him. And when he had gathered all the chief priests and scribes of the people together, he demanded of them where Christ should be born. And they said unto him, In Bethlehem of Judæa: for thus it is written by the prophet, And thou

Bethlehem, in the land of Juda, art not the least among the princes of Juda: for out of thee shall come a Governor, that shall rule my people Israel. Then Herod, when he had privily called the wise men, enquired of them diligently what time the star appeared. And he sent them to Bethlehem, and said, Go and search diligently for the young child; and when ye have found him, bring me word again, that I may come and worship him also. When they had heard the king, they departed; and, lo, the star, *which they saw in the* east, went before them, till it came and stood over where the young child was. When they saw the star, they rejoiced with exceeding great joy. And when they were come into the house, they saw the young child with Mary his mother, and fell down, and worshipped him: and when they had opened their treasures, they presented unto him gifts; gold, and frankincense, and myrrh. And being warned of God in a dream that they should not return to Herod, they departed into their own country another way.

¶ The same Collect, Epistle, and Gospel shall serve for every day after, unto the next Sunday.

The First Sunday after the Epiphany.

The Collect.

O LORD, we beseech thee mercifully to receive the prayers of thy people who call upon thee; and grant that they may both perceive and know what things they ought to do, and also may have grace and power faithfully to fulfil the same; through Jesus Christ our Lord. *Amen.*

The Epistle. Rom. xii. 1.

I BESEECH you therefore, brethren, by the mercies of God, that ye present your bodies a living sacrifice, holy, acceptable unto God, which is your reasonable service. And be not conformed to this world: but be ye transformed by the renewing of your mind, that ye may prove what is that good, and acceptable, and perfect, will of God. For I say, through the grace given unto me, to every man that is among you, not to think of himself more highly than he ought to think; but to think soberly, according as God hath dealt to every man the measure of faith. For as we have many members in one body, and all members have not the same office: so we, being many, are one body in Christ, and every one members one of another.

The Gospel. St. Luke ii. 41.

N OW his parents went to Jerusalem every year at the feast of the passover. And when he was twelve years old, they went up to Jerusalem after the custom of the feast. And when they had fulfilled the days, as they returned, the child Jesus tarried behind in Jerusalem; and Joseph and his mother knew not of it. But they, supposing him to have been in the company, went a day's journey; and they sought him among their kinsfolk and acquaintance. And when they found him not, they turned back again to Jerusalem, seeking him. And it came to pass, that after three days they found him in the temple, sitting in the midst of the doctors, both hearing them, and asking them questions. And all that heard him were astonished at his understanding and answers. And when they saw him, they were amazed: and his mother said unto him, Son, why hast thou thus dealt with us? behold, thy father and I have sought thee sorrowing. And he said unto them, How is it that ye sought me? wist ye not that I must be about my Father's business? And they understood not the saying which he spake unto them. And he went down with them, and came to Nazareth, and was subject unto them: but his mother kept all these sayings in her heart. And Jesus increased in wisdom and stature, and in favour with God and man.

❋

The Second Sunday after the Epiphany.

The Collect.

ALMIGHTY and everlasting God, who dost govern all things in heaven and earth; Mercifully hear the supplications of thy people, and grant us thy peace all the days of our life; through Jesus Christ our Lord. *Amen.*

The Epistle. Rom. xii. 6.

HAVING then gifts differing according to the grace that is given to us, whether prophecy, let us prophesy according to the proportion of faith; or ministry, let us wait on our ministering: or he that teacheth, on teaching; or he that exhorteth, on exhortation: he that giveth, let him do it with simplicity; he that ruleth, with diligence; he that sheweth mercy, with cheerfulness. Let love be without dissimulation. Abhor that which is evil; cleave to that which is good. Be kindly affectioned one to another with brotherly love; in honour preferring one another; not slothful in business; fervent in spirit; serving the Lord; rejoicing in hope; patient in tribulation; continuing instant in prayer; distributing to the necessity of saints; given to hospitality. Bless them which persecute you: bless, and curse not. Rejoice with them that do rejoice, and weep with them that weep. Be of the same mind one toward another. Mind not high things, but condescend to men of low estate.

The Gospel. St. John ii. 1.

AND the third day there was a marriage in Cana of Galilee; and the mother of Jesus was there: and both Jesus was called, and his disciples, to the marriage. And when they wanted wine, the mother of Jesus saith unto him, They have no wine. Jesus saith unto her, Woman, what have I to do with thee? mine hour is not yet come. His mother saith unto the servants, Whatsoever he saith unto you, do it. And there were set there six water-pots of stone, after the manner of the purifying of the Jews, containing two or three firkins apiece. Jesus saith unto them, Fill the water-pots with water. And they filled them up to the brim. And he saith unto them, Draw out now, and bear unto the governor of the feast. And they bare it. When the ruler of the feast had tasted the water that was made wine, and

knew not whence it was: (but the servants which drew the water knew;) the governor of the feast called the bridegroom, and saith unto him, Every man at the beginning doth set forth good wine; and when men have well drunk, then that which is worse: but thou hast kept the good wine until now. This beginning of miracles did Jesus in Cana of Galilee, and manifested forth his glory; and his disciples believed on him.

✠

The Third Sunday after the Epiphany.

The Collect.

ALMIGHTY and everlasting God, mercifully look upon our infirmities, and in all our dangers and necessities stretch forth thy right hand to help and defend us; through Jesus Christ our Lord. *Amen.*

The Epistle. Rom. xii. 16.

BE not wise in your own conceits. Recompense to no man evil for evil. Provide things honest in the sight of all men. If it be possible, as much as lieth in you, live peaceably with all men. Dearly beloved, avenge not yourselves, but rather give place unto wrath: for it is written, Vengeance is mine; I will repay, saith the Lord. Therefore if thine enemy hunger, feed him; if he thirst, give him drink: for in so doing thou shalt heap coals of fire on his head. Be not overcome of evil, but overcome evil with good.

The Gospel. St. Matt. viii. 1.

WHEN he was come down from the mountain, great multitudes followed him. And, behold, there came a leper and worshipped him, saying, Lord, if thou wilt, thou canst make me clean. And Jesus put forth his hand, and touched him, saying, I will; be thou clean. And immediately his leprosy was cleansed. And Jesus saith unto him, See thou tell no man; but go thy way, shew thyself to the priest, and offer the gift that Moses commanded, for a testimony unto them. And when Jesus was entered into Capernaum, there came unto him a centurion, beseeching him, and saying, Lord, my servant lieth at home sick of the palsy, grievously tormented. And Jesus saith unto him, I will come and heal him. The centurion answered and said, Lord, I am not worthy that thou shouldest come under my roof: but speak the word only, and my servant shall be healed. For I am a man under authority, having soldiers under me: and I say to this man, Go, and he goeth; and to another, Come, and he cometh; and to my servant, Do this, and he doeth it. When Jesus heard it, he marvelled, and said to them that followed, Verily I say unto you, I have not found *so great faith, no, not* in Israel. And I say unto you, that many shall come from the east and west, and shall sit down with Abraham, and Isaac, and Jacob, in the kingdom of heaven. But the children of the kingdom shall be cast out into outer darkness: there shall be weeping and gnashing of teeth. And Jesus said unto the centurion, Go thy way; and as thou hast believed, so be it done unto thee. And his servant was healed in the selfsame hour.

The Fourth Sunday after the Epiphany.

The Collect.

O GOD, who knowest us to be set in the midst of so many and great dangers, that by reason of the frailty of our nature we cannot always stand upright; Grant to us such strength and protection, as may support us in all dangers, and carry us through all temptations; through Jesus Christ our Lord. *Amen.*

The Epistle. Rom. xiii. 1.

LET every soul be subject unto the higher powers. For there is no power but of God: the powers that be are ordained of God. Whosoever therefore resisteth the power, resisteth the ordinance of God; and they that resist shall receive to themselves damnation. For rulers are not a terror to good works, but to the evil. Wilt thou then not be afraid of the power? do that which is good, and thou shalt have praise of the same: for he is the minister of God to thee for good. But if thou do that which is evil, be afraid; for he beareth not the sword in vain: for he is the minister of God, a revenger to execute wrath upon him that doeth evil. Wherefore ye must needs be subject, not only for wrath, but also for conscience sake. For for this cause pay ye tribute also: for they are God's ministers, attending continually upon this very thing. Render therefore to all their dues: tribute to whom tribute is due; custom to whom custom; fear to whom fear; honour to whom honour.

The Gospel. St. Matt. viii. 23.

AND when he was entered into a ship, his disciples followed him. And, behold, there arose a great tempest in the sea, insomuch that the ship was covered with the waves: but he was asleep. And his disciples came to him, and awoke him, saying, Lord, save us: we perish. And he saith unto them, Why are ye fearful, O ye of little faith? Then he arose, and rebuked the winds and the sea; and there was a great calm. But the men marvelled, saying, What manner of man is this, that even the winds and the sea obey him! And when he was come to the other side into the country of the Gergesenes, there met him two possessed with devils, coming out of the tombs, exceeding fierce, so that no man might pass by that way. And, behold, they cried out, saying, What have we to do with thee, Jesus, thou Son of God? art thou come hither to torment us before the time? And there was a good way off from them an herd of many swine feeding. So the devils besought him, saying, If thou cast us out, suffer us to go away into the herd of swine. And he said unto them, Go. And when they were come out, they went into the herd of swine: and, behold, the whole herd of swine ran violently down a steep place into the sea, and perished in the waters. And they that kept them fled, and went their ways into the city, and told every thing, and what was befallen to the possessed of the devils. And, behold, the whole city came out to meet Jesus: and when they saw him, they besought him that he would depart out of their coasts.

❧

The Fifth Sunday after the Epiphany.

The Collect.

O LORD, we beseech thee to keep thy Church and household continually in thy true religion; that they who do lean only upon the hope of thy heavenly grace may evermore be defended by thy mighty power; through Jesus Christ our Lord. *Amen.*

The Epistle. Col. iii. 12.

PUT on therefore, as the elect of God, holy and beloved, bowels of mercies, kindness, humbleness of mind, meekness, longsuffering; forbearing one another, and forgiving one another, if any man have a quarrel against any: even as Christ forgave you, so also do ye. And above all these things put on charity, which is the bond of perfectness. And let the peace of God rule in your hearts, to the which also ye are called in one body; and be ye thankful. Let the word of Christ dwell in you richly in all wisdom;

* E

teaching and admonishing one another in psalms and hymns and spiritual songs, singing with grace in your hearts to the Lord. And whatsoever ye do in word or deed, do all in the name of the Lord Jesus, giving thanks to God and the Father by him.

The Gospel. St. Matt. xiii. 24.

THE kingdom of heaven is likened unto a man which sowed good seed in his field : but while men slept, his enemy came and sowed tares among the wheat, and went his way. But when the blade was sprung up, and brought forth fruit, then appeared the tares also. So the servants of the householder came and said unto him, Sir, didst not thou sow good seed in thy field ? from whence then hath it tares? He said unto them, An enemy hath done this. The servants said unto him, Wilt thou then that we go and gather them up ? But he said, Nay ; lest while ye gather up the tares, ye root up also the wheat with them. Let both grow together until the harvest : and in the time of harvest I will say to the reapers,

Gather ye together first the tares, and bind them in bundles to burn them : but gather the wheat into my barn.

The Sixth Sunday after the Epiphany.
The Collect.

O GOD, whose blessed Son was manifested that he might destroy the works of the devil, and make us the sons of God, and heirs of eternal life ; Grant us, we beseech thee, that, having this hope, we may purify ourselves, even as he is pure ; that, when he shall appear again with power and great glory, we may be made like unto him in his eternal and glorious kingdom ; where with thee, O Father, and thee, O Holy Ghost, he liveth and reigneth ever, one God, world without end. *Amen.*

The Epistle. 1 St. John iii. 1.

BEHOLD, what manner of love the Father hath bestowed upon us, that we should be called the sons of God: therefore the world knoweth us not, because it knew him not. Beloved, now are we the sons of God, and it doth not yet appear what we shall be: but we know that, when he shall appear, we shall be like him; for we shall see him as he is. And every man that hath this hope in him purifieth himself, even as he is pure. Whosoever committeth sin transgresseth also the law: for sin is the transgression of the law. And ye know that he was manifested to take away our sins; and in him is no sin. Whosoever abideth in him sinneth not: whosoever sinneth hath not seen him, neither known him. Little children, let no man deceive you: he that doeth righteousness is righteous, even as he is righteous. He that committeth sin is of the devil; for the devil sinneth from the beginning. For this purpose the Son of God was manifested, that he might destroy the works of the devil.

The Gospel. St. Matt. xxiv. 23.

THEN if any man shall say unto you, Lo, here is Christ, or there; believe it not. For there shall arise false Christs, and false prophets, and shall shew great signs and wonders;

insomuch that, if it were possible, they shall deceive the very elect. Behold, I have told you before. Wherefore if they shall say unto you, Behold, he is in the desert; go not forth: behold, he is in the secret chambers; believe it not. For as the lightning cometh out of the east, and shineth even unto the west; so shall also the coming of the Son of man be. For wheresoever the carcase is, there will the eagles be gathered together. Immediately after the tribulation of those days shall the sun be darkened, and the moon shall not give her light, and the stars shall fall from heaven, and the powers of the heavens shall be shaken: and then shall appear the sign of the Son of man in heaven: and then shall all the tribes of the earth mourn, and they shall see the Son of man coming in the clouds of heaven with power and great glory. And he shall send his angels with a great sound of a trumpet, and they shall gather together his elect from the four winds, from one end of heaven to the other.

The Sunday called Septuagesima, or the third Sunday before Lent.

The Collect.

O LORD, we beseech thee favourably to hear the prayers of thy people; that we, who are justly punished for our offences, may be mercifully delivered by thy goodness, for the glory of thy Name; through Jesus Christ our Saviour, who liveth and reigneth with thee and the Holy Ghost ever, one God, world without end. Amen.

The Epistle. 1 Cor. ix. 24.

K NOW ye not that they which run in a race run all, but one receiveth the prize? So run, that ye may obtain. And every man that striveth for the mastery is temperate in all things. Now they do it to obtain a corruptible crown: but we an incorruptible. I therefore so run, not as uncertainly; so fight I, not as one that beateth the air: but I keep under my body, and bring it into subjection: lest that by any means, when I have preached to others, I myself should be a castaway.

The Gospel. St. Matt. xx. 1.

T HE kingdom of heaven is like unto a man that is an householder, which went out early in the morning to hire labourers into his vineyard. And when he had agreed with the labourers for a penny a day, he sent them into his vineyard. And he went out about the third hour, and saw others standing idle in the marketplace, and said unto them; Go ye also into the vineyard, and whatsoever is right I will give you. And they went their way. Again he went out about the sixth and ninth hour, and did likewise. And about the eleventh hour he went out, and found others standing idle, and saith unto them, Why stand ye here all the day idle? They say unto him, Because no man hath hired us. He saith unto them, Go ye also into the vineyard; and whatsoever is right, that shall ye receive. So when even was come, the lord of the vineyard saith unto his steward, Call the labourers, and give them their hire, beginning from the last unto the first. And when they came that were hired about the eleventh hour, they received every man a penny. But when the first came, they supposed that they should have received more; and they likewise received every man a penny. And when they had received it, they murmured against the goodman of the house, saying, These last have wrought but one hour, and thou hast made them equal unto us, which have borne the burden and heat of the day. But he answered one of them, and said, Friend, I do thee no wrong: didst not thou agree with me for a penny? Take that thine is, and go thy way: I will give unto this last, even as unto thee. Is it not lawful for me to do what I will with mine own? Is thine eye evil, because I am good? So the last shall be first, and the first last: for many be called, but few chosen.

The Sunday called Sexagesima, or the second Sunday before Lent.

The Collect.

O LORD God, who seest that we put not our trust in any thing that we do; Mercifully grant that by thy power we may be defended against all adversity; through Jesus Christ our Lord. *Amen.*

The Epistle. 2 Cor. xi. 19.

YE suffer fools gladly, seeing ye yourselves are wise. For ye suffer, if a man bring you into bondage, if a man devour you, if a man take of you, if a man exalt himself, if a man smite you on the face. I speak as concerning reproach, as though we had been weak. Howbeit whereinsoever any is bold, (I speak foolishly,) I am bold also. Are they Hebrews? so am I. Are they Israelites? so am I. Are they the seed of Abraham? so am I. Are they ministers of Christ? (I speak as a fool) I am more; in labours more abundant, in stripes above measure, in prisons more frequent, in deaths oft. Of the Jews five times received I forty stripes save one. Thrice was I beaten with rods, once was I stoned, thrice I suffered shipwreck, a night and a day I have been in the deep; in journeyings often, in perils of waters, in perils of robbers, in perils by mine own countrymen, in perils by the heathen, in perils in the city, in perils in the wilderness, in perils in the sea, in perils among false brethren; in weariness and painfulness, in watchings often, in hunger and thirst, in fastings often, in cold and nakedness. Beside those things that are without, that which cometh upon me daily, the care of all the churches. Who is weak, and I am not weak? who is offended, and I burn not? If I must needs glory, I will glory of the things which concern mine infirmities. The God and Father of our Lord Jesus Christ, which is blessed for evermore, knoweth that I lie not.

The Gospel. St. Luke viii. 4.

WHEN much people were gathered together, and were come to him out of every city, he spake by a parable: A sower went out to sow his seed: and as he sowed, some fell by the way side; and it was trodden down, and the fowls of the air devoured it. And some fell upon a rock; and as soon as it was sprung up, it withered away, because it lacked moisture. And some fell among thorns; and the thorns sprang up with it, and choked it. And other fell on good ground, and sprang up, and bare fruit an hundredfold. And when he had said these things, he cried, He that hath ears to hear, let him hear. And his disciples asked him, saying, What might this parable be? And he said, Unto you it is given to know the mysteries of the kingdom of God: but to others in parables; that seeing they might not see, and hearing they might not understand. Now the parable is this: The seed is the word of God. Those by the way side are they that hear; then cometh the devil, and taketh away the word out of their hearts, lest they should believe and be saved. They on the rock are they, which, when they hear, receive the word with joy; and these have no root, which for a while believe, and in time of temptation fall away. And that which fell among thorns are they, which, when they have heard, go forth, and are choked with cares and riches and pleasures of this life, and bring no fruit to perfection. But that on the good ground are they, which in an honest and good heart, having heard the word, keep it, and bring forth fruit with patience.

✠

The Sunday called Quinquagesima, or the next Sunday before Lent.

The Collect.

O LORD, who hast taught us that all our doings without charity are nothing worth; Send thy Holy Ghost, and pour into our hearts that most excellent gift of charity, the very bond of peace and of all virtues, without which whosoever liveth is counted dead before thee. Grant this for thine only Son Jesus Christ's sake. Amen.

The Epistle. 1 Cor. xiii. 1.

THOUGH I speak with the tongues of men and of angels, and have not charity, I am become as sounding brass, or a tinkling cymbal. And though I have the gift of prophecy, and understand all mysteries, and all knowledge; and though I have all faith, so that I could remove mountains, and have not charity, I am nothing. And though I bestow all my goods to feed the poor, and though I give my body to be burned, and have not charity, it profiteth me nothing. Charity suffereth long, and is kind; charity envieth not; charity vaunteth not itself, is not puffed up, doth not behave itself unseemly, seeketh not her own, is not easily provoked, thinketh no evil; rejoiceth not in iniquity, but rejoiceth in the truth; beareth all things, believeth all things, hopeth all things, endureth all things. Charity never faileth: but whether there be prophecies, they shall fail; whether there be tongues, they shall cease; whether there be knowledge, it shall vanish away. For we know in part, and we prophesy in part. But when that which is perfect is come, then that which is in part shall be done away. When I was a child, I spake as a child, I understood as a child, I thought as a child: but when I became a man, I put away childish things. For now we see through a glass, darkly; but then face to face: now I know in part; but then shall I know even as also I am known. And now abideth faith, hope, charity, these three; but the greatest of these is charity.

The Gospel. St. Luke xviii. 31.

THEN Jesus took unto him the twelve, and said unto them, Behold, we go up to Jerusalem, and all things that are written by the prophets concerning the Son of man shall be accomplished. For he shall be delivered unto the Gentiles, and shall be mocked, and spitefully entreated, and spitted on: *and* they shall scourge him, and put him to death: and the third day he shall rise again. And they understood none of these things: and this saying was hid from them, neither knew they the things which were spoken. And it came to pass, that as he was come nigh unto Jericho, a certain blind man sat by the way side begging: and hearing the multitude pass by, he asked what it meant. And they told him, that Jesus of Nazareth passeth by. And he cried, saying, Jesus, thou son of David, have mercy on me. And they which went before rebuked him, that he should hold his peace: but he cried so much the more, Thou son of David, have mercy on me. And Jesus stood, and commanded him to be brought unto him: and when he was come near, he asked him, saying, What wilt thou that I shall do unto thee? And he said, Lord, that I may receive my sight. And Jesus said unto him, Receive thy sight: thy faith hath saved thee. And immediately he received his sight, and followed him, glorifying God: and all the people, when they saw it, gave praise unto God.

❧

The first day of **Lent**, commonly called Ash-Wednesday.

The Collect.

ALMIGHTY and everlasting God, who hatest

nothing that thou hast made, and dost forgive the sins of all those who are penitent; Create and make in us new and contrite hearts, that we, worthily lamenting our sins and acknowledging our wretchedness, may obtain of thee, the God of all mercy, perfect remission and forgiveness; through Jesus Christ our Lord. *Amen.*

¶ *This Collect is to be read every day in Lent, after the Collect appointed for the day.*

For the Epistle. Joel ii. 12.

TURN ye even to me, saith the LORD, with all your heart, and with fasting, and with weeping, and with mourning: and rend your heart, and not your garments, and turn unto the LORD your God: for he is gracious and merciful, slow to anger, and of great kindness, and repenteth him of the evil. Who knoweth if he will return and repent, and leave a blessing behind him; even a meat offering and a drink offering unto the LORD your God? Blow the trumpet in Zion, sanctify a fast, call a solemn assembly: gather the people, sanctify the congregation, assemble the elders, gather the children, and those that suck the breasts: let the bridegroom go forth of his chamber, and the bride out of her closet. Let the priests, the ministers of the LORD, weep between the porch and the altar, and let them say, Spare thy people, O LORD, and give not thine heritage to reproach, that the heathen should rule over them: wherefore should they say among the people, Where is their God?

The Gospel. St. Matt. vi. 16.

WHEN ye fast, be not, as the hypocrites, of a sad countenance: for they disfigure their faces, that they may appear unto men to fast. Verily I say unto you, They have their reward. But thou, when thou fastest, anoint thine head, and wash thy face; that thou appear not unto men to fast, but unto thy Father which is in secret: and thy Father, which seeth in secret, shall reward thee openly. Lay not up for yourselves treasures upon earth, where moth and rust doth corrupt, and where thieves break through and steal:

but lay up for yourselves treasures in heaven, where neither moth nor rust doth corrupt, and where thieves do not break through nor steal: for where your treasure is, there will your heart be also.

¶ *The same Collect, Epistle, and Gospel shall serve for every day after, unto the next Sunday, except upon the Feast of St. Matthias.*

The First Sunday in Lent.

The Collect.

O LORD, who for our sake didst fast forty days and forty nights; Give us grace to use such abstinence, that, our flesh being subdued to the Spirit, we may ever obey thy godly motions in righteousness, and true holiness, to thy honour and glory, who livest and reignest with the Father and the Holy Ghost, one God, world without end. *Amen.*

The Epistle. 2 Cor. vi. 1.

WE then, as workers together with him, beseech you also that ye receive not the grace of God in vain. (For he saith, I have heard thee in a time accepted, and in the day

of salvation have I succoured thee: behold, now is the accepted time; behold, now is the day of salvation.) Giving no offence in any thing, that the ministry be not blamed: but in all things approving ourselves as the ministers of God, in much patience, in afflictions, in necessities, in distresses, in stripes, in imprisonments, in tumults, in labours, in watchings, in fastings; by pureness, by knowledge, by longsuffering, by kindness, by the Holy Ghost, by love unfeigned, by the word of truth, by the power of God, by the armour of righteousness on the right hand and on the left, by honour and dishonour, by evil report and good report: as deceivers, and yet true; as unknown, and yet well known; as dying, and, behold, we live; as chastened, and not killed; as sorrowful, yet alway rejoicing; as poor, yet making many rich; as having nothing, and yet possessing all things.

The Gospel. St. Matt. iv. 1.

THEN was Jesus led up of the spirit into the wilderness to be tempted of the devil. And when he had fasted forty days and forty nights, he was afterward an hungred. And when the tempter came to him, he said, If thou be the Son of God, command that these stones be made bread. But he answered and said, It is written, Man shall not live by bread alone, but by every word that proceedeth out of the mouth of God. Then the devil taketh him up into the holy city, and setteth him on a pinnacle of the temple, and saith unto him, If thou be the Son of God, cast thyself down: for it is written, He shall give his angels charge concerning thee: and in their hands they shall bear thee up, lest at any time thou dash thy foot against a stone. Jesus said unto him, It is written again, Thou shalt not tempt the Lord thy God. Again, the devil taketh him up into an exceeding high mountain, and sheweth him all the kingdoms of the world, and the glory of them: and saith unto him, All these things will I give thee, if thou wilt fall down and worship me. Then saith Jesus unto him, Get thee

hence, Satan: for it is written, Thou shalt worship the Lord thy God, and him only shalt thou serve. Then the devil leaveth him, and, behold, angels came and ministered unto him.

The Second Sunday in Lent.

The Collect.

ALMIGHTY God, who seest that we have no power of ourselves to help ourselves; Keep us both outwardly in our bodies, and inwardly in our souls; that we may be defended from all adversities which may happen to the body, and from all evil thoughts which may assault and hurt the soul; through Jesus Christ our Lord. *Amen.*

The Epistle. 1 Thess. iv. 1.

WE beseech you, brethren, and exhort you by the Lord Jesus, that as ye have received of us how ye ought to walk and to please God, so ye would abound more and more. For ye know what commandments we gave you by the Lord Jesus. For this is the will of

God, even your sanctifica-
tion, that ye should ab-
stain from fornication:
that every one of you
should know how to pos-
sess his vessel in sanc-
tification and honour;
not in the lust of concu-
piscence, even as the Gentiles which know not God:
that no man go beyond
and defraud his brother
in any matter: because
that the Lord is the avenger of all such, as we also
have forewarned you and
testified. For God hath
not called us unto un-
cleanness, but unto holi-
ness. He therefore that
despiseth, despiseth not
man, but God, who hath
also given unto us his holy
Spirit.

The Gospel. St. Matt. xv. 21.

JESUS went thence, and
departed into the
coasts of Tyre and Sidon.
And, behold, a woman of
Canaan came out of the
same coasts, and cried
unto him, saying, Have
mercy on me, O Lord, thou
son of David; my daugh-
ter is grievously vexed with
a devil. But he answered
her not a word. And his
disciples came and be-
sought him, saying, Send

her away; for she crieth
after us. But he answer-
ed and said, I am not sent
but unto the lost sheep of
the house of Israel. Then
came she and worshipped
him, saying, Lord, help me.
But he answered and said,
It is not meet to take the
children's bread, and to
cast it to dogs. And she
said, Truth, Lord: yet the
dogs eat of the crumbs
which fall from their masters' table. Then Jesus
answered and said unto
her, O woman, great is thy
faith: be it unto thee even
as thou wilt. And her
daughter was made whole
from that very hour.

The Third Sunday in Lent.

The Collect.

WE beseech thee, Al-
mighty God, look
upon the hearty desires
of thy humble servants,
and stretch forth the right
hand of thy Majesty, to be
our defence against all our
enemies; through Jesus
Christ our Lord. *Amen.*

The Epistle. Ephes. v. 1.

BE ye therefore follow-
ers of God, as dear
children; and walk in love,

as Christ also hath loved us, and hath given himself for us an offering and a sacrifice to God for a sweet-smelling savour. But fornication, and all uncleanness, or covetousness, let it not be once named among you, as becometh saints; neither filthiness, nor foolish talking, nor jesting, which are not convenient: but rather giving of thanks. For this ye know, that no whoremonger, nor unclean person, nor covetous man, who is an idolater, hath any inheritance in the kingdom of Christ and of God. Let no man deceive you with vain words: for because of these things cometh the wrath of God upon the children of disobedience. Be not ye therefore partakers with them. For ye were sometimes darkness, but now are ye light in the Lord: walk as children of light: (for the fruit of the Spirit is in all goodness and righteousness and truth;) proving what is acceptable unto the Lord. And have no fellowship with the unfruitful works of darkness, but rather reprove them. For it is a shame even to speak of those things which are done of them in secret. But all things that are reproved are made manifest by the light: for whatsoever doth make manifest is light. Wherefore he saith, Awake thou that sleepest, and arise from the dead, and Christ shall give thee light.

The Gospel. St. Luke xi. 14.

JESUS was casting out a devil, and it was dumb. And it came to pass, when the devil was gone out, the dumb spake; and the people wondered. But some of them said, He casteth out devils through Beelzebub the chief of the devils. And others, tempting him, sought of him a sign from heaven. But he, knowing their thoughts, said unto them, Every kingdom divided against itself is brought to desolation; and a house divided against a house falleth. If Satan also be divided against himself, how shall his kingdom stand? because ye say that I cast out devils through Beelzebub. And if I by Beelzebub cast out devils, by whom do your sons cast them out? therefore shall they be your judges. But if I with the finger of God cast out devils, no doubt the kingdom of God is come upon you. When a strong man armed keepeth his palace, his goods are in peace: but when a stronger than he shall come upon him, and overcome him, he taketh from him all his armour wherein he trusted, and divideth his spoils. He that is not with me is against me: and he that gathereth not with me scattereth. When the unclean spirit is gone out of a man, he walketh through dry places, seeking rest; and finding none, he saith, I will return unto my house whence I came out. And when he cometh, he findeth it swept and garnished. Then goeth he, and taketh to him seven other spirits more wicked than himself; and they enter in, and dwell there: and the last state of that man is worse than the first. And it came to pass, as he spake these things, a certain woman of the company lifted up her voice, and said unto him, Blessed is the womb that bare thee, and the paps which thou hast sucked. But he said, Yea rather, blessed are they that hear the word of God, and keep it.

The Fourth Sunday in Lent.

The Collect.

GRANT, we beseech thee, Almighty God, that we, who for our evil deeds do worthily deserve to be punished, by the comfort of thy grace may mercifully be relieved; through our Lord and Saviour Jesus Christ. *Amen.*

The Epistle. Gal. iv. 21.

TELL me, ye that desire to be under the law, do ye not hear the law? For it is written, that Abraham had two sons, the one by a bondmaid, the other by a freewoman. But he who was of the bondwoman was born after the flesh; but he of the freewoman was by promise. Which things are an allegory: for these are the two covenants; the one from the mount Sinai, which gendereth to bondage, which is Agar. For this Agar is mount Sinai in Arabia, and answereth to Jerusalem which now is, and is in bondage with her children. But Jerusalem which is above is free, which is the mother of us all. For it is written, Rejoice, thou barren that bearest not; break forth and cry, thou that travailest not: for the desolate hath many more children than she which hath an husband. Now we, brethren, as Isaac was, are the children of promise. But as then he that was born after the flesh persecuted him that was born after the Spirit, even so it is now. Nevertheless what saith the scripture? Cast out the bondwoman and her son: for the son of the bondwoman shall not be heir with the son of the freewoman. So then, brethren, we are not children of the bondwoman, but of the free.

The Gospel. St. John vi. 1.

JESUS went over the sea of Galilee, which is the sea of Tiberias. And a great multitude followed him, because they saw his miracles which he did on them that were diseased. And Jesus went up into a mountain, and there he sat with his disciples. And the passover, a feast of the Jews, was nigh. When Jesus then lifted up his eyes, and saw a great company come unto him, he saith unto Philip, Whence shall we buy bread, that these may eat? And this he said to prove him: for he himself knew what he would do. Philip answered him, Two hundred pennyworth of bread is not sufficient for them, that every one of them may take a little. One of his disciples, Andrew, Simon Peter's brother, saith unto him, There is a lad here, which hath five barley loaves, and two small fishes: but what are they among so many? And Jesus said, Make the men sit down. Now there was much grass in the place. So the men sat down, in number about five thousand. And Jesus took the loaves; and when he had given thanks, he distributed to the disciples, and the disciples to them that were set down; and likewise of the fishes as much as they would. When they were filled, he said unto his disciples, Gather up the fragments that remain, that nothing be lost. Therefore they gathered them together, and filled twelve baskets with the fragments of the five barley loaves, which remained over and above unto them that had eaten. Then those men, when they had seen the miracle that Jesus did, said, This is of a truth that prophet that should come into the world.

✳

The Fifth Sunday in Lent.

The Collect.

WE beseech thee, Almighty God, mercifully to look upon thy people; that by thy great goodness they may be governed and preserved evermore, both in body and soul; through Jesus Christ our Lord. *Amen.*

The Epistle. Heb. ix. 11.

CHRIST being come an high priest of good things to come, by a greater and more perfect tabernacle, not made with hands, that is to say, not of this building; neither by the blood of goats and calves, but by his own blood he entered in once into the holy place, having obtained eternal redemption for us. For if the blood of bulls and of goats, and the ashes of an heifer sprinkling the unclean, sanctifieth to the purifying of the flesh: how much more shall the blood of Christ, who through the eternal Spirit offered himself without spot to God, purge your conscience from dead works to serve the living God? And for this cause he is the mediator of the new testament, that by means of death, for the redemption of the transgressions that were under the first testament, they which are called might receive the promise of eternal inheritance.

The Gospel. St. John viii. 46.

JESUS said, Which of you convinceth me of sin? And if I say the truth, why do ye not believe me? He that is of God heareth God's words: ye therefore hear them not, because ye are not of God. Then answered the Jews, and said unto him, Say we not well that thou art a Samaritan, and hast a devil? Jesus answered, I have not a devil; but I honour my Father, and ye do dishonour me. And I seek not mine own glory: there is one that seeketh and judgeth. Verily, verily, I say unto you, If a man keep my saying, he shall never see death. Then said the Jews unto him, Now we know that thou hast a devil. Abraham is dead, and the prophets; and thou sayest, If a man keep my saying, he shall never taste of death. Art thou greater than our father Abraham, which is dead? and the prophets are dead: whom makest thou thyself? Jesus answered, If I honour myself, my honour is nothing: it is my Father that honoureth me; of whom ye say, that he is your God: yet ye have not known him; but I know him: and if I should say, I know him not, I shall be a liar like unto you; but I know him, and keep his saying. Your father Abraham rejoiced to see my day: and he saw it, and was glad. Then said the Jews unto him, Thou art not yet fifty years old, and hast thou

seen Abraham? Jesus said unto them, Verily, verily, I say unto you, Before Abraham was, I am. Then took they up stones to cast at him: but Jesus hid himself, and went out of the temple.

❂

The Sunday next before Easter.

The Collect.

ALMIGHTY and everlasting God, who, of thy tender love towards mankind, hast sent thy Son, our Saviour Jesus Christ, to take upon him our flesh, and to suffer death upon the cross, that all mankind should follow the example of his great humility; Mercifully grant, that we may both follow the example of his patience, and also be made partakers of his resurrection; through the same Jesus Christ our Lord. *Amen.*

The Epistle. Phil. ii. 5.

LET this mind be in you, which was also in Christ Jesus: who, being in the form of God, thought it not robbery to be equal with God: but made himself of no reputation, and took upon him the form of a servant, and was made in the likeness of men: and being found in fashion as a man, he humbled himself, and became obedient unto death, even the death of the cross. Wherefore God also hath highly exalted him, and given him a name which is above every name: that at the name of Jesus every knee should bow, of things in heaven, and things in earth, and things under the earth; and that every tongue should confess that Jesus Christ is Lord, to the glory of God the Father.

The Gospel. St. Matt. xxvii. 1.

WHEN the morning was come, all the chief priests and elders of the people took counsel against Jesus to put him to death: and when they had bound him, they led him away, and delivered him to Pontius Pilate the governor. Then Judas, which had betrayed him, when he saw that he was condemned, repented himself, and brought again the thirty pieces of silver to the chief priests and elders, saying, I have sinned

in that I have betrayed the innocent blood. And they said, What is that to us? see thou to that. And he cast down the pieces of silver in the temple, and departed, and went and hanged himself. And the chief priests took the silver pieces, and said, It is not lawful for to put them into the treasury, because it is the price of blood. And they took counsel, and bought with them the potter's field, to bury strangers in. Wherefore that field was called, The field of blood, unto this day. Then was fulfilled that which was spoken by Jeremy the prophet, saying, And they took the thirty pieces of silver, the price of him that was valued, whom they of the children of Israel did value; and gave them for the potter's field, as the Lord appointed me. And Jesus stood before the governor: and the governor asked him, saying, Art thou the King of the Jews? And Jesus said unto him, Thou sayest. And when he was accused of the chief priests and elders, he answered nothing. Then saith Pilate unto him,

Hearest thou not how many things they witness against thee? And he answered him to never a word; insomuch that the governor marvelled greatly. Now at that feast the governor was wont to release unto the people a prisoner, whom they would. And they had then a notable prisoner, called Barabbas. Therefore when they were gathered together, Pilate said unto them, Whom will ye that I release unto you? Barabbas, or Jesus which is called Christ? For he knew that for envy they had delivered him. When he was set down on the judgment seat, his wife sent unto him, saying, Have thou nothing to do with that just man: for I have suffered many things this day in a dream because of him. But the chief priests and elders persuaded the multitude that they should ask Barabbas, and destroy Jesus. The governor answered and said unto them, Whether of the twain will ye that I release unto you? They said, Barabbas. Pilate saith unto them, What shall I do then with Jesus which is called Christ?

They all say unto him, Let him be crucified. And the governor said, Why, what evil hath he done? But they cried out the more, saying, Let him be crucified. When Pilate saw that he could prevail nothing, but that rather a tumult was made, he took water, and washed his hands before the multitude, saying, I am innocent of the blood of this just person: see ye to it. Then answered all the people, and said, His blood be on us, and on our children. Then released he Barabbas unto them: and when he had scourged Jesus, he delivered him to be crucified. Then the soldiers of the governor took Jesus into the common hall, and gathered unto him the whole band of soldiers. And they stripped him, and put on him a scarlet robe. And when they had platted a crown of thorns, they put it upon his head, and a reed in his right hand: and they bowed the knee before him, and mocked him, saying, Hail, King of the Jews! And they spit upon him, and took the reed, and smote him on the head. And after that they had mocked him, they took the robe off from him, and put his own raiment on him, and led him away to crucify him. And as they came out, they found a man of Cyrene, Simon by name: him they compelled to bear his cross. And when they were come unto a place called Golgotha, that is to say, a place of a skull, they gave him vinegar to drink mingled with gall: and when he had tasted thereof, he would not drink. And they crucified him, and parted his garments, casting lots: that it might be fulfilled which was spoken by the prophet, They parted my garments among them, and upon my vesture did they cast lots. And sitting down they watched him there; and set up over his head his accusation written, THIS IS JESUS THE KING OF THE JEWS. Then were there two thieves crucified with him, one on the right hand, and another on the left. And they that passed by reviled him, wagging their heads, and saying, Thou that destroyest the temple, and buildest it in three days, save thyself. If thou be the Son of God, come down from the cross. Likewise also the chief priests mocking him, with the scribes and elders, said, He saved others; himself he cannot save. If he be the King of Israel, let him now come down from the cross, and we will believe him. He trusted in God; let him deliver him now, if he will have him: for he said, I am the Son of God. The thieves also, which were crucified with him, cast the same in his teeth. Now from the sixth hour there was darkness over all the land unto the ninth hour. And about the ninth hour Jesus cried with a loud voice, saying, Eli, Eli, lama sabachthani? that is to say, My God, my God, why hast thou forsaken me? Some of them that stood there, when they heart that, said, This man calleth for Elias. And straightway one of them ran, and took a spunge, and filled it with vinegar, and put it on a reed, and gave him to drink. The rest said, Let be, let us see whether Elias will come to save him. Jesus, when he had cried again with a loud voice, yielded up the ghost. And, behold, the veil of the temple was rent in twain from the top to the bottom; and the earth did quake, and the rocks rent; and the graves were opened; and many bodies of the saints which slept arose, and came out of the graves after his resurrection, and went into the holy city, and appeared unto many. Now when the centurion, and they that were with him, watching Jesus, saw the earthquake, and those things that were done, they feared greatly, saying, Truly this was the Son of God.

❀

Monday before Easter.

For the Epistle. Isa. lxiii. 1.

WHO is this that cometh from Edom, with dyed garments from Bozrah? this that is glorious in his apparel, travelling in the greatness of his strength? I that speak in righteousness, mighty to save. Wherefore art thou red in thine apparel, and thy garments like him that treadeth in the winefat? I have trodden the winepress alone; and of the people there was none with me: for I will tread them in mine anger, and trample them in my fury; and their blood shall be sprinkled upon my garments, and I will stain all my raiment. For the day of vengeance is in mine heart, and the year of my redeemed is come. And I looked, and there was none to help; and I wondered that there was none to uphold: therefore mine own arm brought salvation unto me; and my fury, it upheld me. And I will tread down the people in mine anger, and make them drunk in my fury, and I will bring down their strength to the earth. I will mention the loving-kindnesses of the LORD, and the praises of the LORD, according to all that the LORD hath bestowed on us, and the great goodness toward the house of Israel, which he hath bestowed on them according to his mercies, and according to the multitude of his lovingkindnesses. For he said, Surely they are my people, children that will not lie: so he was their Saviour. In all their affliction he was afflicted, and the angel of his presence saved them: in his love and in his pity he redeemed them; and he bare them, and carried them all the days of old. But they rebelled, and vexed his holy Spirit; therefore he was turned to be their enemy, and he fought against them. Then he remembered the days of old, Moses, and his people, saying, Where is he that brought them up out of the sea with the shepherd of his flock? where is he that put his holy Spirit within him? that led them by the right hand of Moses with his glorious arm, dividing the water before them, to make himself an everlasting name? that led them through the deep, as an horse in the wilderness, that they should not stumble? As a beast goeth down into the valley, the Spirit of the LORD caused him to rest: so didst thou lead thy people, to make thyself a glorious name. Look down from heaven, and behold from the habitation of thy holiness and of thy glory: where is thy zeal and thy strength, the sounding of thy bowels

and of thy mercies toward me? are they restrained? Doubtless thou art our father, though Abraham be ignorant of us, and Israel acknowledge us not: thou, O LORD, art our father, our redeemer; thy name is from everlasting. O LORD, why hast thou made us to err from thy ways, and hardened our heart from thy fear? Return for thy servants' sake, the tribes of thine inheritance. The people of thy holiness have possessed it but a little while: our adversaries have trodden down thy sanctuary. We are thine: thou never barest rule over them; they were not called by thy name.

The Gospel. St. Mark xiv. 1.

AFTER two days was the feast of the passover, and of unleavened bread: and the chief priests and the scribes sought how they might take him by craft, and put him to death. But they said, Not on the feast day, lest there be an uproar of the people. And being in Bethany in the house of Simon the leper, as he sat at meat, there came a woman having an alabaster box of ointment of spikenard very precious; and she brake the box, and poured it on his head. And there were some that had indignation within themselves, and said, Why was this waste of the ointment made? for it might have been sold for more than three hundred pence, and have been given to the poor. And they murmured against her. And Jesus said, Let her alone; why trouble ye her? she hath wrought a good work on me. For ye have the poor with you always, and whensoever ye will ye may do them good: but me ye have not always. She hath done what she could: she is come aforehand to anoint my body to the burying. Verily I say unto you, Wheresoever this gospel shall be preached throughout the whole world, this also that she hath done shall be spoken of for a memorial of her. And Judas Iscariot, one of the twelve, went unto the chief priests, to betray him unto them. And when they heard it, they were glad, and promised to give him money. And he sought

how he might conveniently betray him. And the first day of unleavened bread, when they killed the passover, his disciples said unto him, Where wilt thou that we go and prepare that thou mayest eat the passover? And he sendeth forth two of his disciples, and saith unto them, Go ye into the city, and there shall meet you a man bearing a pitcher of water: follow him. And wheresoever he shall go in, say ye to the goodman of the house, The Master saith, Where is the guestchamber, where I shall eat the passover with my disciples? And he will shew you a large upper room furnished and prepared: there make ready for us. And his disciples went forth, and came into the city, and found as he had said unto them: and they made ready the passover. And in the evening he cometh with the twelve. And as they sat and did eat, Jesus said, Verily I say unto you, One of you which eateth with me shall betray me. And they began to be sorrowful, and to say unto him one by one, Is it I? and another said, Is it I? And he answered and said unto them, It is one of the twelve, that dippeth with me in the dish. The Son of man indeed goeth, as it is written of him: but woe to that man by whom the Son of man is betrayed! good were it for that man if he had never been born. And as they did eat, Jesus took bread, and blessed, and brake it, and gave to them, and said, Take, eat: this is my body. And he took the cup, and when he had given thanks, he gave it to them: and they all drank of it. And he said unto them, This is my blood of the new testament, which is shed for many. Verily I say unto you, I will drink no more of the fruit of the vine, until that day that I drink it new in the kingdom of God. And when they had sung an hymn, they went out into the mount of Olives. And Jesus saith unto them, All ye shall be offended because of me this night: for it is written, I will smite the shepherd, and the sheep shall be scattered. But after that I am risen, I will go before you into Galilee.

But Peter said unto him, Although all shall be offended, yet will not I. And Jesus saith unto him, Verily I say unto thee, that this day, even in this night, before the cock crow twice, thou shalt deny me thrice. But he spake the more vehemently, If I should die with thee, I will not deny thee in any wise. Likewise also said they all. And they came to a place which was named Gethsemane: and he saith to his disciples, Sit ye here, while I shall pray. And he taketh with him Peter and James and John, and began to be sore amazed, and to be very heavy; and saith unto them, My soul is exceeding sorrowful unto death: tarry ye here, and watch. And he went forward a little, and fell on the ground, and prayed that, if it were possible, the hour might pass from him. And he said, Abba, Father, all things are possible unto thee; take away this cup from me: nevertheless not what I will, but what thou wilt. And he cometh, and findeth them sleeping, and saith unto Peter, Simon, sleepest thou? couldest not thou watch one hour? Watch ye and pray, lest ye enter into temptation. The spirit truly is ready, but the flesh is weak. And again he went away, and prayed, and spake the same words. And when he returned, he found them asleep again, (for their eyes were heavy,) neither wist they what to answer him. And he cometh the third time, and saith unto them, Sleep on now, and take your rest: it is enough, the hour is come; behold, the Son of man is betrayed into the hands of sinners. Rise up, let us go; lo, he that betrayeth me is at hand. And immediately, while he yet spake, cometh Judas, one of the twelve, and with him a great multitude with swords and staves, from the chief priests and the scribes and the elders. And he that betrayed him had given them a token, saying, Whomsoever I shall kiss, that same is he; take him, and lead him away safely. And as soon as he was come, he goeth straightway to him, and saith, Master, master; and kissed him. And they laid their hands on him, and took him. And one of them that stood by drew a sword, and smote a servant of the high priest, and cut off his ear. And Jesus answered and said unto them, Are ye come out, as against a thief, with swords and with staves, to take me? I was daily with you in the temple teaching, and ye took me not: but the scriptures must be fulfilled. And they all forsook him, and fled. And there followed him a certain young man, having a linen cloth cast about his naked body: and the young men laid hold on him: and he left the linen cloth, and fled from them naked. And they led Jesus away to the high priest: and with him were assembled all the chief priests and the elders and the scribes. And Peter followed him afar off, even into the palace of the high priest: and he sat with the servants, and warmed himself at the fire. And the chief priests and all the council sought for witness against Jesus to put him to death; and found none. For many bare false witness against him, but their witness agreed not together. And there arose certain, and bare false witness against him, saying, We heard him say, I will destroy this temple that is made with hands, and within three days I will build another made without hands. But neither so did their witness agree together. And the high priest stood up in the midst, and asked Jesus, saying, Answerest thou nothing? what is it which these witness against thee? But he held his peace, and answered nothing. Again the high priest asked him, and said unto him, Art thou the Christ, the Son of the Blessed? And Jesus said, I am: and ye shall see the Son of man sitting on the right hand of power, and coming in the clouds of heaven. Then the high priest rent his clothes, and saith, What need we any further witnesses? ye have heard the blasphemy: what think ye? And they all condemned him to be guilty of death. And some began to spit on him, and to cover his face, and to buffet him, and to say unto him, Prophesy: and the servants did strike him with the palms of their hands. And as Peter was beneath in the palace, there cometh one of the maids of the high priest: and when she saw Peter warming himself, she looked upon him, and said, And thou also wast with Jesus of Nazareth. But he denied, saying, I know not, neither understand I what thou sayest. And he went out into the porch; and the cock crew. And a maid saw him again, and began to say to them that stood by, This is one of them. And he denied it again. And a little after, they that stood by said again to Peter, Surely thou art one of them: for thou art a Galilæan, and thy speech agreeth thereto. But he began to curse and to swear, saying, I know not this man of whom ye speak. And the second time the cock crew. And Peter called to mind the word that Jesus said unto him, Before the cock crow twice, thou shalt deny me thrice. And when he thought thereon, he wept.

Tuesday before Easter.

For the Epistle. Isa. l. 5.

THE Lord God hath opened mine ear, and I was not rebellious, neither turned away back. I gave my back to the smiters, and my cheeks to them that plucked off the hair: I hid not my face from shame and spitting. For the Lord God will help me; therefore shall I not be confounded: therefore have I set my face like a flint, and I know that I shall not be ashamed. He is near that justifieth me; who will contend with me? let us stand together: who is mine adversary? let him come near to me. Behold, the Lord God will help me; who is he that shall condemn me? lo, they all shall wax old as a garment; the moth shall eat them up. Who is among you that feareth the Lord, that obeyeth the voice of his servant, that walketh in darkness, and hath no light? let him trust in the name of the Lord, and stay upon his God. Behold, all ye that kindle a fire, that compass yourselves about with sparks: walk in the light of your fire, and in the sparks that ye have kindled. This shall ye have of mine hand; ye shall lie down in sorrow.

The Gospel. St. Mark xv. 1.

AND straightway in the morning the chief priests held a consultation with the elders and scribes and the whole council, and bound Jesus, and carried him away, and delivered him to Pilate. And Pilate asked him, Art thou the King of the Jews? And he answering said unto him, Thou sayest it. And the chief priests accused him of many things: but he answered nothing. And Pilate asked him again, saying, Answerest thou nothing? behold how many things they witness against thee. But Jesus yet answered nothing; so that Pilate marvelled. Now at that feast he released unto them one prisoner, whomsoever they desired. And there was one named Barabbas, which lay bound with them that had made insurrection with him, who had committed murder in the insurrection. And the multitude crying aloud began to desire him to do as he had ever done unto them. But Pilate answered them, saying, Will ye that I release unto you the King of the Jews? For he knew that the chief priests had delivered him for envy. But the chief priests moved the people, that he should rather release Barabbas unto them. And Pilate answered and said again unto them, What will ye then that I shall do unto him whom ye call the King of the Jews? And they cried out again, Crucify him. Then Pilate said unto them, Why, what evil hath he done? And they cried out the more exceedingly, Crucify him. And so Pilate, willing to content the people, released Barabbas unto them, and delivered Jesus, when he had scourged him, to be crucified. And the soldiers led him away into the hall, called Prætorium; and they call together the whole band. And they clothed him with purple, and platted a crown of thorns, and put it about his head, and began to salute him, Hail, King of the Jews! And they smote him on the head with a reed, and did spit upon him, and bowing their knees worshipped him. And when they had mocked him, they took off the purple from him, and put his own clothes on him, and led him out to crucify him. And they compel one Simon a Cyrenian, who passed by, coming out of the country, the father of Alexander and Rufus, to bear his cross. And they bring him unto the place Golgotha, which is, being interpreted, The place of a skull. And they gave him to drink wine mingled with myrrh: but he received it not. And when they had crucified him, they parted his garments, casting lots upon them, what every man should take. And it was the third hour, and they crucified him. And the superscription of his accusation was written over, THE KING OF THE JEWS. And with him they crucify two thieves; the one on his right hand, and the other on his left. And the scripture was fulfilled, which saith, And he was numbered with the transgressors. And they that passed by railed on him, wagging their heads, and saying, Ah, thou that destroyest the temple, and buildest it in three days, save thyself, and come down from the cross. Likewise also the chief priests mocking said among themselves with the scribes, He saved others; himself he cannot save. Let Christ the King of Israel descend now from the cross, that we may see and believe. And they that were crucified with him reviled him. And when the sixth hour was come, there was darkness over the whole land until the ninth hour. And at the ninth hour Jesus cried with a loud voice, saying, Eloi, Eloi, lama sabachthani? which is, being interpreted, My God, my God, why hast thou forsaken me? And some of them that stood by, when they heard it, said, Behold, he calleth Elias. And one ran and filled a spunge full of vinegar, and put it on a reed, and gave him to drink, saying, Let alone; let us see whether Elias will come to take him down. And Jesus cried with a loud voice, and

gave up the ghost. And the veil of the temple was rent in twain from the top to the bottom. And when the centurion, which stood over against him, saw that he so cried out, and gave up the ghost, he said, Truly this man was the Son of God.

✠ Wednesday before Easter.

The Epistle. Heb. ix. 16.

WHERE a testament is, there must also of necessity be the death of the testator. For a testament is of force after men are dead: otherwise it is of no strength at all while the testator liveth. Whereupon neither the first testament was dedicated without blood. For when Moses had spoken every precept to all the people according to the law, he took the blood of calves and of goats, with water, and scarlet wool, and hyssop, and sprinkled both the book and all the people, saying, This is the blood of the testament which God hath enjoined unto you. Moreover, he sprinkled with blood both the tabernacle, and all the vessels of the ministry. And almost all things are by the law purged with blood; and without shedding of blood is no remission. It was therefore necessary that the patterns of things in the heavens should be purified with these; but the heavenly things themselves with better sacrifices than these. For Christ is not entered into the holy places made with hands, which are the figures of the true; but into heaven itself, now to appear in the presence of God for us: nor yet that he should offer himself often, as the high priest entereth into the holy place every year with blood of others; for then must he often have suffered since the foundation of the world: but now once in the end of the world hath he appeared to put away sin by the sacrifice of himself. And as it is appointed unto men once to die, but after this the judgment: so Christ was once offered to bear the sins of many; and unto them that look for him shall he appear the second time without sin unto salvation.

The Gospel. St. Luke xxii. 1.

NOW the feast of unleavened bread drew nigh, which is called the Passover. And the chief priests and scribes sought how they might kill him; for they feared the people. Then entered Satan into Judas surnamed Iscariot, being of the number of the twelve. And he went his way, and communed with the chief priests and captains, how he might betray him unto them. And they were glad, and covenanted to give him money. And he promised, and sought opportunity to betray him unto them in the absence of the multitude. Then came the day of unleavened bread, when the passover must be killed. And he sent Peter and John, saying, Go and prepare us the passover, that we may eat. And they said unto him, Where wilt thou that we prepare? And he said unto them, Behold, when ye are entered into the city, there shall a man meet you, bearing a pitcher of water; follow him into the house where he entereth in. And ye shall say unto the goodman of the house, The Master saith unto thee, Where is the guest-chamber, where I shall eat the passover with my disciples? And he shall shew you a large upper room furnished: there make ready. And they went, and found as he had said unto them: and they made ready the passover. And when the hour was come, he sat down, and the twelve apostles with him. And he said unto them, With desire I have desired to eat this passover with you before I suffer: for I say unto you, I will not any more eat thereof, until it be fulfilled in the kingdom of God. And he took the cup, and gave thanks, and said, Take this, and divide it among yourselves: for I say unto you, I will not drink of the fruit of the vine, until the kingdom of God shall come. And he took bread, and gave thanks, and brake it, and gave unto them, saying, This is my body which is given for you: this do in remembrance of me. Likewise also the cup after supper, saying, This cup is the new testament in my blood, which is shed for you. But, behold, the hand of him that betrayeth me is with me on the table. And truly the Son of man goeth as it was determined: but woe unto that man by whom he is betrayed! And they began to enquire among themselves, which of them it was that should do this thing. And there was also a strife among them, which of them should be accounted the greatest. And he said unto them, The kings of the Gentiles exercise lordship over them; and they that exercise authority upon them are called benefactors. But ye shall not be so: but he that is greatest among you, let him be as the younger; and he that is chief, as he that doth serve. For whether is greater, he that sitteth at meat, or he that serveth? is not he that sitteth at meat? but I am among you as he that serveth. Ye are they which have continued with me in my temptations. And I appoint unto you a kingdom, as my Father hath appointed unto me; that ye may e and drink at my table my kingdom, and sit on thrones, judging the twelve tribes of Israel. And the Lord said, Simon, Simon, behold, Satan hath desired to have you, that he may sift you as wheat: but I have prayed for thee, that thy faith fail not; and when thou art converted, strengthen thy brethren. And he said unto him, Lord, I am ready to go with thee, both into prison, and to death. And he said, I tell thee, Peter, the cock shall not crow this day, before that thou shalt thrice deny that thou knowest me. And he said unto them, When I sent you without purse, and scrip, and shoes, lacked ye any thing? And they said, Nothing. Then said he unto them, But now, he that hath a purse, let him take it, and likewise his scrip: and he that hath no sword, let him sell his garment, and buy one. For I say unto you, that this that is written must yet be accomplished in me, And he was reckoned among the transgressors: for the things concerning me have an end. And they said, Lord, behold, here are two swords. And he said unto them, It is enough. And he came out, and went, as he was wont, to the mount of Olives; and his disciples also followed him. And when he was at the place, he said unto them, Pray that ye enter not into temptation. And he was withdrawn from them about a stone's cast, and kneeled down, and prayed, saying, Father, if thou be willing, remove this cup from me: nevertheless not my will, but thine, be done. And there appeared an angel unto him from heaven, strengthening him. And being in an agony he prayed more earnestly: and his sweat was as it were great drops of blood falling down to the ground. And when he rose up from prayer, and was come to his disciples, he found them sleeping for sorrow, and said unto them, Why sleep ye? rise and pray, lest ye enter into temptation. And while he yet spake, behold a multitude, and he that was called Judas, one of the twelve, went before them, and drew near unto Jesus to kiss him. But

Jesus said unto him, Judas, betrayest thou the Son of man with a kiss? When they which were about him saw what would follow, they said unto him, Lord, shall we smite with the sword? And one of them smote the servant of the high priest, and cut off his right ear. And Jesus answered and said, Suffer ye thus far. And he touched his ear, and healed him. Then Jesus said unto the chief priests, and captains of the temple, and the elders, which were come to him, Be ye come out, as against a thief, with swords and staves? When I was daily with you in the temple, ye stretched forth no hands against me: but this is your hour, and the power of darkness. Then took they him, and led him, and brought him into the high priest's house. And Peter followed afar off. And when they had kindled a fire in the midst of the hall, and were set down together, Peter sat down among them. But a certain maid beheld him as he sat by the fire, and earnestly looked upon him, and said, This man was also with him. And he denied him, saying, Woman, I know him not. And after a little while another saw him, and said, Thou art also of them. And Peter said, Man, I am not. And about the space of one hour after another confidently affirmed, saying, Of a truth this fellow also was with him: for he is a Galilæan. And Peter said, Man, I know not what thou sayest. And immediately, while he yet spake, the cock crew. And the Lord turned and looked upon Peter. And Peter remembered the word of the Lord, how he had said unto him, Before the cock crow, thou shalt deny me thrice. And Peter went out, and wept bitterly. And the men that held Jesus mocked him, and smote him. And when they had blindfolded him, they struck him on the face, and asked him, saying, Prophesy, who is it that smote thee? And many other things blasphemously spake they against him. And as soon as it was day, the elders of the people and the chief priests and the scribes came together, and led him into their council, saying, Art thou the Christ? tell us. And he said unto them, If I tell you, ye will not believe: and if I also ask you, ye will not answer me, nor let me go. Hereafter shall the Son of man sit on the right hand of the power of God. Then said they all, Art thou then the Son of God? And he said unto them, Ye say that I am. And they said, What need we any further witness? for we ourselves have heard of his own mouth.

❧

Thursday before Easter.

The Epistle. 1 Cor. xi. 17.

IN this that I declare unto you I praise you not, that ye come together not for the better, but for the worse. For first of all, when ye come together in the church, I hear that there be divisions among you: and I partly believe it. For there must be also heresies among you, that they which are approved may be made manifest among you. When ye come together therefore into one place, this is not to eat the Lord's supper. For in eat-

ing every one taketh before other his own supper: and one is hungry, and another is drunken. What? have ye not houses to eat and to drink in? or despise ye the church of God, and shame them that have not? What shall I say to you? shall I praise you in this? I praise you not. For I have received of the Lord that which also I delivered unto you, That the Lord Jesus the same night in which he was betrayed took bread: and when he had given thanks, he brake it, and said, Take, eat: this is my body, which is broken for you: this do in remembrance of me. After the same manner also he took the cup, when he had supped, saying, This cup is the new testament in my blood: this do ye, as oft as ye drink it, in remembrance of me. For as often as ye eat this bread, and drink this cup, ye do shew the Lord's death till he come. Wherefore whosoever shall eat this bread, and drink this cup of the Lord, unworthily, shall be guilty of the body and blood of the Lord. But let a man examine himself, and so let him eat of that bread, and drink of that cup. For he that eateth and drinketh unworthily, eateth and drinketh damnation to himself, not discerning the Lord's body. For this cause many are weak and sickly among you, and many sleep. For if we would judge ourselves, we should not be judged. But when we are judged, we are chastened of the Lord, that we should not be condemned with the world. Wherefore, my brethren, when ye come together to eat, tarry one for another. And if any man hunger, let him eat at home; that ye come not together unto condemnation. And the rest will I set in order when I come.

The Gospel. St. Luke xxiii. 1.

THE whole multitude of them arose, and led him unto Pilate. And they began to accuse him, saying, We found this fellow perverting the nation, and forbidding to give tribute to Cæsar, saying that he himself is Christ a King. And Pilate asked him, saying, Art thou the King of the Jews? And he answered him and said, Thou sayest it. Then said Pilate to the chief priests and to the people, I find no fault in this man. And they were the more fierce, saying, He stirreth up the people, teaching throughout all Jewry, beginning from Galilee to this place. When Pilate heard of Galilee, he asked whether the man were a Galilæan. And as soon as he knew that he belonged unto Herod's jurisdiction, he sent him to Herod, who himself also was at Jerusalem at that time. And when Herod saw Jesus, he was exceeding glad: for he was desirous to see him of a long season, because he had heard many things of him; and he hoped to have seen some miracle done by him. Then he questioned with him in many words; but he answered him nothing. And the chief priests and scribes stood and vehemently accused him. And Herod with his men of war set him at nought, and mocked him, and arrayed him in a gorgeous robe, and sent him again to Pilate. And the same day Pilate and Herod were made friends together: for before they were at enmity between themselves. And Pilate, when he had called together the chief priests and the rulers and the people, said unto them, Ye have brought this man unto me, as one that perverteth the people: and, behold, I, having examined him before you, have found no fault in this man touching those things whereof ye accuse him: no, nor yet Herod: for I sent you to him; and lo, nothing worthy of death is done unto him. I will therefore chastise him, and release him. (For of necessity he must release one unto them at the feast.) And they cried out all at once, saying, Away with this man, and release unto us Barabbas: (who for a certain sedition made in the city, and for murder, was cast into prison.) Pilate therefore, willing to release Jesus, spake again to them. But they cried, saying, Crucify him, crucify him. And he said unto them the third time, Why, what evil hath he done? I have found no cause of death in him: I will therefore chastise him, and let him go. And they were instant with loud voices, requiring that he might be crucified. And the voices of them and of the chief priests prevailed. And Pilate gave sentence that it should be as they required. And he released unto them him that for sedition and murder was cast into prison, whom they had desired; but he delivered Jesus to their will. And as they led him away, they laid hold upon one Simon, a Cyrenian, coming out of the country, and on him they laid the cross, that he might bear it after Jesus. And there followed him a great company of people, and of women, which also bewailed and lamented him. But Jesus turning unto them said, Daughters of Jerusalem, weep not for me, but weep for yourselves, and for your children. For, behold, the days are coming, in the which they shall say, Blessed are the barren, and the wombs that never bare, and the paps which never gave suck. Then shall they begin to say to the mountains, Fall on us; and to the hills, Cover us. For if they do these things in a green tree, what shall be done in the dry? And there were also two other, malefactors, led with him to be put to death. And when they were come to the place which is called Calvary, there they crucified him, and the malefactors, one on the right hand, and the other on the left. Then said Jesus, Father, forgive him; for they know not what they do. And they parted his raiment, and cast lots. And the people stood beholding. And the rulers also with them derided him, saying, He saved others; let him save himself, if he be Christ, the chosen of God. And the soldiers also mocked him, coming to him, and offering him vinegar, and saying, If thou be the king of the Jews, save thyself. And a superscription also was written over him, in letters of Greek, and Latin, and Hebrew, THIS IS THE KING OF THE JEWS. And one of the malefactors which were hanged railed on him, saying, If thou be Christ, save thyself and us. But the other answering rebuked him, saying, Dost not thou fear God seeing thou art in the same condemnation? And we indeed justly; for we receive the due reward of our deeds: but this man hath done nothing amiss. And he said unto Jesus, Lord, remember me when thou comest into thy kingdom. And Jesus said unto him, Verily I say unto thee, To day shalt thou be with me in paradise. And it was about the sixth hour, and there was a darkness over all the earth until the ninth hour. And the sun was darkened, and the veil of the temple was rent in the midst. And when Jesus had cried with a loud voice, he said, Father, into thy hands I commend my spirit: and having said thus, he gave up the ghost. Now when the centurion saw what was done, he glorified God, saying, Certainly this was a righteous man. And all the people that came together to that sight, beholding the things which were done, smote their breasts, and returned. And all his acquaintance, and the women that followed him from Galilee, stood afar off, beholding these things.

☩

Good Friday.

The Collects.

ALMIGHTY God, we beseech thee graciously

to behold this thy family, for which our Lord Jesus Christ was contented to be betrayed, and given up into the hands of wicked men, and to suffer death upon the cross; who now liveth and reigneth with thee and the Holy Ghost ever, one God, world without end. *Amen.*

ALMIGHTY and everlasting God, by whose Spirit the whole body of the Church is governed and sanctified; Receive our supplications and prayers, which we offer before thee for all estates of men in thy holy Church, that every member of the same, in his vocation and ministry, may truly and godly serve thee; through our Lord and Saviour Jesus Christ. *Amen.*

O MERCIFUL God, who hast made all men, and hatest nothing that thou hast made, nor desirest the death of a sinner, but rather that he should be converted and live; Have mercy upon all Jews, Turks, infidels, and heretics; and take from them all ignorance, hardness of heart, and contempt of thy Word; and so fetch them home, blessed Lord, to thy flock, that they may be saved among the remnant of the true Israelites, and be made one fold under one shepherd, Jesus Christ our Lord, who liveth and reigneth with thee and the Holy Spirit, one God, world without end. *Amen.*

The Epistle. Heb. x. 1.

THE law having a shadow of good things to come, and not the very image of the things, can never with those sacrifices which they offered year by year continually make the comers thereunto perfect. For then would they not have ceased to be offered? because that the worshippers once purged should have had no more conscience of sins. But in those sacrifices there is a remembrance again made of sins every year. For it is not possible that the blood of bulls and of goats should take away sins. Wherefore when he cometh into the world, he saith, Sacrifice and offering thou wouldest not, but a body hast thou prepared me: in burnt offerings and sacrifices for sin thou hast had no pleasure. Then said I, Lo, I come (in the volume of the book it is written of me,) to do thy will, O God. Above when he said, Sacrifice and offering and burnt offerings and offering for sin thou wouldest not, neither hadst pleasure therein; which are offered by the law; then said he, Lo, I come to do thy will, O God. He taketh away the first, that he may establish the second. By the which will we are sanctified through the offering of the body of Jesus Christ once for all. And every priest standeth daily ministering and offering oftentimes the same sacrifices, which can never take away sins: but this man, after he had offered one sacrifice for sins for ever, sat down on the right hand of God; from henceforth expecting till his enemies be made his footstool. For by one offering he hath perfected for ever them that are sanctified. Whereof the Holy Ghost also is a witness to us: for after that he had said before, This is the covenant that I will make with them after those days, saith the Lord, I will put my laws into their hearts, and in their minds will I write them; and

their sins and iniquities will I remember no more. Now where remission of these is, there is no more offering for sin. Having therefore, brethren, boldness to enter into the holiest by the blood of Jesus, by a new and living way, which he hath consecrated for us, through the veil, that is to say, his flesh; and having an high priest over the house of God; let us draw near with a true heart in full assurance of faith, having our hearts sprinkled from an evil conscience, and our bodies washed with pure water. Let us hold fast the profession of our faith without wavering; (for he is faithful that promised;) and let us consider one another to provoke unto love and to good works: not forsaking the assembling of ourselves together, as the manner of some is; but exhorting one another: and so much the more, as ye see the day approaching.

The Gospel. St. John xix. 1.

PILATE therefore took Jesus, and scourged him. And the soldiers platted a crown of thorns, and put it on his head, and they put on him a purple robe, and said, Hail, King of the Jews! and they smote him with their hands. Pilate therefore went forth again, and saith unto them, Behold, I bring him forth to you, that ye may know that I find no fault in him. Then came Jesus forth, wearing the crown of thorns, and the purple robe. And Pilate saith unto them, Behold the man! When the chief priests therefore and officers saw him, they cried out, saying, Crucify him, crucify him. Pilate saith unto them, Take ye him, and crucify him: for I find no fault in him. The Jews answered him, We have a law, and by our law he ought to die, because he made himself the Son of God. When Pilate therefore heard that saying, he was the more afraid; and went again into the judgment hall, and saith unto Jesus, Whence art thou? But Jesus gave him no answer. Then saith Pilate unto him, Speakest thou not unto me? knowest thou not that I have power to crucify thee, and have power to release thee?

Jesus answered, Thou couldest have no power at all against me, except it were given thee from above: therefore he that delivered me unto thee hath the greater sin. And from thenceforth Pilate sought to release him: but the Jews cried out, saying, If thou let this man go, thou art not Cæsar's friend: whosoever maketh himself a king, speaketh against Cæsar. When Pilate therefore heard that saying, he brought Jesus forth, and sat down in the judgment seat in a place that is called the Pavement, but in the Hebrew, Gabbatha. And it was the preparation of the passover, and about the sixth hour: and he saith unto the Jews, Behold your King! But they cried out, Away with him, away with him, crucify him. Pilate saith unto them, Shall I crucify your King? The chief priests answered, We have no king but Cæsar. Then delivered he him therefore unto them to be crucified: And they took Jesus, and led him away. And he bearing his cross went forth into a place called the place of a skull, which is called in the Hebrew Golgotha: where they crucified him, and two other with him, on either side one, and Jesus in the midst. And Pilate wrote a title, and put it on the cross. And the writing was, JESUS OF NAZARETH THE KING OF THE JEWS. This title then read many of the Jews: for the place where Jesus was crucified was nigh to the city; and it was written in Hebrew, and Greek, and Latin. Then said the chief priests of the Jews to Pilate, Write not, The King of the Jews; but that he said, I am King of the Jews. Pilate answered, What I have written I have written. Then the soldiers, when they had crucified Jesus, took his garments, and made four parts, to every soldier a part; and also his coat: now the coat was without seam, woven from the top throughout. They said therefore among themselves, Let us not rend it, but cast lots for it, whose it shall be: that the scripture might be fulfilled, which saith, They parted my raiment among them, and for my vesture they did cast lots. These things therefore the soldiers did. Now there stood by the cross of Jesus his mother, and his mother's sister, Mary the wife of Cleophas, and Mary Magdalene. When Jesus therefore saw his mother, and the disciple standing by, whom he loved, he saith unto his mother, Woman, behold thy son! Then saith he to the disciple, Behold thy mother! And from that hour that disciple took her unto his own home. After this, Jesus knowing that all things were now accomplished, that the scripture might be fulfilled, saith, I thirst. Now there was set a vessel full of vinegar: and they filled a spunge with vinegar, and put it upon hyssop, and put it to his mouth. When Jesus therefore had received the vinegar, he said, It is finished: and he bowed his head, and gave up the ghost. The Jews therefore, because it was the preparation, that the bodies should not remain upon the cross on the sabbath day, (for that sabbath day was an high day,) besought Pilate that their legs might be broken, and that they might be taken away.

Then came the soldiers, and brake the legs of the first, and of the other which was crucified with him. But when they came to Jesus, and saw that he was dead already, they brake not his legs: but one of the soldiers with a spear pierced his side, and forthwith came there out blood and water. And he that saw it bare record, and his record is true: and he knoweth that he saith true, that ye might believe. For these things were done, that the scripture should be fulfilled, A bone of him shall not be broken. And again another scripture saith, They shall look on him whom they pierced.

Easter-Even.

The Collect.

GRANT, O Lord, that as we are baptized into the death of thy blessed Son, our Saviour Jesus Christ, so by continual mortifying our corrupt affections we may be buried with him; and that through the grave, and gate of death, we may pass to our joyful resurrection; for his merits, who died, and was buried, and rose again for us, thy Son Jesus Christ our Lord. *Amen.*

The Epistle. 1 St. Pet. iii. 17.

IT is better, if the will of God be so, that ye suffer for well doing, than for evil doing. For Christ also hath once suffered for sins, the just for the unjust, that he might bring us to God, being put to death in the flesh, but quickened by the Spirit: by which also he went and preached unto the spirits in prison; which sometime were disobedient, when once the long-suffering of God waited in the days of Noah, while the ark was a preparing, wherein few, that is, eight souls were saved by water. The like figure whereunto even baptism doth also now save *us* (not the putting away of the filth of the flesh, but the answer of a good conscience toward God,) by the resurrection of Jesus Christ: who is gone into heaven, and is on the right hand of God; angels and authorities and powers being made subject unto him.

The Gospel. St. Matt. xxvii. 57.

WHEN the even was come, there came a rich man of Arimathæa, named Joseph, who also himself was Jesus' disciple: he went to Pilate, and begged the body of Jesus. Then Pilate commanded the body to be delivered. And when Joseph had taken the body, he wrapped it in a clean linen cloth, and laid it in his own new tomb, which he had hewn out in the rock: and he rolled a great stone to the door of the sepulchre, and departed. And there was Mary Magdalene, and the other Mary, sitting over against the sepulchre. Now the next day, that followed the day of the preparation, the chief priests and Pharisees came together unto Pilate, saying, Sir, we remember that that deceiver said, while he was yet alive, After three days I will rise again. Command therefore that the sepulchre be made sure until the third day, lest his disciples come by night, and steal him away, and say unto the people, He is risen from the dead: so the last error shall be worse than the first. Pilate said unto them, Ye have a watch: go your way, make it as sure as ye can. So they went, and made the sepulchre sure, sealing the stone, and setting a watch.

Easter-day.

¶ *At Morning Prayer, instead of the Psalm, O come, let us sing, etc., these Anthems shall be sung or said.*

CHRIST our Passover is sacrificed for us: therefore let us keep the feast,

Not with old leaven, neither with the leaven of malice and wickedness: but with the unleavened bread of sincerity and truth. 1 *Cor.* v. 7.

CHRIST being raised from the dead dieth no more: death hath no more dominion over him.

For in that he died, he died unto sin once: but in that he liveth, he liveth unto God.

Likewise reckon ye also yourselves to be dead indeed unto sin: but alive unto God through Jesus Christ our Lord. *Rom.* vi. 9.

CHRIST is risen from the dead : and become the firstfruits of them that slept.

For since by man came death : by man came also the resurrection of the dead.

For as in Adam all die : even so in Christ shall all be made alive. 1 *Cor.* xv. 20.

Glory be to the Father, and to the Son : and to the Holy Ghost ;

As it was in the beginning, is now, and ever shall be : world without end. Amen.

The Collect.

ALMIGHTY God, who through thine only-begotten Son Jesus Christ hast overcome death, and opened unto us the gate of everlasting life ; We humbly beseech thee that, as by thy special grace preventing us thou dost put into our minds good desires, so by thy continual help we may bring the same to good effect ; through Jesus Christ our Lord, who liveth and reigneth with thee and the Holy Ghost ever, one God, world without end. *Amen.*

The Epistle. Col. iii. 1.

IF ye then be risen with Christ, seek those things which are above, where Christ sitteth on the right hand of God. Set your affection on things above, not on things on the earth. For ye are dead, and your life is hid with Christ in God. When Christ, who is our life, shall appear, then shall ye also appear with him in glory. Mortify therefore your members which are upon the earth ; fornication, uncleanness, inordinate affection, evil concupiscence, and covetousness, which is idolatry : for which things' sake the wrath of God cometh on the children of disobedience : in the which ye also walked some time, when ye lived in them.

The Gospel. St. John xx. 1.

THE first day of the week cometh Mary Magdalene early, when it was yet dark, unto the sepulchre, and seeth the stone taken away from the sepulchre. Then she runneth, and cometh to Simon Peter, and to the other disciple, whom Jesus loved, and saith unto them, They have taken away the

Lord out of the sepulchre, and we know not where they have laid him. Peter therefore went forth, and that other disciple, and came to the sepulchre. So they ran both together: and the other disciple did outrun Peter, and came first to the sepulchre. And he stooping down, and looking in, saw the linen clothes lying; yet went he not in. Then cometh Simon Peter following him, and went into the sepulchre, and seeth the linen clothes lie, and the napkin, that was about his head, not lying with the linen clothes, but wrapped together in a place by itself. Then went in also that other disciple, which came first to the sepulchre, and he saw, and believed. For as yet they knew not the scripture, that he must rise again from the dead. Then the disciples went away again unto their own home.

¶ *If in any Church the Holy Communion be twice celebrated on Easter-day, the following Collect, Epistle, and Gospel may be used at the first Communion.*

The Collect.

O GOD, who for our redemption didst give thine only-begotten Son to the death of the Cross, and by his glorious resurrection hast delivered us from the power of our enemy; Grant us so to die daily from sin, that we may evermore live with him in the joy of his resurrection; through the same Christ our Lord. *Amen.*

The Epistle. 1 Cor. v. 6.

K NOW ye not that a little leaven leaveneth the whole lump? Purge out therefore the old leaven, that ye may be a new lump, as ye are unleavened. For even Christ our passover is sacrificed for us: therefore let us keep the feast, not with old leaven, neither with the leaven of malice and wickedness; but with the unleavened bread of sincerity and truth.

The Gospel. St. Mark xvi. 1.

W HEN the sabbath was past, Mary Magdalene, and Mary the mother of James, and Salome, had bought sweet spices, that they might come and anoint him. And very early in the morning the first day of the week, they came unto the sepulchre at the rising of the sun. And they said among themselves, Who shall roll us away the stone from the door of the sepulchre? And when they looked, they saw that the stone was rolled away: for it was very great. And entering into the sepulchre, they saw a young man sitting on the right side, clothed in a long white garment; and they were affrighted. And he saith unto them, Be not affrighted: Ye seek Jesus of Nazareth, which was crucified: he is risen; he is not here: behold the place where they laid him. But go your way, tell his disciples and Peter that he goeth before you into Galilee: there shall ye see him, as he said unto you. And they went out quickly, and fled from the sepulchre; for they trembled and were amazed: neither said they any thing to any man; for they were afraid.

❁

Monday in Easter-week.

The Collect.

ALMIGHTY God, who through thine only-begotten Son Jesus Christ

hast overcome death, and opened unto us the gate of everlasting life; We humbly beseech thee that, as by thy special grace preventing us thou dost put into our minds good desires, so by thy continual help we may bring the same to good effect; through Jesus Christ our Lord, who liveth and reigneth with thee and the Holy Ghost ever, one God, world without end. *Amen.*

For the Epistle. Acts x. 34.

PETER opened his mouth, and said, Of a truth I perceive that God is no respecter of persons: but in every nation he that feareth him, and worketh righteousness, is accepted with him. The word which God sent unto the children of Israel, preaching peace by Jesus Christ: (he is Lord of all:) that word, I say, ye know, which was published throughout all Judæa, and began from Galilee, after the baptism which John preached; how God anointed Jesus of Nazareth with the Holy Ghost and with power: who went about doing good, and healing all that were oppressed of the devil; for God was with him. And we are witnesses of all things which he did both in the land of the Jews, and in Jerusalem; whom they slew and hanged on a tree: him God raised up the third day, and shewed him openly; not to all the people, but unto witnesses chosen before of God, even to us, who did eat and drink with him after he rose from the dead. And he commanded us to preach unto the people, and to testify that it is he which was ordained of God to be the Judge of quick and dead. To him give all the prophets witness, that through his name whosoever believeth in him shall receive remission of sins.

The Gospel. St. Luke xxiv. 13.

BEHOLD, two of his disciples went that same day to a village called Emmaus, which was from Jerusalem about threescore furlongs. And they talked together of all these things which had happened. And it came to pass, that, while they communed together and reasoned, Jesus himself drew near, and went with them. But their eyes were holden that they should not know him. And he said unto them, What manner of communications are these that ye have one to another, as ye walk, and are sad? And the one of them, whose name was Cleopas, answering said unto him, Art thou only a stranger in Jerusalem, and hast not known the things which are come to pass there in these days? And he said unto them, What things? And they said unto him, Concerning Jesus of Nazareth, which was a prophet mighty in deed and word before God and all the people: and how the chief priests and our rulers delivered him to be condemned to death, and have crucified him. But we trusted that it had been he which should have redeemed Israel: and beside all this, to day is the third day since these things were done. Yea, and certain women also of our company made us astonished, which were early at the sepulchre; and when they found not his body, they came, saying, that they had also seen a vision of angels, which said that he was alive. And certain of them which were with us went to the sepulchre, and found it even so as the women had said: but him they saw not. Then he said unto them, O fools, and slow of heart to believe all that the prophets have spoken: ought not Christ to have suffered these things, and to enter into his glory? And beginning at Moses and all the prophets, he expounded unto them in all the scriptures the things concerning himself. And they drew nigh unto the village, whither they went: and he made as though he would have gone further. But they constrained him, saying, Abide with us: for it is toward evening, and the day is far spent. And he went in to tarry with them. And it came to pass, as he sat at meat with them, he took bread, and blessed it, and brake, and gave to them. And their eyes were opened, and they knew him; and he vanished out of their sight. And they said one to another, Did not our heart burn within us, while he talked with us by the way, and while he opened to us the scriptures? And they rose up the same hour, and returned to Jerusalem, and found the eleven gathered together, and them that were with them, saying, The Lord is risen indeed, and hath appeared to Simon. And they told what things were done in the way, and how he was known of them in breaking of bread.

Tuesday in Easter-week.

The Collect.

ALMIGHTY God, who through thine only-begotten Son Jesus Christ hast overcome death, and opened unto us the gate of everlasting life; We humbly beseech thee that, as by thy special grace preventing us thou dost put into our minds good desires, so by thy continual help we may bring the same to good effect; through Jesus Christ our Lord, who liveth and reigneth with thee and the Holy Ghost ever, one God, world without end. *Amen.*

For the Epistle. Acts xiii. 26.

MEN and brethren, children of the stock of Abraham, and whosoever among you feareth God, to you is the word of this salvation sent. For they that dwell at Jerusalem, and their rulers, because they knew him not, nor yet the voices of the prophets which are read every sabbath day, they have fulfilled them in condemning him. And though they found no cause of death in him, yet desired they Pilate that he should be slain. And when they had fulfilled all that was written of him, they took him down from the tree, and laid him in a sepulchre. But God raised him from the dead: and he was seen many days of them which came up with him from Galilee to Jerusalem, who are his witnesses unto the people. And we declare unto you glad tidings, how that the promise which was made unto the fathers, God hath fulfilled the same unto us their children, in that he hath raised up Jesus again; as it is also written in the second psalm, Thou art my Son, this day have I begotten thee. And as concerning that he raised him up from the dead, now no more to return to corruption, he said on this wise, I will give you the sure mercies of David. Wherefore he saith also in another psalm, Thou shalt not suffer thine Holy One to see corruption. For David, after he had served his own generation by the will of God, fell on sleep, and was laid unto his fathers, and saw corruption: but he, whom God raised again, saw no corruption. Be it known unto you therefore, men and brethren, that through this man is preached unto you the forgiveness of sins: and by him all that believe are justified from all things, from which ye could not be justified by the law of Moses. Beware therefore, lest that come upon you, which is spoken of in the prophets; Behold, ye despisers, and wonder, and perish: for I work a work in your days, a work which ye shall in no wise believe, though a man declare it unto you.

The Gospel. St. Luke xxiv. 36.

JESUS himself stood in the midst of them, and saith unto them, Peace be unto you. But they were terrified and affrighted, and supposed that they had seen a spirit. And he said unto them, Why are ye troubled? and why do thoughts arise in your hearts? Behold my hands and my feet, that it is I myself: handle me, and see; for a spirit hath not flesh and bones, as ye see me have. And when he had thus spoken, he shewed them his hands and his feet. And while they yet believed not for joy, and wondered, he said unto them, Have ye here any meat? And they gave him a piece of a broiled fish, and of an honeycomb. And he took it, and did eat before them. And he said unto them, These are the words which I spake unto you, while I was yet with you, that all things must be fulfilled, which were written in the law of Moses, and in the prophets, and in the psalms, concerningme. Thenopened he their understanding, that they might understand the scriptures, and said unto them, Thus it is written, and thus it behoved Christ to suffer, and to rise from the dead the third day: and that repentance and remission of sins should be preached in his name among all nations, beginning at Jerusalem. And ye are witnesses of these things.

The First Sunday after Easter.

The Collect.

ALMIGHTY Father, who hast given thine only Son to die for our sins, and to rise again for our justification; Grant us so to put away the leaven of malice and wickedness, that we may always serve thee in pureness of living and truth; through the merits of the same thy Son Jesus Christ our Lord. Amen.

The Epistle. 1 St. John v. 4.

WHATSOEVER is born of God overcometh the world: and this is the victory that overcometh the world, even our faith. Who is he that overcometh the world, but he that believeth that Jesus is the Son of God? This is he that came by water and blood, even Jesus Christ; not by water only, but by water and blood. And it is the Spirit that beareth witness, because the Spirit is truth. For there are three that bear record in heaven, the Father, the Word, and the Holy Ghost: and these three are one. And there are three that bear witness in earth, the spirit, and the water, and the blood: and these three agree in one. If we receive the witness of men, the witness of God is greater: for this is the witness of God which he hath testified of his Son. He that believeth on the Son of God hath the witness in himself: he that believeth not God hath made him a liar; because he believeth not the record that God gave of his Son. And this is the record, that God hath given to us eternal life, and this life is in his Son. He that hath the Son hath life; and he that hath not the Son of God hath not life.

The Gospel. St. John xx. 19.

THE same day at evening, being the first day of the week, when the doors were shut where the disciples were assembled for fear of the Jews, came Jesus and stood in the midst, and saith unto them, Peace be unto you. And when he had so said, he shewed unto them his hands and his side. Then were the disciples glad when they saw the Lord. Then said Jesus to them again, Peace be unto you: as my Father hath sent me, even so send I you. And when he had said this, he breathed on them, and saith unto them, Receive ye the Holy Ghost: whose soever sins ye remit, they are remitted unto them; and whose soever sins ye retain, they are retained.

❦

The Second Sunday after Easter.

The Collect.

ALMIGHTY God, who hast given thine only Son to be unto us both a sacrifice for sin, and also an ensample of godly life; Give us grace that we may always most thankfully receive that his inestimable benefit, and also daily endeavour ourselves to follow the blessed steps of his most holy life; through the same Jesus Christ our Lord. *Amen.*

The Epistle. 1 St. Pet. ii. 19.

THIS is thankworthy, if a man for conscience toward God endure grief, suffering wrongfully. For what glory is it, if, when ye be buffeted for your faults, ye shall take it patiently? but if, when ye do well, and suffer for it, ye take it patiently, this is acceptable with God. For even hereunto were ye called: because Christ also suffered for us, leaving us an example, that ye should follow his steps: who did no sin, neither was guile found in his mouth: who, when he was reviled, reviled not again; when he suffered, he threatened not; but committed himself to him that judgeth *righteously*: who his own self bare our sins in his own body on the tree, that we, being dead to sins, should live unto righteousness: by whose stripes ye were healed. For ye were as sheep going astray; but are now returned unto the Shepherd and Bishop of your souls.

The Gospel. St. John x. 11.

JESUS said, I am the good shepherd: the good shepherd giveth his life for the sheep. But he that is an hireling, and not the shepherd, whose own the sheep are not, seeth the wolf coming, and leaveth the sheep, and fleeth: and the wolf catcheth them, and scattereth the sheep. The hireling fleeth, because he is an hireling, and careth not for the sheep. I am the good shepherd, and know my sheep, and am known of mine. As the Father knoweth me, even so know I the Father: and I lay down my life for the sheep. And other sheep I have, which are not of this fold: them also I must bring, and they shall hear my voice; and there shall be one fold, and one shepherd.

❦

The Third Sunday after Easter.

The Collect.

ALMIGHTY God, who showest to them that are in error the light of thy truth, to the intent that they may return into the way of righteousness;

Grant unto all those who are admitted into the fellowship of Christ's Religion, that they may avoid those things that are contrary to their profession, and follow all such things as are agreeable to the same; through our Lord Jesus Christ. *Amen.*

The Epistle. 1 St. Pet. ii. 11.

DEARLY beloved, I beseech you as strangers and pilgrims, abstain from fleshly lusts, which war against the soul ; having your conversation honest among the Gentiles: that, whereas they speak against you as evildoers, they may by your good works, which they shall behold, glorify God in the day of visitation. Submit yourselves to every ordinance of man for the Lord's sake: whether it be to the king, as supreme; or unto governors, as unto them that are sent by him for the punishment of evildoers, and for the praise of them that do well. For so is the will of God, that with well doing ye may put to silence the ignorance of foolish men : as free, and not using your liberty for a cloke of ma-

liciousness, but as the servants of God. Honour all men. Love the brotherhood. Fear God. Honour the king.

The Gospel. St. John xvi. 16.

JESUS said to his disciples, A little while, and ye shall not see me : and again, a little while, and ye shall see me, because I go to the Father. Then said some of his disciples among themselves, What is this that he saith unto us, A little while, and ye shall not see me: and again, a little while, and ye shall see me: and, Because I go to the Father ? They said therefore, What is this that he saith, A little while? we cannot tell what he saith. Now Jesus knew that they were desirous to ask him, and said unto them, Do ye enquire among yourselves of that I said, A little while, and ye shall not see me: and again, a little while, and ye shall see me ? Verily, verily, I say unto you, That ye shall weep and lament, but the world shall rejoice : and ye shall be sorrowful, but your sorrow shall be turned into joy.

A woman when she is in travail hath sorrow, because her hour is come: but as soon as she is delivered of the child, she remembereth no more the anguish, for joy that a man is born into the world. And ye now therefore have sorrow: but I will see you again, and your heart shall rejoice, and your joy no man taketh from you.

❖

The Fourth Sunday after Easter.

The Collect.

O ALMIGHTY God, who alone canst order the unruly wills and affections of sinful men; Grant unto thy people, that they may love the thing which thou commandest, and desire that which thou dost promise; that so, among the sundry and manifold changes of the world, our hearts may surely there be fixed, where true joys are to be found; through Jesus Christ our Lord. *Amen.*

The Epistle. St. James i. 17.

EVERY good gift and every perfect gift is from above, and cometh down from the Father of lights, with whom is no variableness, neither shadow of turning. Of his own will begat he us with the word of truth, that we should be a kind of firstfruits of his creatures. Wherefore, my beloved brethren, let every man be swift to hear, slow to speak, slow to wrath: for the wrath of man worketh not the righteousness of God. Wherefore lay apart all filthiness and superfluity of naughtiness, and receive with meekness the engrafted word, which is able to save your souls.

The Gospel. St. John xvi. 5.

JESUS said unto his disciples, Now I go my way to him that sent me; and none of you asketh me, Whither goest thou? But because I have said these things unto you, sorrow hath filled your heart. Nevertheless I tell you the truth; It is expedient for you that I go away: for if I go not away, the Comforter will not come unto you; but if I depart, I will send him unto you. And when he is come, he will reprove the world of sin, and of righteousness, and of judgment: of sin, because they believe not on me; of righteousness, because I go to my Father, and ye see me no more; of judgment, because the prince of this world is judged. I have yet many things to say unto you, but ye cannot bear them now. Howbeit when he, the Spirit of truth, is come, he will guide you into all truth: for he shall not speak of himself; but whatsoever he shall hear, that shall he speak: and he will shew you things to come. He shall glorify me: for he shall receive of mine, and shall shew it unto you. All things that the Father hath are mine: therefore said I, that he shall take of mine, and shall shew it unto you.

The Fifth Sunday after Easter.

The Collect.

O LORD, from whom all good things do come: Grant to us thy humble servants, that by thy holy inspiration we may think those things that are good, and by thy merciful guiding may perform the same; through our Lord Jesus Christ. *Amen.*

The Epistle. St. James i. 22.

B E ye doers of the word, and not hearers only, deceiving your own selves. For if any be a hearer of the word, and not a doer, he is like unto a man beholding his natural face in a glass: for he beholdeth himself, and goeth his way, and straightway forgetteth what manner of man he was. But whoso looketh into the perfect law of liberty, and continueth therein, he being not a forgetful hearer, but a doer of the work, this man shall be blessed in his deed. If any man among you seem to be religious, and bridleth not his tongue, but deceiveth his own heart, this man's religion is vain. Pure religion and undefiled before God and the Father is this, To visit the fatherless and widows in their affliction, and to keep himself unspotted from the world.

The Gospel. St. John xvi. 23.

V ERILY, verily, I say unto you, Whatsoever

ye shall ask the Father in my name, he will give it you. Hitherto have ye asked nothing in my name: ask, and ye shall receive, that your joy may be full. These things have I spoken unto you in proverbs: but the time cometh, when I shall no more speak unto you in proverbs, but I shall shew you plainly of the Father. At that day ye shall ask in my name: and I say not unto you, that I will pray the Father for you: for the Father himself loveth you, because ye have loved me, and have believed that I came out from God. I came forth from the Father, and am come into the world: again, I leave the world, and go to the Father. His disciples said unto him, Lo, now speakest thou plainly, and speakest no proverb. Now are we sure that thou knowest all things, and needest not that any man should ask thee: by this we believe that thou camest forth from God. Jesus answered them, Do ye now believe? Behold, the hour cometh, yea, is now come, that ye shall be scattered, every man to his own, and shall leave me alone: and yet I am not alone, because the Father is with me. These things I have spoken unto you, that in me ye might have peace. In the world ye shall have tribulation: but be of good cheer; I have overcome the world.

❁

The Ascension-day.
The Collect.

GRANT, we beseech thee, Almighty God, that like as we do believe thy only-begotten Son our Lord Jesus Christ to have ascended into the heavens; so we may also in heart and mind thither ascend, and with him continually dwell, who liveth and reigneth with thee and the Holy Ghost, one God, world without end. *Amen.*

For the Epistle. Acts i. 1.

THE former treatise have I made, O Theophilus, of all that Jesus began both to do and teach, until the day in which he was taken up, after that he through the Holy Ghost had given commandments unto the apostles whom he had chosen: to whom also he shewed himself alive after his passion by many infallible proofs, being seen of them forty days, and speaking of the things pertaining to the kingdom of God: and, being assembled together with them, commanded them that they should not depart from Jerusalem, but wait for the promise of the Father, which, saith he, ye have heard of me. For John truly baptized with water; but ye shall be baptized with the Holy Ghost not many days hence. When they therefore were come together, they asked of him, saying, Lord, wilt thou at this time restore again the kingdom to Israel? And he said unto them, It is not for you to know the times or the seasons, which the Father hath put in his own power. But ye shall receive power, after that the Holy Ghost is come upon you: and ye shall be witnesses unto me both in Jerusalem, and in all Judæa, and in Samaria, and unto the uttermost part of the earth. And when he had spoken these things, while they beheld, he was taken up; and a cloud received him out of their sight. And while they looked stedfastly toward heaven as he went up, behold, two men stood by them in white apparel; which also said, Ye men of Galilee, why stand ye gazing up into heaven? this same Jesus, which is taken up from you into heaven, shall so come in like manner as ye have seen him go into heaven.

The Gospel. St. Mark xvi. 14.

JESUS appeared unto the eleven as they sat at meat, and upbraided them with their unbelief and hardness of heart, because they believed not them which had seen him after he was risen. And he said unto them, Go ye into all the world, and preach the gospel to every creature. He that believeth and is baptized shall be saved; but he that believeth not shall be damned. And these signs shall follow them that believe; In my name shall they cast out devils; they shall speak with new tongues; they shall take up serpents; and if they drink any deadly thing, it shall not hurt them; they shall lay hands on the sick, and they shall recover. So then after the Lord had spoken unto them, he was received up into heaven, and sat on the right hand of God. And they went forth, and preached every where, the Lord working with them, and confirming the word with signs following.

¶ *The same Collect, Epistle, and Gospel shall serve for every day after, unto the next Sunday, except upon the Feast of St. Philip and St. James.*

Sunday after Ascension-day.

The Collect.

O GOD, the King of glory, who hast exalted thine only Son Jesus Christ with great triumph unto thy kingdom in heaven; We beseech thee, leave us not comfortless; but send to us thine Holy Ghost to comfort us, and exalt us unto the same place whither our Saviour Christ is gone before, who liveth and reigneth with thee and the Holy Ghost, one God, world without end. *Amen.*

The Epistle. 1 St. Pet. iv. 7.

THE end of all things is at hand: be ye therefore sober, and watch unto prayer. And above all things have fervent charity among yourselves: for charity shall cover the multitude of sins. Use hospitality one to another without grudging. As every man hath received the gift, even so minister the same one to another, as good stewards of the manifold grace of God. If any man speak, let him speak as the oracles of God; if any man minister, let him do it as of the ability which God giveth: that God in all things may be glorified through Jesus Christ, to whom be praise and dominion for ever and ever. Amen.

The Gospel. St. John xv. 26, *and part of chap.* xvi.

WHEN the Comforter is come, whom I will send unto you from the Father, even the Spirit of truth, which proceedeth from the Father, he shall testify of me: and ye also shall bear witness, because ye have been with me from the beginning. These things have I spoken unto you, that ye should not be offended. They shall put you out of the synagogues: yea, the time cometh, that whosoever killeth you will think that he doeth God service. And these things will they do unto you, because they have not known the Father, nor me. But these things have I told you, that when the time shall come, ye may remember that I told you of them.

Whitsunday.
The Collect.

O GOD, who as at this time didst teach the hearts of thy faithful people, by sending to them the light of thy Holy Spirit; Grant us by the same Spirit to have a right judgment in all things, and evermore to rejoice in his holy comfort; through the merits of Christ Jesus our Saviour, who liveth and reigneth with thee, in the unity of the same Spirit, one God, world without end. *Amen.*

For the Epistle. Acts ii. 1.

WHEN the day of Pentecost was fully come, they were all with one accord in one place. And suddenly there came a sound from heaven as of a rushing mighty wind, and it filled all the house where they were sitting. And there appeared unto them cloven tongues like as of fire, and it sat upon each of them. And they were all filled with the Holy Ghost, and began to speak with other tongues, as the Spirit gave them utterance. And there were dwelling at Jerusalem Jews, devout men, out of every nation under heaven. Now when this was noised abroad, the multitude came together, and were confounded, because that every man heard them speak in his own language. And they were all amazed and marvelled, saying one to another, Behold, are not all these which speak Galilæans? And how hear we every man in our own tongue, wherein we were born? Parthians, and Medes, and Elamites, and the dwellers in Mesopotamia, and in Judæa, and Cappadocia, in Pontus, and Asia, Phrygia, and Pamphylia, in Egypt, and in the parts of

Libya about Cyrene, and strangers of Rome, Jews and proselytes, Cretes and Arabians, we do hear them speak in our tongues the wonderful works of God.

The Gospel. St. John xiv. 15.

JESUS said unto his disciples, If ye love me, keep my commandments. And I will pray the Father, and he shall give you another Comforter, that he may abide with you for ever; even the Spirit of truth; whom the world cannot receive, because it seeth him not, neither knoweth him: but ye know him; for he dwelleth with you, and shall be in you. I will not leave you comfortless: I will come to you. Yet a little while, and the world seeth me no more; but ye see me: because I live, ye shall live also. At that day ye shall know that I am in my Father, and ye in me, and I in you. He that hath my commandments, and keepeth them, he it is that loveth me: and he that loveth me shall be loved of my Father, and I will love him, and will manifest myself to him. Judas saith unto him, not

Iscariot, Lord, how is it that thou wilt manifest thyself unto us, and not unto the world? Jesus answered and said unto him, If a man love me, he will keep my words; and my Father will love him, and we will come unto him, and make our abode with him. He that loveth me not keepeth not my sayings: and the word which ye hear is not mine, but the Father's which sent me. These things have I spoken unto you, being yet present with you. But the Comforter, which is the Holy Ghost, whom the Father will send in my name, he shall teach you all things, and bring all things to your remembrance, whatsoever I have said unto you. Peace I leave with you, my peace I give unto you: not as the world giveth, give I unto you. Let not your heart be troubled, neither let it be afraid. Ye have heard how I said unto you, I go away, and come again unto you. If ye loved me, ye would rejoice, because I said, I go unto the Father: for my Father is greater than I. And now I have told you before it come to pass, that, when it is come to pass, ye might believe. Hereafter I will not talk much with you: for the prince of this world cometh, and hath nothing in me. But that the world may know that I love the Father; and as the Father gave me commandment, even so I do.

Monday in Whitsunweek.

The Collect.

O GOD, who as at this time didst teach the hearts of thy faithful people, by sending to them the light of thy Holy Spirit; Grant us by the same Spirit to have a right judgment in all things, and evermore to rejoice in his holy comfort; through the merits of Christ Jesus our Saviour, who liveth and reigneth with thee, in the unity of the same Spirit, one God, world without end. *Amen.*

For the Epistle. Acts x. 34.

THEN Peter opened his mouth, and said, Of a truth I perceive that God is no respecter of persons: but in every nation he that feareth him, and worketh righteousness, is accepted with him. The word which God sent unto the children of Israel, preaching peace by Jesus Christ: (he is Lord of all:) that word, I say, ye know, which was published throughout all Judæa, and began from Galilee, after the baptism which John preached; how God anointed Jesus of Nazareth with the Holy Ghost and with power: who went about doing good, and healing all that were oppressed of the devil; for God was with him. And we are witnesses of all things which he did both in the land of the Jews, and in Jerusalem; whom they slew and hanged on a tree: him God raised up the third day, and shewed him openly; not to all the people, but unto witnesses chosen before of God, even to us, who did eat and drink with him after he rose from the dead. And he commanded us to preach unto the people, and to testify that it is he which was ordained of God to be the Judge of quick and dead. To him give all the prophets witness, that through him whosoever believeth in him shall receive remission of sins. While Peter yet spake these words, the Holy Ghost fell on all them which heard the word. And they of the circumcision which believed were astonished, as many as came with Peter, because that on the Gentiles also was poured out the gift of the Holy Ghost. For they heard them speak with tongues, and magnify God. Then answered Peter, Can any man forbid water, that these should not be baptized, which have received the Holy Ghost as well as we? And he commanded them to be baptized in the name of the Lord. Then prayed they him to tarry certain days.

The Gospel. St. John iii. 16.

GOD so loved the world, that he gave his only begotten Son, that whosoever believeth in him should not perish, but have everlasting life. For God sent not his Son into the world to condemn the world; but that the world through him might be saved. He that believeth on him is not condemned: but he that believeth not is condemned already, because he hath not believed in the name of the only begotten Son of God. And this is the condemnation, that light is come into the world, and men loved darkness rather than light, because their deeds were evil. For every one that doeth evil hateth the light, neither cometh to the light, lest his deeds should be reproved. But he that doeth truth cometh to the light, that his deeds may be made manifest, that they are wrought in God.

✠

Tuesday in Whitsun-week.

The Collect.

O GOD, who as at this time didst teach the hearts of thy faithful people, by sending to them the light of thy Holy Spirit; Grant us by the same Spirit to have a right judgment in all things, and evermore to rejoice in his holy comfort; through the merits of Christ Jesus our Saviour, who liveth and reigneth with thee, in the unity of the same Spirit, one God, world without end. *Amen.*

For the Epistle. Acts viii. 14.

WHEN the apostles which were at Jerusalem heard that Samaria had received the word of God, they sent unto them Peter and John: who, when they were come down, prayed for them, that they might receive the Holy Ghost: (for as yet he was fallen upon none of them: only they were baptized in the name of the Lord Jesus.) Then laid they their hands on them, and they received the Holy Ghost.

The Gospel. St. John x. 1.

VERILY, verily, I say unto you, He that entereth not by the door into the sheepfold, but climbeth up some other way, the same is a thief and a robber. But he that entereth in by the door is the shepherd of the sheep. To him the porter openeth; and the sheep hear his voice; and he calleth his own sheep by name, and leadeth them out. And when he putteth forth his own sheep, he goeth before them, and the sheep follow him: for they know his voice. And a stranger will they not follow, but will flee from him: for they know not the voice of strangers. This parable spake Jesus unto them: but they understood not what things they were which he spake unto them. Then said Jesus unto them again, Verily, verily, I say unto you, I am the door of the sheep. All that ever came before me are thieves and robbers: but the sheep did not hear them. I am the door: by me if any man enter in, he shall be saved, and shall go in and out, and find pasture. The thief cometh not, but for to steal, and to kill, and to destroy: I am come that they might have life, and that they might have it more abundantly.

Trinity-Sunday.

The Collect.

ALMIGHTY and everlasting God, who hast given unto us thy servants grace, by the confession of a true faith, to acknowledge the glory of the eternal Trinity, and in the power of the Divine Majesty to worship the Unity; We beseech thee that thou wouldest keep us stedfast in this faith, and evermore defend us from all adversities, who livest and reignest, one God, world without end. *Amen.*

For the Epistle. Rev. iv. 1.

AFTER this I looked, and, behold, a door was opened in heaven: and the first voice which I heard was as it were of a trumpet talking with me; which said, Come up hither, and I will shew thee things which must be hereafter. And immediately I was in the spirit: and, behold, a throne was set in heaven, and one sat on the throne. And he that sat was to look upon like a jasper and a sardine stone: and there was a rainbow round about the throne, in sight like unto an emerald. And round about the throne were four and twenty seats: and upon the seats I saw four and twenty elders sitting, clothed in white raiment; and they had on their heads crowns of gold. And out of the throne proceeded lightnings and thunderings and voices: and there were seven lamps of fire burning before the throne, which are the seven Spirits of God. And before the throne there was a sea of glass like unto crystal: and in the midst of the throne, and round about the throne, were four beasts full of eyes before and behind. And the first beast was like a lion, and the second beast like a calf, and the third beast had a face as a man, and the fourth beast was like a flying eagle. And the four beasts had each of them six wings about him; and they were full of eyes within: and they rest not day and night, saying, Holy, holy, holy, Lord God Almighty, which was, and is, and is to come. And when those beasts give glory and honour and thanks to him that sat on the throne, who liveth for ever and ever, the four and twenty elders fall down before him that sat on the throne, and worship him that liveth for ever and ever, and cast their crowns before the throne, saying, Thou art worthy, O Lord, to receive glory and honour and power: for thou hast created all things, and for thy pleasure they are and were created.

The Gospel. St. John iii. 1.

THERE was a man of the Pharisees, named Nicodemus, a ruler of the Jews: the same came to Jesus by night, and said unto him, Rabbi, we know that thou art a teacher come from God: for no man can do these miracles that thou doest, except God be with him. Jesus answered and said unto him, Verily, verily, I say unto thee, Except a man be born again, he cannot see the kingdom of God. Nicodemus saith unto him, How can a man be born when he is old? can he enter the second time into his mother's womb, and be born? Jesus answered, Verily, verily, I say unto thee, Except a man be born of water and of the Spirit, he cannot enter into the kingdom of God. That which is born of the flesh is flesh; and that which is born of the Spirit is spirit. Marvel not that I said unto thee, Ye must be born again. The wind bloweth where it listeth, and thou hearest the sound

thereof, but canst not tell whence it cometh, and whither it goeth: so is every one that is born of the Spirit. Nicodemus answered and said unto him, How can these things be? Jesus answered and said unto him, Art thou a master of Israel, and knowest not these things? Verily, verily, I say unto thee, We speak that we do know, and testify that we have seen; and ye receive not our witness. If I have told you earthly things, and ye believe not, how shall ye believe, if I tell you of heavenly things? And no man hath ascended up to heaven, but he that came down from heaven, even the Son of man which is in heaven. And as Moses lifted up the serpent in the wilderness, even so must the Son of man be lifted up: that whosoever believeth in him should not perish, but have eternal life.

❧

The First Sunday after Trinity.

The Collect.

O GOD, the strength of all those who put their trust in thee; Mercifully accept our prayers; and because, through the weakness of our mortal nature, we can do no good thing without thee, grant us the help of thy grace, that in keeping thy commandments we may please thee, both in will and deed; through Jesus Christ our Lord. *Amen.*

The Epistle. 1 St. John iv. 7.

BELOVED, let us love one another: for love is of God; and every one that loveth is born of God, and knoweth God. He that loveth not knoweth not God; for God is love. In this was manifested the love of God toward us, because that God sent his only begotten Son into the world, that we might live through him. Herein is love, not that we loved God, but that he loved us, and sent his Son to be the propitiation for our sins. Beloved, if God so loved us, we ought also to love one another. No man hath seen God at any time. If we love one another, God dwelleth in us, and his love is perfected in us. Hereby know we that we dwell in him, and he in us, because he hath

given us of his Spirit. And we have seen and do testify that the Father sent the Son to be the Saviour of the world. Whosoever shall confess that Jesus is the Son of God, God dwelleth in him, and he in God. And we have known and believed the love that God hath to us. God is love; and he that dwelleth in love dwelleth in God, and God in him. Herein is our love made perfect, that we may have boldness in the day of judgment: because as he is, so are we in this world. There is no fear in love; but perfect love casteth out fear: because fear hath torment. He that feareth is not made perfect in love. We love him, because he first loved us. If a man say, I love God, and hateth his brother, he is a liar: for he that loveth not his brother whom he hath seen, how can he love God whom he hath not seen? And this commandment have we from him, That he who loveth God love his brother also.

The Gospel. St. Luke xvi. 19.

THERE was a certain rich man, which was

clothed in purple and fine linen, and fared sumptuously every day: and there was a certain beggar named Lazarus, which was laid at his gate, full of sores, and desiring to be fed with the crumbs which fell from the rich man's table: moreover the dogs came and licked his sores. And it came to pass, that the beggar died, and was carried by the angels into Abraham's bosom: the rich man also died, and was buried; and in hell he lift up his eyes, being in torments, and seeth Abraham afar off, and Lazarus in his bosom. And he cried and said, Father Abraham, have mercy on me, and send Lazarus, that he may dip the tip of his finger in water, and cool my tongue; for I am tormented in this flame. But Abraham said, Son, remember that thou in thy lifetime receivedst thy good things, and likewise Lazarus evil things: but now he is comforted, and thou art tormented. And beside all this, between us and you there is a great gulf fixed: so that they which would pass from hence to you cannot; neither can they pass to us, that would come from thence. Then he said, I pray thee therefore, father, that thou wouldest send him to my father's house: for I have five brethren; that he may testify unto them, lest they also come into this place of torment. Abraham saith unto him, They have Moses and the prophets; let them hear them. And he said, Nay, father Abraham: but if one went unto them from the dead, they will repent. And he said unto him, If they hear not Moses and the prophets, neither will they be persuaded, though one rose from the dead.

✤

The Second Sunday after Trinity.

The Collect.

O LORD, who never failest to help and govern those whom thou dost bring up in thy stedfast fear and love; Keep us, we beseech thee, under the protection of thy good providence, and make us to have a perpetual fear and love of thy holy Name; through Jesus Christ our Lord. *Amen.*

The Epistle. 1 St. John iii. 13.

MARVEL not, my brethren, if the world hate you. We know that we have passed from death unto life, because we love the brethren. He that loveth not his brother abideth in death. Whosoever hateth his brother is a murderer: and ye know that no murderer hath eternal life abiding in him. Hereby perceive we the love of God, because he laid down his life for us: and we ought to lay down our lives for the brethren. But whoso hath this world's good, and seeth his brother have need, and shutteth up his bowels of compassion from him, how dwelleth the love of God in him? My little children, let us not love in word, neither in tongue; but in deed and in truth. And hereby we know that we are of the truth, and shall assure our hearts before him. For if our heart condemn us, God is greater than our heart, and knoweth all things. Beloved, if our heart condemn us not, then have we confidence toward God. And whatsoever we ask, we receive of him, because

we keep his commandments, and do those things that are pleasing in his sight. And this is his commandment, That we should believe on the name of his Son Jesus Christ, and love one another, as he gave us commandment. And he that keepeth his commandments dwelleth in him, and he in him. And hereby we know that he abideth in us, by the Spirit which he hath given us.

The Gospel. St. Luke xiv. 16.

A CERTAIN man made a great supper, and bade many: and sent his servant at supper time to say to them that were bidden, Come; for all things are now ready. And they all with one consent began to make excuse. The first said unto him, I have bought a piece of ground, and I must needs go and see it: I pray thee have me excused. And another said, I have bought five yoke of oxen, and I go to prove them: I pray thee have me excused. And another said, I have married a wife, and therefore I cannot come. So that servant came, and shewed his lord these things. Then the master of the house being angry said to his servant, Go out quickly into the streets and lanes of the city, and bring in hither the poor, and the maimed, and the halt, and the blind. And the servant said, Lord, it is done as thou hast commanded, and yet there is room. And the lord said unto the servant, Go out into the highways and hedges, and compel them to come in, that my house may be filled. For I say unto you, that none of those men which were bidden shall taste of my supper.

❀

The Third Sunday after Trinity.

The Collect.

O LORD, we beseech thee mercifully to hear us; and grant that we, to whom thou hast given an hearty desire to pray, may, by thy mighty aid, be defended and comforted in all dangers and adversities; through Jesus Christ our Lord. *Amen.*

The Epistle. 1 St. Pet. v. 5.

A LL of you be subject one to another, and be clothed with humility: for God resisteth the proud, and giveth grace to the humble. Humble yourselves therefore under the mighty hand of God, that he may exalt you in due time: casting all your care upon him; for he careth for you. Be sober, be vigilant; because your adversary the devil, as a roaring lion, walketh about, seeking whom he may devour: whom resist stedfast in the faith, knowing that the same afflictions are accomplished in your brethren that are in the world. But the God of all grace, who hath called us unto his eternal glory by Christ Jesus, after that ye have suffered a while, make you perfect, stablish, strengthen, settle you. To him be glory and dominion for ever and ever. Amen.

The Gospel. St. Luke xv. 1.

T HEN drew near unto him all the publicans and sinners for to hear him. And the Pharisees and scribes murmured, saying, This man receiveth sinners, and eateth with them. And he spake this parable unto them, saying, What man of you, having a hundred sheep, if he lose one of them, doth not leave the ninety and nine in the wilderness, and go after that which is lost, until he find it? And when he hath found it, he layeth it on his shoulders, rejoicing. And when he cometh home, he calleth together his friends and neighbours, saying unto them, Rejoice with me; for I have found my sheep which was lost. I say unto you, that likewise joy shall be in heaven over one sinner that repenteth, more than over ninety and nine just persons, which need no repentance. Either what woman having ten pieces of silver, if she lose one piece, doth not light a candle, and sweep the house, and seek diligently till she find it? And when she hath found it, she calleth her friends and her neighbours together, saying, Rejoice with me; for I have found the piece which I had lost. Likewise, I say unto you, there is joy in the presence of the angels of God over one sinner that repenteth.

The Fourth Sunday after Trinity.

The Collect.

O GOD, the protector of all that trust in thee, without whom nothing is strong, nothing is holy; Increase and multiply upon us thy mercy; that, thou being our ruler and guide, we may so pass through things temporal, that we finally lose not the things eternal. Grant this, O heavenly Father, for Jesus Christ's sake our Lord. *Amen.*

The Epistle. Rom. viii. 18.

I RECKON that the sufferings of this present time are not worthy to be compared with the glory which shall be revealed in us. For the earnest expectation of the creature waiteth for the manifestation of the sons of God. For the creature was made subject to vanity, not willingly, but by reason of him who hath subjected the same in hope, because the creature itself also shall be delivered from the bondage of corruption into the glorious liberty of the children of God. For we know that the whole creation groaneth and travaileth in pain together until now. And not only they, but ourselves also, which have the firstfruits of the Spirit, even we ourselves groan within ourselves, waiting for the adoption, to wit, the redemption of our body.

The Gospel. St. Luke vi. 36.

BE ye therefore merciful, as your Father also is merciful. Judge not, and ye shall not be judged: condemn not, and ye shall not be condemned: forgive, and ye shall be forgiven: give, and it shall be given unto you; good measure, pressed down, and shaken together, and running over, shall men give into your bosom. For with the same measure that ye mete withal it shall be measured to you again. And he spake a parable unto them, Can the blind lead the blind? shall they not both fall into the ditch? The disciple is not above his master: but every one that is perfect shall be as his master. And why beholdest thou the mote that is in thy brother's eye, but

perceivest not the beam that is in thine own eye? Either how canst thou say to thy brother, Brother, let me pull out the mote that is in thine eye, when thou thyself beholdest not the beam that is in thine own eye? Thou hypocrite, cast out first the beam out of thine own eye, and then shalt thou see clearly to pull out the mote that is in thy brother's eye.

✥

The Fifth Sunday after Trinity.
The Collect.

GRANT, O Lord, we beseech thee, that the course of this world may be so peaceably ordered by thy governance, that thy Church may joyfully serve thee in all godly quietness; through Jesus Christ our Lord. *Amen.*

The Epistle. 1 St. Pet. iii. 8.

BE ye all of one mind, having compassion one of another, love as brethren, be pitiful, be courteous: not rendering evil for evil, or railing for railing: but contrariwise blessing; knowing that ye are thereunto called, that ye should inherit a blessing. For he that will love life, and see good days, let him refrain his tongue from evil, and his lips that they speak no guile: let him eschew evil, and do good; let him seek peace, and ensue it. For the eyes of the Lord are over the righteous, and his ears are open unto their prayers: but the face of the Lord is against them that do evil. And who is he that will harm you, if ye be followers of that which is good? But and if ye suffer for righteousness' sake, happy are ye: and be not afraid of their terror, neither be troubled; but sanctify the Lord God in your hearts.

The Gospel. St. Luke v. 1.

IT came to pass, that, as the people pressed upon him to hear the word of God, he stood by the lake of Gennesaret, and saw two ships standing by the lake: but the fishermen were gone out of them, and were washing their nets. And he entered into one of the ships, which was Simon's, and prayed him that he would thrust out a little from the land. And he sat down, and taught the people out of the ship. Now when he had left speaking, he said unto Simon, Launch out into the deep, and let down your nets for a draught. And Simon answering said unto him, Master, we have toiled all the night, and have taken nothing: nevertheless at thy word I will let down the net. And when they had this done, they enclosed a great multitude of fishes: and their net brake. And they beckoned unto their partners, which were in the other ship, that they should come and help them. And they came, and filled both the ships, so that they began to sink. When Simon Peter saw it, he fell down at Jesus' knees, saying, Depart from me; for I am a sinful man, O Lord. For he was astonished, and all that were with him, at the draught of the fishes which they had taken: and so was also James, and John, the sons of Zebedee, which were partners with Simon. And Jesus said unto Simon, Fear not; from henceforth thou shalt catch men. And when they had brought their ships to land, they forsook all, and followed him.

The Sixth Sunday after Trinity.

The Collect.

O GOD, who hast prepared for those who love thee such good things as pass man's understanding; Pour into our hearts such love toward thee, that we, loving thee above all things, may obtain thy promises, which exceed all that we can desire; through Jesus Christ our Lord. *Amen.*

The Epistle. Rom. vi. 3.

K NOW ye not, that so many of us as were baptized into Jesus Christ were baptized into his death? Therefore we are buried with him by baptism into death: that like as Christ was raised up from the dead by the glory of the Father, even so we also should walk in newness of life. For if we have been planted together in the likeness of his death, we shall be also in the likeness of his resurrection: knowing this, that our old man is cru-cified with him, that the body of sin might be destroyed, that henceforth we should not serve sin. For he that is dead is freed from sin. Now if we be dead with Christ, we believe that we shall also live with him: knowing that Christ being raised from the dead dieth no more; death hath no more dominion over him. For in that he died, he died unto sin once: but in that he liveth, he liveth unto God. Likewise reckon ye also yourselves to be dead indeed unto sin, but alive unto God through Jesus Christ our Lord.

The Gospel. St. Matt. v. 20.

J ESUS said unto his disciples, Except your righteousness shall exceed the righteousness of the scribes and Pharisees, ye shall in no case enter into the kingdom of heaven. Ye have heard that it was said by them of old time, Thou shalt not kill; and whosoever shall kill shall be in danger of the judgment: but I say unto you, That whosoever is angry with his brother without a cause shall be in danger of the judgment: and whosoever shall say to his brother, Raca, shall be in danger of the council: but whosoever shall say, Thou fool, shall be in danger of hell fire. Therefore if thou bring thy gift to the altar, and there rememberest that thy brother hath ought against thee; leave there thy gift before the altar, and go thy way; first be reconciled to thy brother, and then come and offer thy gift. Agree with thine adversary quickly, whiles thou art in the way with him; lest at any time the adversary deliver thee to the judge, and the judge deliver thee to the officer, and thou be cast into prison. Verily I say unto thee, Thou shalt by no means come out thence, till thou hast paid the uttermost farthing.

The Seventh Sunday after Trinity.

The Collect.

LORD of all power and might, who art the author and giver of all good things; Graft in our hearts the love of thy Name, increase in us true religion, nourish us with all goodness, and of thy

great mercy keep us in the same; through Jesus Christ our Lord. *Amen.*

The Epistle. Rom. vi. 19.

I SPEAK after the manner of men because of the infirmity of your flesh: for as ye have yielded your members servants to uncleanness and to iniquity unto iniquity; even so now yield your members servants to righteousness unto holiness. For when ye were the servants of sin, ye were free from righteousness. What fruit had ye then in those things whereof ye are now ashamed? for the end of those things is death. But now being made free from sin, and become servants to God, ye have your fruit unto holiness, and the end everlasting life. For the wages of sin is death; but the gift of God is eternal life through Jesus Christ our Lord.

The Gospel. St. Mark viii. 1.

I N those days the multitude being very great, and having nothing to eat, Jesus called his disciples unto him, and saith unto them, I have compassion on the multitude, because they have now been with me three days, and have nothing to eat: and if I send them away fasting to their own houses, they will faint by the way: for divers of them came from far. And his disciples answered him, From whence can a man satisfy these men with bread here in the wilderness? And he asked them, How many loaves have ye? And they said, Seven. And he commanded the people to sit down on the ground: and he took the seven loaves, and gave thanks, and brake, and gave to his disciples to set before them; and they did set them before the people. And they had a few small fishes: and he blessed, and commanded to set them also before them. So they did eat, and were filled: and they took up of the broken meat that was left seven baskets. And they that had eaten were about four thousand: and he sent them away.

The Eighth Sunday after Trinity.

The Collect.

O GOD, whose never-failing providence or-

dereth all things both in heaven and earth; We humbly beseech thee to put away from us all hurtful things, and to give us those things which are profitable for us; through Jesus Christ our Lord. Amen.

The Epistle. Rom. viii. 12.

BRETHREN, we are debtors, not to the flesh, to live after the flesh. For if ye live after the flesh, ye shall die: but if ye through the Spirit do mortify the deeds of the body, ye shall live. For as many as are led by the Spirit of God, they are the sons of God. For ye have not received the spirit of bondage again to fear; but ye have received the Spirit of adoption, whereby we cry, Abba, Father. The Spirit itself beareth witness with our spirit, that we are the children of God: and if children, then heirs; heirs of God, and joint-heirs with Christ: if so be that we suffer with him, that we may be also glorified together.

The Gospel. St. Matt. vii. 15.

BEWARE of false prophets, which come to

you in sheep's clothing, but inwardly they are ravening wolves. Ye shall know them by their fruits. Do men gather grapes of thorns, or figs of thistles? Even so every good tree bringeth forth good fruit; but a corrupt tree bringeth forth evil fruit. A good tree cannot bring forth evil fruit, neither can a corrupt tree bring forth good fruit. Every tree that bringeth not forth good fruit is hewn down, and cast into the fire. Wherefore by their fruits ye shall know them. Not every one that saith unto me, Lord, Lord, shall enter into the kingdom of heaven; but he that doeth the will of my Father which is in heaven.

✠

The Ninth Sunday after Trinity.

The Collect.

GRANT to us, Lord, we beseech thee, the spirit to think and do always such things as are right; that we, who cannot do any thing that is good without thee, may by thee be enabled to live according to thy will; through Jesus Christ our Lord. Amen.

The Epistle. 1 Cor. x. 1.

BRETHREN, I would not that ye should be ignorant, how that all our fathers were under the cloud, and all passed through the sea; and were all baptized unto Moses in the cloud and in the sea; and did all eat the same spiritual meat; and did all drink the same spiritual drink: for they drank of that spiritual Rock that followed them: and that Rock was Christ. But with many of them God was not well pleased: for they were overthrown in the wilderness. Now these things were our examples, to the intent we should not lust after evil things, as they also lusted. Neither be ye idolaters, as were some of them; as it is written, The people sat down to eat and drink, and rose up to play. Neither let us commit fornication, as some of them committed, and fell in one day three and twenty thousand. Neither let us tempt Christ, as some of them also tempted, and were destroyed of serpents. Neither murmur ye, as some of them also murmured, and were destroyed of the destroyer. Now all these things happened unto them for ensamples: and they are written for our admonition, upon whom the ends of the world are come. Wherefore let him that thinketh he standeth take heed lest he fall. There hath no temptation taken you but such as is common to man: but God is faithful, who will not suffer you to be tempted above that ye are able; but will with the temptation also make a way to escape, that ye may be able to bear it.

The Gospel. St. Luke xvi. 1.

JESUS said unto his disciples, There was a certain rich man, which had a steward; and the same was accused unto him that he had wasted his goods. And he called him, and said unto him, How is it that I hear this of thee? give an account of thy stewardship; for thou mayest be no longer steward. Then the steward said within himself, What shall I do? for my lord taketh away from me the stewardship: I cannot dig; to beg I am ashamed. I am resolved what to do, that, when I am put out of the stewardship, they may receive me into their houses. So he called every one of his lord's debtors unto him, and said unto the first, How much owest thou unto my lord? And he said, An hundred measures of oil. And he said unto him, Take thy bill, and sit down quickly, and write fifty. Then said he to another, And how much owest thou? And he said, An hundred measures of wheat. And he said unto him, Take thy bill, and write fourscore. And the lord commended the unjust steward, because he had done wisely: for the children of this world are in their generation wiser than the children of light. And I say unto you, Make to yourselves friends of the mammon of unrighteousness; that, when ye fail, they may receive you into everlasting habitations.

❈

The Tenth Sunday after Trinity.

The Collect.

LET thy merciful ears, O Lord, be open to the prayers of thy humble servants; and, that they may obtain their petitions, make them to ask such things as shall please thee; through Jesus Christ our Lord. *Amen.*

The Epistle. 1 Cor. xii. 1.

CONCERNING spiritual gifts, brethren, I would not have you ignorant. Ye know that ye were Gentiles, carried away unto these dumb idols, even as ye were led. Wherefore I give you to understand, that no man speaking by the Spirit of God calleth Jesus accursed: and that no man can say that Jesus is the Lord, but by the Holy Ghost. Now there are diversities of gifts, but the same Spirit. And there are differences of administrations, but the same Lord. And there are diversities of operations, but it is the same God which worketh all in all. But the manifestation of the Spirit is given to every man to profit withal. For to one is given by the Spirit the word of wisdom; to another the word of knowledge by the same Spirit; to another faith by the same Spirit; to another the gifts of healing by the same Spirit; to another the working of miracles; to another prophecy; to another discerning of spirits; to another divers kinds of tongues; to another the interpretation of tongues: but all these worketh that one and the selfsame Spirit, dividing to every man severally as he will.

The Gospel. St. Luke xix. 41.

AND when he was come near, he beheld the city, and wept over it, saying, If thou hadst known, even thou, at least in this thy day, the things which belong unto thy peace! but now they are hid from thine eyes. For the days shall come upon thee, that thine enemies shall cast a trench about thee, and compass thee round, and keep thee in on every side, and shall lay thee even with the ground, and thy children within thee; and they shall not leave in thee one stone upon another; because thou knewest not the time of thy visitation. And he went into the temple, and began to cast out them that sold therein, and them that bought;

saying unto them, It is written, My house is the house of prayer: but ye have made it a den of thieves. And he taught daily in the temple.

✤

The Eleventh Sunday after Trinity.

The Collect.

O GOD, who declarest thy almighty power chiefly in showing mercy and pity; Mercifully grant unto us such a measure of thy grace, that we, running the way of thy commandments, may obtain thy gracious promises, and be made partakers of thy heavenly treasure; through Jesus Christ our Lord. *Amen.*

The Epistle. 1 Cor. xv. 1.

BRETHREN, I declare unto you the gospel which I preached unto you, which also ye have received, and wherein ye stand; by which also ye are saved, if ye keep in memory what I preached unto you, unless ye have believed in vain. For I delivered unto you first of all that which I also re-ceived, how that Christ died for our sins according to the scriptures; and that he was buried, and that he rose again the third day according to the scriptures: and that he was seen of Cephas, then of the twelve: after that, he was seen of above five hundred brethren at once; of whom the greater part remain unto this present, but some are fallen asleep. After that, he was seen of James; then of all the apostles. And last of all he was seen of me also, as of one born out of due time. For I am the least of the apostles, that am not meet to be called an apostle, because I persecuted the church of God. But by the grace of God I am what I am: and his grace which was bestowed upon me was not in vain; but I laboured more abundantly than they all: yet not I, but the grace of God which was with me. Therefore whether it were I or they, so we preach, and so ye believed.

The Gospel. St. Luke xviii. 9.

JESUS spake this parable unto certain which

trusted in themselves that they were righteous, and despised others : Two men went up into the temple to pray ; the one a Pharisee, and the other a publican. The Pharisee stood and prayed thus with himself, God, I thank thee, that I am not as other men are, extortioners, unjust, adulterers, or even as this publican. I fast twice in the week, I give tithes of all that I possess. And the publican, standing afar off, would not lift up so much as his eyes unto heaven, but smote upon his breast, saying, God be merciful to me a sinner. I tell you, this man went down to his house justified rather than the other : for every one that exalteth himself shall be abased ; and he that humbleth himself shall be exalted.

❋

The Twelfth Sunday after Trinity.

The Collect.

ALMIGHTY and everlasting God, who art always more ready to hear than we to pray, and art

wont to give more than either we desire or deserve ; Pour down upon us the abundance of thy mercy ; forgiving us those things whereof our conscience is afraid, and giving us those good things which we are not worthy to ask, but through the merits and mediation of Jesus Christ, thy Son, our Lord. *Amen.*

The Epistle. 2 Cor. iii. 4.

SUCH trust have we through Christ to God-ward : not that we are sufficient of ourselves to think any thing as of ourselves ; but our sufficiency is of God ; who also hath made us able ministers of the new testament ; not of the letter, but of the spirit : for the letter killeth, but the spirit giveth life. But if the ministration of death, written and engraven in stones, was glorious, so that the children of Israel could not stedfastly behold the face of Moses for the glory of his countenance ; which glory was to be done away : how shall not the ministration of the spirit be rather glorious ? For if the ministration of condemnation be glory, much more doth the ministration of righteousness exceed in glory.

The Gospel. St. Mark vii. 31.

JESUS, departing from the coasts of Tyre and Sidon, came unto the sea of Galilee, through the midst of the coasts of Decapolis. And they bring unto him one that was deaf, and had an impediment in his speech; and they beseech him to put his hand upon him. And he took him aside from the multitude, and put his fingers into his ears, and he spit, and touched his tongue; and looking up to heaven, he sighed, and saith unto him, Ephphatha, that is, Be opened. And straightway his ears were opened, and the string of his tongue was loosed, and he spake plain. And he charged them that they should tell no man: but the more he charged them, so much the more a great deal they published it; and were beyond measure astonished, saying, He hath done all things well: he maketh both the deaf to hear, and the dumb to speak.

The Thirteenth Sunday after Trinity.

The Collect.

ALMIGHTY and merciful God, of whose only gift it cometh that thy faithful people do unto thee true and laudable service; Grant, we beseech thee, that we may so faithfully serve thee in this life, that we fail not finally to attain thy heavenly promises; through the merits of Jesus Christ our Lord. *Amen.*

The Epistle. Gal. iii. 16.

TO Abraham and his seed were the promises made. He saith not, And to seeds, as of many; but as of one, And to thy seed, which is Christ. And this I say, that the covenant, that was confirmed before of God in Christ, the law, which was four hundred and thirty years after, cannot disannul, that it should make the promise of none effect. For if the inheritance be of the law, it is no more of promise: but God gave it to Abraham by promise. Wherefore then serveth the law? It was added because of transgressions, till the seed should come to whom the promise was made; and it was ordained by angels in the hand of a mediator. Now a mediator is not a mediator of one, but God is one. Is the law then against the promises of God? God forbid: for if there had been a law given which could have given life, verily righteousness should have been by the law. But the scripture hath concluded all under sin, that the promise by faith of Jesus Christ might be given to them that believe.

The Gospel. St. Luke x. 23.

BLESSED are the eyes which see the things that ye see: for I tell you, that many prophets and kings have desired to see those things which ye see, and have not seen them; *and to hear those things which ye hear, and have not heard them.* And, behold, a certain lawyer stood up, and tempted him, saying, Master, what shall I do to inherit eternal life? He said unto him, What is written in the law? how readest thou? And he answering said,

Thou shalt love the Lord thy God with all thy heart, and with all thy soul, and with all thy strength, and with all thy mind; and thy neighbour as thyself. And he said unto him, Thou hast answered right: this do, and thou shalt live. But he, willing to justify himself, said unto Jesus, And who is my neighbour? And Jesus answering said, A certain man went down from Jerusalem to Jericho, and fell among thieves, which stripped him of his raiment, and wounded him, and departed, leaving him half dead. And by chance there came down a certain priest that way: and when he saw him, he passed by on the other side. And likewise a Levite, when he was at the place, came and looked on him, and passed by on the other side. But a certain Samaritan, as he journeyed, came where he was: and when he saw him, he had compassion on him, and went to him, and bound up his wounds, pouring in oil and wine, and set him on his own beast, and brought him to an inn, and took care of him. And on the morrow when he departed, he took out two pence, and gave them to the host, and said unto him, Take care of him; and whatsoever thou spendest more, when I come again, I will repay thee. Which now of these three, thinkest thou, was neighbour unto him that fell among the thieves? And he said, He that shewed mercy on him. Then said Jesus unto him, Go, and do thou likewise.

❋

The Fourteenth Sunday after Trinity.

The Collect.

ALMIGHTY and everlasting God, give unto us the increase of faith, hope, and charity; and, that we may obtain that which thou dost promise, make us to love that which thou dost command; through Jesus Christ our Lord. Amen.

The Epistle. Gal. v. 16.

I SAY then, Walk in the Spirit, and ye shall not fulfil the lust of the flesh. For the flesh lusteth against the Spirit, and the Spirit against the flesh:

and these are contrary the one to the other: so that ye cannot do the things that ye would. But if ye be led of the Spirit, ye are not under the law. Now the works of the flesh are manifest, which are these; Adultery, fornication, uncleanness, lasciviousness, idolatry, witchcraft, hatred, variance, emulations, wrath, strife, seditions, heresies, envyings, murders, drunkenness, revellings, and such like: of the which I tell you before, as I have also told you in time past, that they which do such things shall not inherit the kingdom of God. But the fruit of the Spirit is love, joy, peace, longsuffering, gentleness, goodness, faith, meekness, temperance: against such there is no law. And they that are Christ's have crucified the flesh with the affections and lusts.

The Gospel. St. Luke xvii. 11.

AND it came to pass, as Jesus went to Jerusalem, that he passed through the midst of Samaria and Galilee. And as he entered into a certain village, there met him ten men that were lepers, which stood afar off: and they lifted up their voices, and said, Jesus, Master, have mercy on us. And when he saw them, he said unto them, Go shew yourselves unto the priests. And it came to pass, that, as they went, they were cleansed. And one of them, when he saw that he was healed, turned back, and with a loud voice glorified God, and fell down on his face at his feet, giving him thanks: and he was a Samaritan. And Jesus answering said, Were there not ten cleansed? but where are the nine? There are not found that returned to give glory to God, save this stranger. And he said unto him, Arise, go thy way: thy faith hath made thee whole.

✿

The Fifteenth Sunday after Trinity.

The Collect.

KEEP, we beseech thee, O Lord, thy Church with thy perpetual mercy; and, because the frailty of man without thee cannot but fall, keep us ever by thy help from all things hurtful, and lead us to all things profitable to our salvation; through Jesus Christ our Lord. *Amen.*

The Epistle. Gal. vi. 11.

YE see how large a letter I have written unto you with mine own hand. As many as desire to make a fair shew in the flesh, they constrain you to be circumcised; only lest they should suffer persecution for the cross of Christ. For neither they themselves who are circumcised keep the law; but desire to have you circumcised, that they may glory in your flesh. But God forbid that I should glory, save in the cross of our Lord Jesus Christ, by whom the world is crucified unto me, and I unto the world. For in Christ Jesus neither circumcision availeth any thing, nor uncircumcision, but a new creature. And as many as walk according to this rule, peace be on them, and mercy, and upon the Israel of God. From henceforth let no man trouble me: for I bear in my body the marks of the Lord Jesus. Brethren, the grace of our Lord

Jesus Christ be with your spirit. Amen.

The Gospel. St. Matt. vi. 24.

NO man can serve two masters: for either he will hate the one, and love the other; or else he will hold to the one, and despise the other. Ye cannot serve God and mammon. Therefore I say unto you, Take no thought for your life, what ye shall eat, or what ye shall drink; nor yet for your body, what ye shall put on. Is not the life more than meat, and the body than raiment? Behold the fowls of the air: for they sow not, neither do they reap, nor gather into barns; yet your heavenly Father feedeth them. Are ye not much better than they? Which of you by taking thought can add one cubit unto his stature? And why take ye thought for raiment? Consider the lilies of the field, how they grow; they toil not, neither do they spin: and yet I say unto you, That even Solomon in all his glory was not arrayed like one of these. Wherefore, if God so clothe the grass of the field, which to day is, and to morrow is cast into the oven, shall he not much more clothe you, O ye of little faith? Therefore take no thought, saying, What shall we eat? or, What shall we drink? or, Wherewithal shall we be clothed? (for after all these things do the Gentiles seek;) for your heavenly Father knoweth that ye have need of all these things. But seek ye first the kingdom of God, and his righteousness; and all these things shall be added unto you. Take therefore no thought for the morrow: for the morrow shall take thought for the things of itself. Sufficient unto the day is the evil thereof.

❧

The Sixteenth Sunday after Trinity.
The Collect.

O LORD, we beseech thee, let thy continual pity cleanse and defend thy Church; and, because it cannot continue in safety without thy succour, preserve it evermore by thy help and goodness; through Jesus Christ our Lord. *Amen.*

The Epistle. Ephes. iii. 13.

I DESIRE that ye faint not at my tribulations for you, which is your glory. For this cause I bow my knees unto the Father of our Lord Jesus Christ, of whom the whole family in heaven and earth is named, that he would grant you, according to the riches of his glory, to be strengthened with might by his Spirit in the inner man; that Christ may dwell in your hearts by faith; that ye, being rooted and grounded in love, may be able to comprehend with all saints what is the breadth, and length, and depth, and height; and to know the love of Christ, which passeth knowledge, that ye might be filled with all the fulness of God. Now unto him that is able to do exceeding abundantly above all that we ask or think, according to the power that worketh in us, unto him be glory in the church by Christ Jesus throughout all ages, world without end. Amen.

The Gospel. St. Luke vii. 11.

A ND it came to pass the day after, that Jesus went into a city called Nain; and many of his disciples went with him, and much people. Now when he came nigh to the gate of the city, behold, there was a dead man carried out, the only son of his mother, and she was a widow: and much people of the city was with her. And when the Lord saw her, he had compassion on her, and said unto her, Weep not. And he came and touched the bier: and they that bare him stood still. And he said, Young man, I say unto thee, Arise. And he that was dead sat up, and began to speak. And he delivered him to his mother. And there came a fear on all: and they glorified God, saying, That a great prophet is risen up among us; and, That God hath visited his people. And this rumour of him went forth throughout all Judæa, and throughout all the region round about.

The Seventeenth Sunday after Trinity.

The Collect.

L ORD, we pray thee that thy grace may always

prevent and follow us, and make us continually to be given to all good works; through Jesus Christ our Lord. *Amen.*

The Epistle. Ephes. iv. 1.

I THEREFORE, the prisoner of the Lord, beseech you that ye walk worthy of the vocation wherewith ye are called, with all lowliness and meekness, with longsuffering, forbearing one another in love; endeavouring to keep the unity of the Spirit in the bond of peace. There is one body, and one Spirit, even as ye are called in one hope of your calling; one Lord, one faith, one baptism, one God and Father of all, who is above all, and through all, and in you all.

The Gospel. St. Luke xiv. 1.

I T came to pass, as Jesus went into the house of one of the chief Pharisees to eat bread on the sabbath day, that they watched him. And, behold, there was a certain man before him which had the dropsy. And Jesus answering spake unto the lawyers and Pharisees, say-ing, Is it lawful to heal on the sabbath day? And they held their peace. And he took him, and healed him, and let him go; and answered them, saying, Which of you shall have an ass or an ox fallen into a pit, and will not straightway pull him out on the sabbath day? And they could not answer him again to these things. And he put forth a parable to those which were bidden, when he marked how they chose out the chief rooms; saying unto them, When thou art bidden of any man to a wedding, sit not down in the highest room; lest a more honourable man than thou be bidden of him; and he that bade thee and him come and say to thee, Give this man place; and thou begin with shame to take the lowest room. But when thou art bidden, go and sit down in the lowest room; that when he that bade thee cometh, he may say unto thee, Friend, go up higher: then shalt thou have worship in the presence of them that sit at meat with thee. For whosoever exalteth himself shall be abased; and he that humbleth himself shall be exalted.

❧

The Eighteenth Sunday after Trinity.

The Collect.

LORD, we beseech thee, grant thy people grace to withstand the temptations of the world, the flesh, and the devil ; and with pure hearts and minds to follow thee, the only God; through Jesus Christ our Lord. *Amen.*

The Epistle. 1 Cor. i. 4.

I THANK my God always on your behalf, for the grace of God which is given you by Jesus Christ; that in every thing ye are enriched by him, in all utterance, and in all knowledge ; even as the testimony of Christ was confirmed in you : so that ye come behind in no gift; waiting for the coming of our Lord Jesus Christ: who shall also confirm you unto the end, that ye may be blameless in the day of our Lord Jesus Christ.

The Gospel. St. Matt. xxii. 34.

WHEN the Pharisees had heard that Je-sus had put the Sadducees to silence, they were gathered together. Then one of them, which was a lawyer, asked him a question, tempting him, and saying, Master, which is the great commandment in the law ? Jesus said unto him, Thou shalt love the Lord thy God with all thy heart, and with all thy soul, and with all thy mind. This is the first and great commandment. And the second is like unto it, Thou shalt love thy neighbour as thyself. On these two commandments hang all the law and the prophets. While the Pharisees were gathered together, Jesus asked them, saying, What think ye of Christ? whose son is he ? They say unto him, The son of David. He saith unto them, How then doth David in spirit call him Lord, saying, The LORD said unto my Lord, Sit thou on my right hand, till I make thine enemies thy footstool ? If David then call him Lord, how is he his son ? And no man was able to answer him a word, neither durst any man from that day forth ask him any more questions.

The Nineteenth Sunday after Trinity.

The Collect.

O GOD, forasmuch as without thee we are not able to please thee; Mercifully grant that thy Holy Spirit may in all things direct and rule our hearts; through Jesus Christ our Lord. *A-men.*

The Epistle. Ephes. iv. 17.

THIS I say therefore, and testify in the Lord, that ye henceforth walk not as other Gentiles walk, in the vanity of their mind, having the understanding darkened, being alienated from the life of God through the ignorance that is in them, because of the blindness of their heart: who being past feeling have given themselves over unto lasciviousness, to work all uncleanness with greediness. But ye have not so learned Christ; if so be that ye have heard him, and have been taught by him, as the truth is in Jesus: that ye put off concerning the former conversation the old man, which is corrupt according to the deceitful lusts; and be renewed in the spirit of your mind; and that ye put on the new man, which after God is created in righteousness and true holiness. Wherefore putting away lying, speak every man truth with his neighbour: for we are members one of another. Be ye angry, and sin not: let not the sun go down upon your wrath: neither give place to the devil. Let him that stole steal no more: but rather let him labour, working with his hands the thing which is good, that he may have to give to him that needeth. Let no corrupt communication proceed out of your mouth, but that which is good to the use of edifying, that it may minister grace unto the hearers. And grieve not the holy Spirit of God, whereby ye are sealed unto the day of redemption. Let all bitterness, and wrath, and anger, and clamour, and evil speaking, be put away from you, with all malice: and be ye kind one to another, tenderhearted, forgiving one another, even as God for Christ's sake hath forgiven you.

The Gospel. St. Matt. ix. 1.

JESUS entered into a ship, and passed over, and came into his own city. And, behold, they brought to him a man sick of the palsy, lying on a bed : and Jesus seeing their faith said unto the sick of the palsy ; Son, be of good cheer ; thy sins be forgiven thee. And, behold, certain of the scribes said within themselves, This man blasphemeth. And Jesus knowing their thoughts said, Wherefore think ye evil in your hearts ? For whether is easier, to say, Thy sins be forgiven thee ; or to say, Arise, and walk ? But that ye may know that the Son of man hath power on earth to forgive sins, (then saith he to the sick of the palsy,) Arise, take up thy bed, and go unto thine house. And he arose, and departed to his house. But when the multitudes saw it, they marvelled, and glorified God, which had given such power unto men.

❦

The Twentieth Sunday after Trinity.

The Collect.

O ALMIGHTY and most merciful God,

of thy bountiful goodness keep us, we beseech thee, from all things that may hurt us ; that we, being ready both in body and soul, may cheerfully accomplish those things which thou commandest ; through Jesus Christ our Lord. *Amen.*

The Epistle. Ephes. v. 15.

SEE then that ye walk circumspectly, not as fools, but as wise, redeeming the time, because the days are evil. Wherefore be ye not unwise, but understanding what the will of the Lord is. And be not drunk with wine, wherein is excess ; but be filled with the Spirit ; speaking to yourselves in psalms and hymns and spiritual songs, singing and making melody in your heart to the Lord ; giving thanks always for all things unto God and the Father in the name of our Lord Jesus Christ ; submitting yourselves one to another in the fear of God.

The Gospel. St. Matt. xxii. 1.

JESUS said, The kingdom of heaven is like unto a certain king, which made a marriage for his son, and sent forth his servants to call them that were bidden to the wedding: and they would not come. Again, he sent forth other servants, saying, Tell them which are bidden, Behold, I have prepared my dinner: my oxen and my fatlings are killed, and all things are ready: come unto the marriage. But they made light of it, and went their ways, one to his farm, another to his merchandise: and the remnant took his servants, and entreated them spitefully, and slew them. But when the king heard thereof, he was wroth: and he sent forth his armies, and destroyed those murderers, and burned up their city. Then saith he to his servants, The wedding is ready, but they which were bidden were not worthy. Go ye therefore into the highways, and as many as ye shall find, bid to the marriage. So those servants went out into the highways, and gathered together all as many as they found, both bad and good: and the wedding was furnished with guests. And when the king came in to see the guests, he saw there a man which had not on a wedding garment: and he saith unto him, Friend, how camest thou in hither not having a wedding garment? And he was speechless. Then said the king to the servants, Bind him hand and foot, and take him away, and cast him into outer darkness; there shall be weeping and gnashing of teeth. For many are called, but few are chosen.

❧

The Twenty-first Sunday after Trinity.

The Collect.

GRANT, we beseech thee, merciful Lord, to thy faithful people pardon and peace, that they may be cleansed from all their sins, and serve thee with a quiet mind; through Jesus Christ our Lord. *Amen.*

The Epistle. Ephes. vi. 10.

MY brethren, be strong in the Lord, and in the power of his might. Put on the whole armour of God, that ye may be able to stand against the wiles of the devil. For we wrestle not against flesh and blood, but against principalities, against powers, against the rulers of the darkness of this world, against spiritual wickedness in high places. Wherefore take unto you the whole armour of God, that ye may be able to withstand in the evil day, and having done all, to stand. Stand therefore, having your loins girt about with truth, and having on the breastplate of righteousness; and your feet shod with the preparation of the gospel of peace: above all, taking the shield of faith, wherewith ye shall be able to quench all the fiery darts of the wicked. And take the helmet of salvation, and the sword of the Spirit, which is the word of God: praying always with all prayer and supplication in the Spirit, and watching thereunto with all perseverance and supplication for all saints; and for me, that utterance may be given unto me, that I may open my mouth boldly, to make known the mystery of the gospel, for which I am an ambassador in bonds: that therein I may speak boldly, as I ought to speak.

The Gospel. St. John iv. 46.

THERE was a certain nobleman, whose son was sick at Capernaum. When he heard that Jesus was come out of Judæa into Galilee, he went unto him, and besought him that he would come down, and heal his son: for he was at the point of death. Then said Jesus unto him, Except ye see signs and wonders, ye will not believe. The nobleman saith unto him, Sir, come down ere my child die. Jesus saith unto him, Go thy way; thy son liveth. And the man believed the word that Jesus had spoken unto him, and he went his way. And as he was now going down, his servants met him, and told him, saying, Thy son liveth. Then enquired he of them the hour when he began to amend. And they said unto him, Yesterday at the seventh hour the fever left him. So the father knew that it was at the same hour, in the which Jesus said unto him, Thy son liveth: and himself believed, and his whole house. This is again the second miracle that Jesus did, when he was come out of Judæa into Galilee.

The Twenty-second Sunday after Trinity.

The Collect.

LORD, we beseech thee to keep thy household the Church in continual godliness; that through thy protection it may be free from all adversities, and devoutly given to serve thee in good works, to the glory of thy Name; through Jesus Christ our Lord. *Amen.*

The Epistle. Phil. i. 3.

I THANK my God upon every remembrance of you, always in every prayer of mine for you all making request with joy, for your fellowship in the gospel from the first day until now; being confident of this very thing, that he which hath begun a good work in you will perform it until the day of Jesus Christ: even as it is meet for me to think this of you all, because I have you in my heart; inasmuch as both in my bonds, and in the defence and confirmation of the gospel, ye all are partakers of my grace. For God is my record, how greatly I long after you all in the bowels of Jesus Christ. And this I pray, that your love may abound yet more and more in knowledge and in all judgment; that ye may approve things that are excellent; that ye may be sincere and without offence till the day of Christ; being filled with the fruits of righteousness, which are by Jesus Christ, unto the glory and praise of God.

The Gospel. St. Matt. xviii. 21.

PETER said unto Jesus, Lord, how oft shall my brother sin against me, and I forgive him? till seven times? Jesus saith unto him, I say not unto thee, Until seven times: but, Until seventy times seven. Therefore is the kingdom of heaven likened unto a certain king, which would take account of his servants. And when he had begun to reckon, one was brought unto him, which owed him ten thousand talents. But forasmuch as he had not to pay, his lord commanded him to be sold, and his wife, and children, and all that he had, and payment to be made. The servant therefore fell down, and worshipped him, saying, Lord, have patience with me, and I will pay thee all. Then the lord of that servant was moved with compassion, and loosed him, and forgave him the debt. But the same servant went out, and found one of his fellowservants, which owed him an hundred pence: and he laid hands on him, and took him by the throat, saying, Pay me that thou owest. And his fellowservant fell down at his feet, and besought him, saying, Have patience with me, and I will pay thee all. And he would not: but went and cast him into prison, till he should pay the debt. So when his fellowservants saw what was done, they were very sorry, and came and told unto their lord all that was done. Then his lord, after that he had called him, said unto him, O thou wicked servant, I forgave thee all that debt, because thou desiredst me: shouldest not thou also have had compassion on thy fellowservant, even as I had pity

on thee? And his lord was wroth, and delivered him to the tormentors, till he should pay all that was due unto him. So likewise shall my heavenly Father do also unto you, if ye from your hearts forgive not every one his brother their trespasses.

✠

The Twenty-third Sunday after Trinity.

The Collect.

O GOD, our refuge and strength, who art the author of all godliness; Be ready, we beseech thee, to hear the devout prayers of thy Church; and grant that those things which we ask faithfully we may obtain effectually; through Jesus Christ our Lord. *Amen.*

The Epistle. Phil. iii. 17.

BRETHREN, be followers together of me, and mark them which walk so as ye have us for an ensample. (For many walk, of whom I have told you often, and now tell you even weeping, that they are the enemies of the cross of Christ: whose end is destruction, whose God is their belly, and whose glory is in their shame, who mind earthly things.) For our conversation is in heaven; from whence also we look for the Saviour, the Lord Jesus Christ: who shall change our vile body, that it may be fashioned like unto his glorious body, according to the working whereby he is able even to subdue all things unto himself.

The Gospel. St. Matt. xxii. 15.

THEN went the Pharisees, and took counsel how they might entangle him in his talk. And they sent out unto him their disciples with the Herodians, saying, Master, we know that thou art true, and teachest the way of God in truth, neither carest thou for any man: for thou regardest not the person of men. Tell us therefore, What thinkest thou? Is it lawful to give tribute unto Cæsar, or not? But Jesus perceived their wickedness, and said, Why tempt ye me, ye hypocrites? Shew me the tribute money. And they brought unto him a penny. And he saith unto them, Whose is this image and superscription? They

say unto him, Cæsar's. Then saith he unto them, Render therefore unto Cæsar the things which are Cæsar's; and unto God the things that are God's. When they had heard these words, they marvelled, and left him, and went their way.

�֍

The Twenty-fourth Sunday after Trinity.

The Collect.

O LORD, we beseech thee, absolve thy people from their offences; that through thy bountiful goodness we may all be delivered from the bands of those sins, which by our frailty we have committed. Grant this, O heavenly Father, for Jesus Christ's sake, our blessed Lord and Saviour. *Amen.*

The Epistle. Col. i. 3.

WE give thanks to God and the Father of our Lord Jesus Christ, praying always for you, since we heard of your faith in Christ Jesus, and of the love which ye have to all the saints, for the hope which is laid up for you in heaven, whereof ye heard before in the word of the truth of the gospel; which is come unto you, as it is in all the world; and bringeth forth fruit, as it doth also in you, since the day ye heard of it, and knew the grace of God in truth: as ye also learned of Epaphras our dear fellowservant, who is for you a faithful minister of Christ; who also declared unto us your love in the Spirit. For this cause we also, since the day we heard it, do not cease to pray for you, and to desire that ye might be filled with the knowledge of his will in all wisdom and spiritual understanding; that ye might walk worthy of the Lord unto all pleasing, being fruitful in every good work, and increasing in the knowledge of God; strengthened with all might, according to his glorious power, unto all patience and longsuffering with joyfulness; giving thanks unto the Father, which hath made us meet to be partakers of the inheritance of the saints in light.

The Gospel. St. Matt. ix. 18.

WHILE Jesus spake these things unto John's disciples, behold, there came a certain ruler, and worshipped him, saying, My daughter is even now dead: but come and lay thy hand upon her, and she shall live. And Jesus arose, and followed him, and so did his disciples. And, behold, a woman, which was diseased with an issue of blood twelve years, came behind him, and touched the hem of his garment: for she said within herself, If I may but touch his garment, I shall be whole. But Jesus turned him about, and when he saw her, he said, Daughter, be of good comfort; thy faith hath made thee whole. And the woman was made whole from that hour. And when Jesus came into the ruler's house, and saw the minstrels and the people making a noise, he said unto them, Give place: for the maid is not dead, but sleepeth. And they laughed him to scorn. But when the people were put forth, he went in, and took her by the hand, and the maid arose. And the fame hereof went abroad into all that land.

The Sunday next before Advent.

The Collect.

STIR up, we beseech thee, O Lord, the wills of thy faithful people; that they, plenteously bringing forth the fruit of good works, may by thee be plenteously rewarded; through Jesus Christ our Lord. *Amen.*

For the Epistle.
Jer. xxiii. 5.

BEHOLD, the days come, saith the LORD, that I will raise unto David a righteous Branch, and a King shall reign and prosper, and shall execute judgment and justice in the earth. In his days Judah shall be saved, and Israel shall dwell safely: and this is his name whereby he shall be called, THE LORD OUR RIGHTEOUSNESS. Therefore, behold, the days come, saith the LORD, that they shall no more say, The LORD liveth, which brought up the children of Israel out of the land of Egypt; but, The LORD liveth, which brought up and which led the seed of the house of Israel out of the north country, and from all countries whither I had driven them; and they shall dwell in their own land.

The Gospel. St. John vi. 5.

WHEN Jesus then lifted up his eyes, and saw a great company come unto him, he saith unto Philip, Whence shall we buy bread, that these may eat? And this he said to prove him: for he himself knew what he would do. Philip answered him, Two hundred pennyworth of bread is not sufficient for them, that every one of them may take a little. One of his disciples, Andrew, Simon Peter's brother, saith unto him, There is a lad here, which hath five barley loaves, and two small fishes: but what are they among so many? And Jesus said, Make the men sit down. Now there was much grass in the place. So the men sat down, in number about five thousand. And Jesus took the loaves; and when he had given thanks, he distributed to the disciples, and the disciples to them that were set down; and likewise of the fishes as much as they would. When they

*H

were filled, he said unto his disciples, Gather up the fragments that remain, that nothing be lost. Therefore they gathered them together, and filled twelve baskets with the fragments of the five barley loaves, which remained over and above unto them that had eaten. Then those men, when they had seen the miracle that Jesus did, said, This is of a truth that prophet that should come into the world.

If there be more than twenty-five Sundays after Trinity, the service of some of those Sundays that were omitted after the Epiphany shall be taken in to supply so many as are here wanting. And if there be fewer than twenty-five Sundays, the overplus shall be omitted.

Saint Andrew's Day.

The Collect.

ALMIGHTY God, who didst give such grace unto thy holy Apostle Saint Andrew, that he readily obeyed the calling of thy Son Jesus Christ, and followed him without delay; Grant unto us all, that we, being called by thy holy Word, may forth-with give up ourselves obediently to fulfil thy holy commandments; through the same Jesus Christ our Lord. *Amen.*

The Epistle. Rom. x. 9.

IF thou shalt confess with thy mouth the Lord Jesus, and shalt believe in thine heart that God hath raised him from the dead, thou shalt be saved. For with the heart man believeth unto righteousness; and with the mouth confession is made unto salvation. For the scripture saith, Whosoever believeth on him shall not be ashamed. For there is no difference between the Jew and the Greek: for the same Lord over all is rich unto all that call upon him. For whosoever shall call upon the name of the Lord shall be saved. How then shall they call on him in whom they have not believed? and how shall they believe in him of whom they have not heard? and how shall they hear without a preacher? and how shall they preach, except they be sent? as it is written, How beautiful are the feet of them that preach the gospel of peace, and bring glad tidings of good things! But they have not all obeyed the gospel. For Esaias saith, Lord, who hath believed our report? So then faith cometh by hearing, and hearing by the word of God. But I say, Have they not heard? Yes verily, their sound went into all the earth, and their words unto the ends of the world. But I say, Did not Israel know? First Moses saith, I will provoke you to jealousy by them that are no people, and by a foolish nation I will anger you. But Esaias is very bold, and saith, I was found of them that sought me not; I was made manifest unto them that asked not after me. But to Israel he saith, All day long I have stretched forth my hands unto a disobedient and gainsaying people.

The Gospel. St. Matt. iv. 18.

JESUS, walking by the sea of Galilee, saw two brethren, Simon called Peter, and Andrew his brother, casting a net into the sea: for they were fishers. And he saith unto them, Follow me, and I will make you fishers of men. And they straight-

way left their nets, and followed him. And going on from thence, he saw other two brethren, James the son of Zebedee, and John his brother, in a ship with Zebedee their father, mending their nets; and he called them. And they immediately left the ship and their father, and followed him.

Saint Thomas the Apostle.

The Collect.

ALMIGHTY and ever-living God, who, for the greater confirmation of the faith, didst suffer thy holy Apostle Thomas to be doubtful in thy Son's resurrection; Grant us so perfectly, and without all doubt, to believe in thy Son Jesus Christ, that our faith in thy sight may never be reproved. Hear us, O Lord, through the same Jesus Christ, to whom, with thee and the Holy Ghost, be all honour and glory, now and for evermore. *Amen.*

The Epistle. Ephes. ii. 19.

NOW therefore ye are no more strangers and foreigners, but fellowcitizens with the saints, and of the household of God; and are built upon the foundation of the apostles and prophets, Jesus Christ himself being the chief corner stone; in whom all the building fitly framed together groweth unto an holy temple in the Lord: in whom ye also are builded together for an habitation of God through the Spirit.

The Gospel. St. John xx. 24.

THOMAS, one of the twelve, called Didymus, was not with them when Jesus came. The other disciples therefore said unto him, We have seen the Lord. But he said unto them, Except I shall see in his hands the print of the nails, and put my finger into the print of the nails, and thrust my hand into his side, I will not believe. And after eight days again his disciples were within, and Thomas with them: then came Jesus, the doors being shut, and stood in the midst, and said, Peace be unto you. Then saith he to Thomas, Reach hither thy finger, and behold my hands; and reach hither thy hand, and thrust it into my side: and be not faithless, but believing. And Thomas answered and said unto him, My Lord and my God. Jesus saith unto him, Thomas, because thou hast seen me, thou hast believed: blessed are they that have not seen, and yet have believed. And many other signs truly did Jesus in the presence of his disciples, which are not written in this book: but these are written, that ye might believe that Jesus is the Christ, the Son of God; and that believing ye might have life through his name.

❁

The Conversion of Saint Paul.

The Collect.

O GOD, who, through the preaching of the blessed Apostle Saint Paul, hast caused the light of the Gospel to shine throughout the world; Grant, we beseech thee, that we, having his wonderful conversion in remembrance, may shew forth our thankfulness unto thee for the same, by following the holy doctrine which he taught;

through Jesus Christ our Lord. *Amen.*

For the Epistle. Acts ix. 1.

AND Saul, yet breathing out threatenings and slaughter against the disciples of the Lord, went unto the high priest, and desired of him letters to Damascus to the synagogues, that if he found any of this way, whether they were men or women, he might bring them bound unto Jerusalem. And as he journeyed, he came near Damascus: and suddenly there shined round about him a light from heaven: and he fell to the earth, and heard a voice saying unto him, Saul, Saul, why persecutest thou me? And he said, Who art thou, Lord? And the Lord said, I am Jesus whom thou persecutest: it is hard for thee to kick against the pricks. And he trembling and astonished said, Lord, what wilt thou have me to do? And the Lord said unto him, Arise, and go into the city, and it shall be told thee what thou must do. And the men which journeyed with him stood speechless, hearing a voice, but seeing no man. And Saul arose from the earth; and when his eyes were opened, he saw no man: but they led him by the hand, and brought him into Damascus. And he was three days without sight, and neither did eat nor drink. And there was a certain disciple at Damascus, named Ananias; and to him said the Lord in a vision, Ananias. And he said, Behold, I am here, Lord. And the Lord said unto him, Arise, and go into the street which is called Straight, and enquire in the house of Judas for one called Saul, of Tarsus: for, behold, he prayeth, and hath seen in a vision a man named Ananias coming in, and putting his hand on him, that he might receive his sight. Then Ananias answered, Lord, I have heard by many of this man, how much evil he hath done to thy saints at Jerusalem: and here he hath authority from the chief priests to bind all that call on thy name. But the Lord said unto him, Go thy way: for he is a chosen vessel unto me, to bear my name before the Gentiles, and kings, and the children of Israel: for I will shew him how great things he must suffer for my name's sake. And Ananias went his way, and entered into the house; and putting his hands on him said, Brother Saul, the Lord, even Jesus, that appeared unto thee in the way as thou camest, hath sent me, that thou mightest receive thy sight, and be filled with the Holy Ghost. And immediately there fell from his eyes as it had been scales: and he received sight forthwith, and arose, and was baptized. And when he had received meat, he was strengthened. Then was Saul certain days with the disciples which were at Damascus. And straightway he preached Christ in the synagogues, that he is the Son of God. But all that heard him were amazed, and said; Is not this he that destroyed them which called on this name in Jerusalem, and came hither for that intent, that he might bring them bound unto the chief priests? But Saul increased the more in strength, and confounded the Jews which dwelt at Damascus, proving that this is very Christ.

The Gospel. St. Matt. xix. 27.

PETER answered and said unto Jesus, Behold, we have forsaken all, and followed thee; what shall we have therefore? And Jesus said unto them, Verily I say unto you, That ye which have followed me, in the regeneration when the Son of man shall sit in the throne of his glory, ye also shall sit upon twelve thrones, judging the twelve tribes of Israel. And every one that hath forsaken houses, or brethren, or sisters, or father, or mother, or wife, or children, or lands, for my name's sake, shall receive an hundredfold, and shall inherit everlasting life. But many that are first shall be last; and the last shall be first.

✠

The Presentation of Christ in the Temple, commonly called The Purification of Saint Mary the Virgin.

The Collect.

ALMIGHTY and everliving God, we humbly beseech thy Majesty, that, as thy only-begotten Son was this day presented in the temple in substance of our flesh, so we may be presented unto thee with pure and clean hearts, by the same thy Son Jesus Christ our Lord. *Amen.*

For the Epistle. Mal. iii. 1.

BEHOLD, I will send my messenger, and he shall prepare the way before me: and the Lord, whom ye seek, shall suddenly come to his temple, even the messenger of the covenant, whom ye delight in: behold, he shall come, saith the LORD of hosts. But who may abide the day of his coming? and who shall stand when he appeareth? for he is like a refiner's fire, and like fullers' sope: and he shall sit as a refiner and purifier of silver: and he shall purify the sons of Levi, and purge them as gold and silver, that they may offer unto the LORD an offering in righteousness. Then shall the offering of Judah and Jerusalem be pleasant unto the LORD, as in the days of old, and as in former years. And I will come near to you to judgment; and I will be a swift witness against the sorcerers, and against the adulterers, and against false swearers, and against those that oppress the hireling in his wages, the widow, and the fatherless, and that turn aside the stranger from his right, and fear not me, saith the LORD of hosts.

The Gospel. St. Luke ii. 22.

AND when the days of her purification according to the law of Moses were accomplished, they brought him to Jerusalem, to present him to the Lord; (as it is written in the law of the Lord, Every male that openeth the womb shall be called holy to the Lord;) and to offer a sacrifice according to that which is said in the law of the Lord, A pair of turtle-doves, or two young pigeons. And, behold, there was a man in Jerusalem, whose name was Simeon; and the same man was just and devout, waiting for the consolation of Israel: and the Holy Ghost was upon him. And it was revealed unto him by the Holy Ghost, that he should not see death, before he had seen the Lord's Christ. And he came by the Spirit into the temple: and when the parents brought in the child Jesus, to do for him after the custom of the law, then took he him up in his arms, and blessed God, and said, Lord, now lettest thou thy servant depart in peace, according to thy word: for mine eyes have seen thy salvation, which thou hast prepared before the face of all people; a light to lighten the Gentiles, and the glory of thy people Israel. And Joseph and his mother marvelled at those things which were spoken of him. And Simeon blessed them, and said unto Mary his mother, Behold, this child is set for the fall and rising again of many in Israel; and for a sign which shall be spoken against; (yea, a sword shall pierce through thy own soul also,) that the thoughts of many hearts may be revealed. And there was one Anna, a prophetess, the daughter of Phanuel, of the tribe of Aser: she was of a great age, and had lived with an husband seven years from her virginity; and she was a widow of about fourscore and four years, which departed not from the temple, but served God with fastings

and prayers night and day. And she coming in that instant gave thanks likewise unto the Lord, and spake of him to all them that looked for redemption in Jerusalem. And when they had performed all things according to the law of the Lord, they returned into Galilee, to their own city Nazareth. And the child grew, and waxed strong in spirit, filled with wisdom: and the grace of God was upon him.

Saint Matthias's Day.

The Collect.

O ALMIGHTY God, who into the place of the traitor Judas didst choose thy faithful servant Matthias to be of the number of the twelve Apostles; Grant that thy Church, being alway preserved from false Apostles, may be ordered and guided by faithful and true pastors; through Jesus Christ our Lord. *Amen.*

For the Epistle. Acts i. 15.

IN those days Peter stood up in the midst of the disciples, and said, (the number of names together were about an hundred and twenty,] Men and brethren, this scripture must needs have been fulfilled, which the Holy Ghost by the mouth of David spake before concerning Judas, which was guide to them that took Jesus. For he was numbered with us, and had obtained part of this ministry. Now this man purchased a field with the reward of iniquity; and falling headlong, he burst asunder in the midst, and all his bowels gushed out. And it was known unto all the dwellers at Jerusalem; insomuch as that field is called in their proper tongue, Aceldama, that is to say, The field of blood. For it is written in the book of Psalms, Let his habitation be desolate, and let no man dwell therein: and his bishoprick let another take. Wherefore of these men which have companied with us all the time that the Lord Jesus went in and out among us, beginning from the baptism of John, unto that same day that he was taken up from us, must one be ordained to be a witness with us of his resurrection.

And they appointed two, Joseph called Barsabas, who was surnamed Justus, and Matthias. And they prayed, and said, Thou, Lord, which knowest the hearts of all men, shew whether of these two thou hast chosen, that he may take part of this ministry and apostleship, from which Judas by transgression fell, that he might go to his own place. And they gave forth their lots; and the lot fell upon Matthias; and he was numbered with the eleven apostles.

The Gospel. St. Matt. xi. 25.

AT that time Jesus answered and said, I thank thee, O Father, Lord of heaven and earth, because thou hast hid these things from the wise and prudent, and hast revealed them unto babes. Even so, Father: for so it seemed good in thy sight. All things are delivered unto me of my Father: and no man knoweth the Son, but the Father; neither knoweth any man the Father, save the Son, and he to whomsoever the Son will reveal him. Come unto me, all ye that labour and are heavy laden, and

I will give you rest. Take my yoke upon you, and learn of me: for I am meek and lowly in heart: and ye shall find rest unto your souls. For my yoke is easy, and my burden is light.

✤

The Annunciation of the blessed Virgin Mary.

The Collect.

WE beseech thee, O Lord, pour thy grace into our hearts; that, as we have known the incarnation of thy Son Jesus Christ by the message of an Angel, so by his cross and passion we may be brought unto the glory of his resurrection; through the same Jesus Christ our Lord. *Amen.*

For the Epistle. Isa. vii. 10.

MOREOVER the LORD spake again unto Ahaz, saying, Ask thee a sign of the LORD thy God; ask it either in the depth, or in the height above. But Ahaz said, I will not ask, neither will I tempt the LORD. And he said, Hear ye now, O house of David; Is it a small thing for you to weary men, but will ye weary my God

also? Therefore the Lord himself shall give you a sign; Behold, a virgin shall conceive, and bear a son, and shall call his name Immanuel. Butter and honey shall he eat, that he may know to refuse the evil, and to choose the good.

The Gospel. St. Luke i. 26.

AND in the sixth month the angel Gabriel was sent from God unto a city of Galilee, named Nazareth, to a virgin espoused to a man whose name was Joseph, of the house of David; and the virgin's name was Mary. And the angel came in unto her, and said, Hail, thou that art highly favoured, the Lord is with thee: blessed art thou among women. And when she saw him, she was troubled at his saying, and cast in her mind what manner of salutation this should be. And the angel said unto her, Fear not, Mary: for thou hast found favour with God. And, behold, thou shalt conceive in thy womb, and bring forth a son, and shalt call his name JESUS. He shall be great, and shall be called the Son of the Highest: and the Lord God shall give unto him the throne of his father David: and he shall reign over the house of Jacob for ever; and of his kingdom there shall be no end. Then said Mary unto the angel, How shall this be, seeing I know not a man? And the angel answered and said unto her, The Holy Ghost shall come upon thee, and the power of the Highest shall overshadow thee: therefore also that holy thing which shall be born of thee shall be called the Son of God. And, behold, thy cousin Elisabeth, she hath also conceived a son in her old age: and this is the sixth month with her, who was called barren. For with God nothing shall be impossible. And Mary said, Behold the handmaid of the Lord; be it unto me according to thy word. And the angel departed from her.

❧

Saint Mark's Day.

The Collect.

O ALMIGHTY God, who hast instructed thy holy Church with the heavenly doctrine of thy Evangelist Saint Mark; Give us grace that, being not like children carried away with every blast of vain doctrine, we may be established in the truth of thy holy Gospel; through Jesus Christ our Lord. *Amen.*

The Epistle. Ephes. iv. 7.

U NTO every one of us is given grace according to the measure of the gift of Christ. Wherefore he saith, When he ascended up on high, he led captivity captive, and gave gifts unto men. (Now that he ascended, what is it but that he also descended first into the lower parts of the earth? He that descended is the same also that ascended up far above all heavens, that he might fill all things.) And he gave some, apostles; and some, prophets; and some, evangelists; and some, pastors and teachers; for the perfecting of the saints, for the work of the ministry, for the edifying of the body of Christ: till we all come in the unity of the faith, and of the knowledge of the Son of God, unto a perfect man, unto the measure of the stature of the fulness of Christ: that we henceforth be no more children, tossed to and fro, and carried about with every wind of doctrine, by the sleight of men, and cunning craftiness, whereby they lie in wait to deceive; but speaking the truth in love, may grow up into him in all things, which is the head, even Christ: from whom the whole body fitly joined together and compacted by that which every joint supplieth, according to the effectual working in the measure of every part, maketh increase of the body unto the edifying of itself in love.

The Gospel. St. John xv. 1.

I AM the true vine, and my Father is the husbandman. Every branch in me that beareth not fruit he taketh away: and every branch that beareth fruit, he purgeth it, that it may bring forth more fruit. Now ye are clean through the word which I have spoken unto you. Abide in me, and I in you. As the branch cannot bear fruit of itself, except it abide in the vine; no more can ye, except ye abide in me. I am the vine, ye are the branches: He that abideth in me, and I in him, the same bringeth forth much fruit: for without me ye can do nothing. If a man abide not in me, he is cast forth as a branch, and is withered; and men gather them, and cast them into the fire, and they are burned. If ye abide in me, and my words abide in you, ye shall ask what ye will, and it shall be done unto you. Herein is my Father glorified, that ye bear much fruit; so shall ye be my disciples. As the Father hath loved me, so have I loved you: continue ye in my love. If ye keep my commandments, ye shall abide in my love; even as I have kept my Father's commandments, and abide in his love. These things have I spoken unto you, that my joy might remain in you, and that your joy might be full.

❀

Saint Philip and Saint James's Day.

The Collect.

O ALMIGHTY God, whom truly to know

is everlasting life; Grant us perfectly to know thy Son Jesus Christ to be the way, the truth, and the life; that, following the steps of thy holy Apostles, Saint Philip and Saint James, we may stedfastly walk in the way that leadeth to eternal life; through the same thy Son Jesus Christ our Lord. Amen.

The Epistle. St. James i. 1.

JAMES, a servant of God and of the Lord Jesus Christ, to the twelve tribes which are scattered abroad, greeting. My brethren, count it all joy when ye fall into divers temptations; knowing this, that the trying of your faith worketh patience. But let patience have her perfect work, that ye may be perfect and entire, wanting nothing. If any of you lack wisdom, let him ask of God, that giveth to all men liberally, and upbraideth not; and it shall be given him. But let him ask in faith, nothing wavering. For he that wavereth is like a wave of the sea driven with the wind and tossed. For let not that man think that he shall receive any thing of the Lord. A double minded man is unstable in all his ways. Let the brother of low degree rejoice in that he is exalted: but the rich, in that he is made low: because as the flower of the grass he shall pass away. For the sun is no sooner risen with a burning heat, but it withereth the grass, and the flower thereof falleth, and the grace of the fashion of it perisheth: so also shall the rich man fade away in his ways. Blessed is the man that endureth temptation: for when he is tried, he shall receive the crown of life, which the Lord hath promised to them that love him.

The Gospel. St. John xiv. 1.

AND Jesus said unto his disciples, Let not your heart be troubled: ye believe in God, believe also in me. In my Father's house are many mansions: if it were not so, I would have told you. I go to prepare a place for you. And if I go and prepare a place for you, I will come again, and receive you unto myself;

that where I am, there ye may be also. And whither I go ye know, and the way ye know. Thomas saith unto him, Lord, we know not whither thou goest; and how can we know the way? Jesus saith unto him, I am the way, the truth, and the life: no man cometh unto the Father, but by me. If ye had known me, ye should have known my Father also: and from henceforth ye know him, and have seen him. Philip saith unto him, Lord, shew us the Father, and it sufficeth us. Jesus saith unto him, Have I been so long time with you, and yet hast thou not known me, Philip? he that hath seen me hath seen the Father; and how sayest thou then, Shew us the Father? Believest thou not that I am in the Father, and the Father in me? the words that I speak unto you I speak not of myself: but the Father that dwelleth in me, he doeth the works. Believe me that I am in the Father, and the Father in me: or else believe me for the very works' sake. Verily, verily, I say unto you, He that

believeth on me, the works that I do shall he do also; and greater works than these shall he do; because I go unto my Father. And whatsoever ye shall ask in my name, that will I do, that the Father may be glorified in the Son. If ye shall ask any thing in my name, I will do it.

❊

Saint Barnabas the Apostle.

The Collect.

O LORD God Almighty, who didst endue thy holy Apostle Barnabas with singular gifts of the Holy Ghost; Leave us not, we beseech thee, destitute of thy manifold gifts, nor yet of grace to use them alway to thy honour and glory; through Jesus Christ our Lord. *Amen.*

For the Epistle. Acts xi. 22.

TIDINGS of these things came unto the ears of the church which was in Jerusalem: and they sent forth Barnabas, that he should go as far as Antioch. Who, when he came, and had seen the grace of God, was glad, and exhorted them all, that with purpose of heart they would cleave unto the Lord. For he was a good man, and full of the Holy Ghost and of faith: and much people was added unto the Lord. Then departed Barnabas to Tarsus, for to seek Saul: and when he had found him, he brought him unto Antioch. And it came to pass, that a whole year they assembled themselves with the church, and taught much people. And the disciples were called Christians first in Antioch. And in these days came prophets from Jerusalem unto Antioch. And there stood up one of them named Agabus, and signified by the spirit that there should be great dearth throughout all the world: which came to pass in the days of Claudius Cæsar. Then the disciples, every man according to his ability, determined to send relief unto the brethren which dwelt in Judæa: which also they did, and sent it to the elders by the hands of Barnabas and Saul.

The Gospel. St. John xv. 12.

THIS is my commandment, That ye love one another, as I have loved you. Greater love hath no man than this, that a man lay down his life for his friends. Ye are my friends, if ye do whatsoever I command you. Henceforth I call you not servants; for the servant knoweth not what his lord doeth: but I have called you friends; for all things that I have heard of my Father I have made known unto you. Ye have not chosen me, but I have chosen you, and ordained you, that ye should go and bring forth fruit, and that your fruit should remain: that whatsoever ye shall ask of the Father in my name, he may give it you.

✠

Saint John Baptist's Day.

The Collect.

ALMIGHTY God, by whose providence thy servant John Baptist was wonderfully born, and sent to prepare the way of thy Son our Saviour by preaching repentance; Make us so to follow his doctrine and holy life, that we may truly repent according to his preaching; and after his example constantly speak the truth, boldly rebuke vice, and patiently suffer for the truth's sake; through Jesus Christ our Lord. *Amen.*

For the Epistle. Isa. xl. 1.

COMFORT ye, comfort ye my people, saith your God. Speak ye comfortably to Jerusalem, and cry unto her, that her warfare is accomplished, that her iniquity is pardoned: for she hath received of the LORD's hand double for all her sins. The voice of him that crieth in the wilderness, Prepare ye the way of the LORD, make straight in the desert a highway for our God. Every valley shall be exalted, and every mountain and hill shall be made low: and the crooked shall be made straight, and the rough places plain: and the glory of the LORD shall be revealed, and all flesh shall see it together: for the mouth of the LORD hath spoken it. The voice said, Cry. And he said, What shall I cry? All flesh is grass, and all the goodliness thereof is as the flower

of the field: the grass withereth, the flower fadeth: because the spirit of the LORD bloweth upon it: surely the people is grass. The grass withereth, the flower fadeth: but the word of our God shall stand for ever. O Zion, that bringest good tidings, get thee up into the high mountain; O Jerusalem, that bringest good tidings, lift up thy voice with strength; lift it up, be not afraid; say unto the cities of Judah, Behold your God! Behold, the Lord GOD will come with strong hand, and his arm shall rule for him: behold, his reward is with him, and his work before him. He shall feed his flock like a shepherd: he shall gather the lambs with his arm, and carry them in his bosom, and shall gently lead those that are with young.

The Gospel. St. Luke i. 57.

ELISABETH'S full time came that she should be delivered; and she brought forth a son. And her neighbours and her cousins heard how the Lord had shewed great mercy upon her; and they rejoiced with her. And it came to pass, that on the eighth day they came to circumcise the child; and they called him Zacharias, after the name of his father. And his mother answered and said, Not so; but he shall be called John. And they said unto her, There is none of thy kindred that is called by this name. And they made signs to his father, how he would have him called. And he asked for a writing table, and wrote, saying, His name is John. And they marvelled all. And his mouth was opened immediately, and his tongue loosed, and he spake, and praised God. And fear came on all that dwelt round about them: and all these sayings were noised abroad throughout all the hill country of Judæa. And all they that heard them laid them up in their hearts, saying, What manner of child shall this be! And the hand of the Lord was with him. And his father Zacharias was filled with the Holy Ghost, and prophesied, saying, Blessed be the Lord God of Israel; for he hath visited and redeemed his people, and hath raised up an horn of salvation for us in the house of his servant David; as he spake by the mouth of his holy prophets, which have been since the world began: that we should be saved from our enemies, and from the hand of all that hate us; to perform the mercy promised to our fathers, and to remember his holy covenant; the oath which he sware to our father Abraham, that he would grant unto us, that we being delivered out of the hand of our enemies might serve him without fear, in holiness and righteousness before him, all the days of our life. And thou, child, shalt be called the prophet of the Highest: for thou shalt go before the face of the Lord to prepare his ways; to give knowledge of salvation unto his people by the remission of their sins, through the tender mercy of our God; whereby the dayspring from on high hath visited us, to give light to them that sit in darkness and in the shadow of death, to guide our feet into the way of peace. And the child grew, and waxed strong in spirit, and was in the deserts till the day of his shewing unto Israel.

✦

Saint Peter's Day.

The Collect.

O ALMIGHTY God, who by thy Son Jesus Christ didst give to thy Apostle Saint Peter many excellent gifts, and commandedst him earnestly to feed thy flock ; Make, we beseech thee, all Bishops and Pastors diligently to preach thy holy Word, and the people obediently to follow the same, that they may receive the crown of everlasting glory ; through Jesus Christ our Lord. *Amen.*

For the Epistle. Acts xii. 1.

ABOUT that time Herod the king stretched forth his hands to vex certain of the church. And he killed James the brother of John with the sword. And because he saw it pleased the Jews, he proceeded further to take Peter also. (Then were the days of unleavened bread.) And when he had apprehended him, he put him in prison, and delivered him to four quaternions of soldiers to keep him ; intending after Easter to bring him forth to the people. Peter therefore was kept in prison : but prayer was made without ceasing of the church unto God for him. And when Herod would have brought him forth, the same night Peter was sleeping between two soldiers, bound with two chains : and the keepers before the door kept the prison. And, behold, the angel of the Lord came upon him, and a light shined in the prison : and he smote Peter on the side, and raised him up, saying, Arise up quickly. And his chains fell off from his hands. And the angel said unto him, Gird thyself, and bind on thy sandals. And so he did. And he saith unto him, Cast thy garment about thee, and follow me. And he went out, and followed him ; and wist not that it was true which was done by the angel ; but thought he saw a vision. When they were past the first and the second ward, they came unto the iron gate that leadeth unto the city; which opened to them of his own accord: and they went out, and passed on through one street; and forthwith the angel departed from him. And when Peter was come to himself, he said, Now I know of a surety, that the Lord hath sent his angel, and hath delivered me out of the hand of Herod, and from all the expectation of the people of the Jews. ✠

The Gospel. St. Matt. xvi. 13.

WHEN Jesus came into the coasts of Cæsarea Philippi, he asked his disciples, saying, Whom do men say that I the Son of man am? And they said, Some say that thou art John the Baptist: some, Elias; and others, Jeremias, or one of the prophets. He saith unto them, But whom say ye that I am? And Simon Peter answered and said, Thou art the Christ, the Son of the living God. And Jesus answered and said unto him, Blessed art thou, Simon Bar-jona: for flesh and blood hath not revealed it unto thee, but my Father which is in heaven. And I say also unto thee, That thou art Peter, and upon this rock I will build my church: and the gates of hell shall not prevail against it. And I will give unto thee the keys of the kingdom of heaven: and whatsoever thou shalt bind on earth shall be bound in heaven: and whatsoever thou shalt loose on earth shall be loosed in heaven.

✠

Saint James the Apostle.

The Collect.

GRANT, O merciful God, that, as thine holy Apostle Saint James, leaving his father and all that he had, without delay was obedient unto the calling of thy Son Jesus Christ, and followed him; so we, forsaking all worldly and carnal affections, may be evermore ready to follow thy holy commandments; through Jesus Christ our Lord. *Amen.*

For the Epistle. Acts xi. 27,
and part of chap. xii.

IN these days came pro-
phets from Jerusalem
unto Antioch. And there
stood up one of them
named Agabus, and sig-
nified by the spirit that
there should be great
dearth throughout all
the world: which came
to pass in the days of
Claudius Cæsar. Then
the disciples, every man
according to his ability,
determined to send relief
unto the brethren which
dwelt in Judæa: which
also they did, and sent it
to the elders by the hands
of Barnabas and Saul.
Now about that time He-
rod the king stretched
forth his hands to vex
certain of the church.
And he killed James the
brother of John with the
sword. And because he
saw it pleased the Jews,
he proceeded further to
take Peter also.

The Gospel. St. Matt. xx. 20.

THEN came to him the
mother of Zebedee's
children with her sons,
worshipping him, and de-
siring a certain thing of
him. And he said unto

her, What wilt thou? She
saith unto him, Grant that
these my two sons may
sit, the one on thy right
hand, and the other on
the left, in thy kingdom.
But Jesus answered and
said, Ye know not what
ye ask. Are ye able to
drink of the cup that I
shall drink of, and to be
baptized with the baptism
that I am baptized with?
They say unto him, We
are able. And he saith
unto them, Ye shall drink
indeed of my cup, and be
baptized with the baptism
that I am baptized with:
but to sit on my right
hand, and on my left, is
not mine to give, but it
shall be given to them
for whom it is prepared
of my Father. And when
the ten heard it, they were
moved with indignation
against the two brethren.
But Jesus called them
unto him, and said, Ye
know that the princes of
the Gentiles exercise do-
minion over them, and
they that are great exer-
cise authority upon them.
But it shall not be so a-
mong you: but whosoever
will be great among you,
let him be your minister;
and whosoever will be

chief among you, let him be your servant: even as the Son of man came not to be ministered unto, but to minister, and to give his life a ransom for many.

✠

The Transfiguration of Christ.

The Collect.

O GOD, who on the mount didst reveal to chosen witnesses thine only-begotten Son wonderfully transfigured, in raiment white and glistering; Mercifully grant that we, being delivered from the disquietude of this world, may be permitted to behold the King in his beauty, who with thee, O Father, and thee, O Holy Ghost, liveth and reigneth, one God, world without end. *Amen.*

The Epistle. 2 St. Pet. i. 13.

I THINK it meet, as long as I am in this tabernacle, to stir you up by putting you in remembrance; knowing that shortly I must put off this my tabernacle, even as our Lord Jesus Christ hath shewed me. Moreover I will endeavour that ye may be able after my decease to have these things always in remembrance. For we have not followed cunningly devised fables, when we made known unto you the power and coming of our Lord Jesus Christ, but were eye-witnesses of his majesty. For he received from God the Father honour and glory, when there came such a voice to him from the excellent glory, This is my beloved Son, in whom I am well pleased. And this voice which came from heaven we heard, when we were with him in the holy mount.

The Gospel. St. Luke ix. 28.

A ND it came to pass about an eight days after these sayings, he took Peter and John and James, and went up into a mountain to pray. And as he prayed, the fashion of his countenance was altered, and his raiment was white and glistering. And, behold, there talked with him two men, which were Moses and Elias: who appeared in glory, and spake of his decease which he should accomplish at Jerusalem. But Peter and they that were with him were heavy with sleep: and when they were awake, they saw his glory, and the two men that stood with him. And it came to pass, as they departed from him, Peter said unto Jesus, Master, it is good for us to be here: and let us make three tabernacles; one for thee, and one for Moses, and one for Elias: not knowing what he said. While he thus spake, there came a cloud, and overshadowed them: and they feared as they entered into the cloud. And there came a voice out of the cloud, saying, This is my beloved Son: hear him. And when the voice was past, Jesus was found alone. And they kept it close, and told no man in those days any of those things which they had seen.

❦

Saint Bartholomew the Apostle.

The Collect.

O ALMIGHTY and everlasting God, who didst give to thine Apostle Bartholomew grace truly to believe and to preach thy Word ;. Grant, we beseech thee, unto thy Church, to love that Word which he believed, and both to preach and receive the same ; through Jesus Christ our Lord. *Amen.*

For the Epistle. Acts v. 12.

BY the hands of the apostles were many signs and wonders wrought among the people; (and they were all with one accord in Solomon's porch. And of the rest durst no man join himself to them: but the people magnified them. And believers were the more added to the Lord, multitudes both of men and women.) Insomuch that they brought forth the sick into the streets, and laid them on beds and couches, that at the least the shadow of Peter passing by might overshadow some of them. There came also a multitude out of the cities round about unto Jerusalem, bringing sick folks, and them which were vexed with unclean spirits : and they were healed every one.

The Gospel. St. Luke xxii. 24.

AND there was also a strife among them, which of them should be accounted the greatest. And he said unto them, The kings of the Gentiles exercise lordship over them; and they that exercise authority upon them are called benefactors. But ye shall not be so: but he that is greatest among you, let him be as the younger; and he that is chief, as he that doth serve. For whether is greater, he that sitteth at meat, or he that serveth? is not he that sitteth at meat? but I am among you as he that serveth. Ye are they which have continued with me in my temptations. And I appoint unto you a kingdom, as my Father hath appointed unto me; that ye may eat and drink at my table in my kingdom, and sit on thrones judging the twelve tribes of Israel.

✠

Saint Matthew the Apostle.

The Collect.

O ALMIGHTY God, who by thy blessed Son didst call Matthew from the receipt of custom to be an Apostle and Evangelist; Grant us grace to forsake all covetous desires, and inordinate love of riches, and to follow the same thy Son Jesus Christ, who liveth and reigneth with thee and the Holy Ghost, one God, world without end. *Amen.*

The Epistle. 2 Cor. iv. 1.

THEREFORE seeing we have this ministry, as we have received mercy, we faint not; but have renounced the hidden things of dishonesty, not walking in craftiness, nor handling the word of God deceitfully; but by manifestation of the truth commending ourselves to every man's conscience in the sight of God. But if our gospel be hid, it is hid to them that are lost: in whom the god of this world hath blinded the minds of them which believe not, lest the light of the glorious gospel of Christ, who is the image of God, should shine unto them. For we preach not ourselves, but Christ Jesus the Lord; and ourselves your servants for Jesus' sake. For God, who commanded the light to shine out of darkness, hath shined in our hearts, to give the light of the knowledge of the glory of God in the face of Jesus Christ.

The Gospel. St. Matt. ix. 9.

AND as Jesus passed forth from thence, he saw a man, named Matthew, sitting at the receipt of custom: and he saith unto him, Follow me. And he arose, and followed him. And it came to pass, as Jesus sat at meat in the house, behold, many publicans and sinners came and sat down with him and his disciples. And when the Pharisees saw it, they said unto his disciples, Why eateth your Master with publicans and sinners? But when Jesus heard that, he said unto them, They that be whole need not a physician, but they that are sick. But go ye and learn what that meaneth, I will have mercy, and not sacrifice: for I am not come to call the righteous, but sinners to repentance.

✤

Saint Michael and all Angels.

The Collect.

OEVERLASTING God, who hast ordained and constituted the services of Angels and men in a wonderful order; Mercifully grant that, as thy holy Angels always do thee service in heaven, so, by thy appointment, they may succour and defend us on earth; through Jesus Christ our Lord. *Amen.*

For the Epistle. Rev. xii. 7.

THERE was war in heaven: Michael and his angels fought against the dragon; and the dragon fought and his angels, and prevailed not; neither was their place found any more in heaven. And the great dragon was cast out, that old serpent, called the Devil, and Satan, which deceiveth the whole world: he was cast out into the earth, and his angels were cast out with him. And I heard a loud voice saying in heaven, Now is come salvation, and strength, and the kingdom of our God, *and the power of* his Christ: for the accuser of our brethren is cast down, which accused them before our God day and night. And they overcame him by the blood of the Lamb, and by the word of their testimony; and they loved not their lives unto the death. Therefore rejoice, ye heavens, and ye that dwell in them. Woe to the inhabiters of the earth and of the sea! for the devil is come down unto you, having great wrath, because he knoweth that he hath but a short time.

The Gospel. St. Matt. xviii. 1.

AT the same time came the disciples unto Jesus, saying, Who is the greatest in the kingdom of heaven? And Jesus called a little child unto him, and set him in the midst of them, and said, Verily I say unto you, Except ye be converted, and become as little children, ye shall not enter into the kingdom of heaven. Whosoever therefore shall humble himself as this little child, the same is greatest in the kingdom of heaven. And whoso shall receive one such little child in my name receiveth me. But whoso shall offend one of these little ones which believe in me, it were better for him that a millstone were hanged about his neck, and that he were drowned in the depth of the sea. Woe unto the world because of offences! for it must needs be that offences come; but woe to that man by whom the offence cometh! Wherefore if thy hand or thy foot offend thee, cut them off, and cast them from thee: it is better for thee to enter into life halt or maimed, rather than having two hands or two feet to be cast into everlasting fire. And if thine eye offend thee, pluck it out, and cast it from thee: it is better for thee to enter into life with one eye, rather than having two eyes to be cast into hell fire. Take heed that ye despise not one of these little ones; for I say unto you, That in heaven their angels do always behold the face of my Father which is in heaven.

❋

Saint Luke the Evangelist.

The Collect.

ALMIGHTY God, who calledst Luke the Physician, whose praise is in the Gospel, to be an Evangelist, and Physician of the soul; May it please thee that, by the whole-some medicines of the doctrine delivered by him, all the diseases of our souls may be healed; through the merits of thy Son Jesus Christ our Lord. Amen.

The Epistle. 2 Tim. iv. 5.

WATCH thou in all things, endure afflictions, do the work of an evangelist, make full proof of thy ministry. For I am now ready to be offered, and the time of my departure is at hand. I have fought a good fight, I have finished my course, I have kept the faith: henceforth there is laid up for me a crown of righteousness, which the Lord, the righteous judge, shall give me at that day: and not to me only, but unto all them also that love his appearing. Do thy diligence to come shortly unto me: for Demas hath forsaken me, having loved this present world, and is departed unto Thessalonica; Crescens to Galatia, Titus unto Dalmatia. Only Luke is with me. Take Mark, and bring him with thee: for he is profitable to me for the ministry. And Tychicus have I sent to Ephesus.

The cloke that I left at Troas with Carpus, when thou comest, bring with thee, and the books, but especially the parchments. Alexander the coppersmith did me much evil: the Lord reward him according to his works: of whom be thou ware also; for he hath greatly withstood our words.

The Gospel. St. Luke x. 1.

THE Lord appointed other seventy also, and sent them two and two before his face into every city and place, whither he himself would come. Therefore said he unto them, The harvest truly is great, but the labourers are few: pray ye therefore the Lord of the harvest, that he would send forth labourers into his harvest. Go your ways: behold, I send you forth as lambs among wolves. Carry neither purse, nor scrip, nor shoes: and salute no man by the way. And into whatsoever house ye enter, first say, Peace be to this house. And if the son of peace be there, your peace shall rest upon it: if not, it shall turn to you again. And in the same house remain, eating and drinking such things as they give: for the labourer is worthy of his hire.

Saint Simon and Saint Jude, Apostles.

The Collect.

O ALMIGHTY God, who hast built thy Church upon the foundation of the Apostles and Prophets, Jesus Christ himself being the head corner-stone; Grant us so to be joined together in unity of spirit by their doctrine, that we may be *made an holy temple* acceptable unto thee; through Jesus Christ our Lord. *Amen.*

The Epistle. St. Jude 1.

JUDE, the servant of Jesus Christ, and brother of James, to them that are sanctified by God the Father, and preserved in Jesus Christ, and called: Mercy unto you, and peace, and love, be multiplied. Beloved, when I gave all diligence to write unto you of the common salvation, it was needful for me to write unto you, and exhort you that ye should earnestly contend for the faith which was once delivered unto the saints. For there are certain men crept in unawares, who were before of old ordained to this condemnation, ungodly men, turning the grace of our God into lasciviousness, and denying the only Lord God, and our Lord Jesus Christ. I will therefore put you in remembrance, though ye once knew this, how that the Lord, having saved the people out of the land of Egypt, afterward destroyed them that believed not. And the angels which kept not their first estate, but left their own habitation, he hath reserved in everlasting chains under darkness unto the judgment of the great day. Even as Sodom and Gomorrha, and the cities about them in like manner, giving themselves over to fornication, and going after strange flesh, are set forth for an example, suffering the vengeance of eternal fire. Likewise also these filthy dreamers defile the flesh, despise dominion, and speak evil of dignities.

The Gospel. St. John xv. 17.

THESE things I command you, that ye love one another. If the world hate you, ye know that it hated me before it hated you. If ye were of the world, the world would love his own: but because ye are not of the world, but I have chosen you out of the world, therefore the world hateth you. Remember the word that I said unto you, The servant is not greater than his lord. If they have persecuted me, they will also persecute you; if they have kept my saying, they will keep your's also. But all these things will they do unto you for my name's sake, because they know not him that sent me. If I had not come and spoken unto them, they had not had sin: but now they have no cloke for their sin. He that hateth me hateth my Father also. If I had not done among them the works which none other man did, they had not had sin: but now have they both seen and hated both me and my Father. But this cometh to pass, that the word might be fulfilled that is written in their law, They hated me without a cause. But when the Comforter is come, whom I will send unto you from the Father, even the Spirit of truth, which proceedeth from the Father, he shall testify of me: and ye also shall bear witness, because ye have been with me from the beginning.

☙

All Saints' Day.

The Collect.

O ALMIGHTY God, who hast knit together thine elect in one communion and fellowship, in the mystical body of thy Son Christ our Lord; Grant us grace so to follow thy blessed Saints in all virtuous and godly living, that we may come to those unspeakable joys which thou hast prepared for those who unfeignedly love thee; through Jesus Christ our Lord. A*men.*

For the Epistle. Rev. vii. 2.

AND I saw another angel ascending from the east, having the seal of the living God: and he cried with a loud voice to the four angels, to whom it was given to hurt the earth and the sea, saying, Hurt not the earth, neither the sea, nor the trees, till we have sealed the servants of our God in their foreheads. And I heard the number of them which were sealed: and there were sealed an hundred and forty and four thousand of all the tribes of the children of Israel.

Of the tribe of Juda were sealed twelve thousand. Of the tribe of Reuben were sealed twelve thousand. Of the tribe of Gad were sealed twelve thousand. Of the tribe of Aser were sealed twelve thousand. Of the tribe of Nepthalim were sealed twelve thousand. Of the tribe of Manasses were sealed twelve thousand. Of the tribe of Simeon were sealed twelve thousand. Of the tribe of Levi were sealed twelve thousand. Of the tribe of Issachar were sealed twelve thousand. Of the tribe of Zabulon were sealed twelve thousand. Of the tribe of Joseph were sealed twelve thousand. Of the tribe of Benjamin were sealed twelve thousand.

After this I beheld, and, lo, a great multitude, which no man could number, of all nations, and kindreds, and people, and tongues, stood before the throne, and before the Lamb, clothed with white robes, and palms in their hands; and cried with a loud voice, saying, Salvation to our God which sitteth upon the throne, and unto the Lamb. And all the angels stood round about the throne, and about the elders and the four beasts, and fell before the throne on their faces, and worshipped God, saying, Amen: Blessing, and glory, and wisdom, and thanksgiving, and honour, and power, and might, be unto our God for ever and ever. Amen.

The Gospel. St. Matt. v. 1.

JESUS seeing the multitudes, went up into a mountain: and when he was set, his disciples came unto him: and he opened his mouth, and taught them, saying, Blessed are the poor in spirit: for their's is the kingdom of heaven. Blessed are they that mourn: for they shall be comforted. Blessed are the meek : for they shall inherit the earth. Blessed are they which do hunger and thirst after righteousness : for they shall be filled. Blessed are the merciful : for they shall obtain mercy. Blessed are the pure in heart : for they shall see God. Blessed are the peacemakers : for they shall be called the children of God. Blessed are they which are persecuted for righteousness' sake : for their's is the kingdom of heaven. Blessed are ye, when men shall revile you, and persecute you, and shall say all manner of evil against you falsely, for my sake. Rejoice, and be exceeding glad : for great is your reward in heaven : for so persecuted they the prophets which were before you.

THE ORDER FOR THE
ADMINISTRATION OF THE LORD'S SUPPER,
OR
HOLY COMMUNION.

¶ *If among those who come to be partakers of the Holy Communion, the Minister shall know any to be an open and notorious evil liver, or to have done any wrong to his neighbours by word or deed, so that the Congregation be thereby offended; he shall advertise him, that he presume not to come to the Lord's Table, until he have openly declared himself to have truly repented and amended his former evil life, that the Congregation may thereby be satisfied; and that he hath recompensed the parties to whom he hath done wrong; or at least declare himself to be in full purpose so to do, as soon as he conveniently may.*

¶ *The same order shall the Minister use with those, betwixt whom he perceiveth malice and hatred to reign; not suffering them to be partakers of the Lord's Table, until he know them to be reconciled. And if one of the parties, so at variance, be content to forgive from the bottom of his heart all that the other hath trespassed against him, and to make amends for that wherein he himself hath offended; and the other party will not be persuaded to a godly unity, but remain still in his frowardness and malice; the Minister in that case ought to admit the penitent person to the Holy Communion, and not him that is obstinate. Provided, That every Minister so repelling any, as is herein specified, shall be obliged to give an account of the same to the Ordinary, within fourteen days after, at the furthest.*

¶ *The Table, at the Communion-time having a fair white linen cloth upon it, shall stand in the body of the Church, or in the Chancel. And the Minister, standing at the right side of the Table, or where Morning and Evening Prayer are appointed to be said, shall say the Lord's Prayer and the Collect following, the People kneeling; but the Lord's Prayer may be omitted, if Morning Prayer hath been said immediately before.*

OUR Father, who art in heaven, Hallowed be thy Name. Thy kingdom come. Thy will be done on earth, As it is in heaven. Give us this day our daily bread. And forgive us our trespasses, As we forgive those who trespass against us. And lead us not into temptation; But deliver us from evil. Amen.

The Collect.

ALMIGHTY God, unto whom all hearts are open, all desires known, and from whom no secrets are hid; Cleanse the thoughts of our hearts by the inspiration of thy Holy Spirit, that we may perfectly love thee, and worthily magnify thy holy Name; through Christ our Lord. *Amen.*

¶ *Then shall the Minister, turning to the People, rehearse distinctly* THE TEN COMMANDMENTS; *and the People, still kneeling, shall, after every Commandment, ask God mercy for their transgressions for the time past, and grace to keep the law for the time to come.*

¶ *The Decalogue may be omitted, provided it be said once on each Sunday. But Note, That whenever it is omitted, the Minister shall say the* Summary of the Law, *beginning,* Hear what our Lord Jesus Christ saith.

Minister.

GOD spake these words, and said: I am the LORD thy God; Thou shalt have none other gods but me.

People. Lord, have mercy upon us, and incline our hearts to keep this law.

Minister. Thou shalt not make to thyself any graven image, nor the likeness of any thing that is in heaven above, or in the earth beneath, or in the water under the earth; thou shalt not bow down to them, nor worship them; for I the LORD thy God am a jealous God, and visit the sins of the fathers upon the children, unto the third and fourth generation of them that hate me; and show mercy unto thousands in them that love me and keep my commandments.

People. Lord, have mercy upon us, and incline our hearts to keep this law.

Minister. Thou shalt not take the Name of the LORD thy God in vain; for the LORD will not hold him guiltless, that taketh his Name in vain.

People. Lord, have mercy upon us, and incline our hearts to keep this law.

Minister. Remember that thou keep holy the Sabbath-day. Six days shalt thou labour, and do all that thou hast to do; but the seventh day is the Sabbath of the LORD thy God. In it thou shalt do no manner of work; thou, and thy son, and thy daughter, thy man-servant, and thy maid-servant, thy cattle, and the stranger that is within thy gates. For in six days the LORD made heaven and earth, the sea, and all that in them is, and rested the seventh day: wherefore the LORD blessed the seventh day, and hallowed it.

People. Lord, have mercy upon us, and incline our hearts to keep this law.

Minister. Honour thy father and thy mother; that thy days may be long in the land which the LORD thy God giveth thee.

People. Lord, have mercy upon us, and incline our hearts to keep this law.

Minister. Thou shalt do no murder.

People. Lord, have mercy upon us, and incline our hearts to keep this law.

Minister. Thou shalt not commit adultery.

People. Lord, have mercy upon us, and incline our hearts to keep this law.

Minister. Thou shalt not steal.

People. Lord, have mercy upon us, and incline our hearts to keep this law.

Minister. Thou shalt not bear false witness against thy neighbour.

People. Lord, have mercy upon us, and incline our hearts to keep this law.

Minister. Thou shalt not covet thy neighbour's house, thou shalt not covet thy neighbour's wife, nor his servant, nor his maid, nor his ox, nor his ass, nor any thing that is his.

People. Lord, have mercy upon us, and write all these thy laws in our hearts, we beseech thee.

¶ *Then the Minister may say,*

Hear also what our Lord Jesus Christ saith.

THOU shalt love the Lord thy God with all thy heart, and with all thy soul, and with all thy mind. This is the first and great commandment. And the second is like unto it; Thou shalt love thy neighbour as thyself. On these two com-

* I

mandments hang all the Law and the Prophets.

¶ *Here, if the Decalogue hath been omitted, shall be said,*

Lord, have mercy upon us.

Christ, have mercy upon us.

Lord, have mercy upon us.

¶ *Then the Minister may say,*

Let us pray.

O ALMIGHTY Lord, and everlasting God, vouchsafe, we beseech thee, to direct, sanctify, and govern, both our hearts and bodies, in the ways of thy laws, and in the works of thy commandments; that, through thy most mighty protection, both here and ever, we may be preserved in body and soul; through our Lord and Saviour Jesus Christ. Amen.

¶ *Then shall be said the* COLLECT OF THE DAY. *And immediately after the Collect the Minister shall read the* EPISTLE, *saying,* The Epistle [*or* The portion of Scripture appointed for the Epistle] is written in the—Chapter of—, beginning at the—Verse. *And the Epistle ended, he shall say,* Here endeth the Epistle. *Then, the People shall stand up, shall be read the* GOSPEL, *saying,* The Holy Gospel is written in the—Chapter of——, beginning at the—Verse.

¶ *Here shall be said or sung,*

Glory be to thee, O Lord.

¶ *Then shall be said the Creed commonly called the Nicene, or else the Apostles' Creed; but the Creed may be omitted, if it hath been said immediately before in Morning Prayer; Provided, That the Nicene Creed shall be said on Christmas-day, Easter-day, Ascension-day, Whitsunday, and Trinity-Sunday.*

I BELIEVE in one God the Father Almighty, Maker of heaven and earth, And of all things visible and invisible:

And in one Lord Jesus Christ, the only-begotten Son of God; Begotten of his Father before all worlds, God of God, Light of Light, Very God of very God; Begotten, not made; Being of one substance with the Father; By whom all things were made: Who for us men and for our salvation came down from heaven, And was incarnate by the Holy Ghost of the Virgin Mary, And was made man: And was crucified also for us under Pontius Pilate; He suffered and was buried: And the third day he rose again according to the Scriptures: And ascended into heaven, And sitteth on the right hand of the Father: And he shall come again, with glory, to judge both the quick and the dead; Whose kingdom shall have no end.

And I believe in the Holy Ghost, The Lord, and Giver of Life, Who proceedeth from the Father and the Son; Who with the Father and the Son together is worshipped and glorified; Who spake by the Prophets: And I believe one Catholic and Apostolic Church: I acknowledge one Baptism for the remission of sins: And I look for the Resurrection of the dead: And the Life of the world to come. Amen.

¶ *Then the Minister shall declare unto the People what Holy-days, or Fasting-days, are in the week following to be observed; and (if occasion be) shall Notice be given of the Communion, and of the Banns of Matrimony, and other matters to be published.*

¶ *Then shall follow the Sermon. After which, the Minister, when there is a Communion, shall return to the Lord's Table, and begin the Offertory, saying one or more of these Sentences following, as he thinketh most convenient. And Note, That these Sentences may be used on any other occasion of Public Worship, when the alms of the People are to be received.*

REMEMBER the words of the Lord Jesus, how he said, It is more blessed to give than to receive. *Acts* xx. 35.

Let your light so shine before men, that they may see your good works, and glorify your Father which is in heaven. *St. Matt.* v. 16.

Lay not up for yourselves treasures upon earth, where moth and rust doth corrupt, and where thieves break through and steal: but lay up for yourselves treasures in heaven, where neither moth nor rust doth corrupt, and where thieves do not break through nor steal. *St. Matt.* vi. 19, 20.

Whatsoever ye would that men should do to you, even so do to them: for this is the law and the prophets. *St. Matt.* vii. 12.

Not every one that saith unto me, Lord, Lord, shall enter into the kingdom of heaven; but he that doeth the will of my Father which is in heaven. *St. Matt.* vii. 21.

Zacchæus stood forth, and said unto the Lord, Behold, Lord, the half of my goods I give to the poor; and if I have done any wrong to any man, I restore fourfold. *St. Luke* xix. 8.

Who goeth a warfare at any time of his own cost? Who planteth a vineyard, and eateth not of the fruit thereof? Or who feedeth a flock, and eateth not of the milk of the flock? 1 *Cor.* ix. 7.

If we have sown unto you spiritual things, is it a great matter if we shall reap your worldly things? 1 *Cor.* ix. 11.

Do ye not know, that they who minister about holy things live of the sacrifice; and they who wait at the altar are partakers with the altar? Even so hath the Lord also ordained, that they who preach the gospel should live of the gospel. 1 *Cor.* ix. 13, 14.

He that soweth little shall reap little; and he that soweth plenteously shall reap plenteously. Let every man do according as he is disposed in his heart, not grudgingly, or of necessity: for God loveth a cheerful giver. 2 *Cor.* ix. 6, 7.

Let him that is taught in the Word minister unto him that teacheth, in all good things. Be not deceived; God is not mocked: for whatsoever a man soweth, that shall he reap. *Gal.* vi. 6, 7.

While we have time, let us do good unto all men; and especially unto them that are of the household of faith. *Gal.* vi. 10.

Godliness is great riches, if a man be content with that he hath: for we brought nothing into this world, neither may we carry any thing out. 1 *Tim.* vi. 6, 7.

Charge them who are rich in this world, that they be ready to give, and glad to distribute; laying up in store for themselves a good foundation against the time to come, that they may attain eternal life. 1 *Tim.* vi. 17, 18, 19.

God is not unrighteous, that he will forget your works, and labour that proceedeth of love; which love ye have showed for his Name's sake, who have ministered unto the saints, and yet do minister. *Heb.* vi. 10.

To do good, and to distribute, forget not; for with such sacrifices God is well pleased. *Heb.* xiii. 16.

Whoso hath this world's good, and seeth his brother

have need, and shutteth up his compassion from him, how dwelleth the love of God in him? 1 *St. John* iii. 17.

Give alms of thy goods, and never turn thy face from any poor man; and then the face of the Lord shall not be turned away from thee. *Tobit* iv. 7.

Be merciful after thy power. If thou hast much, give plenteously; if thou hast little, do thy diligence gladly to give of that little: for so gatherest thou thyself a good reward in the day of necessity. *Tobit* iv. 8, 9.

He that hath pity upon the poor lendeth unto the Lord: and look, what he layeth out, it shall be paid him again. *Prov.* xix. 17.

Blessed be the man that provideth for the sick and needy: the Lord shall deliver him in the time of trouble. *Psalm* xli. 1.

Speak unto the children of Israel, that they bring me an offering; of every man that giveth it willingly with his heart ye shall take my offering. *Exod.* xxv. 2.

Ye shall not appear before the Lord empty; every man shall give as

he is able, according to the blessing of the Lord thy God which he hath given thee. *Deut.* xvi. 16, 17.

Thine, O Lord, is the greatness, and the power, and the glory, and the victory, and the majesty: for all that is in the heaven and in the earth is thine; thine is the kingdom, O Lord, and thou art exalted as head above all. 1 *Chron.* xxix. 11.

All things come of thee, O Lord, and of thine own have we given thee. 1 *Chron.* xxix. 14.

¶ *Whilst these Sentences are in reading, the Deacons, Church-wardens, or other fit persons appointed for that purpose, shall receive the Alms for the Poor, and other Devotions of the People, in a decent Bason to be provided by the Parish for that purpose; and reverently bring it to the Priest, who shall humbly present and place it upon the Holy Table.*

¶ *And the Priest shall then place upon the Table so much Bread and Wine as he shall think sufficient.*

¶ *And when the Alms and Oblations are presented, there may be sung a Hymn, or an Offertory Anthem in the words of Holy Scripture or of the Book of Common Prayer, under the direction of the Minister.*

¶ *Then shall the Priest say,*

Let us pray for the whole state of Christ's Church militant.

ALMIGHTY and ever-living God, who by thy holy Apostle hast taught us to make prayers, and supplications, and to give thanks for all men; We humbly beseech thee most mercifully [* to accept our alms and oblations, and] to receive these our prayers, which we offer unto thy Divine Majesty; beseeching thee to inspire continually the Universal Church with the spirit of truth, unity, and concord: And grant that all those who do confess thy holy Name may agree in the truth of thy holy Word, and live in unity and godly love. We beseech thee also, so to direct and dispose the hearts of all Christian Rulers, that they may truly and impartially administer justice, to the punishment of wickedness and vice, and to the mainte-nance of thy true religion, and virtue. Give grace, O heavenly Father, to all Bishops and other Ministers, that they may, both by their life and doctrine, set forth thy true and lively Word, and rightly and duly administer thy holy Sacraments. And to all thy People give thy heavenly grace; and especially to this congregation here present; that, with meek heart and due reverence, they may hear, and receive thy holy Word; truly serving thee in holiness and righteousness all the days of their life. And we most humbly beseech thee, of thy goodness, O Lord, to comfort and succour all those who, in this transitory life, are in trouble, sorrow, need, sickness, or any other adversity. And we also bless thy holy Name for all thy servants departed this life in thy *faith and fear*; beseeching thee to give us grace so to follow their good examples, that with them we may be partakers of thy heavenly kingdom. Grant this, O Father, for *Jesus Christ's sake*, our only Mediator and Advocate. *Amen.*

If there be no alms or oblations, then shall the words [to accept our alms and oblations, and] *be left unsaid.*

¶ *At the time of the Celebration of the Communion, the Priest shall say this* Exhortation. *But Note, That the Exhortation may be omitted if it hath been already said on one Holy-Day in that same month.*

DEARLY beloved in the Lord, ye who mind to come to the holy Communion of the Body and Blood of our Saviour Christ, must consider how Saint Paul exhorteth all persons diligently to try and examine themselves, before they presume to eat of that Bread, and drink of that Cup. For as the benefit is great, if with a true penitent heart and lively faith we receive that holy Sacrament; so is the danger great, if we receive the same unworthily. Judge therefore yourselves, brethren, that ye be not judged of the Lord; repent you truly for your sins past; have a lively and stedfast faith in Christ our Saviour; amend your lives, and be in perfect charity with all men; so shall ye be meet partakers of those holy mysteries. And above all things ye must give most humble and hearty thanks to God, the Father, the Son, and the Holy Ghost, for the redemption of the world by the death and passion of our Saviour Christ, both God and man; who did humble himself, even to the death upon the Cross, for us, miserable sinners, who lay in darkness and the shadow of death; that he might make us the children of God, and exalt us to everlasting life. And to the end that we should always remember the exceeding great love of our Master, and only Saviour, Jesus Christ, thus dying for us, and the innumerable benefits which by his precious blood-shedding he hath obtained for us; he hath instituted and ordained holy mysteries, as pledges of his love, and for a continual remembrance of his death, to our great and endless comfort. To him therefore, with the Father and the Holy Ghost, let us give (as we are most bounden) continual thanks; submitting ourselves wholly to his holy will and pleasure, and studying to serve him in true holiness and righteousness all the days of our life. *Amen.*

¶ *Then shall the Priest say to those who come to receive the Holy Communion.*

YE who do truly and earnestly repent you of your sins, and are in love and charity with your neighbours, and intend to lead a new life, following the commandments of God, and walking from henceforth in his holy ways; Draw near with faith, and take this holy Sacrament to your comfort; and make your humble confession to Almighty God, devoutly kneeling.

¶ *Then shall this General Confession be made, by the Priest and all those who are minded to receive the Holy Communion, humbly kneeling.*

ALMIGHTY God, Father of our Lord Jesus Christ, Maker of all things, Judge of all men; We acknowledge and bewail our manifold sins and wickedness, Which we, from time to time, most grievously have committed, By thought, word, and deed, Against thy Divine Majesty, Provoking most justly thy wrath and indignation against us. We do earnestly repent, And are heartily sorry for these our misdoings; The remembrance of them is grievous unto us; The burden of them is intolerable. Have mercy upon us, Have mercy upon us, most merciful Father; For thy Son our Lord Jesus Christ's sake, Forgive us all that is past; And grant that we may ever hereafter Serve and please thee In newness of life, To the honour and glory of thy Name; Through Jesus Christ our Lord. Amen.

¶ *Then shall the Priest (the Bishop if he be present) stand up, and turning to the People, say,*

ALMIGHTY God, our heavenly Father, who of his great mercy hath promised forgiveness of sins to all those who with hearty repentance and true faith turn unto him; Have mercy upon you; pardon and deliver you from all your sins; confirm and strengthen you in all goodness; and bring you to everlasting life; through Jesus Christ our Lord. Amen.

¶ *Then shall the Priest say,*

Hear what comfortable words our Saviour Christ saith unto all who truly turn to him.

COME unto me, all ye that travail and are

heavy laden, and I will refresh you. *St. Matt.* xi. 28.

So God loved the world, that he gave his only-begotten Son, to the end that all that believe in him should not perish, but have everlasting life. *St. John* iii. 16.

Hear also what Saint Paul saith.

This is a true saying, and worthy of all men to be received, That Christ Jesus came into the world to save sinners. 1 *Tim.* i. 15.

Hear also what Saint John saith.

If any man sin, we have an Advocate with the Father, Jesus Christ the righteous; and he is the Propitiation for our sins. 1 *St. John* ii. 1, 2.

¶ *After which the Priest shall proceed, saying,*

Lift up your hearts.

Answer. We lift them up unto the Lord.

Priest. Let us give thanks unto our Lord God.

Answer. It is meet and right so to do.

¶ *Then shall the Priest turn to the Lord's Table, and say,*

IT is very meet, right, and our bounden duty, that we should at all times, and in all places, give thanks unto thee, O Lord, [*Holy Father,] Almighty, Everlasting God.

* *These words* [Holy Father] *must be omitted on Trinity-Sunday.*

¶ *Here shall follow the PROPER PREFACE, according to the time, if there be any specially appointed; or else immediately shall be said or sung by the Priest,*

Therefore with Angels and Archangels, and with all the company of heaven, we laud and magnify thy glorious Name; evermore praising thee, and saying,

HOLY, HOLY, HOLY, *Priest and People.*

Lord God of hosts, Heaven and earth are full of thy glory: Glory be to thee, O Lord Most High. Amen.

❖

PROPER PREFACES.

Upon Christmas-day, *and seven days after.*

BECAUSE thou didst give Jesus Christ, thine only Son, to be born as at this time for us; who, by the operation of the Holy Ghost, was made very man, of the substance of the Virgin Mary his mother; and that without spot of sin, to make us clean from all sin. Therefore with Angels, *etc.*

Upon Easter-day, *and seven days after.*

BUT chiefly are we bound to praise thee for the glorious Resurrection of thy Son Jesus Christ our Lord: for he is the very Paschal Lamb, which was offered for us, and hath taken away the sin of the world: who by his death hath destroyed death, and by his rising to life again hath restored to us everlasting life. Therefore with Angels, *etc.*

Upon Ascension-day, *and seven days after.*

THROUGH thy most dearly beloved Son Jesus Christ our Lord; who, after his most glorious Resurrection, manifestly appeared to all his Apostles, and in their sight ascended up into heaven, to prepare a place for us; that where he is, thither we might also ascend, and reign with him in glory. Therefore with Angels, *etc.*

Upon Whitsunday, *and six days after.*

THROUGH Jesus Christ our Lord; according to whose most true promise, the Holy Ghost came down as at this time from heaven, with a sudden great sound, as it had been a mighty wind, in the likeness of fiery tongues, lighting upon the Apostles, to teach them, and to lead them to all truth; giving them both the gift of divers languages, and also boldness with fervent zeal constantly to preach the Gospel unto all nations; whereby we have been brought out of darkness and error into the clear light and true knowledge of thee, and of thy Son Jesus Christ. Therefore with Angels, *etc.*

Upon the Feast of Trinity *only, may be said,*

WHO art one God, one Lord; not one only Person, but three Persons in one Substance. For that which we believe of the glory of the Father, the same we believe of the Son, and of the Holy Ghost, without any difference or inequality. Therefore with Angels, *etc.*

¶ *Or else this may be said, the words* [Holy Father] *being retained in the introductory Address.*

FOR the precious death and merits of thy Son Jesus Christ our Lord, and for the sending to us of the Holy Ghost, the Comforter; who are one with thee in thy Eternal Godhead. Therefore with Angels, *etc.*

✠

¶ *Then shall the Priest, kneeling down at the Lord's Table, say, in the name of all those who shall receive the Communion, this Prayer following.*

WE do not presume to come to this thy Table, O merciful Lord, trusting in our own righteousness, but, in thy manifold and great mercies. We are not worthy so much as to gather up the crumbs under the Table. But thou art the same Lord, whose property is always to have mercy: Grant us therefore, gracious Lord, so to eat the flesh of thy dear Son Jesus Christ, and to drink his blood, that our sinful bodies may be made clean by his body, and our souls washed through his most precious blood, and that we may evermore dwell in him, and he in us. *Amen.*

¶ *When the Priest, standing before the Table, hath so ordered the Bread and Wine, that he may with the more readiness and decency break the Bread before the People, and take the Cup into his hands, he shall say the Prayer of Consecration, as followeth.*

ALL glory be to thee, Almighty God, our heavenly Father, for that thou, of thy tender mercy, didst give thine only Son Jesus Christ to suffer death upon the Cross for our redemption; who made there (by his one oblation of himself once offered) a full, perfect, and sufficient sacrifice, oblation, and satisfaction, for the sins of the whole world; and did institute, and in his holy Gospel command us to continue, a perpetual memory of that his precious death and sacrifice, until his coming again: For in the night in *(a) Here the* which he was *Priest is to* betrayed, *(a)* he *take the Pa-* took Bread; and *ten into his* when he had given thanks,

(b) he brake it, and gave it to his disciples, saying, Take, eat, (c) this is my Body, which is given for you; Do this in remembrance of me. Likewise, after supper, (d) he took the Cup; and when he had given thanks, he gave it to them, saying, Drink ye all of this; for (e) this is my Blood of the New Testament, which is shed for you, and for many, for the remission of sins; Do this, as oft as ye shall drink it, in remembrance of me.

(b) And here to break the Bread.

(c) And here he is to lay his hand upon all the Bread.

(d) Here he is to take the Cup into his hands.

(e) And here he is to lay his hand upon every vessel in which there is any Wine to be consecrated.

W HERE-FORE, O Lord and heavenly Father, according to the institution of thy dearly beloved Son our Saviour Jesus Christ, we, thy humble servants, do celebrate and make here before thee thy holy gifts, which we now offer unto thee, the memorial thy Son hath commanded us to make; having in remembrance

The Oblation.

his blessed passion and precious death, his mighty resurrection and glorious ascension ; rendering unto thee most hearty thanks for the innumerable benefits procured unto us by the same.

A ND we most humbly beseech thee, O merciful Father, to hear us; and, of thy almighty goodness, vouchsafe to bless and sanctify, with thy Word and Holy Spirit, these thy gifts and creatures of bread and wine ; that we, receiving them according to thy Son our Saviour Jesus Christ's holy institution, in remembrance of his death and passion, may be partakers of his most blessed Body and Blood.

The Invocation.

A ND we earnestly desire thy fatherly goodness, mercifully to accept this our sacrifice of praise and thanksgiving ; most humbly beseeching thee to grant that, by the merits and death of thy Son Jesus Christ, and through faith in his blood, we, and all thy whole Church, may obtain remission of our sins, and all other benefits of his passion. And here we offer and present unto thee, O Lord, our selves, our souls and bodies, to be a reasonable, holy, and living sacrifice unto thee; humbly beseeching thee, that we, and all others who shall be partakers of this Holy Communion, may worthily receive the most precious Body and Blood of thy Son Jesus Christ, be filled with thy grace and heavenly benediction, and made one body with him, that he may dwell in us, and we in him. And although we are unworthy, through our manifold sins, to offer unto thee any sacrifice; yet we beseech thee to accept this our bounden duty and service; not weighing our merits, but pardoning our offences, through Jesus Christ our Lord; by whom, and with whom, in the unity of the Holy Ghost, all honour and glory be unto thee, O Father Almighty, world without end. *Amen.*

¶ *Here may be sung a Hymn.*

¶ *Then shall the Priest first receive the Holy Communion in both kinds himself, and proceed to deliver the same to the Bishops, Priests, and Deacons, in like manner, (if any be present,) and, after*

that, to the People also in order, into their hands, all devoutly kneeling. And sufficient opportunity shall be given to those present to communicate. And when he delivereth the Bread, he shall say,

THE Body of our Lord Jesus Christ, which was given for thee, preserve thy body and soul unto everlasting life. Take and eat this in remembrance that Christ died for thee, and feed on him in thy heart by faith, with thanksgiving.

¶ *And the Minister who delivereth the Cup shall say,*

THE Blood of our Lord Jesus Christ, which was shed for thee, preserve thy body and soul unto everlasting life. Drink this in remembrance that Christ's Blood was shed for thee, and be thankful.

¶ *If the consecrated Bread or Wine be spent before all have communicated, the Priest is to consecrate more, according to the Form before prescribed; beginning at,* All glory be to thee, Almighty God, *and ending with these words,* partakers of his most blessed Body and Blood.

¶ *When all have communicated, the Minister shall return to the Lord's Table, and reverently place upon it what remaineth of the consecrated Elements, covering the same with a fair linen cloth.*

¶ *Then shall the Minister say the Lord's Prayer, the People repeating after him every Petition.*

OUR Father, who art in heaven, Hallowed be thy Name. Thy kingdom come. Thy will be done on earth, As it is in heaven. Give us this day our daily bread. And forgive us our trespasses, As we forgive those who trespass against us. And lead us not into temptation; But deliver us from evil: For thine is the kingdom, and the power, and the glory, for ever and ever. Amen.

¶ *After shall be said as followeth.*

ALMIGHTY and ever-living God, we most heartily thank thee, for that thou dost vouchsafe to feed us who have duly received these holy mysteries, with the spiritual food of the most precious Body and Blood of thy Son our Saviour Jesus Christ; and dost assure us thereby of thy favour and goodness towards us; and that we are very members incorporate in the mystical body of thy Son, which is the blessed company of all faithful people; and are also heirs through hope of thy everlasting kingdom, by the merits of the most precious death and passion of thy dear Son. And we most humbly beseech thee, O heavenly Father, so to assist us with thy grace, that we may continue in that holy fellowship, and do all such good works as thou hast prepared for us to walk in; through Jesus Christ our Lord, to whom, with thee and the Holy Ghost, be all honour and glory, world without end. *Amen.*

¶ *Then shall be said or sung, all standing,* Gloria in excelsis; *or some proper Hymn from the Selection.*

GLORY be to God on high, and on earth peace, good will towards men. We praise thee, we bless thee, we worship thee, we glorify thee, we give thanks to thee for thy great glory, O Lord God, heavenly King, God the Father Almighty.

O Lord, the only-begotten Son, Jesus Christ; O Lord God, Lamb of God, Son of the Father, that takest away the sins of the world, have mercy upon us. Thou that takest away the sins of the world, have mercy upon us. Thou that takest away the sins of the world, receive our prayer. Thou that sittest at the right hand of God the Father, have mercy upon us.

For thou only art holy; thou only art the Lord; thou only, O Christ, with the Holy Ghost, art most high in the glory of God the Father. Amen.

¶ *Then the Priest (the Bishop if he be present) shall let them depart with this Blessing.*

THE Peace of God, which passeth all understanding, keep your hearts and minds in the knowledge and love of God, and of his Son Jesus Christ our Lord: And the Blessing of God Almighty, the Father, the Son, and the Holy Ghost, be amongst you, and remain with you always. Amen.

✿

¶ *Collects that may be said after the Collects of Morning or Evening Prayer, or Communion, at the discretion of the Minister.*

ASSIST us mercifully, O Lord, in these our supplications and prayers, and dispose the way of thy servants towards the attainment of everlasting salvation; that, among all the changes and chances of this mortal life, they may ever be defended by thy most gracious and ready help; through Jesus Christ our Lord. Amen.

GRANT, we beseech thee, Almighty God, that the words which we have heard this day with our outward ears, may, through thy grace, be so grafted inwardly in our hearts, that they may bring forth in us the fruit of good living, to the honour and praise of thy Name; through Jesus Christ our Lord. Amen.

DIRECT us, O Lord, in all our doings, with thy most gracious favour, and further us with thy continual help; that in all our works begun, continued, and ended in thee, we may glorify thy holy Name, and finally, by thy mercy, obtain everlasting life; through Jesus Christ our Lord. Amen.

ALMIGHTY God, the fountain of all wisdom, who knowest our necessities before we ask, and our ignorance in asking; We beseech thee to have compassion upon our infirmities; and those things which for our unworthiness we dare not, and for our blindness we cannot ask, vouchsafe to give us, for the worthiness of thy Son Jesus Christ our Lord. *Amen.*

A LMIGHTY God, who hast promised to hear the petitions of those who ask in thy Son's Name; We beseech thee mercifully to incline thine ears to us who have now made our prayers and supplications unto thee; and grant that those things which we have faithfully asked according to thy will, may effectually be obtained, to the relief of our necessity, and to the setting forth of thy glory; through Jesus Christ our Lord. *Amen.*

¶ *Upon the Sundays and other Holy-days, (though there be no Sermon or Communion,) shall be said all that is appointed at the Communion, unto the end of the Gospel, concluding with the Blessing.*

¶ *And if any of the consecrated Bread and Wine remain after the Communion, it shall not be carried out of the Church; but the Minister and other Communicants shall, immediately after the Blessing, reverently eat and drink the same.*

¶ *When the Minister giveth warning for the Celebration of the Holy Communion, (which he shall always do upon the Sunday, or some Holy-day, immediately preceding,) he shall read this Exhortation following; or so much thereof as, in his discretion, he may think convenient.*

D EARLY beloved, on —— day next I purpose, through God's assistance, to administer to all such as shall be religiously and devoutly disposed the most comfortable Sacrament of the Body and Blood of Christ; to be by them received in remembrance of his meritorious Cross and Passion; whereby alone we obtain remission of our sins, and are made partakers of the Kingdom of heaven. Wherefore it is our duty to render most humble and hearty thanks to Almighty God, our heavenly Father, for that he hath given his Son our Saviour Jesus Christ, not only to die for us, but also to be our spiritual food and sustenance in that holy Sacrament. Which being so divine and comfortable a thing to them who receive it worthily, and so dangerous to those who will presume to receive it unworthily; my duty is to exhort you, in the mean season to consider the dignity of that holy mystery, and the great peril of the unworthy receiving thereof; and so to search and examine your own consciences, (and that not lightly, and after the manner of dissemblers with God; but so) that ye may come holy and clean to such a heavenly Feast, in the marriage-garment required by God in holy Scripture, and be received as worthy partakers of that holy Table.

The way and means thereto is: *First, to examine your lives and conversations by the rule of God's commandments; and whereinsoever ye shall perceive yourselves to have offended, either by will, word, or deed, there to bewail your own sinfulness, and to confess yourselves to Almighty God, with full purpose of amendment of life. And if ye shall perceive your offences to be such as are not only against God, but also against your neighbours; then ye shall reconcile yourselves unto them; being ready to make restitution and satisfaction, according to the uttermost of your powers, for all injuries and wrongs done by you to any other; and being likewise ready to forgive others who have offended you, as ye would have forgiveness of your offences at God's hand: for otherwise the receiving of the holy Communion doth nothing else but increase your condemnation.* Therefore, if any of you be a blasphemer of God, an hinderer or slanderer of his Word, an adulterer, or be in malice, or envy, or in any other grievous crime; repent you of your sins, or else come not to that holy Table.

And because it is requisite that no man should come to the holy Communion, but with a full trust in God's mercy, and with a quiet conscience; therefore, if there be any of you, who by this means cannot quiet his own conscience herein, but requireth further comfort or counsel, let him come to me, or to some other Minister of God's Word, and open his grief; that he may receive such godly counsel and advice, as may tend to the quieting of his conscience, and the removing of all scruple and doubtfulness.

¶ Or, in case he shall see the People negligent to come to the Holy Communion, instead of the former, he shall use this Exhortation.

DEARLY beloved brethren, on —— I intend, by God's grace, to celebrate the Lord's Supper: unto which, in God's behalf, I bid you all who are here present; and beseech you, for the Lord Jesus Christ's sake, that ye will not refuse to come thereto, being so lovingly called and bidden by God himself. Ye know how grievous and unkind a thing it is, when a man hath prepared a rich feast, decked his table with all kind of provision, so that there lacketh nothing but the guests to sit down; and yet they who are called (without any cause) most unthankfully refuse to come. Which of you in such a case would not be moved? Who would not think a great injury and wrong done unto him? Wherefore, most dearly beloved in Christ, take ye good heed, lest ye, withdrawing yourselves from this holy Supper, provoke God's indignation against you. It is an easy matter for a man to say, I will not communicate, because I am otherwise hindered with worldly business. But such excuses are not so easily accepted and allowed before God. If any man say, I am a grievous sinner, and therefore am afraid to come: wherefore then do ye not repent and amend? When God calleth you, are ye not ashamed to say ye will not come? When ye should return to God, will ye excuse yourselves, and say ye are not ready? Consider earnestly with yourselves how little such feigned excuses will avail before God. Those who refused the feast in the Gospel, because they had bought a farm, or would try their yokes of oxen, or because they were married, were not so excused, but counted unworthy of the heavenly feast. Wherefore, according to mine office, I bid you in the Name of God, I call you in Christ's behalf, I exhort you, as ye love your own salvation,

THE MINISTRATION OF

PUBLIC BAPTISM OF INFANTS,

TO BE USED IN THE CHURCH.

¶ *The People are to be admonished, that it is most convenient that Baptism should not be administered but upon Sundays and other Holy-days, or Prayer-days. Nevertheless, (if necessity so require,) Baptism may be administered upon any other day.*

¶ *There shall be for every Male-child to be baptized, when they can be had, two Godfathers and one Godmother; and for every Female, one Godfather and two Godmothers; and Parents shall be admitted as Sponsors, if it be desired.*

¶ *When there are children to be baptized, the Parents or Sponsors shall give knowledge thereof, before the beginning of Morning Prayer, to the Minister. And then the Godfathers and Godmothers, and the People with the Children, must be ready at the Font, either immediately after the last Lesson at Morning Prayer, or else immediately after the last Lesson at Evening Prayer, as the Minister by his discretion shall appoint. And the Minister coming to the Font, (which is then to be filled with pure Water,) and standing there, shall say,*

HATH this Child been already baptized, or no?

¶ *If they answer, No: then shall the Minister proceed as followeth, the People all standing until the Lord's Prayer.*

DEARLY beloved, forasmuch as all men are conceived and born in sin; and our Saviour Christ saith, None can enter into the kingdom of God, except he be regenerate and born anew of Water and of the Holy Ghost; I beseech you to call upon God the Father, through our Lord Jesus Christ, that of his bounteous mercy he will grant to *this Child* that which by nature *he* cannot have; that *he* may be baptized with Water and the Holy Ghost, and received into Christ's holy Church, and be made *a living member* of the same.

¶ *Then shall the Minister say,*

Let us pray.

ALMIGHTY and ever-lasting God, who of thy great mercy didst save Noah and his family in the ark from perishing by water ; and also didst safely lead the children of Israel thy people through the Red Sea, figuring thereby thy holy Baptism ; and by the Baptism of thy well-beloved Son Jesus Christ in the river Jordan, didst sanctify Water to the mystical washing away of sin ; We beseech thee, for thine infinite mercies, that thou wilt mercifully look upon *this Child ;* wash *him* and sanctify *him* with the Holy Ghost ; that *he,* being delivered from thy wrath, may be received into the ark of Christ's Church ; and being stedfast in faith, joyful through hope, and rooted in charity, may so pass the waves of this troublesome world, that finally *he* may come to the land of everlasting life, there to reign with thee, world without end ; through Jesus Christ our Lord. *Amen.*

¶ *Or this.*

ALMIGHTY and immortal God, the aid of all who need, the helper of all who flee to thee for succour, the life of those who believe, and the resurrection of the dead ; We call upon thee for *this Infant,* that *he,* coming to thy holy Baptism, may receive remission of sin, by spiritual regeneration. Receive *him,* O Lord, as thou hast promised by thy well-beloved Son, saying, Ask, and ye shall have ; seek, and ye shall find ; knock, and it shall be opened unto you. So give now unto us who ask ; let us who seek, find ; open the gate unto us who knock ; that *this Infant* may enjoy the everlasting benediction of thy heavenly washing, and may come to the eternal kingdom which thou hast promised by Christ our Lord. *Amen.*

¶ *Then the Minister shall say as followeth: or else shall pass immediately to the Questions addressed to the Sponsors. But Note, That in every church the intermediate parts of the Service shall be used, once at least in every month, (if there be a baptism,) for the better instructing of the People in the grounds of Infant Baptism.*

Hear the words of the Gospel, written by St. *Mark*, in the tenth Chapter, at the thirteenth Verse.

THEY brought young children to Christ, that he should touch them: and his disciples rebuked those that brought them. But when Jesus saw it, he was much displeased, and said unto them, Suffer the little children to come unto me, and forbid them not: for of such is the kingdom of God. Verily I say unto you, Whosoever shall not receive the kingdom of God as a little child, he shall not enter therein. And he took them up in his hands, put his hands upon them, and blessed them.

¶ *After the Gospel is read, the Minister shall make this brief Exhortation upon the words of the Gospel.*

BELOVED, ye hear in this Gospel the words of our Saviour Christ, that he commanded the children to be brought unto him; how he blamed those who would have kept them from him; how he exhorteth all men to follow their innocency. Ye perceive how, by his outward ges-

ture and deed, he declared his good will toward them; for he embraced them in his arms, he laid his hands upon them, and blessed them. Doubt ye not therefore, but earnestly believe, that he will likewise favourably receive *this* present *Infant*; that he will embrace *him* with the arms of his mercy; that he will give unto *him* the blessing of eternal life, and make *him* partaker of his everlasting kingdom. Wherefore, we being thus persuaded of the good will of our heavenly Father towards *this Infant*, declared by his Son Jesus Christ; and nothing doubting but that he favourably alloweth this charitable work of ours in bringing *this Infant* to his holy Baptism; let us faithfully and devoutly give thanks unto him, and say,

ALMIGHTY and everlasting God, heavenly Father, We give thee humble thanks, That thou hast vouchsafed to call us to the knowledge of thy grace, and faith in thee: Increase this knowledge, And confirm this faith in us evermore. Give thy Holy

Spirit to *this Infant*, That *he* may be born again, And be made *an heir* of everlasting salvation; Through our Lord Jesus Christ, Who liveth and reigneth with thee and the Holy Spirit, Now and for ever. Amen.

¶ *Then shall the Minister speak unto the Godfathers and Godmothers on this wise.*

DEARLY beloved, ye have brought *this Child* here to be baptized; ye have prayed that our Lord Jesus Christ would vouchsafe to receive *him*, to release *him* from sin, to sanctify *him* with the Holy Ghost, to give *him* the kingdom of heaven, and everlasting life. Ye have heard also that our Lord Jesus Christ hath promised in his Gospel to grant all these things that ye have prayed for: which promise he, for his part, will most surely keep and perform.

Wherefore, after this promise made by Christ, *this Infant* must also faithfully, for *his* part, promise by you that are *his* sureties, (until *he* come of age to take it upon *himself*,) that *he* will renounce the devil and all his works,

and constantly believe God's holy Word, and obediently keep his commandments.

¶ *The Minister shall then demand of the Sponsors as followeth: the Questions being considered as addressed to them severally, and the Answers to be made accordingly.*

I demand therefore,

DOST thou, in the name of this Child, renounce the devil and all his works, the vain pomp and glory of the world, with all covetous desires of the same, and the sinful desires of the flesh, so that thou wilt not follow, nor be led by them?

Answer. I renounce them all: and, by God's help, will endeavour not to follow, nor be led by them.

Minister. Dost thou believe all the Articles of the Christian Faith, as contained in the Apostles' Creed?

Answer. I do.

Minister. Wilt thou be baptized in this Faith?

Answer. That is my desire.

Minister. Wilt thou then obediently keep God's holy will and commandments, and walk in the same all the days of thy life?

Answer. I will, by God's help.

¶ *Then shall the Minister say,*

O MERCIFUL God, grant that the old Adam in *this Child* may be so buried, that the new man may be raised up in *him*. *Amen.*

Grant that all sinful affections may die in *him,* and that all things belonging to the Spirit may live and grow in *him*. *Amen.*

Grant that *he* may have power and strength to have victory, and to triumph, against the devil, the world, and the flesh. *Amen.*

Grant that whosoever is here dedicated to thee by our office and ministry, may also be endued with heavenly virtues, and everlastingly rewarded, through thy mercy, O blessed Lord God, who dost live, and govern all things, world without end. *Amen.*

A LMIGHTY, everliving God, whose most dearly beloved Son Jesus Christ, for the forgiveness of our sins, did shed out of his most precious side both water and blood; and gave commandment to his disciples, that they should go teach all nations, and baptize them In the Name of the Father, and of the Son, and of the Holy Ghost; Regard, we beseech thee, the supplications of thy congregation; sanctify this Water to the mystical washing away of sin; and grant that *this Child,* now to be baptized therein, may receive the fulness of thy grace, and ever remain in the number of thy faithful children; through Jesus Christ our Lord. *Amen.*

¶ *Then the Minister shall take the Child into his hands, and shall say to the Godfathers and Godmothers,*

Name this Child.

¶ *And then, naming it after them, he shall dip it in the Water discreetly, or shall pour Water upon it, saying,*

N. I baptize thee In the Name of the Father, and of the Son, and of the Holy Ghost. *Amen.*

¶ *Then the Minister shall say,*

W E receive this Child into the congregation of Christ's flock; and do *sign him   * Here the Minister with the sign   shall make of the Cross,   a Cross up- in token that   on the Child's hereafter   he   forehead. shall not be ashamed to confess the faith of Christ crucified, and manfully to fight under his banner, against sin, the world, and the devil; and to continue Christ's faithful soldier and servant unto *his* life's end. Amen.

¶ *If those who present the Infant shall desire the sign of the Cross to be omitted, although the Church knoweth no worthy cause of scruple concerning the same, yet, in that case, the Minister may omit that part of the above which followeth the Immersion, or the pouring of Water on the Infant.*

¶ *Then shall the Minister say,*

SEEING now, dearly beloved brethren, that *this Child is* regenerate, and grafted into the body of Christ's Church, let us give thanks unto Almighty God for these benefits; and with one *accord* make our prayers unto him, that *this Child* may lead the rest of *his* life according to this beginning.

¶ *Then shall be said, all kneeling,*

OUR Father, who art in heaven, Hallowed be thy Name. Thy kingdom come. Thy will be done on earth, As it is in heaven. Give us this day our daily bread. And forgive us our trespasses, As we forgive those who trespass against us. And lead us not into temptation; But deliver us from evil. Amen.

¶ *Then shall the Minister say,*

WE yield thee hearty thanks, most merciful Father, that it hath pleased thee to regenerate *this Infant* with thy Holy Spirit, to receive *him* for thine own *Child* by adoption, and to incorporate *him* into thy holy Church. And humbly we beseech thee to grant, that *he*, being dead unto sin, and living unto righteousness, and being buried with Christ in his death, may crucify the old man, and utterly abolish the whole body of sin; and that, as *he is* made *partaker* of the death of thy Son, *he* may also be *partaker* of his resurrection; so that finally, with the residue of thy holy Church, *he* may be *an inheritor* of thine everlasting kingdom; through Christ our Lord. Amen.

¶ *Then, all standing up, the Minister shall say to the Godfathers and Godmothers this Exhortation following.*

FORASMUCH as *this Child* hath promised by you *his* sureties to renounce the devil and all his works, to believe in God, and to serve him; ye must remember, that it is your parts and duties to see that *this Infant* be taught, so soon as *he* shall be able to learn, what a solemn vow, promise, and profession, *he hath* here made by you. And that *he* may know these things the better, ye shall call upon *him* to hear Sermons; and chiefly ye shall provide, that *he* may learn the Creed, the Lord's Prayer, and the Ten Commandments, and all other things which a Christian ought to know and believe to his soul's health; and that *this Child* may be virtuously brought up to lead a godly and a Christian life; remembering always, that Baptism doth represent unto us our profession; which is, to follow the example of our Saviour Christ, and to be made like unto him; that, as he died, and rose again for us, so should we, who are baptized, die from sin, and rise again unto righteousness; continually mortifying all our evil and corrupt affections, and daily proceeding in all virtue and godliness of living.

¶ *Then shall he add, and say.*

YE are to take care that *this Child* be brought to the Bishop to be confirmed by him, so soon as *he* can say the Creed, the Lord's Prayer, and the Ten Commandments, and *is* sufficiently instructed in the other parts of the Church - Catechism set forth for that purpose.

THE MINISTRATION OF

PRIVATE BAPTISM OF CHILDREN,

IN HOUSES.

¶ *The Minister of every Parish shall often admonish the People, that they defer not the Baptism of their Children longer than the first or second Sunday next after their birth, or other Holy-day falling between, unless upon a great and reasonable cause.*

¶ *And also he shall warn them, that without like great cause and necessity, they procure not their Children to be baptized at home in their houses. But when need shall compel them so to do, then Baptism shall be administered as followeth.*

¶ *First, let the Minister of the Parish (or, in his absence, any other lawful Minister that can be procured) with those who are present, call upon God, and say the Lord's Prayer, and so many of the Collects appointed to be said before in the Form of Public Baptism, as the time and present exigence will suffer. And then, the Child being named by some one who is present, the Minister shall pour Water upon it, saying these words:*

N. I baptize thee In the Name of the Father, and of the Son, and of the Holy Ghost. Amen.

¶ *Then the Minister shall give thanks unto God, and say.*

WE yield thee hearty thanks, most merciful Father, that it hath pleased thee to regenerate *this Infant* with thy Holy Spirit, to receive *him* for thine own *Child* by adoption, and to incorporate *him* into thy holy Church. And humbly we beseech thee to grant, that *he,* being dead unto sin, and living unto righteousness, and being buried with Christ in his death, may crucify the old man, and utterly abolish the whole body of sin ; and that, as *he is* made *partaker* of the death of thy Son, *he* may also be *partaker* of his resurrection ; so that finally, with the residue of thy holy Church, *he* may be *an inheritor* of thine everlasting kingdom ; through Christ our Lord. *Amen.*

¶ *And let them not doubt, but that the Child so baptized is lawfully and sufficiently baptized, and ought not to be baptized again. Yet nevertheless, if the Child, which is after this sort baptized, do afterward live, it is expedient that it be brought into the Church, to the intent that if the Minister of the same Parish did himself baptize that Child, the Congregation may be certified of the true Form of Baptism, by him privately before used : In which case, all standing, he shall say thus:*

I CERTIFY you, that according to the due and prescribed Order of the Church, *at such a time,* and *at such a place,* before divers witnesses, I baptized *this Child ;* who *is* now by Baptism incorporated into the Christian Church: for our Lord Jesus Christ doth not deny his grace and mercy unto such Infants, but most lovingly doth call them unto him, as the holy Gospel doth witness to our comfort.

❡ *But if the Child were baptized by any other lawful Minister, then the Minister of the Parish where the Child was born or christened, shall examine whether the same hath been lawfully done. And if the Minister shall find, by the answers of such as bring the Child, that all things were done as they ought to be; then shall he not christen the Child again, but shall receive him as one of the flock of true Christian People, saying thus:*

I CERTIFY you, that in this case all is well done, and according unto due order, concerning the baptizing of *this Child*; who *is* now by Baptism incorporated into the Christian Church: for our Lord Jesus Christ doth not deny his grace and mercy unto such Infants, but most lovingly doth call them unto him, as the holy Gospel doth witness to our comfort.

❡ *Then the Minister shall say as followeth.*

Hear the words of the Gospel, written by St. *Mark*, in the tenth Chapter, at the thirteenth Verse.

THEY brought young children to Christ, that he should touch them: and his disciples rebuked those that brought

them. But when Jesus saw it, he was much displeased, and said unto them, Suffer the little children to come unto me, and forbid them not: for of such is the kingdom of God. Verily I say unto you, Whosoever shall not receive the kingdom of God as a little child, he shall not enter therein. And he took them up in his arms, put his hands upon them, and blessed them.

❡ *After the Gospel is read, the Minister shall make this brief Exhortation upon the words of the Gospel.*

BELOVED, ye hear in this Gospel the words of our Saviour Christ, that he commanded the children to be brought unto him; how he blamed those who would have kept them from him; how he exhorteth all men to follow their innocency. Ye perceive how, by his outward gesture and deed, he declared his good will toward them; for he embraced them in his arms, he laid his hands upon them, and blessed them. Doubt ye not therefore, but earnestly believe, that he hath likewise favourably received *this* present *Infant*; that he hath embraced *him* with the arms of his mercy; and, as he hath promised in his holy Word, will give unto *him* the blessing of eternal life, and make *him* partaker of his everlasting kingdom.

Wherefore, we being thus persuaded of the good will of our heavenly Father, declared by his Son Jesus Christ, towards *this Infant*, let us faithfully and devoutly give thanks unto him, and say the Prayer which the Lord himself taught us.

O UR Father, who art in heaven, Hallowed be thy Name. Thy kingdom come. Thy will be done on earth, As it is in heaven. Give us this day our daily bread. And forgive us our trespasses, As we forgive those who trespass against us. And lead us not into temptation; But deliver us from evil. Amen.

¶ *Then shall the Minister demand the name of the Child; which being by the Godfathers and Godmothers pronounced, the Minister shall say as followeth.*

D OST thou, in the name of this Child, renounce the devil and all his works, the vain pomp and glory of the world, with all covetous desires of the same, and the sinful desires of the flesh, so that thou wilt not follow, nor be led by them?

Answer. I renounce them all; and, by God's help, will endeavour not to follow, nor be led by them.

Minister. Dost thou believe all the Articles of the Christian Faith, as contained in the Apostles' Creed?

Answer. I do.

Minister. Wilt thou then obediently keep God's holy will and commandments, and walk in the same all the days of thy life?

Answer. I will, by God's help.

¶ *Then the Minister shall say.*

W E receive this Child into the congregation of Christ's flock; and do *sign *him* with the sign of the Cross, in token that hereafter *he* shall not be ashamed to confess the faith of Christ crucified, and manfully to

¶ *Here the Minister shall make a Cross upon the Child's forehead.*

fight under his banner, against sin, the world, and the devil; and to continue Christ's faithful soldier and servant unto *his* life's end. Amen.

¶ *The same rule is to be observed here, as to the omission of the sign of the Cross, as in the Public Baptism of Infants.*

¶ *Then shall the Minister say,*

SEEING now, dearly beloved brethren, that *this Child is* regenerate, and grafted into the body of Christ's Church, let us give thanks unto Almighty God for these benefits; and with one accord make our prayers unto him, that *this Child* may lead the rest of *his* life according to this beginning.

¶ *Then shall be said, all kneeling,*

WE yield thee hearty thanks, most merciful Father, that it hath pleased thee to regenerate *this Infant* with thy Holy Spirit, to receive *him* for thine own *Child* by adoption, and to incorporate *him* into thy holy Church. And humbly we beseech thee to grant, that *he*, being dead unto sin, and living unto righteousness, and being buried with Christ in his death, may crucify the old man, and utterly abolish the whole body of sin; and that, as *he is* made *partaker* of the death of thy Son, *he* may also be *partaker* of his resurrection; so that finally, with the residue of thy holy Church, *he* may be *an inheritor* of thine everlasting kingdom; through Christ our Lord. *Amen.*

¶ *Then, all standing up, the Minister shall say to the Godfathers and Godmothers this Exhortation following.*

FORASMUCH as *this Child* hath promised by you *his* sureties to renounce the devil and all his works, to believe in God, and to serve him; ye must remember, that it is your parts and duties to see that *this Infant* be taught, so soon as *he* shall be able to learn, what a solemn vow, promise, and profession, *he hath* here made by you. And that *he* may know these things the better, ye shall call upon *him* to hear Sermons; and chiefly ye shall provide, that *he* may learn the Creed, the Lord's Prayer, and the Ten Commandments, and all other things which a Christian ought to know and believe to his soul's health; and that *this Child* may be virtuously brought up to lead a godly and a Christian life; remembering always, that Baptism doth represent unto us our profession; which is to, to follow the example of our Saviour Christ, and to be made like unto him; that, as he died, and rose again for us, so should we, who are baptized, die from sin, and rise again unto righteousness: continually mortifying all our evil and corrupt affections, and daily proceeding in all virtue and godliness of living.

¶ *Then shall he add, and say,*

YE are to take care that *this Child* be brought to the Bishop to be confirmed by him, so soon as *he* can say the Creed, the Lord's Prayer, and the Ten Commandments, and *is* sufficiently instructed in the other parts of the Church-Catechism set forth for that purpose.

¶ *But if they who bring the Infant to the Church do make such uncertain answers to the Minister's questions, as that it cannot appear that the Child was baptized with Water, In the Name of the Father, and of the Son, and of the Holy Ghost, (which are essential parts of Baptism,) then let the Minister baptize it in the Form before appointed for Public Baptism of Infants; saving that at the dipping of the Child in the Font, he shall use this Form of words:*

IF thou art not already baptized, *N.,* I baptize thee In the Name of the Father, and of the Son, and of the Holy Ghost. Amen.

¶ *If Infant Baptism, and the receiving of Infants baptized in private, are to be at the same time, the Minister may make the Questions to the Sponsors, and the succeeding Prayers, serve for both. And again, after the Immersion, or the pouring of Water, and the receiving into the Church, the Minister may use the remainder of the Service for both.*

THE MINISTRATION OF

BAPTISM TO SUCH AS ARE
OF RIPER YEARS,

AND ABLE TO ANSWER FOR THEMSELVES.

¶ *When any such Persons as are of riper years are to be baptized, timely notice shall be given to the Minister; that so due care may be taken for their examination, whether they be sufficiently instructed in the Principles of the Christian Religion; and that they may be exhorted to prepare themselves, with Prayers and Fasting, for the receiving of this holy Sacrament.*

¶ *And if they shall be found fit, then the Godfathers and Godmothers (the People being assembled upon the Sunday, Holyday or Prayer-day appointed) shall be ready to present them at the Font, immediately after the second Lesson, either at Morning or Evening Prayer, as the Minister, in his discretion, shall think fit. And standing there, the Minister shall say,*

HATH this Person been already baptized, or no?

¶ *If they answer, No: then shall the Minister (the People all standing until the Lord's Prayer) proceed as followeth.*

DEARLY beloved, forasmuch as all men are conceived and born in sin, (and that which is born of the flesh is flesh,) and they who are in the flesh cannot please God, but live in sin, committing many actual transgressions; and our Saviour Christ saith, None can enter into the kingdom of God, except he be regenerate and born anew of water and of the Holy Ghost: I beseech you to call upon God the Father, through our Lord Jesus Christ, that of his bounteous goodness he will grant to *these Persons* that which by nature *they* cannot have; that *they* may be baptized with Water and the Holy Ghost, and received into Christ's holy Church, and be made lively *members* of the same.

¶ Then shall the Minister say,

Let us pray.

ALMIGHTY and ever-lasting God, who of thy great mercy didst save Noah and his family in the ark from perishing by water; and also didst safely lead the children of Israel thy people through the Red Sea, figuring thereby thy holy Baptism; and by the Baptism of thy well-beloved Son Jesus Christ in the river Jordan, didst sanctify the element of Water to the mystical washing away of sin; We beseech thee, for thine infinite mercies, that thou wilt mercifully look upon *these* thy *Servants;* wash *them* and sanctify *them* with the Holy Ghost; that *they,* being delivered from thy wrath, may be received into the ark of Christ's Church; and being stedfast in faith, joyful through hope, and rooted in charity, may so pass the waves of this troublesome world, that finally *they* may come to the land of everlasting life, there to reign with thee, world without end; through Jesus Christ our Lord. *Amen.*

¶ Or this.

ALMIGHTY and immortal God, the aid of all who need, the helper of all who flee to thee for succour, the life of those who believe, and the resurrection of the dead; We call upon thee for *these* thy *Servants,* that *they,* coming to thy holy Baptism, may receive remission of *their* sins, by spiritual regeneration. Receive *them,* O Lord, as thou hast promised by thy well-beloved Son, saying, Ask, and ye shall receive; seek, and ye shall find; knock, and it shall be opened unto you. So give now unto us who ask; let us who seek, find; open the gate unto us who knock; that *these* thy *Servants* may enjoy the everlasting benediction of thy heavenly washing, and may come to the eternal kingdom which thou hast promised by Christ our Lord. *Amen.*

¶ Then the Minister shall say,

Hear the words of the Gospel, written by St. *John,* in the third Chapter, beginning at the first Verse.

THERE was a man of the Pharisees, named Nicodemus, a ruler of the Jews: the same came to Jesus by night, and said unto him, Rabbi, we know that thou art a teacher come from God: for no man can do these miracles that thou doest, except God be with him. Jesus answered and said unto him, Verily, verily, I say unto thee, Except a man be born again, he cannot see the kingdom of God. Nicodemus saith unto him, How can a man be born when he is old? can he enter the second time into his mother's womb, and be born? Jesus answered, Verily, verily, I say unto thee, Except a man be born of water and of the Spirit, he cannot enter into the kingdom of God. That which is born of the flesh is flesh; and that which is born of the Spirit is spirit. Marvel not that I said unto thee, Ye must be born again. The wind bloweth where it listeth, and thou hearest the sound thereof, but canst not tell whence it cometh, and whither it goeth: so is every one that is born of the Spirit.

¶ After which he shall say this Exhortation following.

BELOVED, ye hear in this Gospel the express words of our Saviour Christ, that except a man be born of water and of the Spirit, he cannot enter into the kingdom of God. Whereby ye may perceive the great necessity of this Sacrament, where it may be had. Likewise, immediately before his ascension into heaven, (as we read in the last Chapter of Saint Mark's Gospel,) he gave command to his disciples, saying, Go ye into all the world, and preach the Gospel to every creature. He that believeth and is baptized shall be saved; but he that believeth not shall be damned. Which also showeth unto us the great benefit we reap thereby. For which cause Saint Peter the Apostle, when upon his first preaching of the Gospel many were pricked at the heart, and said to him and the rest of the Apostles, Men and brethren, what shall we do? replied and said unto them, Repent, and be baptized every one of you for the remission of sins, and ye shall receive the gift of the Holy Ghost. For the promise is to you and your children, and to all that are afar off, even as many as the Lord our God shall call. And with many other words exhorted he them, saying, Save yourselves from this untoward generation. For (as the same Apostle testifieth in another place) even Baptism doth also now save us, (not the putting away of the filth of the flesh, but the answer of a good conscience towards God,) by the resurrection of Jesus Christ. Doubt ye not therefore, but *earnestly believe*, that he will favourably receive *these* present *Persons*, truly repenting, and coming unto him by faith; that he will grant *them* remission of *their* sins, and bestow upon *them* the Holy Ghost: that he will give *them* the blessing of eternal life, and make *them partakers* of his everlasting kingdom.

Wherefore, we being thus persuaded of the good will of our heavenly Father toward *these Persons*, declared by his Son Jesus Christ; let us faithfully and devoutly give thanks to him, and say,

ALMIGHTY and everlasting God, heavenly Father, We give thee humble thanks, For that thou hast vouchsafed to call us to the knowledge of thy grace, and faith in thee: Increase this knowledge, And confirm this faith in us evermore. Give thy Holy Spirit to *these* thy *Servants*, That *they* may be born again, And be made *heirs* of everlasting salvation; Through our Lord Jesus Christ, Who liveth and reigneth with thee and the Holy Spirit, Now and for ever. Amen.

¶ *Then the Minister shall speak to the Persons to be baptized on this wise.*

WELL-BELOVED, who are come hither desiring to receive holy Baptism, *ye* have heard how the congregation hath prayed, that our Lord Jesus Christ would vouchsafe to receive you and bless you, to release you of your sins, to give you the kingdom of heaven, and everlasting life. *Ye* have heard also, that our Lord Jesus Christ hath promised in his holy

Word to grant all those things that we have prayed for; which promise he, for his part, will most surely keep and perform.

Wherefore, after this promise made by Christ, *ye* must also faithfully, for your part, in the presence of these your Witnesses, and this whole congregation, promise and answer to the following questions.

¶ *The Minister shall then demand of the Persons to be baptized as followeth; the Questions being considered as addressed to them severally, and the Answers to be made accordingly.*

Question.

DOST thou renounce the devil and all his works, the vain pomp and glory of the world, with all covetous desires of the same, and the sinful desires of the flesh, so that thou wilt not follow, nor be led by them?

Answer. I renounce them all; and, by God's help, will endeavour not to follow, nor be led by them.

Minister. Dost thou believe all the Articles of the Christian Faith, as contained in the Apostles' Creed?

Answer. I do.

Question. Wilt thou be baptized in this Faith?

Answer. That is my desire.

Question. Wilt thou then obediently keep God's holy will and commandments, and walk in the same all the days of thy life?

Answer. I will, by God's help.

¶ *Then shall the Minister say,*

O MERCIFUL God, grant that the old Adam in *these* thy *Servants* may be so buried, that the new man may be raised up in *them. Amen.*

Grant that all sinful affections may die in *them*, and that all things belonging to the Spirit may live and grow in *them. Amen.*

Grant that *they* may have power and strength to have victory, and to triumph, against the devil, the world, and the flesh. *Amen.*

Grant that *they,* being here dedicated to thee by our office and ministry, may also be endued with heavenly virtues, and everlastingly rewarded, through thy mercy, O blessed Lord God, who dost live, and govern all things, world without end. *Amen.*

ALMIGHTY, everliving God, whose most dearly beloved Son Jesus Christ, for the forgiveness of our sins, did shed out of his most precious side both water and blood; and gave commandment to his disciples, that they should go teach all nations, and baptize them In the Name of the Father, and of the Son, and of the Holy Ghost; Regard, we beseech thee, the supplications of thy congregation; sanctify this Water to the mystical *washing away of sin;* and grant that *these* thy *Servants,* now to be baptized therein, may receive the fulness of thy grace, and ever remain in the number of thy faithful children; through Jesus Christ our Lord. *Amen.*

¶ *Then shall the Minister take each Person to be baptized by the right hand; and placing him conveniently by the Font, according to his discretion, shall ask the Godfathers and Godmothers the Name; and then shall dip him in the water, or pour water upon him, saying,*

N. I baptize thee In the Name of the Father,

and of the Son, and of the Holy Ghost. *Amen.*

¶ *Then shall the Minister say,*

WE receive this Person into the congregation of Christ's flock; and do * sign *him* with the sign of the Cross, in token that hereafter *he* shall not be ashamed to confess the faith of Christ crucified, and manfully to fight under his banner, against sin, the world, and the devil; and to continue Christ's faithful soldier and servant unto *his* life's end. *Amen.*

* *Here the Minister shall make a Cross upon the Person's forehead.*

¶ *The same rule, as to the omission of the sign of the Cross, is to be observed here as in the Baptism of Infants.*

¶ *Then shall the Minister say,*

SEEING now, dearly beloved brethren, that *these Persons are* regenerate, and grafted into the body of Christ's Church, let us give thanks unto Almighty God for these benefits; and with one accord make our prayers unto him, that *they* may lead the rest of *their* life according to this beginning.

¶ *Then shall be said the* Lord's Prayer, *all kneeling.*

OUR Father, who art in heaven, Hallowed be thy Name. Thy kingdom come. Thy will be done on earth, As it is in heaven. Give us this day our daily bread. And forgive us our trespasses, As we forgive those who trespass against us. And lead us not into temptation; But deliver us from evil. Amen.

WE yield thee hearty thanks, most merciful Father, that it hath pleased thee to regenerate *these* thy *Servants* with thy Holy Spirit, to receive *them* for thine own *children* by adoption, and to incorporate *them* into thy holy Church. And humbly we beseech thee to grant, that *they*, being dead unto sin, and living unto righteousness, and being buried with Christ in his death, may crucify the old man, and utterly abolish the whole body of sin; and that, as *they are* made *partakers* of the death of thy Son, *they* may also be *partakers* of his resurrection; so that finally, with the residue of thy holy Church, *they* may be *inheritors* of thine everlasting kingdom; through Christ our Lord. *Amen.*

¶ *Then, all standing up, the Minister shall use this Exhortation following; speaking to the Godfathers and Godmothers first.*

FORASMUCH as *these Persons* have promised, in your presence, to renounce the devil and all his works, to believe in God, and to serve him; ye must remember, that it is your part and duty to put *them* in mind, what a solemn vow, promise, and profession, *they have* now made before this congregation, and especially before you *their* chosen witnesses. And ye are also to call upon *them* to use all diligence to be rightly instructed in God's holy Word; that so they may grow in grace, and in the knowledge of our Lord Jesus Christ, and live godly, righteously, and soberly, in this present world.

¶ *And then, speaking to the baptized* Persons, *he shall proceed and say,*

AND as for you, who have now by Baptism put on Christ, it is your part and duty also, being made the *children* of God and of the light, by faith in Jesus Christ, to walk answerably to your Christian calling, and as becometh the children of light; remembering always, that Baptism doth represent unto us our profession; which is, to follow the example of our Saviour Christ, and to be made like unto him; that, as he died, and rose again for us, so should we, who are baptized, die from sin, and rise again unto righteousness; continually mortifying all our evil and corrupt affections, and daily proceeding in all virtue and godliness of living.

¶ *It is expedient that every Person, thus baptized, should be confirmed by the Bishop, so soon after his Baptism as conveniently may be; that so he may be admitted to the Holy Communion.*

¶ *Whereas necessity may require the baptizing of Adults in private houses, in consideration of extreme sickness; the same is hereby allowed in that case. And a convenient number of persons shall be assembled in the house where the Sacrament is to be administered. And in the exhortation, Well-beloved, etc., instead of these words, come hither desiring, shall be inserted this word, desirous. And in case of great necessity, the Minister may begin with the questions addressed to the candidate, and end with the thanksgiving following the baptism.*

¶ *If there be occasion for the Office of Infant Baptism and that of Adults at the same time, the Minister shall use the exhortation and one of the prayers next following in the Office for Adults: only, in the exhortation and prayer, after the words, these Persons, and these thy Servants, adding, and these Infants. Then the Minister shall proceed to the questions to be demanded in the cases respectively. After the immersion, or the pouring of water, the prayer shall be as in this service: only, after the words, these thy Servants, shall be added, and these Infants. After which the remaining part of each service shall be used; first, that for Adults, and lastly that for Infants.*

¶ *If any persons, not baptized in their infancy, shall be brought to be baptized before they come to years of discretion to answer for themselves, it may suffice to use the Office for Public Baptism of Infants; or, in case of extreme danger, the Office for Private Baptism; only changing the word Infant, for Child, or Person, as occasion requireth.*

¶ *If there be reasonable doubt concerning the baptism of any person, such person may be baptized in the manner herein appointed; saving that, at the immersion or the pouring of water, the Minister shall use this form of words:*

IF thou art not already baptized, *N.* I baptize thee In the Name of the Father, and of the Son, and of the Holy Ghost. Amen.

A CATECHISM;

THAT IS TO SAY,

AN INSTRUCTION, TO BE LEARNED BY EVERY PERSON BEFORE HE BE BROUGHT TO BE CONFIRMED BY THE BISHOP.

Question.

WHAT is your Name?
Answer. N. or M.

Question. Who gave you this Name?

Answer. My Sponsors in Baptism; wherein I was made a member of Christ, the child of God, and an inheritor of the kingdom of heaven.

Question. What did your Sponsors then for you?

Answer. They did promise and vow three things in my name: First, that I should renounce the devil and all his works, the pomps and vanity of this wicked world, and all the sinful lusts of the flesh; Secondly, that I should believe all the Articles of the Christian Faith; And Thirdly, that I should keep God's holy will and commandments, and walk in the same all the days of my life.

Question. Dost thou not think that thou art bound to believe, and to do, as they have promised for thee?

Answer. Yes, verily; and by God's help so I will. And I heartily thank our heavenly Father, that he hath called me to this state of salvation, through Jesus Christ our Saviour. And I pray unto God to give me his grace, that I may continue in the same unto my life's end.

Catechist. Rehearse the Articles of thy Belief.

Answer.

I BELIEVE in God the Father Almighty, Maker of heaven and earth:

And in Jesus Christ his only Son our Lord: Who was conceived by the Holy Ghost, Born of the Virgin Mary: Suffered under Pontius Pilate, Was crucified, dead, and buried: He descended into hell;

The third day he rose again from the dead: He ascended into heaven, And sitteth on the right hand of God the Father Almighty: From thence he shall come to judge the quick and the dead.

I believe in the Holy Ghost: The holy Catholic Church; The Communion of Saints: The Forgiveness of sins: The Resurrection of the body: And the Life everlasting. Amen.

Question. What dost thou chiefly learn in these Articles of thy Belief?

Answer. First, I learn to believe in *God* the Father, who hath made me, and all the world.

Secondly, in God the Son, who hath redeemed me, and all mankind.

Thirdly, in *God* the Holy Ghost, who sanctifieth me, and all the people of God.

Question. You said that your Sponsors did promise for you, that you should keep God's Commandments. Tell me how many there are?

Answer. Ten.

Question. Which are they?

Answer.

THE same which God spake in the twentieth Chapter of Exodus, saying, I am the LORD thy God, who brought thee out of the land of Egypt, out of the house of bondage.

I. Thou shalt have none other gods but me.

II. Thou shalt not make to thyself any graven image, nor the likeness of any thing that is in heaven above, or in the earth beneath, or in the water under the earth; thou shalt not bow down to them, nor worship them; for I the LORD thy God am a jealous God, and visit the sins of the fathers upon the children, unto the third and fourth generation of them that hate me; and show mercy unto thousands in them that love me and keep my commandments.

III. Thou shalt not take the Name of the LORD thy God in vain; for the LORD will not hold him guiltless, that taketh his Name in vain.

IV. Remember that thou keep holy the Sabbath-day. Six days shalt thou labour, and do all that thou hast to do; but the seventh day

*k 3

is the Sabbath of the LORD thy God. In it thou shalt do no manner of work; thou, and thy son, and thy daughter, thy man-servant, and thy maid-servant, and thy cattle, and the stranger that is within thy gates. For in six days the LORD made heaven and earth, the sea, and all that in them is, and rested the seventh day: wherefore the LORD blessed the seventh day, and hallowed it.

V. Honour thy father and thy mother; that thy days may be long in the land which the LORD thy God giveth thee.

VI. Thou shalt do no murder.

VII. Thou shalt not commit adultery.

VIII. Thou shalt not steal.

IX. Thou shalt not bear false witness against thy neighbour.

X. Thou shalt not covet thy neighbour's house, thou shalt not covet thy neighbour's wife, nor his servant, nor his maid, nor his ox, nor his ass, nor any thing that is his.

Question. What dost thou chiefly learn by these Commandments?

Answer. I learn two things; my duty towards God, and my duty towards my Neighbour.

Question. What is thy duty towards God?

Answer. My duty towards God is To believe in him, to fear him, And to love him with all my heart, with all my mind, with all my soul, and with all my strength: To worship him, to give him thanks: To put my whole trust in him, to call upon him: To honour his holy Name and his Word: And to serve him truly all the days of my life.

Question. What is thy duty towards thy Neighbour?

Answer. My duty towards my Neighbour is To love him as myself, and to do to all men as I would they should do unto me: To love, honour, and succour my father and mother: To honour and obey the civil authority: To submit myself to all my governors, teachers, spiritual pastors and masters: To order myself lowly and reverently to all my betters: To hurt nobody by word or deed: To be true and just in all my dealings: To bear no malice nor hatred in my heart: To keep my hands from picking and stealing, and my tongue from evil speaking, lying, and slandering: To keep my body in temperance, soberness, and chastity: Not to covet nor desire other men's goods; But to learn and labour truly to get mine own living, And to do my duty in that state of life unto which it shall please God to call me.

Catechist. My good Child, know this; that thou art not able to do these things of thyself, nor to walk in the Commandments of God, and to serve him, without his special grace; which thou must learn at all times to call for by diligent prayer. Let me hear, therefore, if thou canst say the Lord's Prayer.

Answer.

OUR Father, who art in heaven, Hallowed be thy Name. Thy kingdom come. Thy will be done on earth, As it is in heaven. Give us this day our daily bread. And forgive us our trespasses, As we forgive those who trespass against us. And lead us not into temptation; But deliver us from evil. Amen.

Question. What desirest thou of God in this Prayer?

Answer. I desire my Lord God, our heavenly Father, who is the giver of all goodness, to send his grace unto me, and to all people; that we may worship him, serve him, and obey him, as we ought to do. And I pray unto God, that he will send us all things that are needful both for our souls and bodies; and that he will be merciful unto us, and forgive us our sins; and that it will please him to save and defend us in all dangers both of soul and body; and that he will keep us from all sin and wickedness, and from our spiritual enemy, and from everlasting death. And this I trust he will do of his mercy and goodness, through our Lord Jesus Christ. And therefore, I say, Amen. So be it.

Question.

HOW many Sacraments hath Christ ordained in his Church?

Answer. Two only, as generally necessary to salvation; that is to say, Baptism, and the Supper of the Lord.

Question. What meanest thou by this word *Sacrament?*

Answer. I mean an outward and visible sign of an inward and spiritual grace given unto us; ordained by Christ himself, as a means whereby we receive the same, and a pledge to assure us thereof.

Question. How many parts are there in a Sacrament?

Answer. Two; the outward visible sign, and the inward spiritual grace.

Question. What is the outward visible sign or form in Baptism?

Answer. Water; wherein the person is baptized, *In the Name of the Father, and of the Son, and of the Holy Ghost.*

Question. What is the inward and spiritual grace?

Answer. A death unto sin, and a new birth unto righteousness: for being by nature born in sin, and the children of wrath, we are hereby made the children of grace.

Question. What is required of persons to be baptized?

Answer. Repentance, whereby they forsake sin; and Faith, whereby they stedfastly believe the promises of God made to them in that Sacrament.

Question. Why then are Infants baptized, when by reason of their tender age they cannot perform them?

Answer. Because they promise them both by their Sureties; which promise, when they come to age, themselves are bound to perform.

Question. Why was the Sacrament of the Lord's Supper ordained?

Answer. For the continual remembrance of the sacrifice of the death of Christ, and of the benefits which we receive thereby.

Question. What is the outward part or sign of the Lord's Supper?

Answer. Bread and Wine, which the Lord hath commanded to be received.

Question. What is the inward part, or thing signified?

Answer. The Body and Blood of Christ, which are spiritually taken and received by the faithful in the Lord's Supper.

Question. What are the

benefits whereof we are partakers thereby?

Answer. The strengthening and refreshing of our souls by the Body and Blood of Christ, as our bodies are by the Bread and Wine.

Question. What is required of those who come to the Lord's Supper?

Answer. To examine themselves, whether they repent them truly of their former sins, stedfastly purposing to lead a new life; have a lively faith in God's mercy through Christ, with a thankful remembrance of his death; and be in charity with all men.

¶ *The Minister of every Parish shall diligently, upon Sundays and Holy-days, or on some other convenient occasions, openly in the Church, instruct or examine so many Children of his Parish, sent unto him, as he shall think convenient, in some part of this Catechism.*

¶ *And all Fathers, Mothers, Masters, and Mistresses, shall cause their Children, Servants, and Apprentices, who have not learned their Catechism, to come to the Church at the time appointed, and obediently to hear and to be ordered by the Minister, until such time as they have learned all that is here appointed for them to learn.*

¶ *So soon as Children are come to a competent age, and can say the Creed, the Lord's Prayer, and the Ten Commandments, and can answer to the other questions of this short Catechism, they shall be brought to the Bishop.*

¶ *And whensoever the Bishop shall give knowledge for Children to be brought unto him for their Confirmation, the Minister of every Parish shall either bring, or send in writing, with his hand subscribed thereunto, the Names of all such Persons within his Parish, as he shall think fit to be presented to the Bishop to be confirmed.*

THE ORDER OF
CONFIRMATION,
OR LAYING ON OF HANDS UPON THOSE WHO ARE BAPTIZED, AND COME TO YEARS OF DISCRETION.

¶ Upon the day appointed, all that are to be then confirmed, being placed and standing in order before the Bishop, sitting in his chair near to the Holy Table, he, or some other Minister appointed by him, may read this Preface following ; the People standing until the Lord's Prayer.

TO the end that Confirmation may be ministered to the more edifying of such as shall receive it, the Church hath thought good to order, That none shall be confirmed, but such as can say the Creed, the Lord's Prayer, and the Ten Commandments ; and can also answer to such other Questions, as in the short Catechism are contained : which order is very convenient to be observed ; to the end that children, being now come to the years of discretion, and having learned what their Godfathers and Godmothers promised for them in Baptism, may themselves, with their own mouth and consent, openly before the Church, ratify and confirm the same ; and also promise, that, by the grace of God, they will evermore endeavour themselves faithfully to observe such things, as they, by their own confession, have assented unto.

¶ Then the Minister shall present unto the Bishop those who are to be confirmed, and shall say,

REVEREND Father in God, I present unto you these children [*or* these persons] to receive the Laying on of Hands.

¶ Then the Bishop, or some Minister appointed by him, may say,

Hear the words of the Evangelist Saint *Luke*, in

the eighth Chapter of the Book of the *Acts of the Apostles.*

WHEN the apostles which were at Jerusalem heard that Samaria had received the word of God, they sent unto them Peter and John: who, when they were come down, prayed for them, that they might receive the Holy Ghost: (for as yet he was fallen upon none of them: only they were baptized in the name of the Lord Jesus.) Then laid they their hands on them, and they received the Holy Ghost.

¶ *Then shall the Bishop say,*

DO ye here, in the presence of God, and of this congregation, renew the solemn promise and vow that ye made, or that was made in your name, at your Baptism; ratifying and confirming the same; and acknowledging yourselves bound to believe and to do all those things which ye then undertook, or your Sponsors then undertook for you?

¶ *And every one shall audibly answer,*

I do.

Bishop.

OUR help is in the Name of the Lord;
Answer. Who hath made heaven and earth.
Bishop. Blessed be the Name of the Lord;
Answer. Henceforth, world without end.
Bishop. Lord hear our prayer.
Answer. And let our cry come unto thee.

Bishop. Let us pray.

ALMIGHTY and ever-living God, who hast vouchsafed to regenerate these thy servants by Water and the Holy Ghost, and hast given unto them forgiveness of all their sins; Strengthen them, we beseech thee, O Lord, with the Holy Ghost, the Comforter, and daily increase in them thy manifold gifts of grace: the spirit of wisdom and understanding, the spirit of counsel and ghostly strength, the spirit of knowledge and true godliness; and fill them, O Lord, with the spirit of thy holy fear, now and for ever. *Amen.*

¶ *Then all of them in order kneeling before the Bishop, he shall lay his hands upon the head of every one severally, saying,*

DEFEND, O Lord, this thy Child [or this thy Servant] with thy heavenly grace; that *he* may continue thine for ever; and daily increase in thy Holy Spirit more and more, until *he* come unto thy everlasting kingdom. Amen.

¶ *Then shall the Bishop say,*

The Lord be with you.

Answer. And with thy spirit.

¶ *And all kneeling down, the Bishop shall add,*

Let us pray.

OUR Father, who art in heaven, Hallowed be thy Name. Thy kingdom come. Thy will be done on earth, As it is in heaven. Give us this day our daily bread. And forgive us our trespasses, As we forgive those who trespass against us. And lead us not into temptation; But deliver us from evil. Amen.

¶ *And these Collects.*

ALMIGHTY and ever-living God, who makest us both to will and to do those things which are good, and acceptable unto thy Divine Majesty; We make our humble supplications unto thee for these thy servants, upon whom, after the example of thy holy Apostles, we have now laid our hands, to certify them, by this sign, of thy favour and gracious goodness towards them. Let thy fatherly hand, we beseech thee, ever be over them; let thy Holy Spirit ever be with them; and so lead them in the knowledge and obedience of thy Word, that in the end they may obtain everlasting life; through our Lord Jesus Christ, who with thee and the Holy Ghost liveth and reigneth ever, one God, world without end. *Amen.*

O ALMIGHTY Lord, and everlasting God, vouchsafe, we beseech thee, to direct, sanctify, and govern, both our hearts and bodies, in the ways of thy laws, and in the works of thy commandments; that, through thy most mighty protection, both here and ever, we may be preserved in body and soul; through our Lord and Saviour Jesus Christ. *Amen.*

¶ *Then the Bishop shall bless them, saying thus.*

THE Blessing of God Almighty, the Father, the Son, and the Holy Ghost, be upon you, and remain with you for ever. *Amen.*

¶ *The Minister shall not omit earnestly to move the Persons confirmed to come, without delay, to the Lord's Supper.*

¶ *And there shall none be admitted to the Holy Communion, until such time as he be confirmed, or be ready and desirous to be confirmed.*

THE FORM OF
SOLEMNIZATION OF MATRIMONY.

¶ *The laws respecting Matrimony, whether by publishing the Banns in Churches, or by Licence, being different in the several States, every Minister is left to the direction of those laws, in every thing that regards the civil contract between the parties.*

¶ *And when the Banns are published, it shall be in the following form: I publish the Banns of Marriage between M. of —, and N. of —. If any of you know cause, or just impediment, why these two persons should not be joined together in holy Matrimony, ye are to declare it. This is the first [second or third] time of asking.*

¶ *At the day and time appointed for Solemnization of Matrimony, the Persons to be married shall come into the body of the Church, or shall be ready in some proper house, with their friends and neighbours; and there standing together, the Man on the right hand, and the Woman on the left, the Minister shall say,*

DEARLY beloved, we are gathered together here in the sight of God, and in the face of this company, to join together this Man and this Woman in holy Matrimony; which is an honourable estate, instituted of God in the time of man's innocency, signifying unto us the mystical union that is betwixt Christ and his Church: which holy estate Christ adorned and beautified with his presence and first miracle that he wrought in Cana of Galilee, and is commended of Saint Paul to be honourable among all men: and therefore is not by any to be entered into unadvisedly or lightly; but reverently, discreetly, advisedly, soberly, and in the fear of God. Into this holy estate these two persons present come now to be joined. If any man can show just cause, why they may not lawfully be joined together, let him now speak, or else hereafter for ever hold his peace.

¶ *And also speaking unto the Persons who are to be married, he shall say,*

I REQUIRE and charge you both, as ye will answer at the dreadful day of judgment when the secrets of all hearts shall be disclosed, that if either of you know any impediment, why ye may not be lawfully joined together in Matrimony, ye do now confess it. For be ye well assured, that if any persons are joined together otherwise than as God's Word doth allow, their marriage is not lawful.

¶ *The Minister, if he shall have reason to doubt of the lawfulness of the proposed Marriage, may demand sufficient surety for his indemnification: but if no impediment shall be alleged, or suspected, the Minister shall say to the Man,*

M. WILT thou have this Woman to thy wedded wife, to live together after God's ordinance in the holy estate of Matrimony? Wilt thou love her, comfort her, honour, and keep her in sickness and in health; and, forsaking all others, keep thee only unto her, so long as ye both shall live?

¶ *The Man shall answer,*

I will.

¶ *Then shall the Minister say unto the Woman,*

N. WILT thou have this Man to thy wedded husband, to live together after God's ordinance in the holy estate of Matrimony? Wilt thou obey him, and serve him, love, honour, and keep him in sickness and in health; and, forsaking all others, keep thee only unto him, so long as ye both shall live?

¶ *The Woman shall answer,*

I will.

¶ *Then shall the Minister say,*

WHO giveth this Woman to be married to this Man?

¶ *Then shall they give their troth to each other in this manner. The Minister, receiving the Woman at her father's or friend's hands, shall cause the Men with his right hand to take the Woman by her right hand, and to say after him as followeth.*

I M. take thee N. to my wedded Wife, to have and to hold from this day forward, for better for worse, for richer for poorer, in sickness and in health, to love and to cherish, till death us do part, according to God's holy ordinance; and thereto I plight thee my troth.

¶ *Then shall they loose their hands; and the Woman with her right hand taking the Man by his right hand, shall likewise say after the Minister:*

I N. take thee M. to my wedded Husband, to have and to hold from this day forward, for better for worse, for richer for poorer, in sickness and in health, to love, cherish, and to obey, till death us do part, according to God's holy ordinance; and thereto I give thee my troth.

¶ *Then shall they again loose their hands; and the Man shall give unto the Woman a Ring. And the Minister taking the Ring shall deliver it unto the Man, to put it upon the fourth finger of the Woman's left hand. And the Man holding the Ring there, and taught by the Minister, shall say,*

WITH this Ring I thee wed, and with all my worldly goods I thee endow: In the Name of the Father, and of the Son, and of the Holy Ghost. Amen.

¶ *Then, the Man leaving the Ring upon the fourth finger of the Woman's left hand, the Minister shall say,*

Let us pray.

OUR Father, who art in heaven, Hallowed be thy Name. Thy kingdom come. Thy will be done on earth, As it is in heaven. Give us this day our daily bread. And forgive us our trespasses, As we forgive those who trespass against us. And lead us not into temptation: But deliver us from evil. Amen.

O ETERNAL God, Creator and Preserver of all mankind, Giver of all spiritual grace, the Author of everlasting life; Send thy blessing upon these thy servants, this man and this woman, whom we bless in thy Name; that, as Isaac and Rebecca lived faithfully together, so these persons may surely perform and keep the vow and covenant betwixt them made, (whereof this Ring given and received is a token and pledge,) and may ever remain in perfect love and peace together, and live according to thy laws; through Jesus Christ our Lord. *Amen.*

¶ *Then shall the Minister join their right hands together, and say,*

THOSE whom God hath joined together let no man put asunder.

¶ *Then shall the Minister speak unto the company.*

FORASMUCH as *M.* and *N.* have consented together in holy wed-

lock, and have witnessed the same before God and this company, and thereto have given and pledged their troth, each to the other, and have declared the same by giving and receiving a Ring, and by joining hands; I pronounce that they are Man and Wife, In the Name of the Father, and of the Son, and of the Holy Ghost. *Amen.*

¶ *And the Minister shall add this Blessing.*

GOD the Father, God the Son, God the Holy Ghost, bless, preserve, and keep you; the Lord mercifully with his favour look upon you, and fill you with all spiritual benediction and grace; that ye may so live together in this life, that in the world to come ye may have life everlasting. *Amen.*

THE ORDER FOR
THE VISITATION OF THE SICK.

❦

¶ When any person is sick, notice shall be given thereof to the Minister of the Parish; who, coming into the sick person's house, shall say,

PEACE be to this house, and to all that dwell in it.

¶ When he cometh into the sick man's presence, he shall say, kneeling down,

REMEMBER not, Lord, our iniquities, nor the iniquities of our forefathers: Spare us, good Lord, spare thy people, whom thou hast redeemed with thy most precious blood, and be not angry with us for ever.

Answer. Spare us, good Lord.

¶ Then the Minister shall say,

Let us pray.

Lord, have mercy upon us.

Christ, have mercy upon us.

Lord, have mercy upon us.

OUR Father, who art in heaven, Hallowed be thy Name. Thy kingdom come. Thy will be done on earth, As it is in heaven. Give us this day our daily bread. And forgive us our trespasses, As we forgive those who trespass against us. And lead us not into temptation; But deliver us from evil. Amen.

Minister. O Lord, save thy servant;

Answer. Who putteth *his* trust in thee.

Minister. Send *him* help from thy holy place;

Answer. And evermore mightily defend *him.*

Minister. Let the enemy have no advantage of *him;*

Answer. Nor the wicked approach to hurt *him.*

Minister. Be unto *him,* O Lord, a strong tower;

Answer. From the face of *his* enemy.

Minister. O Lord, hear our prayer.

Answer. And let our cry come unto thee.

Minister.

O LORD, look down from heaven, behold,

visit, and relieve this thy servant. Look upon *him* with the eyes of thy mercy, give *him* comfort and sure confidence in thee, defend *him* from the danger of the enemy, and keep *him* in perpetual peace and safety; through Jesus Christ our Lord. *Amen.*

HEAR us, Almighty and most merciful God and Saviour; extend thy accustomed goodness to this thy servant, who is grieved with sickness. Sanctify, we beseech thee, this thy fatherly correction to *him;* that the sense of *his* weakness may add strength to *his* faith, and seriousness to *his* repentance: that, if it shall be thy good pleasure to restore *him* to *his* former health, *he* may lead the residue of *his* life in thy fear, and to thy glory: or else, give *him* grace so to take thy visitation, that, after this painful life ended, *he* may dwell with thee in life everlasting; through Jesus Christ our Lord. *Amen.*

¶ *Then shall the Minister exhort the sick Person after this form, or other like.*

DEARLY beloved, know this, that Almighty God is the Lord of life and death, and of all things to them pertaining; as youth, strength, health, age, weakness, and sickness. Wherefore, whatsoever your sickness be, know you certainly that it is God's visitation. And for what cause soever this sickness be sent unto you; whether it be to try your patience for the example of others, and that your faith may be found, in the day of the Lord, laudable, glorious, and honourable, to the increase of glory and endless felicity; or else it be sent unto you to correct and amend in you whatsoever doth offend the eyes of your heavenly Father; know you certainly, that if you truly repent you of your sins, and bear your sickness patiently, trusting in God's mercy for his dear Son Jesus Christ's sake, and render unto him humble thanks for his fatherly visitation, submitting yourself wholly unto his will, it shall turn to your profit, and help you forward in the right way that leadeth unto everlasting life.

¶ *If the Person visited be very sick, then the Minister may end his Exhortation in this place, or else proceed.*

TAKE therefore in good part the chastisement of the Lord: for (as Saint Paul saith in the twelfth Chapter to the Hebrews) whom the Lord loveth he chasteneth, and scourgeth every son whom he receiveth. If ye endure chastening, God dealeth with you as with sons; for what son is he whom the father chasteneth not? But if ye be without chastisement, whereof all are partakers, then are ye bastards, and not sons. Furthermore we have had fathers of our flesh which corrected us, and we gave them reverence: shall we not much rather be in subjection unto the Father of spirits, and live? For they verily for a few days chastened us after their own pleasure; but he for our profit, that we might be partakers of his holiness. These words, good *brother*, are written in holy Scripture for our comfort and instruction; that we should patiently, and with thanksgiving, bear our heavenly Father's correction, whensoever, by any manner of adversity, it shall please his gracious goodness to visit us. And there should be no greater comfort to Christian persons, than to be made like unto Christ, by suffering patiently adversities, troubles, and sicknesses. For he himself went not up to joy, but first he suffered pain; he entered not into his glory before he was crucified. So truly our way to eternal joy is to suffer here with Christ; and our door to enter into eternal life is gladly to die with Christ; that we may rise again from death, and dwell with him in everlasting life. Now therefore, taking your sickness, which is thus profitable for you, patiently, I exhort you, in the Name of God, to remember the profession which you made unto God in your Baptism. And forasmuch as after this life there is an account to be given unto the righteous Judge, by whom all must be judged, without respect of persons, I require you to examine yourself and your estate, both toward God and man; so that, accusing and condemning yourself for your own faults, you may find mercy at our heavenly Father's hand for Christ's sake, and not be accused and condemned in that fearful judgment. Therefore I shall rehearse to you the Articles of our Faith; that you may know whether you do believe as a Christian man should, or no.

¶ *Here the Minister shall rehearse the Articles of the Faith, saying thus.*

DOST thou believe in God the Father Almighty, Maker of heaven and earth?

And in Jesus Christ his only-begotten Son our Lord? And that he was conceived by the Holy Ghost, born of the Virgin Mary: that he suffered under Pontius Pilate, was crucified, dead, and buried: that he went down into hell, and also did rise again the third day: that he ascended into heaven, and sitteth on the right hand of God the Father Almighty: and from thence shall come again, at the end of the world, to judge the quick and the dead?

And dost thou believe in the Holy Ghost: the holy Catholic Church; the Communion of Saints: the Remission of sins: the Resurrection of the flesh: and everlasting Life after death?

¶ *The sick person shall answer,*

All this I stedfastly believe.

¶ *Then shall the Minister examine whether he repent him truly of his sins, and be in charity with all the world; exhorting him to forgive, from the bottom of his heart, all persons that have offended him; and if he hath offended any other, to ask them forgiveness; and where he hath done injury or wrong to any man, that he make amends to the uttermost of his power. And if he hath not before disposed of his goods, let him then be admonished to make his Will, and to declare his Debts, what he oweth, and what is owing unto him, for the better discharging of his conscience, and the quietness of his Executors. But men should often be put in remembrance to take order for the settling of their temporal estates, whilst they are in health.*

¶ *The Exhortation before rehearsed, may be said before the Minister begin his Prayer, as he shall see cause.*

¶ *The Minister shall not omit earnestly to move such sick persons as are of ability, to be liberal to the poor.*

¶ *And then the Minister shall say the Collect following.*

Let us pray.

O MOST merciful God, who, according to the

multitude of thy mercies, dost so put away the sins of those who truly repent, that thou rememberest them no more; Open thine eye of mercy upon this thy servant, who most earnestly desireth pardon and forgiveness. Renew in *him*, most loving Father, whatsoever hath been decayed by the fraud and malice of the devil, or by *his* own carnal will and frailness; preserve and continue this sick member in the unity of the Church; consider *his* contrition, accept *his* tears, assuage *his* pain, as shall seem to thee most expedient for *him*. And forasmuch as *he* putteth *his* full trust only in thy mercy, impute not unto *him his* former sins, but strengthen *him* with thy blessed Spirit; and, when thou art pleased to take *him* hence, take *him* unto thy favour; through the merits of thy most dearly beloved Son, Jesus Christ our Lord. *Amen.*

¶ *Then shall the Minister say this Psalm.*

PSALM 130. *De profundis.*

OUT of the deep have I called unto thee, O LORD: Lord, hear my voice.

O let thine ears consider well: the voice of my complaint.

If thou, LORD, wilt be extreme to mark what is done amiss: O Lord, who may abide it?

For there is mercy with thee: therefore shalt thou be feared.

I look for the LORD; my soul doth wait for him: in his word is my trust.

My soul fleeth unto the Lord: before the morning watch, I say, before the morning watch.

O Israel, trust in the LORD; for with the LORD there is mercy: and with him is plenteous redemption.

And he shall redeem Israel: from all his sins.

¶ *Adding this.*

O SAVIOUR of the world, who by thy Cross and precious Blood hast redeemed us; Save us, and help us, we humbly beseech thee, O Lord.

¶ *Then shall the Minister say.*

THE Almighty Lord, who is a most strong tower to all those who put their trust in him, to whom all things in heaven, in earth, and under the earth, do bow and obey, Be now and evermore thy defence; and make thee know and feel, that there is none other Name under heaven given to man, in whom, and through whom, thou mayest receive health and salvation, but only the Name of our Lord Jesus Christ. *Amen.*

⁋ Here the Minister may use any part of the service of this Book, which, in his discretion, he shall think convenient to the occasion; and after that shall say,

UNTO God's gracious mercy and protection we commit thee. The LORD bless thee, and keep thee. The LORD make his face to shine upon thee, and be gracious unto thee. The LORD lift up his countenance upon thee, and give thee peace, both now and evermore. *Amen.*

✠

Prayers which may be said with the foregoing Service, or any part thereof, at the discretion of the Minister.

A Prayer for a sick Child.

O ALMIGHTY God, and merciful Father, to whom alone belong the issues of life and death; Look down from heaven, we humbly beseech thee, with the eyes of mercy, upon this child now lying upon the bed of sickness: Visit *him,* O Lord, with thy salvation; deliver *him* in thy good appointed time from *his* bodily pain, and save *his* soul for thy mercies' sake: that, if it shall be thy pleasure to prolong *his* days here on earth, *he* may live to thee, and be an instrument of thy glory, by serving thee faithfully, and doing good in *his* generation; or else receive *him* into those heavenly habitations, where the souls of those who sleep in the Lord Jesus enjoy perpetual rest and felicity. Grant this, O Lord, for thy mercies' sake in the same thy Son our Lord Jesus Christ, who liveth and reigneth with thee and the Holy Ghost ever, one God, world without end. *Amen.*

A Prayer for a sick Person, when there appeareth but small hope of recovery.

O FATHER of mercies, and God of all comfort, our only help in time of need; We fly unto thee for succour in behalf of this thy servant, here lying under thy hand in great weakness of body. Look graciously upon *him*, O Lord; and the more the outward man decayeth, strengthen *him*, we beseech thee, so much the more continually with thy grace and Holy Spirit in the inner man. Give *him* unfeigned repentance for all the errors of *his* life past, and stedfast faith in thy Son Jesus; that *his* sins may be done away by thy mercy, and *his* pardon sealed in heaven, before *he* go hence, and be no more seen. We know, O Lord, that there is no word impossible with thee; and that, if thou wilt, thou canst even yet raise *him* up, and grant *him* a longer continuance amongst us; yet, forasmuch as in all appearance the time of *his* dissolution draweth near, so fit and prepare *him*, we beseech thee, against the hour of death, that after *his* departure hence in peace, and in thy favour, *his* soul may be received into thine everlasting kingdom; through the merits and mediation of Jesus Christ thine only Son, our Lord and Saviour. *Amen.*

A Commendatory Prayer for a sick Person at the point of departure.

O ALMIGHTY God, with whom do live the spirits of just men made perfect, after they are delivered from their earthly prisons; We humbly commend the soul of this thy servant, our dear *brother*, into thy hands, as into the hands of a faithful Creator, and most merciful Saviour; most humbly beseeching thee, that it may be precious in thy sight. Wash it, we pray thee, in the blood of that immaculate Lamb, that was slain to take away the sins of the world; *that* whatsoever defilements it may have contracted in the midst of this miserable and naughty world, through the lusts of the flesh, or the wiles of Satan, being purged and done away, it may be presented pure and without spot before thee; through the merits of Jesus Christ thine only Son our Lord. *Amen.*

A Prayer for Persons troubled in mind or in conscience.

O BLESSED Lord, the Father of mercies, and the God of all comfort; We beseech thee, look down in pity and compassion upon this thy afflicted servant. Thou writest bitter things against *him*, and makest *him* to possess *his* former iniquities; thy wrath lieth hard upon *him*, and *his* soul is full of trouble. But, O merciful God, who hast written thy holy Word for our learning, that we, through patience and comfort of thy holy Scriptures, might have hope; give *him* a right understanding of *himself*, and of thy threats and promises; that *he* may neither cast away *his* confidence in thee, nor place it any where but in thee. Give *him* strength against all *his* temptations, and heal all *his* distempers. Break not the bruised reed, nor quench the smoking flax. Shut not up thy tender mercies in displeasure; but make *him* to hear of joy and gladness, that the bones which thou hast broken may rejoice. Deliver *him* from fear of the enemy, and lift up the light of thy countenance upon *him*, and give *him* peace, through the merits and mediation of Jesus Christ our Lord. *Amen.*

A Prayer which may be said by the Minister in behalf of all present at the Visitation.

O GOD, whose days are without end, and whose mercies cannot be numbered; Make us, we beseech thee, deeply sensible of the shortness and uncertainty of human life; and let thy Holy Spirit lead us through this vale of misery, in holiness and righteousness, all the days of our lives: that, when we shall have served thee in our generation, we may be gathered unto our fathers, having the testimony of a good conscience; in the communion of the catholic Church; in the confidence of a certain faith; in the comfort of a reasonable, religious, and holy hope; in favour with thee our God, and in perfect charity with the world. All which we ask through Jesus Christ our Lord. *Amen.*

A Prayer which may be said in case of sudden surprise and immediate danger.

O MOST gracious Father, we fly unto thee for mercy in behalf of this thy servant, here lying under the sudden visitation of thine hand. If it be thy will, preserve *his* life, that there may be place for repentance; but if thou hast otherwise appointed, let thy mercy supply to *him* the want of the usual opportunity for the trimming of *his* lamp. Stir up in *him* such sorrow for sin, and such fervent love to thee, as may in a short time do the work of many days: that among the praises which thy saints and holy angels shall sing to the honour of thy mercy through eternal ages, it may be to thy unspeakable glory, that thou hast redeemed the soul of this thy servant from eternal death, and made *him* partaker of the everlasting life, which is through Jesus Christ our Lord. *Amen.*

A Thanksgiving for the beginning of a Recovery.

GREAT and mighty God, who bringest down to the grave, and bringest up again; We bless thy wonderful goodness, for having turned our heaviness into joy and our mourning into gladness, by restoring this our *brother* to some degree of *his* former health. Blessed be thy Name that thou didst not forsake *him* in *his* sickness; but didst visit *him* with comforts from above; didst support *him* in patience and submission to thy will; and at last didst send *him* seasonable relief. Perfect, we beseech thee, this thy mercy towards *him*; and prosper the means which shall be made use of for *his* cure: that, being restored to health of body, vigour of mind, and cheerfulness of spirit, *he* may be able to go to thine house, to offer thee an oblation with great gladness, and to bless thy holy Name for all thy goodness towards *him*; through Jesus Christ our Saviour, to whom, with thee and the Holy Spirit, be all honour and glory, world without end. *Amen.*

THE
COMMUNION OF THE SICK.

¶ *Forasmuch as all mortal men are subject to many sudden perils, diseases, and sicknesses, and ever uncertain what time they shall depart out of this life; therefore, to the intent they may be always in readiness to die, whensoever it shall please Almighty God to call them, the Ministers shall diligently from time to time (but especially in the time of pestilence, or other infectious sickness) exhort their parishioners to the often receiving of the Holy Communion of the Body and Blood of our Saviour Christ, when it shall be publicly administered in the Church; that so doing, they may, in case of sudden visitation, have the less cause to be disquieted for lack of the same. But if the sick person be not able to come to the Church, and yet is desirous to receive the Communion in his house; then he must give timely notice to the Minister, signifying also how many there are to communicate with him, (which shall be two at the least;) and all things necessary being prepared, the Minister shall there celebrate the Holy Communion, beginning with the Collect, Epistle, and Gospel, here following.*

The Collect.

ALMIGHTY, everliving God, Maker of mankind, who dost correct those whom thou dost love, and chastise every one whom thou dost receive; We beseech thee to have mercy upon this thy servant visited with thine hand, and to grant that *he* may take *his* sickness patiently, and recover *his* bodily health, if it be thy gracious will: and that, whensoever *his* soul shall depart from the body, it may be without spot presented unto thee; through Jesus Christ our Lord. *Amen.*

The Epistle. Heb. xii. 5.

MY son, despise not thou the chastening of the Lord, nor faint when thou art rebuked of him: for whom the Lord loveth he chasteneth, and scourgeth every son whom he receiveth.

The Gospel. St. John v. 24.

VERILY, verily, I say unto you, He that

heareth my word, and believeth on him that sent me, hath everlasting life, and shall not come into condemnation; but is passed from death unto life.

¶ *After which the Minister shall proceed according to the form before prescribed for the Holy Communion, beginning at these words,* Ye who do truly, etc.

¶ *At the time of the distribution of the holy Sacrament, the Minister shall first receive the Communion himself, and after minister unto those who are appointed to communicate with the sick, and last of all to the sick person.*

¶ *In the times of contagious sickness or disease, or when extreme weakness renders it expedient, the following form shall suffice:* The Confession *and the* Absolution; Lift up your hearts, etc., *through the* Sanctus; The Prayer of Consecration, *ending with these words,* partakers of his most blessed Body and Blood; The Communion; The Lord's Prayer; The Blessing.

¶ *But if a man, either by reason of extremity of sickness, or for want of warning in due time to the Minister, or for lack of company to receive with him, or by any other just impediment, do not receive the Sacrament of Christ's Body and Blood, the Minister shall instruct him, that if he do truly repent him of his sins, and stedfastly believe that Jesus Christ hath suffered death upon the Cross for him, and shed his Blood for his redemption, earnestly remembering the benefits he hath thereby, and giving him hearty thanks therefor, he doth eat and drink the Body and Blood of our Saviour Christ profitably to his soul's health, although he do not receive the Sacrament with his mouth.*

¶ *When the sick person is visited, and receiveth the Holy Communion all at one time, then the Minister, for more expedition, shall cut off the form of the Visitation at the Psalm, and go straight to the Communion.*

¶ *In the times of contagious sickness or disease, when none of the Parish or neighbours can be gotten to communicate with the sick in their houses, for fear of the infection, upon special request of the diseased, the Minister alone may communicate with him.*

¶ *This Office may be used with aged and bed-ridden persons, or such as are not able to attend the public Ministration in Church, substituting the Collect, Epistle, and Gospel for the Day, for those appointed above.*

THE ORDER FOR
THE BURIAL OF THE DEAD.

❁

¶ *Here is to be noted, that the Office ensuing is not to be used for any unbaptized adults, any who die excommunicate, or who have laid violent hands upon themselves.*

¶ *The Minister, meeting the Corpse at the entrance of the Churchyard, and going before it, either into the Church or towards the Grave, shall say or sing,*

I AM the resurrection and the life, saith the Lord: he that believeth in me, though he were dead, yet shall he live: and whosoever liveth and believeth in me, shall never die. *St. John* xi. 25, 26.

I KNOW that my redeemer liveth, and that he shall stand at the latter day upon the earth: and though after my skin worms destroy this body, yet in my flesh shall I see God: whom I shall see for myself, and mine eyes shall behold, and not another. *Job* xix. 25, 26, 27.

WE brought nothing into this world, and it is certain we can carry nothing out. The LORD gave, and the LORD hath taken away; blessed be the name of the LORD. 1 *Tim.* vi. 7. *Job* i. 21.

¶ *After they are come into the Church, shall be said or sung one or both of the following Selections, taken from the 39th and 90th Psalms.*

LORD, let me know mine end, and the number of my days : that I may be certified how long I have to live.

Behold, thou hast made my days as it were a span long : and mine age is even as nothing in respect of thee ; and verily every man living is altogether vanity.

For man walketh in a vain shadow, and disquieteth himself in vain : he heapeth up riches, and cannot tell who shall gather them.

And now, Lord, what is my hope : truly my hope is even in thee.

Deliver me from all mine offences : and make me not a rebuke unto the foolish.

When thou with rebukes dost chasten man for sin, thou makest his beauty to consume away, like as it were a moth fretting a garment : every man therefore is but vanity.

Hear my prayer, O Lord, and with thine ears consider my calling : hold not thy peace at my tears.

For I am a stranger with thee, and a sojourner : as all my fathers were.

O spare me a little, that I may recover my strength : before I go hence, and be no more seen.

Glory be to the Father, and to the Son : and to the Holy Ghost ;

As it was in the beginning, is now, and ever shall be : world without end. Amen.

LORD, thou hast been our refuge : from one generation to another.

Before the mountains were brought forth, or ever the earth and the world were made : thou art God from everlasting, and world without end.

Thou turnest man to destruction : again thou sayest, Come again, ye children of men.

For a thousand years in thy sight are but as yesterday : seeing that is past as a watch in the night.

As soon as thou scatterest them they are even as a sleep : and fade away suddenly like the grass.

In the morning it is green, and groweth up : but in the evening it is cut down, dried up, and withered.

For we consume away in thy displeasure : and are afraid at thy wrathful indignation.

Thou hast set our misdeeds before thee : and our secret sins in the light of thy countenance.

For when thou art angry all our days are gone : we bring our years to an end, as it were a tale that is told.

The days of our age are threescore years and ten ; and though men be so strong that they come to fourscore years : yet is their strength then but labour and sorrow ; so soon passeth it away, and we are gone.

* L

O teach us to number our days : that we may apply our hearts unto wisdom.

Glory be to the Father, and to the Son : and to the Holy Ghost;

As it was in the beginning, is now, and ever shall be : world without end. Amen.

¶ *Then shall follow the Lesson, taken out of the fifteenth Chapter of the first Epistle of St. Paul to the Corinthians.*

1 *Cor.* xv. 20.

NOW is Christ risen from the dead, and become the firstfruits of them that slept. For since by man came death, by man came also the resurrection of the dead. For as in Adam all die, even so in Christ shall all be made alive. But every man in his own order: Christ the firstfruits; afterward they that are Christ's at his coming. Then cometh the end, when he shall have delivered up the kingdom to God, even the Father; when he shall have put down all rule and all authority and power. For he must reign, till he hath put all enemies under his feet. The last enemy that shall be destroyed is death. For he hath put all things under his feet. But when he saith all things are put under him, it is manifest that he is excepted, which did put all things under him. And when all things shall be subdued unto him, then shall the Son also himself be subject unto him that put all things under him, that God may be all in all. Else what shall they do which are baptized for the dead, if the dead rise not at all? why are they then baptized for the dead? and why stand we in jeopardy every hour? I protest by your rejoicing which I have in Christ Jesus our Lord, I die daily. If after the manner of men I have fought with beasts at Ephesus, what advantageth it me, if the dead rise not? let us eat and drink; for to morrow we die. Be not deceived: evil communications corrupt good manners. Awake to righteousness, and sin not; for some have not the knowledge of God: I speak this to your shame. But some man will say, How are the dead raised up? and with what body do they come? Thou fool, that which thou sowest is not quickened, except it die: and that which thou sowest, thou sowest not that body that shall be, but bare grain, it may chance of wheat, or of some other grain: but God giveth it a body as it hath pleased him, and to every seed his own body. All flesh is not the same flesh: but there is one kind of flesh of men, another flesh of beasts, another of fishes, and another of birds. There are also celestial bodies, and bodies terrestrial: but the glory of the celestial is one, and the glory of the terrestrial is another. There is one glory of the sun, and another glory of the moon, and another glory of the stars: for one star differeth from another star in glory. So also is the resurrection of the dead. It is sown in corruption; it is raised in incorruption: it is sown in dishonour; it is raised in glory: it is sown in weakness; it is raised in power: it is sown a natural body; it is raised a spiritual body. There is a natural body, and there is a spiritual body. And so it is written, The first man Adam was made a living soul; the last Adam was made a quickening spirit. Howbeit that was not first which is spiritual, but that which is natural; and afterward that which is spiritual. The first man is of the earth, earthy: the second man is the Lord from heaven. As is the earthy, such are they also that are earthy: and as is the heavenly, such are they also that are heavenly. And as we have borne the image of the earthy, we shall also bear the image of the heavenly. Now this I say, brethren, that flesh and blood cannot inherit the kingdom of God; neither doth corruption inherit incorruption. Behold, I shew you a mystery; We shall not all sleep, but we shall all be changed, in a moment, in the twinkling of an eye, at the last trump: for the trumpet shall sound, and the dead shall be raised incorruptible, and we shall be changed. For this corruptible must put on incorruption, and this mortal must put on immortality. So when this corruptible shall have put on incorruption, and this mortal shall have put on immortality, then shall be brought to pass the saying that is written, Death is swallowed up in victory. O death, where is thy sting? O grave, where is thy victory? The sting of death is sin; and the strength of sin is the law. But thanks be to God, which giveth us the victory through our Lord Jesus Christ. Therefore, my beloved brethren, be ye stedfast, unmoveable, always abounding in the work of the Lord, forasmuch as ye know that your labour is not in vain in the Lord.

¶ *Here may be sung a Hymn or an Anthem; and, at the discretion of the Minister, the* CREED, *and such fitting* PRAYERS *as are elsewhere provided in this Book, may be added.*

¶ *When they come to the Grave, while the Corpse is made ready to be laid into the earth, shall be sung or said,*

MAN, that is born of a woman, hath but a short time to live, and is full of misery. He cometh up, and is cut down, like a flower; he fleeth as it were a shadow, and never continueth in one stay.

In the midst of life we are in death; of whom may we seek for succour, but of thee, O Lord, who for our sins art justly displeased?

Yet, O Lord God most holy, O Lord most mighty, O holy and most merciful Saviour, deliver us not into the bitter pains of eternal death.

Thou knowest, Lord, the secrets of our hearts; shut not thy merciful ears to our prayer; but spare us, Lord most holy, O God most mighty, O holy and merciful Saviour, thou most worthy Judge eternal, suffer us not, at our last hour, for any pains of death, to fall from thee.

¶ *Then, while the earth shall be cast upon the Body by some standing by, the Minister shall say,*

FORASMUCH as it hath pleased Almighty God, in his wise providence, to take out of this world the soul of our deceased *brother,* we therefore commit *his* body to the ground; earth to earth, ashes to ashes, dust to dust; looking for the general Resurrection in the last day, *and the life of the world to come, through our Lord Jesus Christ; at whose second coming in glorious majesty to judge the world, the earth and the sea shall give up their dead; and the corruptible bodies of those who sleep in him shall be changed, and made like unto his own glorious body; according to the mighty working whereby he is able to subdue all things unto himself.*

¶ *Then shall be said or sung,*

I HEARD a voice from heaven, saying unto me, Write, From henceforth blessed are the dead who die in the Lord: even so saith the Spirit; for they rest from their labours. *Rev. xiv. 13.*

¶ *Then the Minister shall say,*

Lord, have mercy upon us.

Christ, have mercy upon us.

Lord, have mercy upon us.

O UR Father, who art in heaven, Hallowed be thy Name. Thy kingdom come. Thy will be done on earth, As it is in heaven. Give us this day our daily bread. And forgive us our trespasses, As we forgive those who trespass against us. And lead us not into temptation; But deliver us from evil. Amen.

¶ *Then the Minister shall say one or both of the following Prayers, at his discretion.*

A LMIGHTY God, with whom do live the spirits of those who depart hence in the Lord, and with whom the souls of the faithful, after they are delivered from the burden of the flesh, are in joy and felicity; We give thee hearty thanks for the good examples of all those thy servants, who, having finished their course in faith, do now rest from their labours. And we beseech thee, that we, with all those who are departed in the true faith of thy holy Name, may have our perfect consummation and bliss, both in body and soul, in thy eternal and everlasting glory; through Jesus Christ our Lord. *Amen.*

O MERCIFUL God, the Father of our Lord Jesus Christ, who is the

Resurrection and the Life; in whom whosoever believeth, shall live, though he die; and whosoever liveth, and believeth in him, shall not die eternally; who also hath taught us, by his holy Apostle Saint Paul, not to be sorry, as men without hope, for those who sleep in him; We humbly beseech thee, O Father, to raise us from the death of sin unto the life of righteousness; that, when we shall depart this life, we may rest in him; and that, at the general Resurrection in the last day, we may be found acceptable in thy sight; and receive that blessing, which thy well-beloved Son shall then pronounce to all who love and fear thee, saying, Come, ye blessed children of my Father, receive the kingdom prepared for you from the beginning of the world. Grant this, we beseech thee, O merciful Father, through Jesus Christ, our Mediator and Redeemer. *Amen.*

THE grace of our Lord Jesus Christ, and the love of God, and the fellowship of the Holy Ghost, be with us all evermore. *Amen.*

Additional Prayers.

MOST merciful Father, who hast been pleased to take unto thyself the soul of this thy servant [*or* this child]; Grant to us who are still in our pilgrimage, and who walk as yet by faith, that having served thee with constancy on earth, we may be joined hereafter with thy blessed saints in glory everlasting; through Jesus Christ our Lord. *Amen.*

O LORD Jesus Christ, who by thy death didst take away the sting of death; Grant unto us thy servants so to follow in faith where thou hast led the way, that we may at length fall asleep peacefully in thee, and awake up after thy likeness; through thy mercy, who livest with the Father and the Holy Ghost, one God, world without end. *Amen.*

ALMIGHTY and everliving God, we yield unto thee most high praise and hearty thanks, for the wonderful grace and virtue declared in all thy saints, who have been the choice vessels of thy grace, and the lights of the world in their several generations; most humbly beseeching thee to give us grace so to follow the example of their stedfastness in thy faith, and obedience to thy holy commandments, that at the day of the general Resurrection, we, with all those who are of the mystical body of thy Son, may be set on his right hand, and hear that his most joyful voice: Come, ye blessed of my Father, inherit the kingdom prepared for you from the foundation of the world. Grant this, O Father, for Jesus Christ's sake, our only Mediator and Advocate. *Amen.*

¶ *Inasmuch as it may sometimes be expedient to say under shelter of the Church the whole or a part of the service appointed to be said at the Grave, the same is hereby allowed for weighty cause.*

At the Burial of the Dead at Sea.

¶ *The same office may be used; but in the Sentence of Committal, the Minister shall say,*

We therefore commit *his* body to the deep, looking for the general Resurrection in the last day, and the life of the world to come, through our Lord Jesus Christ; at whose second coming in glorious majesty to judge the world, the sea shall give up her dead; and the corruptible bodies of those who sleep in him shall be changed, and made like unto his glorious body; according to the mighty working whereby he is able to subdue all things unto himself.

THE THANKSGIVING OF WOMEN
AFTER CHILD-BIRTH;
COMMONLY CALLED,
THE CHURCHING OF WOMEN.

❖

¶ *This Service, or the concluding prayer alone, as it stands among the Occasional Prayers and Thanksgivings, may be used at the discretion of the Minister.*

¶ *The Woman, at the usual time after her delivery, shall come into the Church decently apparelled, and there shall kneel down in some convenient place, as hath been accustomed, or as the Ordinary shall direct; and then the Minister shall say unto her,*

FORASMUCH as it hath pleased Almighty God, of his goodness, to give you safe deliverance, and to preserve you in the great danger of Child-birth; you shall therefore give hearty thanks unto God, and say,

¶ *Then shall be said by both of them the following* Hymn, *the woman still kneeling.*

Dilexi, quoniam.

I AM well pleased: that the LORD hath heard the voice of my prayer;

That he hath inclined his ear unto me: therefore will I call upon him as long as I live.

I found trouble and heaviness, and I called upon the Name of the LORD: O LORD, I beseech thee, deliver my soul.

Gracious is the LORD, and righteous: yea, our God is merciful.

What reward shall I give unto the LORD: for all the benefits that he hath done unto me?

I will receive the cup of salvation: and call upon the Name of the LORD.

I will pay my vows now in the presence of all his people: in the courts of the LORD's house, even in the midst of thee, O Jerusalem. Praise the LORD.

Glory be to the Father, and to the Son: and to the Holy Ghost;

As it was in the beginning, is now, and ever shall be : world without end. Amen.

¶ *Then shall the Minister say the Lord's Prayer, with what followeth: but the Lord's Prayer may be omitted, if this be used with the Morning or Evening Prayer.*

OUR Father, who art in heaven, Hallowed be thy Name. Thy kingdom come. Thy will be done on earth, As it is in heaven. Give us this day our daily bread. And forgive us our trespasses, As we forgive those who trespass against us. And lead us not into temptation ; But deliver us from evil. Amen.

Minister. O Lord, save this woman thy servant ;

Answer. Who putteth her trust in thee.

Minister. Be thou to her a strong tower ;

Answer. From the face of her enemy.

Minister. Lord, hear our prayer.

Answer. And let our cry come unto thee.

Minister. Let us pray.

O ALMIGHTY God, we give thee humble thanks for that thou hast been graciously pleased to preserve, through the great pain and peril of child-birth, this woman, thy servant, who desireth now to offer her praises and thanksgivings unto thee. Grant, we beseech thee, most merciful Father, that she, through thy help, may both faithfully live and walk according to thy will in this life present, and also may be partaker of everlasting glory in the life to come ; through Jesus Christ our Lord. Amen.

¶ *The Woman, that cometh to give her Thanks, must offer accustomed offerings, which shall be applied by the Minister and the Church-wardens to the relief of distressed women in child-bed ; and if there be a Communion, it is convenient that she receive the Holy Communion.*

FORMS OF
PRAYER TO BE USED AT SEA.

❧

¶ The Morning and Evening Service to be used daily at Sea, shall be the same which is appointed in the Book of Common Prayer.

¶ These two following Prayers may be also used in Ships of war.

ETERNAL Lord God, who alone spreadest out the heavens, and rulest the raging of the sea; who hast compassed the waters with bounds, until day and night come to an end; Be pleased to receive into thy almighty and most gracious protection, the persons of us thy servants, and the Fleet [*or* Ship] in which we serve. Preserve us from the dangers of the sea, and from the violence of the enemy; that we may be a safeguard unto the United States of America, and a security for such as pass on the seas upon their lawful occasions; that the inhabitants of our land may in peace and quietness serve thee our God; and that we may return in safety to enjoy the blessings of the land, with the fruits of our labour; and, with a thankful remembrance of thy mercies, to praise and glorify thy holy Name; through Jesus Christ our Lord. *Amen.*

The Collect.

DIRECT us, O Lord, in all our doings, with thy most gracious favour, and further us with thy continual help; that in all our works begun, continued, and ended in thee, we may glorify thy holy Name, and finally, by thy mercy, obtain everlasting life; through Jesus Christ our Lord. *Amen.*

Prayers to be used in all Ships in Storms at Sea.

O MOST powerful and glorious Lord God, at whose command the winds blow, and lift up the waves of the sea, and who stillest the rage thereof; We, thy creatures, but miserable sinners, do in this our great distress cry unto thee for help: Save, Lord, or else we perish. We confess, when we have been safe, and seen all things quiet about us, we have forgotten thee our God, and refused to hearken to the still voice of thy word, and to obey thy commandments: but now we see how terrible thou art in all thy works of wonder, the great God to be feared above all: and therefore we adore thy Divine Majesty, acknowledging thy power, and imploring thy goodness. Help, Lord, and save us for thy mercy's sake in Jesus Christ, thy Son our Lord. *Amen.*

¶ Or this.

O MOST glorious and gracious Lord God, who dwellest in heaven, but beholdest all things below; Look down, we beseech thee, and hear us, calling out of the depth of misery, and out of the jaws of this death, which is now ready to swallow us up: Save, Lord, or else we perish. The living, the living shall praise thee. O send thy word of command to rebuke the raging winds and the roaring sea; that we, being delivered from this distress, may live to serve thee, and to glorify thy Name all the days of our life. Hear, Lord, and save us, for the infinite merits of our blessed Saviour, thy Son, our Lord Jesus Christ. Amen.

Short Prayers in respect of a Storm.

THOU, O Lord, who stillest the raging of the sea, hear, hear us, and save us, that we perish not.

O blessed Saviour, who didst save thy disciples ready to perish in a storm, hear us, and save us, we beseech thee.

Lord, have mercy upon us.
Christ, have mercy upon us.
Lord, have mercy upon us.
O Lord, hear us.
O Christ, hear us.

God the Father, God the Son, God the Holy Ghost, have mercy upon us, save us now and evermore. Amen.

¶ *When there shall be imminent danger, as many as can be spared from necessary service in the Ship shall be called together, and make an humble Confession of their sin to God; in which every one ought seriously to reflect upon those particular sins of which his conscience shall accuse him; saying as followeth.*

The Confession.

ALMIGHTY God, Father of our Lord Jesus Christ, Maker of all things, Judge of all men: We acknowledge and bewail our manifold sins and wickedness, Which we from time to time most grievously have committed, By thought, word, and deed, Against thy Divine Majesty, Provoking most justly thy

wrath and indignation against us. We do earnestly repent, And are heartily sorry for these our misdoings; The remembrance of them is grievous unto us; The burden of them is intolerable. Have mercy upon us, Have mercy upon us, most merciful Father; For thy Son our Lord Jesus Christ's sake, Forgive us all that is past; And grant that we may ever hereafter Serve and please thee In newness of life, To the honour and glory of thy Name; Through Jesus Christ our Lord. Amen.

¶ *Then shall the Priest, if there be any in the Ship, say,*

ALMIGHTY God, our heavenly Father, who of his great mercy hath promised forgiveness of sins to all those who with hearty repentance and true faith turn unto him; Have mercy upon you; pardon and deliver you from all your sins; confirm and strengthen you in all goodness; and bring you to everlasting life; through Jesus Christ our Lord. Amen.

¶ *Then shall they together say the Lord's Prayer.*

OUR Father, who art in heaven, Hallowed be thy Name, Thy kingdom come, Thy will be done on earth, As it is in heaven. Give us this day our daily bread. And forgive us our trespasses, As we forgive those who trespass against us. And lead us not into temptation; But deliver us from evil. Amen.

The Prayer to be said before a Fight at sea against any enemy.

O MOST powerful and glorious Lord God, the Lord of hosts, that rulest and commandest all things; Thou sittest in the throne judging right, and therefore we make our address to thy Divine Majesty in this our necessity, that thou wouldest take the cause into thine own hand, and judge between us and our enemies. Stir up thy strength, O Lord, and come and help us; for thou givest not alway the battle to the strong, but canst save by many or by few. O let not our sins now cry against us for vengeance; but hear us, thy poor servants, begging mercy and imploring thy help, and that thou wouldest be a defence unto us against the face of the enemy. Make it appear that thou art our Saviour and mighty Deliverer, through Jesus Christ our Lord. *Amen.*

Short Prayers for single persons, who cannot meet to join in Prayer with others, by reason of the Fight, or Storm.

General Prayers.

LORD, be merciful to us sinners, and save us for thy mercy's sake.

Thou art the great God, who hast made and rulest all things: O deliver us for thy Name's sake.

Thou art the great God to be feared above all: O save us, that we may praise thee.

Special Prayers with respect to the Enemy.

THOU, O Lord, art just and powerful: O defend our cause against the face of the enemy.

O God, thou art a strong tower of defence to all who fly unto thee: O save us from the violence of the enemy.

O Lord of hosts, fight for us, that we may glorify thee.

O suffer us not to sink under the weight of our sins, or the violence of the enemy.

O Lord, arise, help us, and deliver us for thy Name's sake.

※

Thanksgiving after a Storm.

From PSALM 66. *Jubilate Deo.*

OBE joyful in God, all ye lands: sing praises unto the honour of his Name; make his praise to be glorious.

Say unto God, O how wonderful art thou in thy works: through the greatness of thy power shall thine enemies be found liars unto thee.

For all the world shall worship thee: sing of thee, and praise thy Name.

O come hither, and behold the works of God: how wonderful he is in his doing toward the children of men.

He ruleth with his power for ever: his eyes behold the people: and such as will not believe shall not be able to exalt themselves.

O praise our God, ye people: and make the voice of his praise to be heard:

Who holdeth our soul in life: and suffereth not our feet to slip.

For thou, O God, hast proved us: thou also hast tried us, like as silver is tried.

Thou broughtest us into the snare: and laidest trouble upon our loins.

I will go into thine house with burnt-offerings: and will pay thee my vows, which I promised with my lips, and spake with my mouth, when I was in trouble.

O come hither, and hearken, all ye that fear God: and I will tell you what he hath done for my soul.

I called unto him with my

mouth : and gave him praises with my tongue.

If I incline unto wickedness with mine heart : the Lord will not hear me.

But God hath heard me : and considered the voice of my prayer.

Praised be God, who hath not cast out my prayer : nor turned his mercy from me.

Glory be to the Father, and to the Son : and to the Holy Ghost;

As it was in the beginning, is now, and ever shall be : world without end. Amen.

From PSALM 107. *Confitemini Domino.*

O THAT men would praise the LORD for his goodness: and declare the wonders that he doeth for the children of men !

That they would offer unto him the sacrifice of thanksgiving : and tell out his works with gladness !

They that go down to the sea in ships : and occupy their business in great waters;

These men see the works of the LORD : and his wonders in the deep.

For at his word the stormy wind ariseth : which lifteth up the waves thereof.

They are carried up to the heaven, and down again to the deep : their soul melteth away because of the trouble.

They reel to and fro, and stagger like a drunken man : and are at their wit's end.

So when they cry unto the LORD in their trouble : he delivereth them out of their distress.

For he maketh the storm to cease : so that the waves thereof are still.

Then are they glad, because they are at rest : and so he bringeth them unto the haven where they would be.

O that men would therefore praise the LORD for his goodness: and declare the wonders that he doeth for the children of men !

That they would exalt him also in the congregation of the people : and praise him in the seat of the elders !

Glory be to the Father, and to the Son : and to the Holy Ghost;

As it was in the beginning, is now, and ever shall be : world without end. Amen.

A Hymn of Praise and Thanksgiving after a dangerous Tempest.

O COME, let us give thanks unto the Lord, for he is gracious : and his mercy endureth for ever.

Great is the Lord, and greatly to be praised : let the redeemed of the Lord say so : whom he hath delivered from the merciless rage of the sea.

The Lord is gracious, and full of compassion : slow to anger, and of great mercy.

He hath not dealt with us according to our sins : neither rewarded us according to our iniquities.

But as the heaven is high above the earth : so great hath been his mercy towards us.

We found trouble and heaviness : we were even at death's door.

The waters of the sea had well-nigh covered us : the proud waters had well-nigh gone over our soul.

The sea roared : and the stormy wind lifted up the waves thereof.

We were carried up as it were to heaven, and then down again into the deep : our soul melted within us, because of trouble.

Then cried we unto thee, O Lord : and thou didst deliver us out of our distress.

Blessed be thy Name, who didst not despise the prayer of thy servants : but didst hear our cry, and hast saved us.

Thou didst send forth thy commandment : and the windy storm ceased, and was turned into a calm.

O let us therefore praise the Lord for his goodness : and declare the wonders that he hath done, and still doeth for the children of men!

Praised be the Lord daily : even the Lord that helpeth us, and poureth his benefits upon us.

He is our God, even the God of whom cometh salvation : God is the Lord, by whom we have escaped death.

Thou, Lord, hast made us glad through the operation of thy hands : and we will triumph in thy praise.

Blessed be the Lord God : even the Lord God, who only doeth wondrous things ;

And blessed be the Name of his Majesty for ever : and let every one of us say, Amen, Amen.

Glory be to the Father, and to the Son : and to the Holy Ghost ;

As it was in the beginning, is now, and ever shall be : world without end. Amen.

Collects of Thanksgiving.

O MOST blessed and glorious Lord God, who art of infinite goodness and mercy ; We, thy poor creatures, whom thou hast made and preserved, holding our souls in life, and now rescuing us out of the jaws of death, humbly present ourselves again before thy Divine Majesty, to offer a sacrifice of praise and thanksgiving, for that thou heardest us when we called in our trouble, and didst not cast out our prayer, which we made before thee in our great distress : even when we gave all for lost, our ship, our goods, our lives, then didst thou mercifully look upon us, and wonderfully command a deliverance : for which we, now being in safety, do give all praise and glory to thy holy Name : through Jesus Christ our Lord. Amen.

¶ Or this.

O MOST mighty and gracious good God, thy mercy is over all thy works, but in special manner hath been extended towards us, whom thou hast so powerfully and wonderfully defended. Thou hast showed us terrible things, and wonders in the deep, that we might see how powerful and gracious a God thou art ; how able and ready to help those who trust in thee. Thou hast showed us how both winds and seas obey thy command : that we may learn, even from them, hereafter to obey thy voice, and to do thy will. We therefore bless and glorify thy Name, for this thy mercy in saving us when we were ready to perish. And, we beseech thee, make us as truly sensible now of thy mercy, as we were then of the danger : and give us hearts always ready to express our thankfulness, not only by words, but also by our lives, in being more obedient to thy holy commandments. Continue, we beseech thee, this thy goodness to us : that we, whom thou hast saved, may serve thee in holiness and righteousness all the days of our life : through Jesus Christ our Lord and Saviour. Amen.

Thanksgiving after a Victory.

A Psalm or Hymn of Praise and Thanksgiving.

IF the Lord had not been on our side, now may we say : if the Lord himself had not been on our side, when men rose up against us ;

They that swallowed us up quick : when they were so wrathfully displeased at us.

Yea, the waters had drowned us, and the stream had gone over our soul : the deep waters of the proud had gone over our soul.

But praised be the Lord : who hath not given us over as a prey unto them.

The Lord hath wrought : a mighty salvation for us.

We got not this by our own sword, neither was it our own arm that saved us : but thy right hand, and thine arm, and the light of thy countenance, because thou hadst a favour unto us.

The Lord hath appeared for us : the Lord hath covered our heads, and made us to stand in the day of battle.

The Lord hath appeared for us : the Lord hath overthrown our enemies, and dashed in pieces those that rose up against us.

Therefore not unto us, O Lord, not unto us : but unto thy Name be given the glory.

The Lord hath done great things for us : the Lord hath done great things for us, for which we rejoice.

Our help standeth in the Name of the Lord : who hath made heaven and earth.

Blessed be the Name of the Lord : from this time forth for evermore.

Glory be to the Father, and to the Son : and to the Holy Ghost ;

As it was in the beginning, is now, and ever shall be : world without end. Amen.

¶ *After this Hymn may be said the* Te Deum.

¶ *Then this Collect.*

O ALMIGHTY God, the Sovereign Commander of all the world, in whose hand is power and might, which none is able to withstand ; We bless and magnify thy great and glorious Name for this happy Victory, the whole glory whereof we do ascribe to thee, who art the only giver of victory. And, we beseech thee, give us grace to improve this great mercy to thy glory, the advancement of thy Gospel, the honour of our country, and, as much as in us lieth, to the good of all mankind. And, we beseech thee, give us such a sense of this great mercy, as may engage us to a true thankfulness, such as may appear in our lives by an humble, holy, and obedient walking before thee all our days ; through Jesus Christ our Lord, to whom, with thee and the Holy Spirit, as for all thy mercies, so in particular for this Victory and Deliverance, be all glory and honour, world without end. *Amen.*

2 *Cor.* xiii. 14.

THE grace of our Lord Jesus Christ, and the love of God, and the fellowship of the Holy Ghost, be with us all evermore. *Amen.*

A FORM OF PRAYER FOR
THE VISITATION OF PRISONERS.

¶ When Morning or Evening Prayer shall be read in any Prison, instead of the Psalm, O come, let us sing, etc., shall be read the 130th Psalm: and the Minister shall insert, after the Collect for the day, the Collect in the following Service, O God, who sparest, etc., and at such times as the Litany is not read, he shall add the prayer, O God, merciful Father, who despisest not, etc.

¶ And when notice is given to the Minister, that a Prisoner is confined for some great or capital crime, he shall visit him; and when he cometh into the place where the Prisoner is, he shall say, kneeling down,

REMEMBER not, Lord, our iniquities, nor the iniquities of our forefathers; neither take thou vengeance of our sins: Spare us, good Lord, spare thy people, whom thou hast redeemed with thy most precious blood, and be not angry with us for ever.

Answer. Spare us, good Lord.

Let us pray.

Lord, have mercy upon us.
Christ, have mercy upon us.
Lord, have mercy upon us.

O Lord, show thy mercy upon us ;

And grant us thy salvation.

Turn thy face from our sins ;

And blot out all our iniquities.

Send us help from thy holy place ;

For thine indignation lieth hard upon us.

O Lord, hear our prayer ;

And let the sighing of the prisoners come before thee.

¶ Then shall the Minister exhort the Prisoner or Prisoners after this form, or other like.

DEARLY beloved, know this, that Almighty God, whose never-failing providence governeth all things both in heaven and earth, hath so wisely and mercifully ordered the course of this world, that his judgments are often sent as fatherly corrections to us ; and if with due submission and resignation to his holy will we receive the same, they will work together for our good.

It is your part and duty, therefore, to humble *yourself* under the mighty hand of God, to acknowledge the righteousness of his judgments, and to endeavour that, by his grace, this present visitation may lead you to a sincere and hearty repentance.

The way and means thereto is, to examine your life and conversation by the rule of God's commandments; and wherein-soever you shall perceive *yourself* to have offended, either by will, word, or deed, there to bewail your own sinfulness, and to confess *yourself* to Almighty God, with full purpose of amendment of life. And if you shall perceive your offences to be such as are not only against God, but also against your neighbours; then to reconcile *yourself* to them, being ready to make restitution and satisfaction, according to the uttermost of your power, for all injuries and wrongs done by you to any other; and being likewise ready to forgive others who have offended you, as you would have forgiveness of your offences at God's hand. And to this true repentance and change of mind you must add a lively and stedfast faith, and dependence upon the merits of the death of Christ, with an entire resignation of *yourself* to the will of God. Except you repent, and believe, we can give you no hope of salvation. But if you do sincerely repent and believe, God hath declared, though your sins be as red as scarlet, they shall be made white as snow; though your wickedness have gone over your head, yet shall they not be your destruction.

We exhort you therefore in the Name of God, and of his dear Son Jesus Christ our Saviour, and as you tender your own salvation, to take good heed of these things in time, while the day of salvation lasteth; for the night cometh, when no man can work. While you have the light, believe in the light, and walk as children of the light, that you be not cast into outer darkness; that you may not knock, when the door shall be

shut; and cry for mercy, when it is the time of justice. Now, you are the object of God's mercy, if by repentance and true faith you turn unto him; but if you neglect these things, you will be the object of his justice and vengeance. Now, you may claim the merits of Christ; but if you die in your sins, his sufferings will tend to your greater condemnation. O beloved, consider in this your day, how fearful a thing it will be to fall into the hands of the living God, when you can neither fly to his mercy to protect you, nor to the merits of Christ to cover you in that terrible day.

¶ *Here the Minister shall examine him concerning his faith, and rehearse the Articles of the Creed,* Dost thou believe in God, etc. *And the Prisoner shall answer,*

All this I stedfastly believe.

¶ *Then shall the Minister examine whether he repent him truly of his sins, and be in charity with all the world, and further admonish him particularly concerning the crimes wherewith he is charged; and exhort him, if he have any scruples, that he would declare the same, and prepare himself for the Holy Communion, against the time that it may be proper to administer it to him.*

¶ *Then, all kneeling, the Minister shall say the fifty-first Psalm of the Psalter,* Miserere mei, Deus.

¶ *Here the Minister, as he shall see convenient, may recited certain or all of these Prayers following, the Prayer for all Conditions of Men, or any other Prayer which he shall judge proper.*

O GOD, whose nature and property is ever to have mercy and to forgive; Receive our humble petitions; and though we be tied and bound with the chain of our sins, yet let the pitifulness of thy great mercy loose us; for the honour of Jesus Christ, our Mediator and Advocate. *Amen.*

O GOD, who sparest when we deserve punishment, and in thy wrath rememberest mercy; We humbly beseech thee, of thy goodness, to comfort and succour all those who are under reproach and misery in the house of bondage; correct them not in thine anger, neither chasten them in thy sore displeasure. Give them a right understanding of themselves, and of thy threats and promises; that they may neither cast away their confidence in thee, nor place it any where but in thee. Relieve the distressed, protect the innocent, and awaken the guilty: and forasmuch as thou alone bringest light out of darkness, and good out of evil, grant that the pains and punishments which these thy servants endure, through their bodily confinement, may tend to setting free their souls from the chains of sin; through Jesus Christ our Lord. *Amen.*

O LORD, we beseech thee, mercifully hear our prayers, and spare all those who confess their sins unto thee; that they, whose consciences by sin are accused, by thy merciful pardon may be absolved; through Christ our Lord. *Amen.*

O GOD, whose mercy is everlasting, and power infinite; Look down with pity and compassion upon the sufferings of *this* thy *servant*; and whether thou visitest for trial of *his* patience, or punishment of *his* of-

fences, enable *him* by thy grace cheerfully to submit *himself* to thy holy will and pleasure. Go not far from those, O Lord, whom thou hast laid in a place of darkness, and in the deep; and forasmuch as thou hast not cut *him* off suddenly, but chastenest *him* as a father, grant that *he*, duly considering thy great mercies, may be unfeignedly thankful, and turn unto thee with true repentance and sincerity of heart; through Jesus Christ our Lord. *Amen.*

A Form of Prayer for Persons under sentence of death.

¶ *When a Criminal is under sentence of death, the Minister shall proceed to exhort him after this form, or other like.*

DEARLY beloved, it hath pleased Almighty God, in his justice, to bring you under the sentence and condemnation of the law. You are shortly to suffer death in such a manner, that others, warned by your example, may be the more afraid to offend; and we pray God, that you may make such use of your punishments in this world, that your soul may be saved in the world to come.

Wherefore we come to you in *the* bowels of compassion; and, being desirous that *you* should avoid presumption on the one hand, and despair on the other, shall plainly lay before you the wretchedness of your condition, and declare how far you ought to depend on the mercies of God and the merits of our Saviour. Consider then seriously with yourself, in all appearance the time of your dissolution draweth near; your sins have laid fast hold upon you; you are soon to be removed from among men by a violent death; and you shall fade away suddenly like the grass, which in the morning is green and groweth up, but in the evening is cut down, dried up, and withered. After you have thus finished the course of a sinful and miserable life, you shall appear before the Judge of all flesh; who, as he pronounces blessings on the righteous, shall likewise say, with a terrible voice of most just judgment, to the wicked, Go, ye accursed, into the fire everlasting, prepared for the devil and his angels.

Your sins have brought you too near this dreadful sentence: it is therefore your part and duty, my brother, humbly to confess and bewail your great and manifold offences, and to repent you truly of your sins, as you tender the eternal salvation of your soul.

Be not deceived with a vain and presumptuous expectation of God's favour, nor say within yourself, Peace, peace, where there is no peace; for there is no peace, saith my God, to the wicked. God is not mocked: he is of purer eyes than to behold iniquity; and without holiness no man shall see the Lord. On the other hand, despair not of God's mercy, though trouble is on every side; for God shutteth not up his mercies for ever in displeasure; but if we confess our sins, he is faithful and just to forgive us our sins, and to cleanse us from all unrighteousness. Do not either way abuse the goodness of God, who calleth us mercifully to amendment, and of his endless pity promiseth us forgiveness of that which is past, if with a

perfect and a true heart we return unto him.

Since therefore you are soon to pass into an endless and unchangeable state, and your future happiness or misery depends upon the few moments which are left you, I require you strictly to examine yourself, and your estate both towards God and towards man; and let no worldly consideration hinder you from making a true and full confession of your sins, and giving all the satisfaction which is in your power to every one whom you have wronged or injured; that you may find mercy at your heavenly Father's hand, for Christ's sake, and not be condemned in the dreadful day of judgment.

Lastly, beloved, submit yourself with Christian resignation to the just judgment of God, which your own crimes have brought upon you, and be in charity with all men; being ready sincerely to forgive all such as have offended you, not excepting those who have prosecuted you even unto death: and, though this may seem a hard saying, yet know assuredly, that without it your charity is not yet perfect. And fail not earnestly to endeavour and pray for this blessed temper and composure of mind. So may you cast yourself with an entire dependence upon the mercies of God, through the merits of our Saviour and Redeemer Jesus Christ.

¶ *Here the Minister shall examine him concerning his faith, and rehearse the Articles of the* CREED, *Dost thou believe in God, etc. And the Criminal shall answer,*

All this I stedfastly believe.

¶ *Then shall the Minister examine whether he repent him truly of his sins, exhorting him to a particular confession of the sin for which he is condemned; and upon confession, he shall instruct him what satisfaction ought to be made to those whom he has offended thereby; and if he knoweth any combinations in wickedness, or any evil practices designed against others, let him be admonished to the utmost of his power to discover and prevent them.*

¶ *After his confession, the Priest shall declare to him the pardoning mercy of God, in the form which is used in the Communion Service.*

¶ *After which shall be said the Collect following.*

O HOLY Jesus, who, of thine infinite goodness, didst accept the conversion of a sinner on the cross; Open thine eye of mercy upon this thy servant, who desireth pardon and forgiveness, though in his latest hour he turneth unto thee. Renew in him whatsoever hath been decayed by the fraud and malice of the devil, or by his own carnal will and frailness. Consider his contrition; accept his repentance; and forasmuch as he putteth his full trust only in thy mercy, impute not unto him his former sins, but strengthen him with thy blessed Spirit; and when thou art pleased to take him hence, take him unto thy favour. This we beg through thy merits, O Lord, our Saviour and our Redeemer. Amen.

¶ *Then shall the Minister say,*

O FATHER of mercies, and God of all comfort; We fly unto thee for succour in behalf of this thy servant, who is now under the sentence of condemnation. The day of his calamity is at hand, and he is accounted as one of those who go down into the pit. Blessed Lord, remember thy mercies; look upon his infirmities; hear the voice of his complaint; give him, we beseech thee, patience in this his time of adversity, and support under the terrors which encompass him; set before his eyes the things he hath done in the body, which have justly provoked thee to anger; and forasmuch as his continuance appeareth to be short amongst us, quicken him so much the more by thy grace and Holy Spirit; that he, being converted and reconciled unto thee, before thy judgments have cut him off from the earth, may at the hour of his death depart in peace, and be received into thine everlasting kingdom; through Jesus Christ our Lord. Amen.

¶ *Adding this.*

O SAVIOUR of the world, who by thy Cross and precious Blood hast redeemed us: Save us, and help us, we humbly beseech thee, O Lord.

¶ *Then the Minister, standing, shall say,*

IN the midst of life we are in death; of whom may we seek for succour, but of thee, O Lord, who for our sins art justly displeased?

Yet, O Lord God most holy, O Lord most mighty, O holy and most merciful Saviour, deliver us not into the bitter pains of eternal death.

Thou knowest, Lord, the secrets of our hearts; shut not thy merciful ears to our prayer; but spare us, Lord most holy, O God most mighty, O holy and merciful Saviour, thou most worthy Judge eternal, suffer us not, at our last hour, for any pains of death, to fall from thee.

¶ *Then the Minister shall say,*

THE Almighty God, who is a most strong tower to all those who put their trust in him, to whom all things in heaven, in earth, and under the earth, do bow and obey, Be now and evermore thy defence; and make thee know and feel, that there is none other Name under heaven given to man, in whom, and through whom, thou mayest receive salvation, but only the Name of our Lord Jesus Christ. *Amen.*

¶ *And after that shall say,*

UNTO God's gracious mercy and protection we commit thee. The LORD bless thee, and keep thee. The LORD make his face to shine upon thee, and be gracious unto thee. The LORD lift up his countenance upon thee, and give thee peace, both now and evermore. *Amen.*

¶ *At the time of Execution, the Minister shall use such devotions as he shall think proper.*

Notice. *It is judged best that the Criminal should not make any public profession or declaration.*

The Collect for the Communion Service.

O GOD, who declarest thy almighty power chiefly in showing mercy and pity; We beseech thee to have mercy upon this thy servant, who for *his* transgressions is appointed to die. Grant that *he* may take thy judgments patiently, and repent *him* truly of *his* sins; that *he* recovering thy favour, the fearful reward of *his* actions may end with this life; and whensoever *his* soul shall depart from the body, it may be without spot presented unto thee; through Jesus Christ our Lord. *Amen.*

The Epistle. Heb. xii. 11.

NO chastening for the present seemeth to be joyous, but grievous: nevertheless afterward it yieldeth the peaceable fruit of righteousness unto them which are exercised thereby.

The Gospel. St. John v. 24.

VERILY, verily, I say unto you, He that heareth my word, and believeth on him that sent me, hath everlasting life, and shall not come into condemnation: but is passed from death unto life.

A FORM OF
PRAYER AND THANKSGIVING
TO ALMIGHTY GOD,

For the fruits of the earth, and all the other blessings of his merciful Providence; to be used yearly on the first Thursday in November, or on such other day as shall be appointed by the Civil Authority.

¶ *The service shall be as usual, except where it is hereby otherwise appointed.*

¶ *Among the Sentences at the beginning of Morning Prayer shall be the following.*

HONOUR the LORD with thy substance, and with the firstfruits of all thine increase: so shall thy barns be filled with plenty, and thy presses shall burst out with new wine. *Prov.* iii. 9, 10.

The LORD by wisdom hath founded the earth; by understanding hath he established the heavens. By his knowledge the depths are broken up, and the clouds drop down the dew. *Prov.* iii. 19, 20.

The eternal God is thy refuge, and underneath are the everlasting arms. *Deut.* xxxiii. 27.

Israel then shall dwell in safety alone: the fountain of Jacob shall be upon a land of corn and wine; also his heavens shall drop down dew. *Deut.* xxxiii. 28.

Happy art thou, O Israel: who is like unto thee, O people saved by the LORD, the shield of thy help, and who is the sword of thy excellency! *Deut.* xxxiii. 29.

¶ *Instead of* O come, let us sing, *etc., the following shall be said or sung.*

O PRAISE the LORD, for it is a good thing to sing praises unto our God: yea, a joyful and pleasant thing it is to be thankful.

The LORD doth build up Jerusalem: and gather together the outcasts of Israel.

He healeth those that are broken in heart : and giveth medicine to heal their sickness.

O sing unto the LORD with thanksgiving : sing praises upon the harp unto our God :

Who covereth the heaven with clouds, and prepareth rain for the earth : and maketh the grass to grow upon the mountains, and herb for the use of men ;

Who giveth fodder unto the cattle : and feedeth the young ravens that call upon him.

Praise the LORD, O Jerusalem : praise thy God, O Sion.

For he hath made fast the bars of thy gates : and hath blessed thy children within thee.

He maketh peace in thy borders : and filleth thee with the flour of wheat.

Glory be to the Father, and to the Son : and to the Holy Ghost ;

As it was in the beginning, is now, and ever shall be : world without end. Amen.

¶ *Then shall be said or sung one of the* Selections, *or some other portion of the* Psalms, *at the discretion of the Minister.*

¶ *The* First Lesson *shall be* Deut. 8, *and the* Second Lesson *shall be* 1 Thess. 5, *v.* 12 *to v.* 24.

¶ *After the General Thanksgiving, shall be said this which followeth.*

MOST gracious God, by whose knowledge the depths are broken up, and the clouds drop down the dew ; We yield thee unfeigned thanks and praise for the return of seed-time and harvest, for the increase of the ground and the gathering in of the fruits thereof, and for all the other blessings of thy merciful providence bestowed upon this nation and people. And, we beseech thee, give us a just sense of these great mercies ; such as may appear in our lives by an humble, holy, and obedient walking before thee all our days ; through Jesus Christ our Lord, to whom, with thee and the Holy Ghost, be all glory and honour, world without end. *Amen.*

❋

The Collect to be used instead of that for the day.

O MOST merciful Father, who hast blessed the labours of the husbandman in the returns of the fruits of the earth: We give thee humble and hearty thanks for this thy bounty: beseeching thee to continue thy loving-kindness to us, that our land may still yield her increase, to thy glory and our comfort; through Jesus Christ our Lord. Amen.

The Epistle. St. James i. 16.

DO not err, my beloved brethren. Every good gift and every perfect gift is from above, and cometh down from the Father of lights, with whom is no variableness, neither shadow of turning. Of his own will begat he us with the word of truth, that we should be a kind of first-fruits of his creatures. Wherefore, my beloved brethren, let every man be swift to hear, slow to speak, slow to wrath: for the wrath of man worketh not the righteousness of God. Wherefore lay apart all filthiness and superfluity of naughtiness, and receive with meekness the engrafted word, which is able to save your souls. But be ye doers of the word, and not hearers only,

deceiving your own selves. For if any be a hearer of the word, and not a doer, he is like unto a man beholding his natural face in a glass: for he beholdeth himself, and goeth his way, and straightway forgetteth what manner of man he was. But whoso looketh into the perfect law of liberty, and continueth therein, he being not a forgetful hearer, but a doer of the work, this man shall be blessed in his deed. If any man among you seem to be religious, and bridleth not his tongue, but deceiveth his own heart, this man's religion is vain. Pure religion and undefiled before God and the Father is this, To visit the fatherless and widows in their affliction, and to keep himself unspotted from the world.

The Gospel. St. Matt. v. 43.

YE have heard that it hath been said, Thou shalt love thy neighbour, and hate thine enemy. But I say unto you, Love your enemies, bless them that curse you, do good to them that hate you, and pray for them which despitefully use you, and persecute you; that ye may be the children of your Father which is in heaven: for he maketh his sun to rise on the evil and on the good, and sendeth rain on the just and on the unjust. For if ye love them which love you, what reward have ye? do not even the publicans the same? And if ye salute your brethren only, what do ye more than others? do not even the publicans so? Be ye therefore perfect, even as your Father which is in heaven is perfect.

FORMS OF

PRAYER TO BE USED IN FAMILIES.

MORNING PRAYER.

¶ The Master or Mistress having called together as many of the Family as can conveniently be present, let one of them, or any other whom they shall think proper, say as follows, all kneeling.

OUR Father, who art in heaven, Hallowed be thy Name. Thy kingdom come. Thy will be done on earth, As it is in heaven. Give us this day our daily bread. And forgive us our trespasses, As we forgive those who trespass against us. And lead us not into temptation; But deliver us from evil: For thine is the kingdom, and the power, and the glory, for ever and ever. Amen.

ALMIGHTY and ever-lasting God, in whom we live and move and have our being; We, thy needy creatures, render thee our humble praises, for thy preservation of us from the beginning of our lives to this day, and especially for having delivered us from the dangers of the past night. To thy watchful

Acknowledgment of God's mercy and preservation, especially through the night past.

providence we owe it, [*that no disturbance hath come nigh us or our dwelling: but that we are brought in safety to the beginning of this day.] For these thy mercies, we bless and magnify thy glorious Name; humbly beseeching thee to accept this our morning sacrifice of praise and thanksgiving; for his sake who lay down in the grave, and rose again for us, thy Son our Saviour Jesus Christ. *Amen.*

When disturbances of any kind befall a family, instead of this, say, that notwithstanding our dangers, we are brought in safety to the beginning of this day.

AND since it is of thy mercy, O gracious Father, that another day is added to our lives; We here dedicate both our souls and our bodies to thee and thy service, in a sober, righteous, and godly life: in which resolution, do thou, O merciful God, confirm and strengthen us; that, as we grow in age, we may grow in grace, and in the knowledge of our Lord and

Dedication of soul and body to God's service, with a resolution to be growing daily in goodness.

Saviour Jesus Christ. *Amen.*

BUT, O God, who knowest the weakness and corruption of our nature, and the manifold temptations which we daily meet with; We humbly beseech thee to have compassion on our infirmities, and to give us the constant assistance of thy Holy Spirit; that we may be effectually restrained from sin, and excited to our duty. Imprint upon our hearts such a dread of thy judgments, and such a grateful sense of thy goodness to us, as may make us both afraid and ashamed to offend thee. And, above all, keep in our minds a lively remembrance of that great day, in which we must give a strict account of our thoughts, words, and actions; and according to the works done in the body, be eternally rewarded or punished, by him whom thou hast appointed the Judge of quick and dead, thy Son Jesus Christ our Lord. *Amen.*

Prayer for grace to enable us to perform that resolution.

IN particular, we implore thy grace and protection for the ensuing day. Keep us temperate in our meats and drinks, and diligent in our several callings. Grant us patience under any afflictions[*] thou shalt see fit to lay on us, and minds always contented with our present condition. Give us grace to be just and upright in all our dealings; quiet and peaceable; full of compassion; and ready to do good to all men, according to our abilities and opportunities. Direct us in all our ways, [* and prosper the works of our hands in the business of our several stations.] Defend

For grace to guide us and the following day, and for God's blessing on the business of the same.

On Sunday morning, instead of this, say, and let thy Holy Spirit accompany us

us from all dangers and adversities; and be graciously pleased to take us, and all things belonging to us, under thy fatherly care and protection. These things, and whatever else thou shalt see necessary and convenient to us, we humbly beg, through the merits and mediation of thy Son Jesus Christ, our Lord and Saviour. *Amen.*

to the place of thy public worship, making us serious and attentive, and raising our minds from the thoughts of this world to the consideration of the next; that we may fervently join in the prayers and praises of thy Church, and listen to our duty with honest hearts, in order to practise it.

THE grace of our Lord Jesus Christ, and the love of God, and the fellowship of the Holy Ghost, be with us all evermore. *Amen.*

❀

EVENING PRAYER.

¶ *The Family being together, a little before bed-time, let the Master or Mistress, or any other whom they shall think proper, say as follows, all kneeling.*

OUR Father, who art in heaven, Hallowed be thy Name. Thy kingdom come. Thy will be done on earth, As it is in heaven. Give us this day our daily bread. And forgive us our trespasses, As we forgive those who trespass against us. And lead us not into temptation; But deliver us from evil: For thine is the kingdom, and the power, and the glory, for ever and ever. Amen.

MOST merciful God, who art of purer eyes than to behold iniquity, and hast promised forgiveness to all those who confess and forsake their sins; We come before thee in a humble sense of our own unworthiness, acknowledging our manifold transgressions of thy righteous *Confession of sin, with a prayer for contrition and pardon.* laws. * But, O gracious Father, who desirest not the death of a sinner, look upon us, we beseech thee, in mercy, and forgive us all our transgressions. Make us deeply sensible of the great evil of them; and work in us an hearty contrition; that we may obtain forgiveness at thy hands, who art ever ready to receive humble and penitent sinners; for the sake of thy Son Jesus Christ, our only Saviour and Redeemer. *Amen.*

* Here let him who reads make a short pause, that every one may secretly confess the sins and failings of that day.

AND lest, through our own frailty, or the temptations which encompass us, we be drawn again into sin, vouchsafe us, we beseech thee, the direction and *Prayer for grace to reform and grow better.*

assistance of thy Holy Spirit. Reform whatever is amiss in the temper and disposition of our souls; that no unclean thoughts, unlawful designs, or inordinate desires, may rest there. Purge our hearts from envy, hatred, and malice; that we may never suffer the sun to go down upon our wrath; but may always go to our rest in peace, charity, and good-will, with a conscience void of offence towards thee, and towards men; that so we may be preserved pure and blameless, unto the coming of our Lord and Saviour Jesus Christ. *Amen.*

The Intercession. AND accept, O Lord, our intercessions for all mankind. Let the light of thy Gospel shine upon all nations; and may as many as have received it, live as becomes it. Be gracious unto thy Church; and grant that every member of the same, in his vocation and ministry, may serve thee faithfully. Bless all in authority over us; and so rule their hearts and strengthen their hands, that they may punish wickedness and vice, and maintain thy true religion and virtue. Send down thy blessings, temporal and spiritual, upon all our relations, friends, and neighbours. Reward all who have done us good, and pardon all those who have done or wish us evil, and give them repentance and better minds. Be merciful to all who are in any trouble; and do thou, the God of pity, administer to them according to their several necessities; for his sake who went about doing good, thy Son our Saviour Jesus Christ. *Amen.*

The Thanksgiving. TO our prayers, O Lord, we join our unfeigned thanks for all thy mercies; for our being, our reason, and all other endowments and faculties of soul and body; for our health, friends, food, and raiment, and all the other comforts and conveniences of life. Above all, we adore thy mercy in sending thy only Son into the world, to redeem us from sin and eternal death, and in giving us the knowledge and sense of our duty towards thee. We bless thee for thy patience with us, notwithstanding our many and great provocations; for all the directions, assistances, and comforts of thy Holy Spirit; for thy continual care and watchful providence over us through the whole course of our lives; and particularly for the mercies and benefits of the past day; beseeching thee to continue these thy blessings to us, and to give us grace to show our thankfulness in a sincere obedience to his laws, through whose merits and intercession we received them all, thy Son our Saviour Jesus Christ. *Amen.*

I N particular, we beseech thee to continue thy gracious protection to us *Prayer for God's protection through the night following.*

this night. Defend us from all dangers and mischiefs, and from the fear of them; that we may enjoy such refreshing sleep as may fit us for the duties of the following day. Make us ever mindful of the time when we shall lie down in the dust; and grant us grace always to live in such a state that we may never be afraid to die; so that, living and dying, we may be thine, through the merits and satisfaction of thy Son Christ Jesus, in whose Name we offer up these our imperfect prayers. *Amen.*

T HE grace of our Lord Jesus Christ, and the love of God, and the fellowship of the Holy Ghost, be with us all evermore. *Amen.*

¶ *On Sundays, and on other days when it may be convenient, it will be proper to begin with a Chapter, or part of a Chapter, from the New Testament.*

Table of Proper Psalms on certain Days.

First Sunday in Advent.	Morning. 8, 50	Evening. 96, 97	Easter-even.	Morning. 4, 16, 17	Evening. 30, 31
Christmas-day.	19, 45, 85	89, 110, 132	Easter-day.	2, 57, 111	113, 114, 118
Circumcision.	40, 90	65, 103	Ascension-day.	8, 15, 21	24, 47, 108
Epiphany.	46, 47, 48	72, 117, 135	Whitsunday.	48, 68	104, 145
Purification.	20, 86, 87	84, 113, 134	Trinity-Sunday.	29, 33	93, 97, 150
Ash-Wednesday.	6, 32, 38	102, 130, 143	Transfiguration.	27, 61, 93	84, 99, 133
Annunciation.	89	131, 132, 138	St. Michael's.	91, 103	34, 148
Good Friday.	22, 40, 54	69, 88	All Saints' Day.	1, 15, 146	112, 121, 149

Table of Selections of Psalms.

First.	Psalms. 1, 15, 91	Eleventh.	Psalms. 80, 81
Second.	4, 31 to v. 7, 91, 134	Twelfth.	84, 122, 131
Third.	19, 24, 103	Thirteenth.	85, 93, 97
Fourth.	23, 34, 65	Fourteenth.	102
Fifth.	26, 43, 141	Fifteenth.	107
Sixth.	32, 130, 121	Sixteenth.	118
Seventh.	37	Seventeenth.	123, 124, 125
Eighth.	51, 42	Eighteenth.	139, 145
Ninth.	72, 96	Nineteenth.	147
Tenth.	77	Twentieth.	148, 149, 150

The Psalter,

OR

PSALMS OF DAVID.

❀

THE FIRST DAY.

Morning Prayer.

PSALM 1.

Beatus vir qui non abiit.

BLESSED is the man that hath not walked in the counsel of the ungodly, nor stood in the way of sinners : and hath not sat in the seat of the scornful.

2 But his delight is in the law of the LORD : and in his law will he exercise himself day and night.

3 And he shall be like a tree planted by the water-side : that will bring forth his fruit in due season:

4 His leaf also shall not wither : and look, whatsoever he doeth, it shall prosper.

5 As for the ungodly, it is not so with them : but they are like the chaff, which the wind scattereth away from the face of the earth.

6 Therefore the ungodly shall not be able to stand in the judgment : neither the sinners in the congregation of the righteous.

7 But the LORD knoweth the way of the righteous : and the way of the ungodly shall perish.

PSALM 2.

Quare fremuerunt gentes ?

WHY do the heathen so furiously rage together : and why do the people imagine a vain thing ?

2 The kings of the earth stand up, and the rulers take counsel together : against the LORD, and against his Anointed :

3 Let us break their bonds asunder : and cast away their cords from us.

4 He that dwelleth in heaven shall laugh them to scorn : the Lord shall have them in derision.

5 Then shall he speak unto them in his wrath : and vex them in his sore displeasure :

6 Yet have I set my King : upon my holy hill of Sion.

7 I will preach the law, whereof the Lord hath said unto me : Thou art my Son, this day have I begotten thee.

8 Desire of me, and I shall give thee the heathen for *thine inheritance* : and the utmost parts of the earth for thy possession.

9 Thou shalt bruise them with a rod of iron : and break them in pieces like a potter's vessel.

10 Be wise now therefore, O ye kings : be learned, ye that are judges of the earth.

11 Serve the Lord in fear : and rejoice unto him with reverence.

12 Kiss the Son, lest he be angry, and so ye perish from the right way : if his wrath be kindled, yea but

a little. Blessed are all they that put their trust in him.

PSALM 3.

Domine, quid multiplicati?

LORD, how are they increased that trouble me : many are they that rise against me.

2 Many one there be that say of my soul : There is no help for him in his God.

3 But thou, O Lord, art my defender : thou art my worship, and the lifter up of my head.

4 I did call upon the Lord with my voice : and he heard me out of his holy hill.

5 I laid me down and slept, and rose up again : for the Lord sustained me.

6 I will not be afraid for ten thousands of the people : that have set themselves against me round about.

7 Up, Lord, and help me, O my God : for thou smitest all mine enemies upon the cheek-bone ; thou hast broken the teeth of the ungodly.

8 Salvation belongeth unto the Lord : and thy blessing is upon thy people.

PSALM 4.

Cum invocarem.

HEAR me when I call, O God of my righteousness : thou hast set me at liberty when I was in trouble ; have mercy upon me, and hearken unto my prayer.

2 O ye sons of men, how long will ye blaspheme mine honour : and have such pleasure in vanity, and seek after falsehood?

3 Know this also, that the LORD hath chosen to himself the man that is godly : when I call upon the LORD he will hear me.

4 Stand in awe, and sin not : commune with your own heart, and in your chamber, and be still.

5 Offer the sacrifice of righteousness : and put your trust in the LORD.

6 There be many that say : Who will show us any good?

7 LORD, lift thou up : the light of thy countenance upon us.

8 Thou hast put gladness in my heart : since the time that their corn and wine and oil increased.

9 I will lay me down in peace, and take my rest : for it is thou, LORD, only, that makest me dwell in safety.

PSALM 5.

Verba mea auribus.

PONDER my words, O LORD : consider my meditation.

2 O hearken thou unto the voice of my calling, my King and my God : for unto thee will I make my prayer.

3 My voice shalt thou hear betimes, O LORD : early in the morning will I direct my prayer unto thee, and will look up.

4 For thou art the God that hast no pleasure in wickedness : neither shall any evil dwell with thee.

5 Such as be foolish shall not stand in thy sight : for thou hatest all them that work vanity.

6 Thou shalt destroy them that speak lies : the LORD will abhor both the blood-thirsty and deceitful man.

7 But as for me, I will come into thine house, even upon the multitude of thy mercy : and in thy fear will I worship toward thy holy temple.

8 Lead me, O LORD, in

thy righteousness, because of mine enemies: make thy way plain before my face.

9 For there is no faithfulness in his mouth: their inward parts are very wickedness.

10 Their throat is an open sepulchre: they flatter with their tongue.

11 Destroy thou them, O God; let them perish through their own imaginations: cast them out in the multitude of their ungodliness; for they have rebelled against thee.

12 And let all them that put their trust in thee rejoice: they shall ever be giving of thanks, because thou defendest them; they *that* love thy Name shall be joyful in thee;

13 For thou, LORD, wilt give thy blessing unto the righteous: and with thy favourable kindness wilt thou defend him as with a shield.

❁

Evening Prayer.

PSALM 6.

Domine, ne in furore.

O LORD, rebuke me not in thine indignation: neither chasten me in thy displeasure.

2 Have mercy upon me, O LORD, for I am weak: O LORD, heal me, for my bones are vexed.

3 My soul also is sore troubled: but, LORD, how long wilt thou punish me?

4 Turn thee, O LORD, and deliver my soul: O save me, for thy mercy's sake.

5 For in death no man remembereth thee: and who will give thee thanks in the pit?

6 I am weary of my groaning, every night wash I my bed: and water my couch with my tears.

7 My beauty is gone for very trouble: and worn away because of all mine *enemies.*

8 Away from me, all ye that work vanity: for the LORD hath heard the voice of my weeping.

9 The LORD hath heard my petition: the LORD will receive my prayer.

10 All mine enemies shall be confounded, and sore vexed: they shall be turned back, and put to shame suddenly.

PSALM 7.

Domine, Deus meus.

O LORD my God, in thee have I put my trust: save me from all them that persecute me, and deliver me;

2 Lest he devour my soul like a lion, and tear it in pieces : while there is none to help.

3 O LORD my God, if I have done any such thing : or if there be any wickedness in my hands ;

4 If I have rewarded evil unto him that dealt friendly with me : yea, I have delivered him that without any cause is mine enemy ;

5 Then let mine enemy persecute my soul, and take me : yea, let him tread my life down upon the earth, and lay mine honour in the dust.

6 Stand up, O LORD, in thy wrath, and lift up thyself, because of the indignation of mine enemies : arise up for me in the judgment that thou hast commanded.

7 And so shall the congregation of the people come about thee : for their sakes therefore lift up thyself again.

8 The LORD shall judge the people ; give sentence with me, O LORD : according to my righteousness, and according to the innocency that is in me.

9 O let the wickedness of the ungodly come to an end : but guide thou the just.

10 For the righteous God : trieth the very hearts and reins.

11 My help cometh of God : who preserveth them that are true of heart.

12 God is a righteous Judge, strong, and patient : and God is provoked every day.

13 If a man will not turn, he will whet his sword : he hath bent his bow, and made it ready.

14 He hath prepared for him the instruments of death : he ordaineth his arrows against the persecutors.

15 Behold, he travaileth with mischief : he hath conceived sorrow, and brought forth ungodliness.

16 He hath graven and digged up a pit : and is fallen himself into the destruction that he made for other.

17 For his travail shall come upon his own head : and his wickedness shall fall on his own pate.

18 I will give thanks unto the LORD, according to his righteousness : and I will praise the Name of the LORD Most High.

PSALM 8.

Domine, Dominus noster.

O LORD our Governor, how excellent is thy Name in all the world : thou that hast set thy glory above the heavens !

2 Out of the mouth of very babes and sucklings hast thou ordained strength, because of thine enemies : that thou mightest still the enemy and the avenger.

3 For I will consider thy heavens, even the works of thy fingers : the moon and the stars which thou hast ordained.

4 What is man, that *thou art mindful of him* : and the son of man, that thou visitest him ?

5 Thou madest him lower than the angels : to crown him with glory and worship.

6 Thou makest him to have dominion of the works of thy hands : and thou hast put all things in subjection under his feet :

7 All sheep and oxen : yea, and the beasts of the field ;

8 The fowls of the air, and the fishes of the sea : and whatsoever walketh through the paths of the seas.

9 O LORD our Governor : how excellent is thy Name in all the world !

❧

THE SECOND DAY.

Morning Prayer.

PSALM 9.

Confitebor tibi.

I WILL give thanks unto thee, O LORD, with my whole heart : I will speak of all thy marvellous works.

2 I will be glad and rejoice in thee : yea, my songs will I make of thy Name, O thou Most Highest.

3 While mine enemies are driven back : they shall fall and perish at thy presence.

4 For thou hast maintained my right and my cause : thou art set in the throne that judgest right.

5 Thou hast rebuked the heathen, and destroyed the ungodly : thou hast put out their name for ever and ever.

6 O thou enemy, destructions are come to a perpetual end : even as the cities which thou hast destroyed, their memorial is perished with them.

7 But the LORD shall endure for ever : he hath also prepared his seat for judgment.

8 For he shall judge the world in righteousness : and minister true judgment unto the people.

9 The LORD also will be a defence for the oppressed : even a refuge in due time of trouble.

10 And they that know thy Name will put their trust in thee : for thou, LORD, hast never failed them that seek thee.

11 O praise the LORD which dwelleth in Sion : show the people of his doings.

12 For when he maketh inquisition for blood, he remembereth them : and forgetteth not the complaint of the poor.

13 Have mercy upon me, O LORD : consider the trouble which I suffer of them that hate me : thou that liftest me up from the gates of death ;

14 That I may show all thy praises within the ports of the daughter of Sion : I will rejoice in thy salvation.

15 The heathen are sunk down in the pit that they made : in the same net which they hid privily is their foot taken.

16 The LORD is known to execute judgment : the ungodly is trapped in the work of his own hands.

17 The wicked shall be turned into hell : and all the people that forget God.

18 For the poor shall not alway be forgotten : the patient abiding of the meek shall not perish for ever.

19 Up, LORD, and let not man have the upper hand : let the heathen be judged in thy sight.

20 Put them in fear, O LORD : that the heathen may know themselves to be but men.

PSALM 10.

Ut quid, Domine?

WHY standest thou so far off, O LORD : and hidest thy face in the needful time of trouble ?

2 The ungodly, for his own lust, *doth* persecute the poor : let them be taken in the crafty wiliness that they have imagined.

3 For the ungodly hath made boast of his own heart's desire : and speaketh good of the covetous, whom God abhorreth.

4 The ungodly is so

proud, that he careth not for God : neither is God in all his thoughts.

5 His ways are alway grievous : thy judgments are far above out of his sight, and therefore defieth he all his enemies.

6 For he hath said in his heart, Tush, I shall never be cast down : there shall no harm happen unto me.

7 His mouth is full of cursing, deceit, and fraud : under his tongue is ungodliness and vanity.

8 He sitteth lurking in the thievish corners of the streets : and privily in his lurking dens doth he murder the innocent ; his eyes are set against the poor.

9 For he lieth waiting secretly ; even as a lion lurketh he in his den : that he may ravish the poor.

10 He doth ravish the poor : when he getteth him into his net.

11 He falleth down, and humbleth himself : that the congregation of the poor may fall into the hands of his captains.

12 He hath said in his heart, Tush, God hath forgotten : he hideth away his face, and he will never see it.

13 Arise, O LORD God, and lift up thine hand : forget not the poor.

14 Wherefore should the wicked blaspheme God : while he doth say in his heart, Tush, thou God carest not for it ?

15 Surely thou hast seen it : for thou beholdest ungodliness and wrong,

16 That thou mayest take the matter into thy hand : the poor committeth himself unto thee ; for thou art the helper of the friendless.

17 Break thou the power of the ungodly and malicious : take away his ungodliness, and thou shalt find none.

18 The LORD is King for ever and ever : and the heathen are perished out of the land.

19 LORD, thou hast heard the desire of the poor : thou preparest their heart, and thine ear hearkeneth thereto ;

20 To help the fatherless and poor unto their right : that the man of the earth be no more exalted against them.

PSALM 11.

In Domino confido.

IN the LORD put I my trust : how say ye then

to my soul, that she should flee as a bird unto the hill?

2 For lo, the ungodly bend their bow, and make ready their arrows within the quiver: that they may privily shoot at them which are true of heart.

3 For the foundations will be cast down: and what hath the righteous done?

4 The LORD is in his holy temple: the LORD's seat is in heaven.

5 His eyes consider the poor: and his eyelids try the children of men.

6 The LORD alloweth the righteous: but the ungodly, and him that delighteth in wickedness, doth his soul abhor.

7 Upon the ungodly he shall rain snares, fire and brimstone, storm and tempest: this shall be their portion to drink.

8 For the righteous LORD loveth righteousness: his countenance will behold the thing that is just.

Evening Prayer.

PSALM 12.

Salvum me fac.

HELP me, LORD, for there is not one godly man left: for the faithful are minished from among the children of men.

2 They talk of vanity every one with his neighbour: they do but flatter with their lips, and dissemble in their double heart.

3 The LORD shall root out all deceitful lips: and the tongue that speaketh proud things;

4 Which have said, With our tongue will we prevail: we are they that ought to speak, who is lord over us?

5 Now, for the comfortless troubles' sake of the needy: and because of the deep sighing of the poor,

6 I will up, saith the LORD: and will help every one from him that swelleth against him, and will set him at rest.

7 The words of the LORD are pure words: even as the silver which from the earth is tried, and purified seven times in the fire.

8 Thou shalt keep them, O LORD: thou shalt preserve him from this generation for ever.

9 The ungodly walk on every side: when they are exalted, the children of men are put to rebuke.

PSALM 13.

Usquequo, Domine?

HOW long wilt thou forget me, O LORD; for ever: how long wilt thou hide thy face from me?

2 How long shall I seek counsel in my soul, and be so vexed in my heart: how long shall mine enemies triumph over me?

3 Consider, and hear me, O LORD my God: lighten mine eyes, that I sleep not in death;

4 Lest mine enemy say, I have prevailed against him: for if I be cast down, they that trouble me will rejoice at it.

5 *But my trust is in thy mercy: and my heart is joyful in thy salvation.*

6 I will sing of the LORD, because he hath dealt so lovingly with me: yea, I will praise the Name of the Lord most highest.

PSALM 14.

Dixit insipiens.

THE fool hath said in his heart: There is no God.

2 They are corrupt, and become abominable in their doings: there is none that doeth good, no not one.

3 The LORD looked down from heaven upon the children of men: to see if there were any that would understand, and seek after God.

4 But they are all gone out of the way, they are altogether become abominable: there is none that doeth good, no not one.

5 Their throat is an open sepulchre; with their tongues have they deceived: the poison of asps is under their lips.

6 Their mouth is full of cursing and bitterness: their feet are swift to shed blood.

7 Destruction and unhappiness is in their ways, and the way of peace have they not known: there is no fear of God before their eyes.

8 Have they no knowledge, that they are all such workers of mischief: eating up my people as it were bread, and call not upon the LORD?

9 There were they brought in great fear, even where no fear was: for God is in the generation of the righteous.

10 As for you, ye have made a mock at the counsel of the poor: because

he putteth his trust in the LORD.

11 Who shall give salvation unto Israel out of Sion? When the LORD turneth the captivity of his people : then shall Jacob rejoice, and Israel shall be glad.

THE THIRD DAY.
Morning Prayer.

PSALM 15.
Domine, quis habitabit?

LORD, who shall dwell in thy tabernacle : or who shall rest upon thy holy hill?

2 Even he that leadeth an uncorrupt life : and doeth the thing which is right, and speaketh the truth from his heart.

3 He that hath used no deceit in his tongue, nor done evil to his neighbour : and hath not slandered his neighbour.

4 He that setteth not by himself, but is lowly in his own eyes : and maketh much of them that fear the LORD.

5 He that sweareth unto his neighbour, and disappointeth him not : though it were to his own hindrance.

6 He that hath not given his money upon usury : nor taken reward against the innocent.

7 Whoso doeth these things : shall never fall.

PSALM 16.
Conserva me, Domine.

PRESERVE me, O God : for in thee have I put my trust.

2 O my soul, thou hast said unto the LORD : Thou art my God ; my goods are nothing unto thee.

3 All my delight is upon the saints that are in the earth : and upon such as excel in virtue.

4 But they that run after another god : shall have great trouble.

5 Their drink-offerings of blood will I not offer : neither make mention of their names within my lips.

6 The LORD himself is the portion of mine inheritance, and of my cup : thou shalt maintain my lot.

7 The lot is fallen unto me in a fair ground : yea, I have a goodly heritage.

8 I will thank the LORD for giving me warning : my reins also chasten me in the night season.

9 I have set God alway before me : for he is on my right hand, therefore I shall not fall.

10 Wherefore my heart was glad, and my glory rejoiced : my flesh also shall rest in hope.

11 For why ? thou shalt not leave my soul in hell : neither shalt thou suffer thy Holy One to see corruption.

12 Thou shalt show me the path of life : in thy presence is the fulness of joy : and at thy right hand there is pleasure for evermore.

PSALM 17.

Exaudi, Domine.

HEAR the right, O Lord, consider my complaint : and hearken unto my prayer, that goeth not out of feigned lips.

2 Let my sentence come forth from thy presence : and let thine eyes look upon the thing that is equal.

3 Thou hast proved and visited mine heart in the night season ; thou hast tried me, and shalt find no wickedness in me : for I am utterly purposed that my mouth shall not offend.

4 Because of men's works that are done against the words of thy lips : I have kept me from the ways of the destroyer.

5 O hold thou up my goings in thy paths : that my footsteps slip not.

6 I have called upon thee, O God, for thou shalt hear me : incline thine ear to me, and hearken unto my words.

7 Show thy marvellous loving-kindness, thou that art the Saviour of them which put their trust in thee : from such as resist thy right hand.

8 Keep me as the apple of an eye : hide me under the shadow of thy wings,

9 From the ungodly, that trouble me : mine enemies compass me round about, to take away my soul.

10 They are inclosed in their own fat : and their mouth speaketh proud things.

11 They lie waiting in our way on every side : turning their eyes down to the ground ;

12 Like as a lion that is greedy of his prey : and as it were a lion's whelp lurking in secret places.

13 Up, Lord, disappoint

him, and cast him down : deliver my soul from the ungodly, which is a sword of thine ;

14 From the men of thy hand, O LORD, from the men, I say, and from the evil world : which have their portion in this life, whose bellies thou fillest with thy hid treasure.

15 They have children at their desire : and leave the rest of their substance for their babes.

16 But as for me, I will behold thy presence in righteousness : and when I awake up after thy likeness, I shall be satisfied with it.

Evening Prayer.

PSALM 18.

Diligam te, Domine.

I WILL love thee, O LORD, my strength. The LORD is my stony rock, and my defence : my Saviour, my God, and my might, in whom I will trust ; my buckler, the horn also of my salvation, and my refuge.

2 I will call upon the LORD, which is worthy to be praised : so shall I be safe from mine enemies.

3 The sorrows of death compassed me : and the overflowings of ungodliness made me afraid.

4 The pains of hell came about me : the snares of death overtook me.

5 In my trouble I will call upon the LORD : and complain unto my God :

6 So shall he hear my voice out of his holy temple : and my complaint shall come before him ; it shall enter even into his ears.

7 The earth trembled and quaked : the very foundations also of the hills shook, and were removed, because he was wroth.

8 There went a smoke out in his presence : and a consuming fire out of his mouth, so that coals were kindled at it.

9 He bowed the heavens also, and came down : and it was dark under his feet.

10 He rode upon the Cherubim, and did fly : he came flying upon the wings of the wind.

11 He made darkness his secret place : his pavilion round about him with dark water, and thick clouds to cover him.

12 At the brightness of

his presence his clouds removed : hailstones and coals of fire.

13 The Lord also thundered out of heaven, and the Highest gave his thunder : hailstones and coals of fire.

14 He sent out his arrows, and scattered them : he cast forth lightnings, and destroyed them.

15 The springs of waters were seen, and the foundations of the round world were discovered at thy chiding, O Lord : at the blasting of the breath of thy displeasure.

16 He shall send down from on high to fetch me : and shall *take me out of* many waters.

17 He shall deliver me from my strongest enemy, and from them which hate me : for they are too mighty for me.

18 They prevented me in the day of my trouble : but the Lord was my upholder.

19 He brought me forth also into a place of liberty : he brought me forth, even because he had a favour unto me.

20 The Lord shall reward me after my righteous dealing : according

to the cleanness of my hands shall he recompense me.

21 Because I have kept the ways of the Lord : and have not forsaken my God, as the wicked doth.

22 For I have an eye unto all his laws : and will not cast out his commandments from me.

23 I was also uncorrupt before him : and eschewed mine own wickedness.

24 Therefore shall the Lord reward me after my righteous dealing : and according unto the cleanness of my hands in his eyesight.

25 With the holy thou shalt be holy : and with a perfect man thou shalt be perfect.

26 With the clean thou shalt be clean : and with the froward thou shalt learn frowardness.

27 For thou shalt save the people that are in adversity : and shalt bring down the high looks of the proud.

28 Thou also shalt light my candle : the Lord my God shall make my darkness to be light.

29 For in thee I shall discomfit an host of men : and with the help of my

God I shall leap over the wall.

30 The way of God is an undefiled way : the word of the LORD also is tried in the fire ; he is the defender of all them that put their trust in him.

31 For who is God, but the LORD : or who hath any strength, except our God ?

32 It is God that girdeth me with strength of war : and maketh my way perfect.

33 He maketh my feet like harts' feet : and setteth me up on high.

34 He teacheth mine hands to fight : and mine arms shall break even a bow of steel.

35 Thou hast given me the defence of thy salvation : thy right hand also shall hold me up, and thy loving correction shall make me great.

36 Thou shalt make room enough under me for to go : that my footsteps shall not slide.

37 I will follow upon mine enemies, and overtake them : neither will I turn again till I have destroyed them.

38 I will smite them, that they shall not be able to stand : but fall under my feet.

39 Thou hast girded me with strength unto the battle : thou shalt throw down mine enemies under me.

40 Thou hast made mine enemies also to turn their backs upon me : and I shall destroy them that hate me.

41 They shall cry, but there shall be none to help them : yea, even unto the LORD shall they cry, but he shall not hear them.

42 I will beat them as small as the dust before the wind : I will cast them out as the clay in the streets.

43 Thou shalt deliver me from the strivings of the people : and thou shalt make me the head of the heathen.

44 A people whom I have not known : shall serve me.

45 As soon as they hear of me, they shall obey me : but the strange children shall dissemble with me.

46 The strange children shall fail : and be afraid out of their prisons.

47 The LORD liveth ; and blessed be my strong helper : and praised be the God of my salvation :

48 Even the God that seeth that I be avenged : and subdueth the people unto me.

49 It is he that delivereth me from my cruel enemies, and setteth me up above mine adversaries : thou shalt rid me from the wicked man.

50 For this cause will I give thanks unto thee, O LORD, among the Gentiles : and sing praises unto thy Name.

51 Great prosperity giveth he unto his King : and showeth loving-kindness unto David his anointed, and unto his seed for evermore.

❀

THE FOURTH DAY.

Morning Prayer.

PSALM 19.

Cæli enarrant.

THE heavens declare the glory of God : and the firmament showeth his handy-work.

2 One day telleth another : and one night certifieth another.

3 There is neither speech nor language : but their voices are heard among them.

4 Their sound is gone out into all lands : and their words into the ends of the world.

5 In them hath he set a tabernacle for the sun : which cometh forth as a bridegroom out of his chamber, and rejoiceth as a giant to run his course.

6 It goeth forth from the uttermost part of the heaven, and runneth about unto the end of it again : and there is nothing hid from the heat thereof.

7 The law of the LORD is an undefiled law, converting the soul : the testimony of the LORD is sure, and giveth wisdom unto the simple.

8 The statutes of the LORD are right, and rejoice the heart : the commandment of the LORD is pure, and giveth light unto the eyes.

9 The fear of the LORD is clean, and endureth for ever : the judgments of the LORD are true, and righteous altogether.

10 More to be desired are they than gold, yea, than much fine gold : sweeter also than honey, and the honey-comb.

11 Moreover, by them is thy servant taught : and

in keeping of them there is great reward.

12 Who can tell how oft he offendeth : O cleanse thou me from my secret faults.

13 Keep thy servant also from presumptuous sins, lest they get the dominion over me : so shall I be undefiled, and innocent from the great offence.

14 Let the words of my mouth, and the meditation of my heart : be alway acceptable in thy sight,

15 O LORD : my strength and my redeemer.

PSALM 20.

Exaudiat te Dominus.

THE LORD hear thee in the day of trouble : the Name of the God of Jacob defend thee ;

2 Send thee help from the sanctuary : and strengthen thee out of Sion ;

3 Remember all thy offerings : and accept thy burnt-sacrifice ;

4 Grant thee thy heart's desire : and fulfil all thy mind.

5 We will rejoice in thy salvation, and triumph in the Name of the Lord our

God : the LORD perform all thy petitions.

6 Now know I that the LORD helpeth his anointed, and will hear him from his holy heaven : even with the wholesome strength of his right hand.

7 Some put their trust in chariots, and some in horses : but we will remember the Name of the LORD our God.

8 They are brought down and fallen : but we are risen and stand upright.

9 Save, LORD ; and hear us, O King of heaven : when we call upon thee.

PSALM 21.

Domine, in virtute tua.

THE King shall rejoice in thy strength, O LORD : exceeding glad shall he be of thy salvation.

2 Thou hast given him his heart's desire : and hast not denied him the request of his lips.

3 For thou shalt prevent him with the blessings of goodness : and shalt set a crown of pure gold upon his head.

4 He asked life of thee ; and thou gavest him a long life : even for ever and ever.

5 His honour is great in

thy salvation : glory and great worship shalt thou lay upon him.

6 For thou shalt give him everlasting felicity : and make him glad with the joy of thy countenance.

7 And why? because the King putteth his trust in the LORD : and in the mercy of the Most Highest he shall not miscarry.

8 All thine enemies shall feel thine hand : thy right hand shall find out them that hate thee.

9 Thou shalt make them like a fiery oven in time of thy wrath : the LORD shall destroy them in his displeasure, and the fire shall consume them.

10 Their fruit shalt thou root out of the earth : and their seed from among the children of men.

11 For they intended mischief against thee : and imagined such a device as they are not able to perform.

12 Therefore shalt thou put them to flight : and the strings of thy bow shalt thou make ready against the face of them.

13 Be thou exalted, LORD, in thine own strength : so will we sing, and praise thy power.

Evening Prayer.

PSALM 22.

Deus, Deus meus.

MY God, my God, look upon me; why hast thou forsaken me : and art so far from my health, and from the words of my complaint?

2 O my God, I cry in the day-time, but thou hearest not : and in the night season also I take no rest.

3 And thou continuest holy : O thou Worship of Israel.

4 Our fathers hoped in thee : they trusted in thee, and thou didst deliver them.

5 They called upon thee, and were holpen : they put their trust in thee, and were not confounded.

6 But as for me, I am a worm, and no man : a very scorn of men, and the outcast of the people.

7 All they that see me laugh me to scorn : they shoot out their lips, and shake their heads, saying,

8 He trusted in God, that he would deliver him : let him deliver him, if he will have him.

9 But thou art he that took me out of my mother's womb : thou wast

my hope, when I hanged yet upon my mother's breasts.

10 I have been left unto thee ever since I was born : thou art my God even from my mother's womb.

11 O go not from me ; for trouble is hard at hand : and there is none to help me.

12 Many oxen are come about me : fat bulls of Basan close me in on every side.

13 They gape upon me with their mouths : as it were a ramping and a roaring lion.

14 I am poured out like water, and all my bones are out of joint : my heart also in the midst of my body is even like melting wax.

15 My strength is dried up like a potsherd, and my tongue cleaveth to my gums : and thou shalt bring me into the dust of death.

16 For many dogs are come about me : and the council of the wicked layeth siege against me.

17 They pierced my hands and my feet ; I may tell all my bones : they stand staring and looking upon me.

18 They part my garments among them : and cast lots upon my vesture.

19 But be not thou far from me, O LORD : thou art my succour, haste thee to help me.

20 Deliver my soul from the sword : my darling from the power of the dog.

21 Save me from the lion's mouth : thou hast heard me also from among the horns of the unicorns.

22 I will declare thy Name unto my brethren : in the midst of the congregation will I praise thee.

23 O praise the LORD, ye that fear him : magnify him, all ye of the seed of Jacob ; and fear him, all ye seed of Israel.

24 For he hath not despised nor abhorred the low estate of the poor : he hath not hid his face from him ; but when he called unto him he heard him.

25 My praise is of thee in the great congregation : my vows will I perform in the sight of them that fear him.

26 The poor shall eat, and be satisfied : they that seek after the LORD shall praise him ; your heart shall live for ever.

27 All the ends of the world shall remember themselves, and be turned unto the LORD : and all the kindreds of the nations shall worship before him.

28 For the kingdom is the LORD'S : and he is the Governor among the people.

29 All such as be fat upon earth : have eaten, and worshipped.

30 All they that go down into the dust shall kneel before him : and no man hath quickened his own soul.

31 My seed shall serve him : they shall be counted unto the Lord for a generation.

32 They shall come, and the heavens shall declare his righteousness : unto a people that shall be born, whom the Lord hath made.

PSALM 23.

Dominus regit me.

THE LORD is my shepherd : therefore can I lack nothing.

2 He shall feed me in a green pasture : and lead me forth beside the waters of comfort.

3 He shall convert my soul : and bring me forth in the paths of righteousness for his Name's sake.

4 Yea, though I walk through the valley of the shadow of death, I will fear no evil : for thou art with me ; thy rod and thy staff comfort me.

5 Thou shalt prepare a table before me against them that trouble me : thou hast anointed my head with oil, and my cup shall be full.

6 But thy loving-kindness and mercy shall follow me all the days of my life : and I will dwell in the house of the LORD for ever.

✿

THE FIFTH DAY.

Morning Prayer.

PSALM 24.

Domini est terra.

THE earth is the LORD'S, and all that therein is : the compass of the world, and they that dwell therein.

2 For he hath founded it upon the seas : and prepared it upon the floods.

3 Who shall ascend into the hill of the LORD : or who shall rise up in his holy place?

4 Even he that hath clean hands, and a pure heart : and that hath not

lift up his mind unto vanity, nor sworn to deceive his neighbour.

5 He shall receive the blessing from the Lord : and righteousness from the God of his salvation.

6 This is the generation of them that seek him : even of them that seek thy face, O Jacob.

7 Lift up your heads, O ye gates ; and be ye lift up, ye everlasting doors : and the King of glory shall come in.

8 Who is this King of glory : It is the Lord strong and mighty, even the Lord mighty in battle.

9 Lift up your heads, O ye gates ; and be ye lift up, ye everlasting doors : and the King of glory shall come in.

10 Who is this King of glory : Even the Lord of hosts, he is the King of glory.

Psalm 25.

Ad te, Domine, levavi.

UNTO thee, O Lord, will I lift up my soul ; my God, I have put my trust in thee : O let me not be confounded, neither let mine enemies triumph over me.

2 For all they that hope in thee shall not be ashamed : but such as transgress without a cause shall be put to confusion.

3 Show me thy ways, O Lord : and teach me thy paths.

4 Lead me forth in thy truth, and learn me : for thou art the God of my salvation ; in thee hath been my hope all the day long.

5 Call to remembrance, O Lord, thy tender mercies : and thy loving-kindnesses, which have been ever of old.

6 O remember not the sins and offences of my youth : but according to thy mercy think thou upon me, O Lord, for thy goodness.

7 Gracious and righteous is the Lord : therefore will he teach sinners in the way.

8 Them that are meek shall he guide in judgment : and such as are gentle, them shall he learn his way.

9 All the paths of the Lord are mercy and truth : unto such as keep his covenant and his testimonies.

10 For thy Name's sake,

O LORD : be merciful unto my sin ; for it is great.

11 What man is he that feareth the LORD : him shall he teach in the way that he shall choose.

12 His soul shall dwell at ease : and his seed shall inherit the land.

13 The secret of the LORD is among them that fear him : and he will show them his covenant.

14 Mine eyes are ever looking unto the LORD : for he shall pluck my feet out of the net.

15 Turn thee unto me, and have mercy upon me : for I am desolate, and in misery.

16 The sorrows of my heart are enlarged : O bring thou me out of my troubles.

17 Look upon my adversity and misery : and forgive me all my sin.

18 Consider mine enemies, how many they are : and they bear a tyrannous hate against me.

19 O keep my soul, and deliver me : let me not be confounded, for I have put my trust in thee.

20 Let perfectness and righteous dealing wait upon me : for my hope hath been in thee.

21 Deliver Israel, O God : out of all his troubles.

PSALM 26.

Judica me, Domine.

BE thou my Judge, O LORD, for I have walked innocently : my trust hath been also in the LORD, therefore shall I not fall.

2 Examine me, O LORD, and prove me : try out my reins and my heart.

3 For thy loving-kindness is ever before mine eyes : and I will walk in thy truth.

4 I have not dwelt with vain persons : neither will I have fellowship with the deceitful.

5 I have hated the congregation of the wicked : and will not sit among the ungodly.

6 I will wash my hands in innocency, O LORD : and so will I go to thine altar ;

7 That I may show the voice of thanksgiving : and tell of all thy wondrous works.

8 LORD, I have loved the habitation of thy house : and the place where thine honour dwelleth.

9 O shut not up my

soul with the sinners : nor my life with the blood-thirsty ;

10 In whose hands is wickedness : and their right hand is full of gifts.

11 But as for me, I will walk innocently : O deliver me, and be merciful unto me.

12 My foot standeth right : I will praise the LORD in the congregations.

❊

Evening Prayer.

PSALM 27.

Dominus illuminatio.

THE LORD is my light and my salvation ; whom then shall I fear : the LORD is the strength of my life ; of whom then shall I be afraid ?

2 When the wicked, even mine enemies and my foes, came upon me to eat up my flesh : they stumbled and fell.

3 Though an host of men were laid against me, yet shall not my heart be afraid : and though there rose up war against me, yet will I put my trust in him.

4 One thing have I desired of the LORD, which I will require : even that I may dwell in the house of the LORD all the days of my life, to behold the fair beauty of the LORD, and to visit his temple.

5 For in the time of trouble he shall hide me in his tabernacle : yea, in the secret place of his dwelling shall he hide me, and set me up upon a rock of stone.

6 And now shall he lift up mine head : above mine enemies round about me.

7 Therefore will I offer in his dwelling an oblation, with great gladness : I will sing and speak praises unto the LORD.

8 Hearken unto my voice, O LORD, when I cry unto thee : have mercy upon me, and hear me.

9 My heart hath talked of thee, Seek ye my face : Thy face, LORD, will I seek.

10 O hide not thou thy face from me : nor cast thy servant away in displeasure.

11 Thou hast been my succour : leave me not, neither forsake me, O God of my salvation.

12 When my father and my mother forsake me : the LORD taketh me up.

13 Teach me thy way, O

LORD : and lead me in the right way, because of mine enemies.

14 Deliver me not over into the will of mine adversaries : for there are false witnesses risen up against me, and such as speak wrong.

15 I should utterly have fainted : but that I believe verily to see the goodness of the LORD in the land of the living.

16 O tarry thou the LORD's leisure : be strong, and he shall comfort thine heart ; and put thou thy trust in the LORD.

PSALM 28.

Ad te, Domine.

UNTO thee will I cry, O LORD, my strength : think no scorn of me ; lest, if thou make as though thou hearest not, I become like them that go down into the pit.

2 Hear the voice of my humble petitions, when I cry unto thee : when I hold up my hands towards the mercy-seat of thy holy temple.

3 O pluck me not away, neither destroy me with the ungodly and wicked doers : which speak friendly to their neighbours, but imagine mischief in their hearts.

4 Reward them according to their deeds : and according to the wickedness of their own inventions.

5 Recompense them after the work of their hands : pay them that they have deserved.

6 For they regard not in their mind the works of the LORD, nor the operation of his hands : therefore shall he break them down, and not build them up.

7 Praised be the LORD : for he hath heard the voice of my humble petitions.

8 The LORD is my strength, and my shield ; my heart hath trusted in him, and I am helped : therefore my heart danceth for joy, and in my song will I praise him.

9 The LORD is my strength : and he is the wholesome defence of his anointed.

10 O save thy people, and give thy blessing unto thine inheritance : feed them, and set them up for ever.

PSALM 29.

Afferte Domino.

BRING unto the LORD, O ye mighty, bring

young rams unto the LORD: ascribe unto the LORD worship and strength.

2 Give the LORD the honour due unto his Name: worship the LORD with holy worship.

3 It is the LORD that commandeth the waters: it is the glorious God that maketh the thunder.

4 It is the LORD that ruleth the sea; the voice of the LORD is mighty in operation: the voice of the LORD is a glorious voice.

5 The voice of the LORD breaketh the cedar-trees: yea, the LORD breaketh the cedars of Libanus.

6 He maketh them also to skip like a calf: Libanus also, and Sirion, like a young unicorn.

7 The voice of the LORD divideth the flames of fire; the voice of the LORD shaketh the wilderness: yea, the LORD shaketh the wilderness of Cades.

8 The voice of the LORD maketh the hinds to bring forth young, and discovereth the thick bushes: in his temple doth every man speak of his honour.

9 The LORD sitteth above the water-flood: and the LORD remaineth a King for ever.

10 The LORD shall give strength unto his people: the LORD shall give his people the blessing of peace.

☙

THE SIXTH DAY.

Morning Prayer.

PSALM 30.

Exaltabo te, Domine.

I WILL magnify thee, O LORD; for thou hast set me up: and not made my foes to triumph over me.

2 O LORD my God, I cried unto thee: and thou hast healed me.

3 Thou, LORD, hast brought my soul out of hell: thou hast kept my life from them that go down to the pit.

4 Sing praises unto the LORD, O ye saints of his: and give thanks unto him, for a remembrance of his holiness.

5 For his wrath endureth but the twinkling of an eye, and in his pleasure is life: heaviness may endure for a night, but joy cometh in the morning.

6 And in my prosperity I said, I shall never be removed: thou, LORD, of thy goodness, hast made my hill so strong.

7 Thou didst turn thy

face from me : and I was troubled.

8 Then cried I unto thee, O LORD : and gat me to my LORD right humbly.

9 What profit is there in my blood : when I go down to the pit ?

10 Shall the dust give thanks unto thee : or shall it declare thy truth ?

11 Hear, O LORD, and have mercy upon me : LORD, be thou my helper.

12 Thou hast turned my heaviness into joy : thou hast put off my sackcloth, and girded me with gladness :

13 Therefore shall every good man sing of thy praise without ceasing : O my God, I will give thanks unto thee for ever.

PSALM 31.

In te, Domine, speravi.

IN thee, O LORD, have I put my trust : let me never be put to confusion ; deliver me in thy righteousness.

2 Bow down thine ear to me : make haste to deliver me.

3 And be thou my strong rock, and house of defence : that thou mayest save me.

4 For thou art my strong rock, and my castle : be

thou also my guide, and lead me for thy Name's sake.

5 Draw me out of the net that they have laid privily for me : for thou art my strength.

6 Into thy hands I commend my spirit : for thou hast redeemed me, O LORD, thou God of truth.

7 I have hated them that hold of superstitious vanities : and my trust hath been in the LORD.

8 I will be glad and rejoice in thy mercy : for thou hast considered my trouble, and hast known my soul in adversities.

9 Thou hast not shut me up into the hand of the enemy : but hast set my feet in a large room.

10 Have mercy upon me, O LORD, for I am in trouble : and mine eye is consumed for very heaviness ; yea, my soul and my body.

11 For my life is waxen old with heaviness : and my years with mourning.

12 My strength faileth me, because of mine iniquity : and my bones are consumed.

13 I became a reproof among all mine enemies, but especially among my neighbours : and they of

mine acquaintance were afraid of me; and they that did see me without, conveyed themselves from me.

14 I am clean forgotten as a dead man out of mind : I am become like a broken vessel.

15 For I have heard the blasphemy of the multitude : and fear is on every side ; while they conspire together against me, and take their counsel to take away my life.

16 But my hope hath been in thee, O LORD : I have said, Thou art my God.

17 My time is in thy hand; deliver me from the hand of mine enemies : and from them that persecute me.

18 Show thy servant the light of thy countenance : and save me for thy mercy's sake.

19 Let me not be confounded, O LORD, for I have called upon thee : let the ungodly be put to confusion, and be put to silence in the grave.

20 Let the lying lips be put to silence : which cruelly, disdainfully, and despitefully speak against the righteous.

21 O how plentiful is thy goodness, which thou hast laid up for them that fear thee : and that thou hast prepared for them that put their trust in thee, even before the sons of men!

22 Thou shalt hide them privily by thine own presence from the provoking of all men : thou shalt keep them secretly in thy tabernacle from the strife of tongues.

23 Thanks be to the LORD : for he hath showed me marvellous great kindness in a strong city.

24 And when I made haste, I said : I am cast out of the sight of thine eyes.

25 Nevertheless, thou heardest the voice of my prayer : when I cried unto thee.

26 O love the LORD, all ye his saints : for the LORD preserveth them that are faithful, and plenteously rewardeth the proud doer.

27 Be strong, and he shall establish your heart: all ye that put your trust in the LORD.

❖

Evening Prayer.

PSALM 32.

Beati quorum.

BLESSED is he whose unrighteousness is forgiven : and whose sin is covered.

2 Blessed is the man unto whom the Lord imputeth no sin : and in whose spirit there is no guile.

3 For whilst I held my tongue : my bones consumed away through my daily complaining.

4 For thy hand is heavy upon me day and night : and my moisture is like the drought in summer.

5 I will acknowledge my sin unto thee : and mine unrighteousness have I not hid.

6 I said, I will confess my sins unto the Lord : and so thou forgavest the wickedness of my sin.

7 For this shall every one that is godly make his prayer unto thee, in a time when thou mayest be found : but in the great water-floods they shall not come nigh him.

8 Thou art a place to hide me in ; thou shalt preserve me from trouble : thou shalt compass me about with songs of deliverance.

9 I will inform thee, and teach thee in the way wherein thou shalt go : and I will guide thee with mine eye.

10 Be ye not like to horse and mule, which have no understanding : whose mouths must be held with bit and bridle, lest they fall upon thee.

11 Great plagues remain for the ungodly : but whoso putteth his trust in the Lord, mercy embraceth him on every side.

12 Be glad, O ye righteous, and rejoice in the Lord : and be joyful, all ye that are true of heart.

PSALM 33.
Exultate, justi.

REJOICE in the Lord, O ye righteous : for it becometh well the just to be thankful.

2 Praise the Lord with harp : sing praises unto him with the lute, and instrument of ten strings.

3 Sing unto the Lord a new song : sing praises lustily unto him with a good courage.

4 For the word of the Lord is true : and all his works are faithful.

5 He loveth righteousness and judgment : the earth is full of the goodness of the Lord.

6 By the word of the Lord were the heavens made : and all the hosts

of them by the breath of his mouth.

7 He gathereth the waters of the sea together, as it were upon an heap : and layeth up the deep, as in a treasure-house.

8 Let all the earth fear the LORD : stand in awe of him, all ye that dwell in the world.

9 For he spake, and it was done : he commanded, and it stood fast.

10 The LORD bringeth the counsel of the heathen to nought : and maketh the devices of the people to be of none effect, and casteth out the counsels of princes.

11 The counsel of the LORD shall endure for ever : and the thoughts of his heart from generation to generation.

12 Blessed are the people whose God is the Lord JEHOVAH : and blessed are the folk that he hath chosen to him, to be his inheritance.

13 The LORD looked down from heaven, and beheld all the children of men : from the habitation of his dwelling, he considereth all them that dwell on all the earth.

14 He fashioneth all the hearts of them : and understandeth all their works.

15 There is no king that can be saved by the multitude of an host : neither is any mighty man delivered by much strength.

16 A horse is counted but a vain thing to save a man : neither shall he deliver any man by his great strength.

17 Behold, the eye of the LORD is upon them that fear him : and upon them that put their trust in his mercy ;

18 To deliver their soul from death : and to feed them in the time of dearth.

19 Our soul hath patiently tarried for the LORD : for he is our help and our shield.

20 For our heart shall rejoice in him : because we have hoped in his holy Name.

21 Let thy merciful kindness, O LORD, be upon us : like as we do put our trust in thee.

PSALM 34.

Benedicam Dominum.

I WILL alway give thanks unto the LORD : his praise shall ever be in my mouth.

2 My soul shall make her boast in the LORD : the humble shall hear thereof, and be glad.

3 O praise the LORD with me : and let us magnify his Name together.

4 I sought the LORD, and he heard me : yea, he delivered me out of all my fear.

5 They had an eye unto him, and were lightened : and their faces were not ashamed.

6 Lo, the poor crieth, and the LORD heareth him : yea, and saveth him out of all his troubles.

7 The angel of the LORD tarrieth round about them that fear him : and delivereth them.

8 O taste, and see, how gracious the LORD is : blessed is the man that trusteth in him.

9 O fear the LORD, ye that are his saints : for they that fear him lack nothing.

10 The lions do lack, and suffer hunger : but they who seek the LORD shall want no manner of thing that is good.

11 Come, ye children, and hearken unto me : I will teach you the fear of the LORD.

12 What man is he that lusteth to live : and would fain see good days?

13 Keep thy tongue from evil : and thy lips, that they speak no guile.

14 Eschew evil, and do good : seek peace, and ensue it.

15 The eyes of the LORD are over the righteous : and his ears are open unto their prayers.

16 The countenance of the LORD is against them that do evil : to root out the remembrance of them from the earth.

17 The righteous cry, and the LORD heareth them : and delivereth them out of all their troubles.

18 The LORD is nigh unto them that are of a contrite heart : and will save such as be of an humble spirit.

19 Great are the troubles of the righteous : but the LORD delivereth him out of all.

20 He keepeth all his bones : so that not one of them is broken.

21 But misfortune shall slay the ungodly : and they that hate the righteous shall be desolate.

22 The LORD delivereth

the souls of his servants : and all they that put their trust in him shall not be destitute.

❦

THE SEVENTH DAY.

Morning Prayer.

PSALM 35.

Judica, Domine.

PLEAD thou my cause, O LORD, with them that strive with me : and fight thou against them that fight against me.

2 Lay hand upon the shield and buckler : and stand up to help me.

3 Bring forth the spear, and stop the way against them that persecute me : say unto my soul, I am thy salvation.

4 Let them be confounded, and put to shame, that seek after my soul : let them be turned back, and brought to confusion, that imagine mischief for me.

5 Let them be as the dust before the wind : and the angel of the LORD scattering them.

6 Let their way be dark and slippery : and let the angel of the LORD persecute them.

7 For they have privily laid their net to destroy me without a cause : yea, even without a cause have they made a pit for my soul.

8 Let a sudden destruction come upon him unawares, and his net that he hath laid privily catch himself : that he may fall into his own mischief.

9 And, my soul, be joyful in the LORD : it shall rejoice in his salvation.

10 All my bones shall say, LORD, who is like unto thee, who deliverest the poor from him that is too strong for him : yea, the poor, and him that is in misery, from him that spoileth him?

11 False witnesses did rise up : they laid to my charge things that I knew not.

12 They rewarded me evil for good : to the great discomfort of my soul.

13 Nevertheless, when they were sick, I put on sackcloth, and humbled my soul with fasting : and my prayer shall turn into mine own bosom.

14 I behaved myself as though it had been my friend or my brother : I went heavily, as one that mourneth for his mother.

15 But in mine adversity they rejoiced, and gathered themselves together : yea, the very abjects came together against me unawares, making mouths at me, and ceased not.

16 With the flatterers were busy mockers : who gnashed upon me with their teeth.

17 Lord, how long wilt thou look upon this : O deliver my soul from the calamities which they bring on me, and my darling from the lions.

18 So will I give thee thanks in the great congregation : I will praise thee among much people.

19 O let not them that are mine enemies triumph over me ungodly : neither let them wink with their eyes, that hate me without a cause.

20 And why? their communing is not for peace : but they imagine deceitful words against them that are quiet in the land.

21 They gaped upon me with their mouths, and said : Fie on thee! fie on thee! we saw it with our eyes.

22 This thou hast seen, O LORD : hold not thy tongue then, go not far from me, O Lord.

23 Awake, and stand up to judge my quarrel : avenge thou my cause, my God and my Lord.

24 Judge me, O LORD my God, according to thy righteousness : and let them not triumph over me.

25 Let them not say in their hearts, There! there! so would we have it : neither let them say, We have devoured him.

26 Let them be put to confusion and shame together, that rejoice at my trouble : let them be clothed with rebuke and dishonour, that boast themselves against me.

27 Let them be glad and rejoice, that favour my righteous dealing : yea, let them say alway, Blessed be the LORD, who hath pleasure in the prosperity of his servant.

28 And as for my tongue, it shall be talking of thy righteousness : and of thy praise, all the day long.

PSALM 36.

Dixit injustus.

MY heart showeth me the wickedness of

the ungodly: that there is no fear of God before his eyes.

2 For he flattereth himself in his own sight: until his abominable sin be found out.

3 The words of his mouth are unrighteous and full of deceit: he hath left off to behave himself wisely, and to do good.

4 He imagineth mischief upon his bed, and hath set himself in no good way: neither doth he abhor any thing that is evil.

5 Thy mercy, O Lord, reacheth unto the heavens: and thy faithfulness unto the clouds.

6 Thy righteousness standeth like the strong mountains: thy judgments are like the great deep.

7 Thou, Lord, shalt save both man and beast; how excellent is thy mercy, O God: and the *children of men* shall put their trust under the shadow of thy wings.

8 They shall be satisfied with the plenteousness of thy house: and thou shalt give them drink of thy pleasures, as out of the river.

9 For with thee is the well of life: and in thy light shall we see light.

10 O continue forth thy loving-kindness unto them that know thee: and thy righteousness unto them that are true of heart.

11 O let not the foot of pride come against me: and let not the hand of the ungodly cast me down.

12 There are they fallen, all that work wickedness: they are cast down, and shall not be able to stand.

Evening Prayer.

Psalm 37.

Noli æmulari.

FRET not thyself because of the ungodly: neither be thou envious against the evil doers.

2 For they shall soon be cut down like the grass: and be withered even as the green herb.

3 Put thou thy trust in the Lord, and be doing good: dwell in the land, and verily thou shalt be fed.

4 Delight thou in the Lord: and he shall give thee thy heart's desire.

5 Commit thy way unto the Lord, and put thy

trust in him : and he shall bring it to pass.

6 He shall make thy righteousness as clear as the light : and thy just dealing as the noon-day.

7 Hold thee still in the LORD, and abide patiently upon him : but grieve not thyself at him whose way doth prosper, against the man that doeth after evil counsels.

8 Leave off from wrath, and let go displeasure : fret not thyself, else shalt thou be moved to do evil.

9 Wicked doers shall be rooted out : and they that patiently abide the LORD, those shall inherit the land.

10 Yet a little while, and the ungodly shall be clean gone : thou shalt look after his place, and he shall be away.

11 But the meek-spirited shall possess the earth : and shall be refreshed in the multitude of peace.

12 The ungodly seeketh counsel against the just : and gnasheth upon him with his teeth.

13 The Lord shall laugh him to scorn : for he hath seen that his day is coming.

14 The ungodly have drawn out the sword, and have bent their bow : to cast down the poor and needy, and to slay such as are of a right conversation.

15 Their sword shall go through their own heart : and their bow shall be broken.

16 A small thing that the righteous hath : is better than great riches of the ungodly.

17 For the arms of the ungodly shall be broken : and the LORD upholdeth the righteous.

18 The LORD knoweth the days of the godly : and their inheritance shall endure for ever.

19 They shall not be confounded in the perilous time : and in the days of dearth they shall have enough.

20 As for the ungodly, they shall perish, and the enemies of the LORD shall consume as the fat of lambs : yea, even as the smoke shall they consume away.

21 The ungodly borroweth, and payeth not again : but the righteous is merciful and liberal.

22 Such as are blessed of God, shall possess the

* N

land : and they that are cursed of him, shall be rooted out.

23 The LORD ordereth a good man's going : and maketh his way acceptable to himself.

24 Though he fall, he shall not be cast away : for the LORD upholdeth him with his hand.

25 I have been young, and now am old : and yet saw I never the righteous forsaken, nor his seed begging their bread.

26 The righteous is ever merciful, and lendeth : and his seed is blessed.

27 Flee from evil, and do the thing that is good : and dwell for evermore.

28 For the LORD loveth the thing that is right : he forsaketh not his that be godly, but they are preserved for ever.

29 The unrighteous shall be punished : as for the seed of the ungodly, it shall be rooted out.

30 The righteous shall inherit the land : and dwell therein for ever.

31 The mouth of the righteous is exercised in wisdom : and his tongue will be talking of judgment.

32 The law of his God is in his heart : and his goings shall not slide.

33 The ungodly seeth the righteous : and seeketh occasion to slay him.

34 The LORD will not leave him in his hand : nor condemn him when he is judged.

35 Hope thou in the LORD, and keep his way, and he shall promote thee, that thou shalt possess the land : when the ungodly shall perish, thou shalt see it.

36 I myself have seen the ungodly in great power : and flourishing like a green bay-tree.

37 I went by, and lo, he was gone : I sought him, but his place could no where be found.

38 Keep innocency, and take heed unto the thing that is right : for that shall bring a man peace at the last.

39 As for the transgressors, they shall perish together : and the end of the ungodly is, they shall be rooted out at the last.

40 But the salvation of the righteous cometh of the LORD : who is also their strength in the time of trouble.

41 And the LORD shall

stand by them, and save them : he shall deliver them from the ungodly, and shall save them, because they put their trust in him.

☙

THE EIGHTH DAY.

Morning Prayer.

PSALM 38.

Domine, ne in furore.

PUT me not to rebuke, O LORD, in thine anger : neither chasten me in thy heavy displeasure :

2 For thine arrows stick fast in me : and thy hand presseth me sore.

3 There is no health in my flesh, because of thy displeasure : neither is there any rest in my bones, by reason of my sin.

4 For my wickednesses are gone over my head : and are like a sore burden, too heavy for me to bear.

5 My wounds stink, and are corrupt : through my foolishness.

6 I am brought into so great trouble and misery : that I go mourning all the day long.

7 For my loins are filled with a sore disease : and there is no whole part in my body.

8 I am feeble and sore smitten : I have roared for the very disquietness of my heart.

9 Lord, thou knowest all my desire : and my groaning is not hid from thee.

10 My heart panteth, my strength hath failed me : and the light of mine eyes is gone from me.

11 My lovers and my neighbours did stand looking upon my trouble : and my kinsmen stood afar off.

12 They also that sought after my life laid snares for me : and they that went about to do me evil talked of wickedness,and imagined deceit all the day long.

13 As for me, I was like a deaf man,and heard not : and as one that is dumb, who doth not open his mouth.

14 I became even as a man that heareth not : and in whose mouth are no reproofs.

15 For in thee, O LORD, have I put my trust : thou shalt answer for me, O Lord my God.

16 I have required that they, even mine enemies, should not triumph over

me : for when my foot slipt, they rejoiced greatly against me.

17 And I truly am set in the plague : and my heaviness is ever in my sight.

18 For I will confess my wickedness : and be sorry for my sin.

19 But mine enemies live, and are mighty : and they that hate me wrongfully are many in number.

20 They also that reward evil for good are against me : because I follow the thing that good is.

21 Forsake me not, O LORD my God : be not thou far from me.

22 Haste thee to help me : O Lord God of my salvation.

PSALM 39.

Dixi, Custodiam.

I SAID, I will take heed to my ways : that I offend not in my tongue.

2 I will keep my mouth as it were with a bridle : while the ungodly is in my sight.

3 I held my tongue, and spake nothing : I kept silence, yea, even from good words; but it was pain and grief to me.

4 My heart was hot with-

in me ; and while I was thus musing the fire kindled : and at the last I spake with my tongue:

5 LORD, let me know mine end, and the number of my days : that I may be certified how long I have to live.

6 Behold, thou hast made my days as it were a span long : and mine age is even as nothing in respect of thee ; and verily every man living is altogether vanity.

7 For man walketh in a vain shadow, and disquieteth himself in vain : he heapeth up riches, and cannot tell who shall gather them.

8 And now, Lord, what is my hope : truly my hope is even in thee.

9 Deliver me from all mine offences : and make me not a rebuke unto the foolish.

10 I became dumb, and opened not my mouth : for it was thy doing.

11 Take thy plague away from me : I am even consumed by the means of thy heavy hand.

12 When thou with rebukes dost chasten man for sin, thou makest his beauty to consume away,

like as it were a moth fretting a garment : every man therefore is but vanity.

13 Hear my prayer, O Lord, and with thine ears consider my calling : hold not thy peace at my tears :

14 For I am a stranger with thee, and a sojourner : as all my fathers were.

15 O spare me a little, that I may recover my strength : before I go hence, and be no more seen.

PSALM 40.

Expectans expectavi.

I WAITED patiently for the Lord : and he inclined unto me, and heard my calling.

2 He brought me also out of the horrible pit, out of the mire and clay : and set my feet upon the rock, and ordered my goings.

3 And he hath put a new song in my mouth : even a thanksgiving unto our God.

4 Many shall see it, and fear : and shall put their trust in the Lord.

5 Blessed is the man that hath set his hope in the Lord : and turned not unto the proud, and to such as go about with lies.

6 O Lord my God, great are the wondrous works which thou hast done, like as be also thy thoughts, which are to us-ward : and yet there is no man that ordereth them unto thee.

7 If I should declare them, and speak of them : they should be more than I am able to express.

8 Sacrifice and meat-offering thou wouldest not : but mine ears hast thou opened.

9 Burnt-offerings and sacrifice for sin hast thou not required : then said I, Lo, I come ;

10 In the volume of the book it is written of me, that I should fulfil thy will, O my God : I am content to do it ; yea, thy law is within my heart.

11 I have declared thy righteousness in the great congregation : lo, I will not refrain my lips, O Lord, and that thou knowest.

12 I have not hid thy righteousness within my heart : my talk hath been of thy truth, and of thy salvation.

13 I have not kept back thy loving mercy

and truth : from the great congregation.

14 Withdraw not thou thy mercy from me, O LORD : let thy loving-kindness and thy truth alway preserve me.

15 For innumerable troubles are come about me ; my sins have taken such hold upon me, that I am not able to look up : yea, they are more in number than the hairs of my head, and my heart hath failed me.

16 O LORD, let it be thy pleasure to deliver me : make haste, O LORD, to help me.

17 Let them be ashamed, and confounded together, that seek after my soul to destroy it : let them be driven backward, and put to rebuke, that wish me evil.

18 Let them be desolate, and rewarded with shame : that say unto me, Fie upon thee ! fie upon thee !

19 Let all those that seek thee, be joyful and glad in thee : and let such as love thy salvation, say alway, The LORD be praised.

20 As for me, I am poor and needy : but the Lord careth for me.

21 Thou art my helper and redeemer : make no long tarrying, O my God.

❊

Evening Prayer.

PSALM 41.
Beatus qui intelligit.

BLESSED is he that considereth the poor and needy : the LORD shall deliver him in the time of trouble.

2 The LORD preserve him, and keep him alive, that he may be blessed upon earth : and deliver not thou him into the will of his enemies.

3 The LORD comfort him when he lieth sick upon his bed : make thou all his bed in his sickness.

4 I said, LORD, be merciful unto me : heal my soul, for I have sinned against thee.

5 Mine enemies speak evil of me : When shall he die, and his name perish ?

6 And if he come to see me, he speaketh vanity : and his heart conceiveth falsehood within himself ; and when he cometh forth, he telleth it.

7 All mine enemies whisper together against me :

even against me do they imagine this evil:

8 Let the sentence of guiltiness proceed against him : and now that he lieth, let him rise up no more.

9 Yea, even mine own familiar friend whom I trusted : who did also eat of my bread, hath laid great wait for me.

10 But be thou merciful unto me, O LORD : raise thou me up again, and I shall reward them.

11 By this I know thou favoured me : that mine enemy doth not triumph against me.

12 And when I am in *my health, thou uphold-est* me : and shalt set me before thy face for ever.

13 Blessed be the LORD God of Israel : world without end. Amen.

PSALM 42.
Quemadmodum.

LIKE as the hart desir-eth the water-brooks : so longeth my soul after thee, O God.

2 My soul is athirst for God, yea, even for the living God : when shall I come to appear before the presence of God?

3 My tears have been my meat day and night : while they daily say unto me, Where is now thy God?

4 Now when I think thereupon, I pour out my heart by myself : for I went with the multitude, and brought them forth into the house of God :

5 In the voice of praise and thanksgiving : among such as keep holy-day.

6 Why art thou so full of heaviness, O my soul : and why art thou so disquieted within me?

7 Put thy trust in God : for I will yet give him thanks for the help of his countenance.

8 *My God, my soul is* vexed within me : therefore will I remember thee concerning the land of Jordan, and the little hill of Hermon.

9 One deep calleth another, because of the noise of thy water-pipes : all thy waves and storms are gone over me.

10 The LORD hath granted his loving-kindness in the day-time : and in the night season did I sing of him, and made my prayer unto the God of my-life.

11 I will say unto the God of my strength, Why

hast thou forgotten me : why go I thus heavily, while the enemy oppresseth me ?

12 My bones are smitten asunder as with a sword : while mine enemies that trouble me cast me in the teeth :

13 Namely, while they say daily unto me : Where is now thy God ?

14 Why art thou so vexed, O my soul : and why art thou so disquieted within me ?

15 O put thy trust in God : for I will yet thank him, which is the help of my countenance, and my God.

PSALM 43.
Judica me, Deus.

GIVE sentence with me, O God, and defend my cause against the ungodly people : O deliver me from the deceitful and wicked man.

2 For thou art the God of my strength ; why hast thou put me from thee : and why go I so heavily, while the enemy oppresseth me ?

3 O send out thy light and thy truth, that they may lead me : and bring me unto thy holy hill, and to thy dwelling.

4 And that I may go unto the altar of God, even unto the God of my joy and gladness : and upon the harp will I give thanks unto thee, O God, my God.

5 Why art thou so heavy, O my soul : and why art thou so disquieted within me ?

6 O put thy trust in God : for I will yet give him thanks, which is the help of my countenance, and my God.

✦

THE NINTH DAY.
Morning Prayer.
PSALM 44.
Deus, auribus.

WE have heard with our ears, O God, our fathers have told us : what thou hast done in their time of old :

2 How thou hast driven out the heathen with thy hand, and planted them in : how thou hast destroyed the nations, and cast them out.

3 For they gat not the land in possession through their own sword : neither was it their own arm that helped them :

4 But thy right hand,

and thine arm, and the light of thy countenance : because thou hadst a favour unto them.

5 Thou art my King, O God : send help unto Jacob.

6 Through thee will we overthrow our enemies : and in thy Name will we tread them under that rise up against us.

7 For I will not trust in my bow : it is not my sword that shall help me ;

8 But it is thou that savest us from our enemies : and puttest them to confusion that hate us.

9 We make our boast of God all day long : and will praise thy Name for ever.

10 But now thou art far off, and puttest us to confusion : and goest not forth with our armies.

11 Thou makest us to turn our backs upon our enemies : so that they which hate us spoil our goods.

12 Thou lettest us be eaten up like sheep : and hast scattered us among the heathen.

13 Thou sellest thy people for nought : and takest no money for them.

14 Thou makest us to be rebuked of our neighbours : to be laughed to scorn, and had in derision of them that are round about us.

15 Thou makest us to be a by-word among the heathen : and that the people shake their heads at us.

16 My confusion is daily before me : and the shame of my face hath covered me;

17 For the voice of the slanderer and blasphemer: for the enemy and avenger.

18 And though all this be come upon us, yet do we not forget thee : nor behave ourselves frowardly in thy covenant.

19 Our heart is not turned back : neither our steps gone out of thy way ;

20 No, not when thou hast smitten us into the place of dragons : and covered us with the shadow of death.

21 If we have forgotten the Name of our God, and holden up our hands to any strange god : shall not God search it out? for he knoweth the very secrets of the heart.

22 For thy sake also are we killed all the day long : and are counted as sheep appointed to be slain.

* N 3

23 Up, Lord, why sleepest thou : awake, and be not absent from us for ever.

24 Wherefore hidest thou thy face : and forgettest our misery and trouble?

25 For our soul is brought low, even unto the dust : our belly cleaveth unto the ground.

26 Arise, and help us : and deliver us, for thy mercy's sake.

PSALM 45.

Eructavit cor meum.

MY heart is inditing of a good matter : I speak of the things which I have made unto the King.

2 My tongue is the pen : of a ready writer.

3 Thou art fairer than the children of men : full of grace are thy lips, because God hath blessed thee for ever.

4 Gird thee with thy sword upon thy thigh, O thou Most Mighty : according to thy worship and renown.

5 Good luck have thou with thine honour : ride on, because of the word of truth, of meekness, and righteousness ; and thy

right hand shall teach thee terrible things.

6 Thy arrows are very sharp, and the people shall be subdued unto thee : even in the midst among the King's enemies.

7 Thy seat, O God, endureth for ever : the sceptre of thy kingdom is a right sceptre.

8 Thou hast loved righteousness, and hated iniquity : wherefore God, even thy God, hath anointed thee with the oil of gladness above thy fellows.

9 All thy garments smell of myrrh, aloes, and cassia : out of the ivory palaces, whereby they have made thee glad.

10 Kings' daughters were among thy honourable women : upon thy right hand did stand the queen in a vesture of gold, wrought about with divers colours.

11 Hearken, O daughter, and consider, incline thine ear : forget also thine own people, and thy father's house.

12 So shall the King have pleasure in thy beauty : for he is thy Lord God, and worship thou him.

13 And the daughter of

Tyre shall be there with a gift : like as the rich also among the people shall make their supplication before thee.

14 The King's daughter is all glorious within : her clothing is of wrought gold.

15 She shall be brought unto the King in raiment of needlework : the virgins that be her fellows shall bear her company, and shall be brought unto thee.

16 With joy and gladness shall they be brought : and shall enter into the King's palace.

17 Instead of thy fathers, thou shalt have children : whom thou mayest make princes in all lands.

18 I will remember thy Name from one generation to another : therefore shall the people give thanks unto thee, world without end.

PSALM 46.

Deus noster refugium.

God is our hope and strength : a very present help in trouble.

2 Therefore will we not fear, though the earth be moved : and though the hills be carried into the midst of the sea ;

3 Though the waters thereof rage and swell : and though the mountains shake at the tempest of the same.

4 The rivers of the flood thereof shall make glad the city of God : the holy place of the tabernacle of the Most Highest.

5 God is in the midst of her, therefore shall she not be removed : God shall help her, and that right early.

6 The heathen make much ado, and the kingdoms are moved : but God hath showed his voice, and the earth shall melt away.

7 The LORD of hosts is with us : the God of Jacob is our refuge.

8 O come hither, and behold the works of the LORD : what destruction he hath brought upon the earth.

9 He maketh wars to cease in all the world : he breaketh the bow, and knappeth the spear in sunder, and burneth the chariots in the fire.

10 Be still then, and know that I am God : I will be exalted among the heathen, and I will be exalted in the earth.

11 The LORD of hosts is

with us : the God of Jacob is our refuge.

✠

Evening Prayer.

PSALM 47.

Omnes gentes, plaudite.

O CLAP your hands together, all ye people : O sing unto God with the voice of melody.

2 For the LORD is high, and to be feared : he is the great King upon all the earth.

3 He shall subdue the people under us : and the nations under our feet.

4 He shall choose out an heritage for us : even the worship of Jacob, whom he loved.

5 God is gone up with a merry noise : and the LORD with the sound of the trump.

6 O sing praises, sing praises unto our God : O sing praises, sing praises unto our King.

7 For God is the King of all the earth : sing ye praises with understanding.

8 God reigneth over the heathen : God sitteth upon his holy seat.

9 The princes of the people are joined unto the people of the God of Abraham : for God, which is very high exalted, doth defend the earth, as it were with a shield.

PSALM 48.

Magnus Dominus.

G REAT is the LORD, and highly to be praised : in the city of our God, even upon his holy hill.

2 The hill of Sion is a fair place, and the joy of the whole earth : upon the north side lieth the city of the great King ; God is well known in her palaces as a sure refuge.

3 For lo, the kings of the earth : are gathered, and gone by together.

4 They marvelled to see such things : they were astonished, and suddenly cast down.

5 Fear came there upon them, and sorrow : as upon a woman in her travail.

6 Thou shalt break the ships of the sea : through the east-wind.

7 Like as we have heard, so have we seen in the city of the LORD of hosts, in the city of our God : God upholdeth the same for ever.

8 We wait for thy lovingkindness, O God : in the midst of thy temple.

9 O God, according to thy Name, so is thy praise unto the world's end : thy right hand is full of righteousness.

10 Let the mount Sion rejoice, and the daughter of Judah be glad : because of thy judgments.

11 Walk about Sion, and go round about her : and tell the towers thereof.

12 Mark well her bulwarks, set up her houses : that ye may tell them that come after.

13 For this God is our God for ever and ever : he shall be our guide unto death.

PSALM 49.

Audite hæc, omnes.

O HEAR ye this, all ye people : ponder it with your ears, all ye that dwell in the world ;

2 High and low, rich and poor : one with another.

3 My mouth shall speak of wisdom : and my heart shall muse of understanding.

4 I will incline mine ear to the parable : and show my dark speech upon the harp.

5 Wherefore should I fear in the days of wickedness : and when the wickedness of my heels compasseth me round about ?

6 There be some that put their trust in their goods : and boast themselves in the multitude of their riches.

7 But no man may deliver his brother : nor make agreement unto God for him ;

8 For it cost more to redeem their souls : so that he must let that alone for ever ;

9 Yea, though he live long : and see not the grave.

10 For he seeth that wise men also die and perish together : as well as the ignorant and foolish, and leave their riches for other.

11 And yet they think that their houses shall continue for ever : and that their dwelling-places shall endure from one generation to another ; and call the lands after their own names.

12 Nevertheless, man will not abide in honour : seeing he may be compared unto the beasts that perish ; this is the way of them.

13 This is their foolishness : and their posterity praise their saying.

14 They lie in the hell

like sheep; death gnaweth upon them, and the righteous shall have domination over them in the morning: their beauty shall consume in the sepulchre out of their dwelling.

15 But God hath delivered my soul from the place of hell: for he shall receive me.

16 Be not thou afraid, though one be made rich: or if the glory of his house be increased;

17 For he shall carry nothing away with him when he dieth: neither shall his pomp follow him.

18 For while he lived, he counted himself an happy man: and so long as thou doest well unto thyself, men will speak good of thee.

19 He shall follow the generation of his fathers: and shall never see light.

20 Man being in honour hath no understanding: but is compared unto the beasts that perish.

✠

THE TENTH DAY.

Morning Prayer.

PSALM 50.

Deus deorum.

THE LORD, even the Most Mighty God, hath

spoken: and called the world, from the rising up of the sun unto the going down thereof.

2 Out of Sion hath God appeared: in perfect beauty.

3 Our God shall come, and shall not keep silence: there shall go before him a consuming fire, and a mighty tempest shall be stirred up round about him.

4 He shall call the heaven from above: and the earth, that he may judge his people.

5 Gather my saints together unto me: those that have made a covenant with me with sacrifice.

6 And the heavens shall declare his righteousness: for God is Judge himself.

7 Hear, O my people, and I will speak: I myself will testify against thee, O Israel; for I am God, even thy God.

8 I will not reprove thee because of thy sacrifices, or for thy burnt-offerings: because they were not alway before me.

9 I will take no bullock out of thine house: nor he-goats out of thy folds.

10 For all the beasts of the forest are mine: and so

are the cattle upon a thousand hills.

11 I know all the fowls upon the mountains : and the wild beasts of the field are in my sight.

12 If I be hungry, I will not tell thee : for the whole world is mine, and all that is therein.

13 Thinkest thou that I will eat bulls' flesh : and drink the blood of goats ?

14 Offer unto God thanksgiving : and pay thy vows unto the Most Highest.

15 And call upon me in the time of trouble : so will I hear thee, and thou shalt praise me.

16 But unto the ungodly said God : Why dost thou preach my laws, and takest my covenant in thy mouth ;

17 Whereas thou hatest to be reformed : and hast cast my words behind thee ?

18 When thou sawest a thief, thou consentedst unto him : and hast been partaker with the adulterers.

19 Thou hast let thy mouth speak wickedness : and with thy tongue thou hast set forth deceit.

20 Thou sattest and spakest against thy brother : yea, and hast slandered thine own mother's son.

21 These things hast thou done, and I held my tongue, and thou thoughtest wickedly, that I am even such a one as thyself : but I will reprove thee, and set before thee the things that thou hast done.

22 O consider this, ye that forget God : lest I pluck you away, and there be none to deliver you.

23 Whoso offereth me thanks and praise, he honoureth me : and to him that ordereth his conversation right, will I show the salvation of God.

PSALM 51.

Miserere mei, Deus.

HAVE mercy upon me, O God, after thy great goodness : according to the multitude of thy mercies do away mine offences.

2 Wash me throughly from my wickedness : and cleanse me from my sin.

3 For I acknowledge my faults : and my sin is ever before me.

4 Against thee only have I sinned, and done this

evil in thy sight : that thou mightest be justified in thy saying, and clear when thou art judged.

5 Behold, I was shapen in wickedness : and in sin hath my mother conceived me.

6 But lo, thou requirest truth in the inward parts : and shalt make me to understand wisdom secretly.

7 Thou shalt purge me with hyssop, and I shall be clean : thou shalt wash me, and I shall be whiter than snow.

8 Thou shalt make me hear of joy and gladness : that the bones which thou hast broken may rejoice.

9 Turn thy face from my sins : and put out all my misdeeds.

10 Make me a clean heart, O God : and renew a right spirit within me.

11 Cast me not away from thy presence : and take not thy holy Spirit from me.

12 O give me the comfort of thy help again : and stablish me with thy free Spirit.

13 Then shall I teach thy ways unto the wicked : and sinners shall be converted unto thee.

14 Deliver me from blood-guiltiness, O God, thou that art the God of my health : and my tongue shall sing of thy righteousness.

15 Thou shalt open my lips, O Lord : and my mouth shall show thy praise.

16 For thou desirest no sacrifice, else would I give it thee : but thou delightest not in burnt-offerings.

17 The sacrifice of God is a troubled spirit : a broken and contrite heart, O God, shalt thou not despise.

18 O be favourable and gracious unto Sion : build thou the walls of Jerusalem.

19 Then shalt thou be pleased with the sacrifice of righteousness, with the burnt-offerings and oblations : then shall they offer young bullocks upon thine altar.

PSALM 52.

Quid gloriaris?

WHY boastest thou thyself, thou tyrant : that thou canst do mischief;

2 Whereas the goodness of God : endureth yet daily ?

3 Thy tongue imagineth wickedness : and with lies thou cuttest like a sharp razor.

4 Thou hast loved unrighteousness more than goodness : and to talk of lies more than righteousness.

5 Thou hast loved to speak all words that may do hurt : O thou false tongue.

6 Therefore shall God destroy thee for ever : he shall take thee, and pluck thee out of thy dwelling, and root thee out of the land of the living.

7 The righteous also shall see this, and fear : and shall laugh him to scorn :

8 Lo, this is the man that took not God for his strength : but trusted unto the multitude of his riches, and strengthened himself in his wickedness.

9 As for me, I am like a green olive-tree in the house of God : my trust is in the tender mercy of God for ever and ever.

10 I will alway give thanks unto thee for that thou hast done : and I will hope in thy Name, for thy saints like it well.

Evening Prayer.

PSALM 53.

Dixit insipiens.

THE foolish body hath said in his heart : There is no God.

2 Corrupt are they, and become abominable in their wickedness : there is none that doeth good.

3 God looked down from heaven upon the children of men : to see if there were any that would understand, and seek after God.

4 But they are all gone out of the way, they are altogether become abominable : there is also none that doeth good, no not one.

5 Are not they without understanding that work wickedness : eating up my people as if they would eat bread ? they have not called upon God.

6 They were afraid where no fear was : for God hath broken the bones of him that besieged thee ; thou hast put them to confusion, because God hath despised them.

7 O that the salvation were given unto Israel

out of Sion : O that the Lord would deliver his people out of captivity !

8 Then should Jacob rejoice : and Israel should be right glad.

PSALM 54.
Deus, in Nomine.

SAVE me, O God, for thy Name's sake : and avenge me in thy strength.

2 Hear my prayer, O God : and hearken unto the words of my mouth.

3 For strangers are risen up against me : and tyrants, which have not God before their eyes, seek after my soul.

4 Behold, God is my helper : the Lord is with them that uphold my soul.

5 He shall reward evil unto mine enemies : destroy thou them in thy truth.

6 An offering of a free heart will I give thee, and praise thy Name, O LORD : because it is so comfortable.

7 For he hath delivered me out of all my trouble : and mine eye hath seen his desire upon mine enemies.

PSALM 55.
Exaudi, Deus.

HEAR my prayer, O God : and hide not thyself from my petition.

2 Take heed unto me, and hear me : how I mourn in my prayer, and am vexed ;

3 The enemy crieth so, and the ungodly cometh on so fast : for they are minded to do me some mischief, so maliciously are they set against me.

4 My heart is disquieted within me : and the fear of death is fallen upon me.

5 Fearfulness and trembling are come upon me : and an horrible dread hath overwhelmed me.

6 And I said, O that I had wings like a dove : for then would I flee away, and be at rest.

7 Lo, then would I get me away far off : and remain in the wilderness.

8 I would make haste to escape : because of the stormy wind and tempest.

9 Destroy their tongues, O Lord, and divide them : for I have spied unrighteousness and strife in the city.

10 Day and night they go about within the walls thereof : mischief also and sorrow are in the midst of it.

11 Wickedness is there-

in : deceit and guile go not out of her streets.

12 For it is not an open enemy that hath done me this dishonour : for then I could have borne it ;

13 Neither was it mine adversary that did magnify himself against me : for then peradventure I would have hid myself from him ;

14 But it was even thou, my companion : my guide, and mine own familiar friend.

15 We took sweet counsel together : and walked in the house of God as friends.

16 Let death come hastily upon them, and let them go down quick into hell : for wickedness is in their dwellings, and among them.

17 As for me, I will call upon God : and the Lord shall save me.

18 In the evening, and morning, and at noon-day will I pray, and that instantly : and he shall hear my voice.

19 It is he that hath delivered my soul in peace from the battle that was against me : for there were many with me.

20 Yea, even God, that endureth for ever, shall hear me, and bring them down : for they will not turn, nor fear God.

21 He laid his hands upon such as be at peace with him : and he brake his covenant.

22 The words of his mouth were softer than butter, having war in his heart ; his words were smoother than oil, and yet be they very swords.

23 O cast thy burden upon the Lord, and he shall nourish thee : and he shall not suffer the righteous to fall for ever.

24 And as for them : thou, O God, shalt bring them into the pit of destruction.

25 The blood-thirsty and deceitful men shall not live out half their days : nevertheless, my trust shall be in thee, O Lord.

❧

THE ELEVENTH DAY.

Morning Prayer.

Psalm 56.

Miserere mei, Deus.

BE merciful unto me, O God, for man goeth about to devour me : he is daily fighting, and troubling me.

2 Mine enemies are daily in hand to swallow me up: for they be many that fight against me, O thou most Highest.

3 Nevertheless, though I am sometime afraid : yet put I my trust in thee.

4 I will praise God, because of his word : I have put my trust in God, and will not fear what flesh can do unto me.

5 They daily mistake my words : all that they imagine is to do me evil.

6 They hold all together, and keep themselves close: and mark my steps, when they lay wait for my soul.

7 Shall they escape for their wickedness : thou, O God, in thy displeasure shalt cast them down.

8 Thou tellest my wanderings ; put my tears into thy bottle : are not these things noted in thy book ?

9 Whensoever I call upon thee, then shall mine enemies be put to flight : this I know ; for God is on my side.

10 In God's word will I rejoice : in the Lord's word will I comfort me.

11 Yea, in God have I put my trust : I will not be afraid what man can do unto me.

12 Unto thee, O God, will I pay my vows : unto thee will I give thanks.

13 For thou hast delivered my soul from death, and my feet from falling : that I may walk before God in the light of the living.

PSALM 57.

Miserere mei, Deus.

BE merciful unto me, O God, be merciful unto me ; for my soul trusteth in thee : and under the shadow of thy wings shall be my refuge, until this tyranny be overpast.

2 I will call unto the Most High God : even unto the God that shall perform the cause which I have in hand.

3 He shall send from heaven : and save me from the reproof of him that would eat me up.

4 God shall send forth his mercy and truth : my soul is among lions :

5 And I lie even among the children of men, that are set on fire : whose teeth are spears and arrows, and their tongue a sharp sword.

6 Set up thyself, O God, above the heavens : and thy glory above all the earth.

7 They have laid a net for my feet, and pressed down my soul : they have digged a pit before me, and are fallen into the midst of it themselves.

8 My heart is fixed, O God, my heart is fixed : I will sing and give praise.

9 Awake up, my glory ; awake, lute and harp : I myself will awake right early.

10 I will give thanks unto thee, O Lord, among the people : and I will sing unto thee among the nations.

11 For the greatness of thy mercy reacheth unto the heavens : and thy truth unto the *clouds.*

12 Set up thyself, O God, above the heavens : and thy glory above all the earth.

Psalm 58.

Si vere utique.

ARE your minds set upon righteousness, O ye congregation : and do ye judge the thing that is right, O ye sons of men?

2 Yea, ye imagine mischief in your heart upon the earth : and your hands deal with wickedness.

3 The ungodly are froward, even from their mother's womb : as soon as they are born, they go astray, and speak lies.

4 They are as venomous as the poison of a serpent : even like the deaf adder, that stoppeth her ears ;

5 Which refuseth to hear the voice of the charmer : charm he never so wisely.

6 Break their teeth, O God, in their mouths ; smite the jaw-bones of the lions, O LORD : let them fall away like water that runneth apace ; and when they shoot their arrows let them be rooted out.

7 Let them consume away like a snail, and be like the untimely fruit of a woman : and let them not see the sun.

8 Or ever your pots be made hot with thorns ; so let indignation vex him, even as a thing that is raw.

9 The righteous shall rejoice when he seeth the vengeance : he shall wash his footsteps in the blood of the ungodly.

10 So that a man shall say, Verily there is a reward for the righteous : doubtless there is a God that judgeth the earth.

Evening Prayer.

PSALM 59.

Eripe me de inimicis.

DELIVER me from mine enemies, O God : defend me from them that rise up against me.

2 O deliver me from the wicked doers : and save me from the blood-thirsty men.

3 For lo, they lie waiting for my soul : the mighty men are gathered against me, without any offence or fault of me, O LORD.

4 They run and prepare themselves without my fault : arise thou therefore to help me, and behold.

5 Stand up, O LORD God of hosts, thou God of Israel, to visit all the heathen : and be not merciful unto them that offend of malicious wickedness.

6 They go to and fro in the evening : they grin like a dog, and run about through the city.

7 Behold, they speak with their mouth, and swords are in their lips : for who doth hear ?

8 But thou, O LORD, shalt have them in derision : and thou shalt laugh all the heathen to scorn.

9 My strength will I ascribe unto thee : for thou art the God of my refuge.

10 God showeth me his goodness plenteously : and God shall let me see my desire upon mine enemies.

11 Slay them not, lest my people forget it : but scatter them abroad among the people, and put them down, O Lord our defence.

12 For the sin of their mouth, and for the words of their lips, they shall be taken in their pride : and why ? their preaching is of cursing and lies.

13 Consume them in thy wrath, consume them, that they may perish : and know that it is God that ruleth in Jacob, and unto the ends of the world.

14 And in the evening they will *return* : grin like a dog, and will go about the city.

15 They will run here and there for meat : and grudge if they be not satisfied.

16 As for me, I will sing of thy power, and will

praise thy mercy betimes in the morning : for thou hast been my defence and refuge in the day of my trouble.

17 Unto thee, O my strength, will I sing : for thou, O God, art my refuge, and my merciful God.

Psalm 60.

Deus, repulisti nos.

O God, thou hast cast us out, and scattered us abroad : thou hast also been displeased ; O turn thee unto us again.

2 Thou hast moved the land, and divided it : heal the sores thereof, for it shaketh.

3 Thou hast showed thy people heavy things : thou hast given us a drink of deadly wine.

4 Thou hast given a token for such as fear thee : that they may triumph because of the truth.

5 Therefore were thy beloved delivered : help me with thy right hand, and hear me.

6 God hath spoken in his holiness, I will rejoice, and divide Sichem : and mete out the valley of Succoth.

7 Gilead is mine, and Manasses is mine : Eph-

raim also is the strength of my head ; Judah is my lawgiver ;

8 Moab is my wash-pot; over Edom will I cast out my shoe: Philistia, be thou glad of me.

9 Who will lead me into the strong city : who will bring me into Edom ?

10 Hast not thou cast us out, O God : wilt not thou, O God, go out with our hosts ?

11 O be thou our help in trouble : for vain is the help of man.

12 Through God will we do great acts : for it is he that shall tread down our enemies.

Psalm 61.

Exaudi, Deus.

HEAR my crying, O God : give ear unto my prayer.

2 From the ends of the earth will I call upon thee : when my heart is in heaviness.

3 O set me up upon the rock that is higher than I : for thou hast been my hope, and a strong tower for me against the enemy.

4 I will dwell in thy tabernacle for ever : and my trust shall be under the covering of thy wings.

5 For thou, O Lord, hast heard my desires : and hast given an heritage unto those that fear thy Name.

6 Thou shalt grant the King a long life : that his years may endure throughout all generations.

7 He shall dwell before God for ever : O prepare thy lovingmercy and faithfulness, that they may preserve him.

8 So will I alway sing praise unto thy Name : that I may daily perform my vows.

❁

THE TWELFTH DAY.

Morning Prayer.

PSALM 62.

Nonne Deo?

MY soul truly waiteth still upon God : for of him cometh my salvation.

2 He verily is my strength and my salvation : he is my defence, so that I shall not greatly fall.

3 How long will ye imagine mischief against every man : ye shall be slain all the sort of you ; yea, as a tottering wall shall ye be, and like a broken hedge.

4 Their device is only how to put him out whom God will exalt : their delight is in lies ; they give good words with their mouth, but curse with their heart.

5 Nevertheless, my soul, wait thou still upon God : for my hope is in him.

6 He truly is my strength and my salvation : he is my defence, so that I shall not fall.

7 In God is my health and my glory : the rock of my might ; and in God is my trust.

8 O put your trust in him alway, ye people : pour out your hearts before him, for God is our hope.

9 As for the children of men, they are but vanity : the children of men are deceitful upon the weights; they are altogether lighter than vanity itself.

10 O trust not in wrong and robbery ; give not *yourselves unto* vanity : if riches increase, set not your heart upon them.

11 God spake once, and twice I have also heard the same : that power belongeth unto God ;

12 And that thou, Lord, art merciful : for thou re-

wardest every man according to his work.

PSALM 63.

Deus, Deus meus.

O GOD, thou art my God: early will I seek thee.

2 My soul thirsteth for thee; my flesh also longeth after thee : in a barren and dry land where no water is.

3 Thus have I looked for thee in holiness : that I might behold thy power and glory.

4 For thy loving-kindness is better than the life itself : my lips shall praise thee.

5 As long as I live will I *magnify thee* in this manner : and lift up my hands in thy Name.

6 My soul shall be satisfied, even as it were with marrow and fatness : when my mouth praiseth thee with joyful lips.

7 Have I not remembered thee in my bed : and thought upon thee when I was waking?

8 Because thou hast been my helper : therefore under the shadow of thy wings will I rejoice.

9 My soul hangeth upon thee : thy right hand hath upholden me.

10 These also that seek the hurt of my soul : they shall go under the earth.

11 Let them fall upon the edge of the sword : that they may be a portion for foxes.

12 But the King shall rejoice in God; all they also that swear by him shall be commended : for the mouth of them that speak lies shall be stopped.

PSALM 64.

Exaudi, Deus.

H EAR my voice, O God, in my prayer : preserve my life from fear of the enemy.

2 Hide me from the gathering together of the froward : and from the insurrection of wicked doers ;

3 Who have whet their tongue like a sword : and shoot out their arrows, even bitter words;

4 That they may privily shoot at him that is perfect : suddenly do they hit him, and fear not.

5 They encourage themselves in mischief : and commune among themselves, how they may lay snares; and say, that no man shall see them.

6 They imagine wicked-

ness, and practise it : that they keep secret among themselves, every man in the deep of his heart.

7 But God shall suddenly shoot at them with a swift arrow : that they shall be wounded.

8 Yea, their own tongues shall make them fall : insomuch that whoso seeth them shall laugh them to scorn.

9 And all men that see it shall say, This hath God done : for they shall perceive that it is his work.

10 The righteous shall rejoice in the LORD, and put his trust in him : and all they that are true of heart shall be glad.

✤

Evening Prayer.

PSALM 65.

Te decet hymnus.

THOU, O God, art praised in Sion : and unto thee shall the vow be performed in Jerusalem.

2 Thou that hearest the prayer : unto thee shall all flesh come.

3 My misdeeds prevail against me : O be thou merciful unto our sins.

4 Blessed is the man whom thou choosest, and

receivest unto thee : he shall dwell in thy court, and shall be satisfied with the pleasures of thy house, even of thy holy temple.

5 Thou shalt show us wonderful things in thy righteousness, O God of our salvation : thou that art the hope of all the ends of the earth, and of them that remain in the broad sea.

6 Who in his strength setteth fast the mountains : and is girded about with power.

7 Who stilleth the raging of the sea : and the noise of his waves, and the madness of the people.

8 They also that dwell in the uttermost parts of the earth shall be afraid at thy tokens : thou that makest the out-goings of the morning and evening to praise thee.

9 Thou visitest the earth, and blessest it : thou makest it very plenteous.

10 The river of God is full of water : thou preparest their corn, for so thou providest for the earth.

11 Thou waterest her furrows ; thou sendest rain into the little valleys thereof : thou makest it soft

with the drops of rain, and blessest the increase of it.

12 Thou crownest the year with thy goodness : and thy clouds drop fatness.

13 They shall drop upon the dwellings of the wilderness : and the little hills shall rejoice on every side.

14 The folds shall be full of sheep : the valleys also shall stand so thick with corn, that they shall laugh and sing.

PSALM 66.

Jubilate Deo.

O BE joyful in God, all ye lands : sing praises unto the honour of his Name ; make his praise to be glorious.

2 Say unto God, O how wonderful art thou in thy works : through the greatness of thy power shall thine enemies be found liars unto thee.

3 For all the world shall worship thee : sing of thee, and praise thy Name.

4 O come hither, and behold the works of God : how wonderful he is in his doing toward the children of men.

5 He turned the sea into dry land : so that they went through the water on foot ; there did we rejoice thereof.

6 He ruleth with his power for ever ; his eyes behold the people : and such as will not believe shall not be able to exalt themselves.

7 O praise our God, ye people : and make the voice of his praise to be heard ;

8 Who holdeth our soul in life : and suffereth not our feet to slip.

9 For thou, O God, hast proved us : thou also hast tried us, like as silver is tried.

10 Thou broughtest us into the snare : and laidest trouble upon our loins.

11 Thou sufferedst men to ride over our heads : we went through fire and water, and thou broughtest us out into a wealthy place.

12 I will go into thine house with burnt-offerings : and will pay thee my vows, which I promised with my lips, and spake with my mouth, when I was in trouble.

13 I will offer unto thee fat burnt-sacrifices, with the incense of rams : I will offer bullocks and goats.

14 O come hither, and hearken, all ye that fear God : and I will tell you what he hath done for my soul.

15 I called unto him with my mouth : and gave him praises with my tongue.

16 If I incline unto wickedness with mine heart : the Lord will not hear me.

17 But God hath heard me : and considered the voice of my prayer.

18 Praised be God, who hath not cast out my prayer : nor turned his mercy from me.

PSALM 67.

Deus misereatur.

GOD be merciful unto us, and bless us : and show us the light of his countenance, and be merciful unto us ;

2 That thy way may be known upon earth : thy saving health among all nations.

3 Let the people praise thee, O God : yea, let all the people praise thee.

4 O let the nations rejoice and be glad : for thou shalt judge the folk righteously, and govern the nations upon earth.

5 Let the people praise thee, O God : yea, let all the people praise thee.

6 Then shall the earth bring forth her increase : and God, even our own God, shall give us his blessing.

7 God shall bless us : and all the ends of the world shall fear him.

✵

THE THIRTEENTH DAY.

Morning Prayer.

PSALM 68.

Exsurgat Deus.

LET God arise, and let his enemies be scattered : let them also that hate him flee before him.

2 Like as the smoke vanisheth, so shalt thou drive them away : and like as wax melteth at the fire, so let the ungodly perish at the presence of God.

3 But let the righteous be glad, and rejoice before God : let them also be merry and joyful.

4 O sing unto God, and sing praises unto his Name : magnify him that rideth upon the heavens, as it were upon an horse ; praise him in his Name JAH, and rejoice before him.

5 He is a Father of the fatherless, and defendeth the cause of the widows : even God in his holy habitation.

6 He is the God that maketh men to be of one mind in an house, and bringeth the prisoners out of captivity : but letteth the runagates continue in scarceness.

7 O God, when thou wentest forth before the people : when thou wentest through the wilderness,

8 The earth shook, and the heavens dropped at the presence of God : even as Sinai also was moved at the presence of God, who is the God of Israel.

9 Thou, O God, sentest a gracious rain upon thine inheritance : and refreshedst it when it was weary.

10 Thy congregation shall dwell therein : for thou, O God, hast of thy goodness prepared for the poor.

11 The Lord gave the word : great was the company of the preachers.

12 Kings with their armies did flee, and were discomfited : and they of the household divided the spoil.

13 Though ye have lain among the pots, yet shall ye be as the wings of a dove : that is covered with silver wings, and her feathers like gold.

14 When the Almighty scattered kings for their sake : then were they as white as snow in Salmon.

15 As the hill of Basan, so is God's hill : even an high hill, as the hill of Basan.

16 Why hop ye so, ye high hills ? this is God's hill, in the which it pleaseth him to dwell : yea, the Lord will abide in it for ever.

17 The chariots of God are twenty thousand, even thousands of angels : and the Lord is among them as in the holy place of Sinai.

18 Thou art gone up on high, thou hast led captivity captive, and received gifts for men : yea, even for thine enemies, that the Lord God might dwell among them.

19 Praised be the Lord daily : even the God who helpeth us, and poureth his benefits upon us.

20 He is our God, even the God of whom cometh salvation : God is the

Lord, by whom we escape death.

21 God shall wound the head of his enemies : and the hairy scalp of such a one as goeth on still in his wickedness.

22 The Lord hath said, I will bring my people again, as I did from Basan : mine own will I bring again, as I did sometime from the deep of the sea.

23 That thy foot may be dipped in the blood of thine enemies : and that the tongue of thy dogs may be red through the same.

24 It is well seen, O God, how thou goest : how thou, my God and King, goest in the sanctuary.

25 The singers go before, the minstrels follow after : in the midst are the damsels playing with the timbrels.

26 Give thanks, O Israel, unto God the Lord in the congregations : from the ground of the heart.

27 There is little Benjamin their ruler, and the princes of Judah their council : the princes of Zabulon, and the princes of Nephthali.

28 Thy God hath sent forth strength for thee : stablish the thing, O God, that thou hast wrought in us,

29 For thy temple's sake at Jerusalem : so shall kings bring presents unto thee.

30 When the company of the spearmen and multitude of the mighty are scattered abroad among the beasts of the people, so that they humbly bring pieces of silver : and when he hath scattered the people that delight in war ;

31 Then shall the princes come out of Egypt : the Morians' land shall soon stretch out her hands unto God.

32 Sing unto God, O ye kingdoms of the earth : O sing praises unto the Lord ;

33 Who sitteth in the heavens over all, from the beginning : lo, he doth send out his voice ; yea, and that a mighty voice.

34 Ascribe ye the power to God over Israel : his worship and strength is in the clouds.

35 O God, wonderful art thou in thy holy places : even the God of Israel, he will give strength and power unto his people. Blessed be God.

Evening Prayer.

Psalm 69.

Salvum me fac.

SAVE me, O God : for the waters are come in, even unto my soul.

2 I stick fast in the deep mire, where no ground is : I am come into deep waters, so that the floods run over me.

3 I am weary of crying ; my throat is dry : my sight faileth me for waiting so long upon my God.

4 They that hate me without a cause are more than the hairs of my head : they that are mine enemies, and would destroy me guiltless, are mighty.

5 I paid them the things that I never took : O God, thou knowest my simpleness, and my faults are not hid from thee.

6 Let not them that trust in thee, O Lord God of hosts, be ashamed for my cause : let not those that seek thee be confounded through me, O Lord God of Israel.

7 And why? for thy sake have I suffered reproof : shame hath covered my face.

8 I am become a stranger unto my brethren : even an alien unto my mother's children.

9 For the zeal of thine house hath even eaten me : and the rebukes of them that reproved thee are fallen upon me.

10 I wept, and chastened myself with fasting : and that was turned to my reproof.

11 I put on sackcloth also : and they jested upon me.

12 They that sit in the gate speak against me : and the drunkards make songs upon me.

13 But, Lord, I make my prayer unto thee : in an acceptable time.

14 Hear me, O God, in the multitude of thy mercy : even in the truth of thy salvation.

15 Take me out of the mire, that I sink not : O let me be delivered from them that hate me, and out of the deep waters.

16 Let not the waterflood drown me, neither let the deep swallow me up : and let not the pit shut her mouth upon me.

17 Hear me, O Lord, for thy loving-kindness is comfortable : turn thee unto me according to the multitude of thy mercies.

18 And hide not thy face from thy servant, for I am in trouble : O haste thee, and hear me.

19 Draw nigh unto my soul, and save it : O deliver me, because of mine enemies.

20 Thou hast known my reproof, my shame, and my dishonour : mine adversaries are all in thy sight.

21 Thy rebuke hath broken my heart; I am full of heaviness : I looked for some to have pity on me, but there was no man, neither found I any to comfort me.

22 They gave me gall to eat : and when I was thirsty they gave me vinegar to drink.

23 Let their table be made a snare to take themselves withal : and let the things that should have been for their wealth be unto them an occasion of falling.

24 Let their eyes be blinded, that they see not : and ever bow thou down their backs.

25 Pour out thine indignation upon them : and let thy wrathful displeasure take hold of them.

26 Let their habitation be void : and no man to dwell in their tents.

27 For they persecute him whom thou hast smitten : and they talk how they may vex them whom thou hast wounded.

28 Let them fall from one wickedness to another : and not come into thy righteousness.

29 Let them be wiped out of the book of the living : and not be written among the righteous.

30 As for me, when I am poor and in heaviness : thy help, O God, shall lift me up.

31 I will praise the Name of God with a song : and magnify it with thanksgiving.

32 This also shall please the Lord : better than a bullock that hath horns and hoofs.

33 The humble shall consider this, and be glad : seek ye after God, and your soul shall live.

34 For the Lord heareth the poor : and despiseth not his prisoners.

35 Let heaven and earth praise him : the sea, and all that moveth therein.

36 For God will save Sion, and build the cities of Judah : that men may dwell there, and have it in possession.

37 The posterity also of his servants shall inherit it : and they that love his Name shall dwell therein.

Psalm 70.

Deus, in adjutorium.

HASTE thee, O God, to deliver me : make haste to help me, O LORD.

2 Let them be ashamed and confounded that seek after my soul : let them be turned backward and put to confusion that wish me evil.

3 Let them for their reward be soon brought to shame : that cry over me, There ! there !

4 But let all those that seek thee be joyful and glad in thee : and let all such as delight in thy salvation say alway, The Lord be praised.

5 As for me, I am poor and in misery : haste thee unto me, O God.

6 Thou art my helper, and my redeemer : O LORD, make no long tarrying.

✿

THE FOURTEENTH DAY.

Morning Prayer.

Psalm 71.

In te, Domine, speravi.

IN thee, O LORD, have I put my trust ; let me never be put to confusion : but rid me, and deliver me, in thy righteousness ; incline thine ear unto me, and save me.

2 Be thou my stronghold, whereunto I may alway resort : thou hast promised to help me, for thou art my house of defence, and my castle.

3 Deliver me, O my God, out of the hand of the ungodly : out of the hand of the unrighteous and cruel man.

4 For thou, O Lord GOD, art the thing that I long for : thou art my hope, even from my youth.

5 Through thee have I been holden up ever since I was born : thou art he that took me out of my mother's womb ; my praise shall be alway of thee.

6 I am become as it were a monster unto many : but my sure trust is in thee.

7 O let my mouth be filled with thy praise : that I may sing of thy glory and honour all the day long.

8 Cast me not away in the time of age : forsake me not when my strength faileth me.

9 For mine enemies

speak against me: and they that lay wait for my soul take their counsel together, saying : God hath forsaken him; persecute him, and take him, for there is none to deliver him.

10 Go not far from me, O God : my God, haste thee to help me.

11 Let them be confounded and perish that are against my soul : let them be covered with shame and dishonour that seek to do me evil.

12 As for me, I will patiently abide alway : and will praise thee more and more.

13 My mouth shall daily speak of thy righteousness and salvation : for I know no end thereof.

14 I will go forth in the strength of the Lord GOD : and will make mention of thy righteousness only.

15 Thou, O God, hast taught me from my youth up until now : therefore will I tell of thy wondrous works.

16 Forsake me not, O God, in mine old age, when I am gray-headed : until I have shewed thy strength unto this generation, and thy power to all them that are yet for to come.

17 Thy righteousness, O God, is very high : and great things are they that thou hast done; O God, who is like unto thee!

18 O what great troubles and adversities hast thou showed me! and yet didst thou turn and refresh me : yea, and broughtest me from the deep of the earth again.

19 Thou hast brought me to great honour : and comforted me on every side :

20 Therefore will I praise thee, and thy faithfulness, O God, playing upon an instrument of music : unto thee will I sing upon the harp, O thou Holy One of Israel.

21 My lips will be fain when I sing unto thee : and so will my soul whom thou hast delivered.

22 My tongue also shall talk of thy righteousness all the day long : for they are confounded and brought unto shame that seek to do me evil.

PSALM 72.

Deus, judicium.

GIVE the King thy judgments, O God :

and thy righteousness unto the King's son.

2 Then shall he judge thy people according unto right : and defend the poor.

3 The mountains also shall bring peace : and the little hills righteousness unto the people.

4 He shall keep the simple folk by their right : defend the children of the poor, and punish the wrong doer.

5 They shall fear thee, as long as the sun and moon endureth : from one generation to another.

6 He shall come down like the rain into a fleece of wool : even as the drops that water the earth.

7 In his time shall the righteous flourish : yea, and abundance of peace, so long as the moon endureth.

8 His dominion shall be also from the one sea to the other : and from the flood unto the world's end.

9 They that dwell in the wilderness shall kneel before him : his enemies shall lick the dust.

10 The kings of Tharsis and of the isles shall give presents : the kings of Arabia and Saba shall bring gifts.

11 All kings shall fall down before him : all nations shall do him service.

12 For he shall deliver the poor when he crieth : the needy also, and him that hath no helper.

13 He shall be favourable to the simple and needy : and shall preserve the souls of the poor.

14 He shall deliver their souls from falsehood and wrong : and dear shall their blood be in his sight.

15 He shall live, and unto him shall be given of the gold of Arabia : prayer shall be made ever unto him, and daily shall he be praised.

16 There shall be an heap of corn in the earth, high upon the hills : his fruit shall shake like Libanus, and shall be green in the city like grass upon the earth.

17 His Name shall endure for ever ; his Name shall remain under the sun among the posterities : which shall be blessed through him ; and all the heathen shall praise him.

18 Blessed be the Lord God, even the God of

Israel : which only doeth wondrous things ;

19 And blessed be the Name of his majesty for ever : and all the earth shall be filled with his majesty. Amen, Amen.

✸

Evening Prayer.

PSALM 73.

Quam bonus Israel!

TRULY God is loving unto Israel : even unto such as are of a clean heart.

2 Nevertheless, my feet were almost gone : my treadings had well-nigh slipt.

3 And why? I was grieved at the wicked : I do also see the ungodly in such prosperity.

4 For they are in no peril of death : but are lusty and strong.

5 They come in no misfortune like other folk : neither are they plagued like other men.

6 And this is the cause that they are so holden with pride : and overwhelmed with cruelty.

7 Their eyes swell with fatness : and they do even what they lust.

8 They corrupt other, and speak of wicked blasphemy : their talking is against the most High.

9 For they stretch forth their mouth unto the heaven : and their tongue goeth through the world.

10 Therefore fall the people unto them : and thereout suck they no small advantage.

11 Tush, say they, how should God perceive it : is there knowledge in the Most High?

12 Lo, these are the ungodly, these prosper in the world, and these have riches in possession : and I said, Then have I cleansed my heart in vain, and washed my hands in innocency.

13 All the day long have I been punished : and chastened every morning.

14 Yea, and I had almost said even as they : but lo, then I should have condemned the generation of thy children.

15 Then thought I to understand this : but it was too hard for me,

16 Until I went into the sanctuary of God : then understood I the end of these men ;

17 Namely, how thou dost set them in slippery

places : and castest them down, and destroyest them.

18 O how suddenly do they consume : perish, and come to a fearful end!

19 Yea, even like as a dream when one awaketh : so shalt thou make their image to vanish out of the city.

20 Thus my heart was grieved : and it went even through my reins.

21 So foolish was I, and ignorant : even as it were a beast before thee.

22 Nevertheless, I am alway by thee : for thou hast holden me by my right hand.

23 Thou shalt guide me with thy counsel : and after that receive me with glory.

24 Whom have I in heaven but thee : and there is none upon earth that I desire in comparison of thee.

25 My flesh and my heart faileth : but God is the strength of my heart, and my portion for ever.

26 For lo, they that forsake thee shall perish : thou hast destroyed all them that commit fornication against thee.

27 But it is good for me

to hold me fast by thee, to put my trust in the Lord God : and to speak of all thy works in the gates of the daughter of Sion.

Psalm 74.
Ut quid, Deus?

O God, wherefore art thou absent from us so long : why is thy wrath so hot against the sheep of thy pasture?

2 O think upon thy congregation : whom thou hast purchased, and redeemed of old.

3 Think upon the tribe of thine inheritance : and Mount Sion, wherein thou hast dwelt.

4 Lift up thy feet, that thou mayest utterly destroy every enemy : which hath done evil in thy sanctuary.

5 Thine adversaries roar in the midst of thy congregations : and set up their banners for tokens.

6 He that hewed timber afore out of the thick trees : was known to bring it to an excellent work.

7 But now they break down all the carved work thereof : with axes and hammers.

8 They have set fire upon

thy holy places : and have defiled the dwelling-place of thy Name, even unto the ground.

9 Yea, they said in their hearts, Let us make havoc of them altogether : thus have they burnt up all the houses of God in the land.

10 We see not our tokens ; there is not one prophet more : no, not one is there among us, that understandeth any more.

11 O God, how long shall the adversary do this dishonour : how long shall the enemy blaspheme thy Name ? for ever ?

12 Why withdrawest thou thy hand : why pluckest thou not thy right hand out of thy bosom to consume the enemy ?

13 For God is my King of old : the help that is done upon earth, he doeth it himself.

14 Thou didst divide the sea through thy power : thou brakest the heads of the dragons in the waters.

15 Thou smotest the heads of leviathan in pieces : and gavest him to be meat for the people in the wilderness.

16 Thou broughtest out fountains and waters out of the hard rocks : thou driedst up mighty waters.

17 The day is thine, and the night is thine : thou hast prepared the light and the sun.

18 Thou hast set all the borders of the earth : thou hast made summer and winter.

19 Remember this, O Lord, how the enemy hath rebuked : and how the foolish people hath blasphemed thy Name.

20 O deliver not the soul of thy turtle-dove unto the multitude of the enemies : and forget not the congregation of the poor for ever.

21 Look upon the covenant : for all the earth is full of darkness and cruel habitations.

22 O let not the simple go away ashamed : but let the poor and needy give praise unto thy Name.

23 Arise, O God, maintain thine own cause : remember how the foolish man blasphemeth thee daily.

24 Forget not the voice of thine enemies : the presumption of them that

hate thee increaseth ever more and more.

❊

THE FIFTEENTH DAY.

Morning Prayer.

PSALM 75.

Confitebimur tibi.

UNTO thee, O God, do we give thanks : yea, unto thee do we give thanks.

2 Thy Name also is so nigh : and that do thy wondrous works declare.

3 When I receive the congregation : I shall judge according unto right.

4 The earth is weak, and all the inhabiters thereof : I bear up the pillars of it.

5 I said unto the fools, Deal not so madly : and to the ungodly, Set not up your horn.

6 Set not up your horn on high : and speak not with a stiff neck.

7 For promotion cometh neither from the east, nor from the west : nor yet from the south.

8 And why? God is the Judge : he putteth down one, and setteth up another.

9 For in the hand of the LORD there is a cup, and the wine is red : it is full mixt, and he poureth out of the same.

10 As for the dregs thereof : all the ungodly of the earth shall drink them, and suck them out.

11 But I will talk of the God of Jacob : and praise him for ever.

12 All the horns of the ungodly also will I break : and the horns of the righteous shall be exalted.

PSALM 76.

Notus in Judæa.

IN Jewry is God known : his Name is great in Israel.

2 At Salem is his tabernacle : and his dwelling in Sion.

3 There brake he the arrows of the bow : the shield, the sword, and the battle.

4 Thou art of more honour and might : than the hills of the robbers.

5 The proud are robbed, they have slept their sleep : and all the men whose hands were mighty have found nothing.

6 At thy rebuke, O God of Jacob : both the chariot and horse are fallen.

7 Thou, even thou art

to be feared : and who may stand in thy sight when thou art angry ?

8 Thou didst cause thy judgment to be heard from heaven : the earth trembled, and was still,

9 When God arose to judgment : and to help all the meek upon earth.

10 The fierceness of man shall turn to thy praise : and the fierceness of them shalt thou refrain.

11 Promise unto the LORD your God, and keep it, all ye that are round about him : bring presents unto him that ought to be feared.

12 He shall refrain the spirit of princes : and is wonderful among the kings of the earth.

PSALM 77.

Voce mea ad Dominum.

I WILL cry unto God with my voice : even unto God will I cry with my voice, and he shall hearken unto me.

2 In the time of my trouble I sought the Lord : my sore ran, and ceased not in the night season ; my soul refused comfort.

3 When I am in heaviness, I will think upon God : when my heart is vexed, I will complain.

4 Thou holdest mine eyes waking : I am so feeble that I cannot speak.

5 I have considered the days of old : and the years that are past.

6 I call to remembrance my song : and in the night I commune with mine own heart, and search out my spirit.

7 Will the Lord absent himself for ever : and will he be no more intreated?

8 Is his mercy clean gone for ever : and is his promise come utterly to an end for evermore ?

9 Hath God forgotten to be gracious : and will he shut up his loving-kindness in displeasure ?

10 And I said, It is mine own infirmity : but I will remember the years of the right hand of the Most Highest.

11 I will remember the works of the LORD : and call to mind thy wonders of old time.

12 I will think also of all thy works : and my talking shall be of thy doings.

13 Thy way, O God, is holy : who is so great a God as our God?

14 Thou art the God that doest wonders : and

hast declared thy power among the people.

15 Thou hast mightily delivered thy people: even the sons of Jacob and Joseph.

16 The waters saw thee, O God, the waters saw thee, and were afraid: the depths also were troubled.

17 The clouds poured out water, the air thundered: and thine arrows went abroad.

18 The voice of thy thunder was heard round about: the lightnings shone upon the ground; the earth was moved, and shook withal.

19 Thy way is in the sea, and thy paths in the great waters: and thy footsteps are not known.

20 Thou leddest thy people like sheep: by the hand of Moses and Aaron.

Evening Prayer.

Psalm 78.

Attendite, popule.

HEAR my law, O my people: incline your ears unto the words of my mouth.

2 I will open my mouth in a parable: I will declare hard sentences of old;

3 Which we have heard and known: and such as our fathers have told us;

4 That we should not hide them from the children of the generations to come: but to show the honour of the LORD, his mighty and wonderful works that he hath done.

5 He made a covenant with Jacob, and gave Israel a law: which he commanded our forefathers to teach their children;

6 That their posterity might know it: and the children which were yet unborn;

7 To the intent that when they came up: they might show their children the same;

8 That they might put their trust in God: and not to forget the works of God, but to keep his commandments;

9 And not to be as their forefathers, a faithless and stubborn generation: a generation that set not their heart aright, and whose spirit cleaveth not stedfastly unto God;

10 Like as the children of Ephraim: who being harnessed, and carrying bows, turned themselves back in the day of battle.

11 They kept not the covenant of God : and would not walk in his law ;

12 But forgat what he had done : and the wonderful works that he had showed for them.

13 Marvellous things did he in the sight of our forefathers, in the land of Egypt : even in the field of Zoan.

14 He divided the sea, and let them go through : he made the waters to stand on an heap.

15 In the day-time also he led them with a cloud : and all the night through with a light of fire.

16 He clave the hard rocks in the wilderness : and gave them drink thereof, as it had been out of the great depth.

17 He brought waters out of the stony rock : so that it gushed out like the rivers.

18 Yet for all this they sinned more against him : and provoked the Most Highest in the wilderness.

19 They tempted God in their hearts : and required meat for their lust.

20 They spake against God also, saying : Shall God prepare a table in the wilderness ?

21 He smote the stony rock indeed, that the water gushed out, and the streams flowed withal : but can he give bread also, or provide flesh for his people ?

22 When the Lord heard this, he was wroth : so the fire was kindled in Jacob, and there came up heavy displeasure against Israel ;

23 Because they believed not in God : and put not their trust in his help.

24 So he commanded the clouds above : and opened the doors of heaven.

25 He rained down manna also upon them for to eat : and gave them food from heaven.

26 So man did eat angels' food : for he sent them meat enough.

27 He caused the east-wind to blow under heaven : and through his power he *brought in the* southwest-wind.

28 He rained flesh upon them as thick as dust : and feathered fowls like as the sand of the sea.

29 He let it fall among their tents : even round about their habitation.

30 So they did eat, and

were well filled; for he gave them their own desire: they were not disappointed of their lust.

31 But while the meat was yet in their mouths, the heavy wrath of God came upon them, and slew the wealthiest of them: yea, and smote down the chosen men that were in Israel.

32 But for all this they sinned yet more: and believed not his wondrous works.

33 Therefore their days did he consume in vanity: and their years in trouble.

34 When he slew them, they sought him: and turned them early, and inquired after God.

35 And they remembered that God was their strength: and that the High God was their redeemer.

36 Nevertheless, they did but flatter him with their mouth: and dissembled with him in their tongue.

37 For their heart was not whole with him: neither continued they stedfast in his covenant.

38 But he was so merciful, that he forgave their misdeeds: and destroyed them not.

39 Yea, many a time turned he his wrath away: and would not suffer his whole displeasure to arise.

40 For he considered that they were but flesh: and that they were even a wind that passeth away, and cometh not again.

41 Many a time did they provoke him in the wilderness: and grieved him in the desert.

42 They turned back, and tempted God: and moved the Holy One in Israel.

43 They thought not of his hand: and of the day when he delivered them from the hand of the enemy;

44 How he had wrought his miracles in Egypt: and his wonders in the field of Zoan.

45 He turned their waters into blood: so that they might not drink of the rivers.

46 He sent lice among them, and devoured them up: and frogs to destroy them.

47 He gave them their fruit unto the caterpillar: and their labour unto the grasshopper.

48 He destroyed their

vines with hailstones : and their mulberry-trees with the frost.

49 He smote their cattle also with hailstones : and their flocks with hot thunderbolts.

50 He cast upon them the furiousness of his wrath, anger, displeasure, and trouble : and sent evil angels among them.

51 He made a way to his indignation, and spared not their soul from death : but gave their life over to the pestilence ;

52 And smote all the firstborn in Egypt : the most principal and mightiest in the dwellings of Ham.

53 But as for his own people, he led them forth like sheep : and carried them in the wilderness like a flock.

54 He brought them out safely, that they should not fear : and overwhelmed their enemies with the sea.

55 And brought them within the borders of his sanctuary : even to his mountain, which he purchased with his right hand.

56 He cast out the heathen also before them : caused their land to be divided among them for an heritage, and made the tribes of Israel to dwell in their tents.

57 So they tempted and displeased the Most High God : and kept not his testimonies ;

58 But turned their backs, and fell away like their forefathers : starting aside like a broken bow.

59 For they grieved him with their hill-altars : and provoked him to displeasure with their images.

60 When God heard this, he was wroth : and took sore displeasure at Israel ;

61 So that he forsook the tabernacle in Silo : even the tent that he had pitched among men.

62 He delivered their power into captivity : and their beauty into the enemy's hand.

63 He gave his people over also unto the sword : and was wroth with his inheritance.

64 The fire consumed their young men : and their maidens were not given to marriage.

65 Their priests were slain with the sword : and there were no widows to make lamentation.

66 So the Lord awaked as one out of sleep: and like a giant refreshed with wine.

67 He smote his enemies in the hinder parts: and put them to a perpetual shame.

68 He refused the tabernacle of Joseph: and chose not the tribe of Ephraim;

69 But chose the tribe of Judah: even the hill of Sion which he loved.

70 And there he built his temple on high: and laid the foundation of it like the ground which he hath made continually.

71 He chose David also his servant: and took him away from the sheep-folds:

72 As he was following the ewes great with young ones he took him: that he might feed Jacob his people, and Israel his inheritance.

73 So he fed them with a faithful and true heart: and ruled them prudently with all his power.

✠

THE SIXTEENTH DAY.
Morning Prayer.
PSALM 79.
Deus, venerunt.

O God, the heathen are come into thine inheritance: thy holy temple have they defiled, and made Jerusalem an heap of stones.

2 The dead bodies of thy servants have they given to be meat unto the fowls of the air: and the flesh of thy saints unto the beasts of the land.

3 Their blood have they shed like water on every side of Jerusalem: and there was no man to bury them.

4 We are become an open shame to our enemies: a very scorn and derision unto them that are round about us.

5 LORD, how long wilt thou be angry: shall thy jealousy burn like fire for ever?

6 Pour out thine indignation upon the heathen that have not known thee: and upon the kingdoms that have not called upon thy Name.

7 For they have devoured Jacob: and laid waste his dwelling-place.

8 O remember not our old sins, but have mercy upon us, and that soon: for we are come to great misery.

9 Help us, O God of our salvation, for the glory of

thy Name : O deliver us, and be merciful unto our sins, for thy Name's sake.

10 Wherefore do the heathen say : Where is now their God?

11 O let the vengeance of thy servants' blood that is shed : be openly showed upon the heathen, in our sight.

12 O let the sorrowful sighing of the prisoners come before thee : according to the greatness of thy power, preserve thou those that are appointed to die.

13 And for the blasphemy wherewith our neighbours have blasphemed thee : reward thou them, O Lord, seven-fold into their bosom.

14 So we, that are thy people, and sheep of thy pasture, shall give thee thanks for ever : and will alway be showing forth thy praise from generation to generation.

PSALM 80.

Qui regis Israel.

HEAR, O thou Shepherd of Israel, thou that leadest Joseph like a sheep : show thyself also, thou that sittest upon the Cherubim.

2 Before Ephraim, Benjamin, and Manasses : stir up thy strength, and come and help us.

3 Turn us again, O God : show the light of thy countenance, and we shall be whole.

4 O Lord God of hosts : how long wilt thou be angry with thy people that prayeth?

5 Thou feedest them with the bread of tears : and givest them plenteousness of tears to drink.

6 Thou hast made us a very strife unto our neighbours : and our enemies laugh us to scorn.

7 Turn us again, thou God of hosts : show the light of thy countenance, and we shall be whole.

8 Thou hast brought a vine out of Egypt : thou hast cast out the heathen, and planted it.

9 Thou madest room for it : and when it had taken root, it filled the land.

10 The hills were covered with the shadow of it : and the boughs *thereof* were like the goodly cedar-trees.

11 She stretched out her branches unto the sea : and her boughs unto the river.

12 Why hast thou then

broken down her hedge : that all they that go by pluck off her grapes ?

13 The wild boar out of the wood doth root it up : and the wild beasts of the field devour it.

14 Turn thee again, thou God of hosts, look down from heaven : behold, and visit this vine.

15 And the place of the vineyard that thy right hand hath planted : and the branch that thou madest so strong for thyself.

16 It is burnt with fire, and cut down : and they shall perish at the rebuke of thy countenance.

17 Let thy hand be upon the man of thy right hand : and upon the son of man, whom thou madest so strong for thine own self.

18 And so will not we go back from thee : O let us live, and we shall call upon thy Name.

19 Turn us again, O LORD God of hosts : show the light of thy countenance, and we shall be whole.

PSALM 81.

Exultate Deo.

SING we merrily unto God our strength :

make a cheerful noise unto the God of Jacob.

2 Take the psalm, bring hither the tabret : the merry harp with the lute.

3 Blow up the trumpet in the new moon : even in the time appointed, and upon our solemn feast-day.

4 For this was made a statute for Israel : and a law of the God of Jacob.

5 This he ordained in Joseph for a testimony : when he came out of the land of Egypt, and had heard a strange language.

6 I eased his shoulder from the burden : and his hands were delivered from making the pots.

7 Thou calledst upon me in troubles, and I delivered thee : and heard thee what time as the storm fell upon thee.

8 I proved thee also : at the waters of strife.

9 Hear, O my people, and I will assure thee, O Israel : if thou wilt hearken unto me,

10 There shall no strange god be in thee : neither shalt thou worship any other god.

11 I am the LORD thy God, who brought thee out of the land of Egypt :

open thy mouth wide, and I shall fill it.

12 But my people would not hear my voice : and Israel would not obey me ;

13 So I gave them up unto their own hearts' lusts : and let them follow their own imaginations.

14 O that my people would have hearkened unto me : for if Israel had walked in my ways,

15 I should soon have put down their enemies : and turned my hand against their adversaries.

16 The haters of the LORD should have been found liars : but their time should have endured for ever.

17 He should have fed them also with the finest wheat-flour : and with honey out of the stony rock should I have satisfied thee.

Evening Prayer.

PSALM 82.
Deus stetit.

GOD standeth in the congregation of princes : he is a Judge among gods.

2 How long will ye give wrong judgment : and accept the persons of the ungodly ?

3 Defend the poor and fatherless : see that such as are in need and necessity have right.

4 Deliver the outcast and poor : save them from the hand of the ungodly

5 They will not be learned, nor understand, but walk on still in darkness : all the foundations of the earth are out of course.

6 I have said, Ye are gods : and ye are all the children of the Most Highest.

7 But ye shall die like men : and fall like one of the princes.

8 Arise, O God, and judge thou the earth : for thou shalt take all heathen to thine inheritance.

PSALM 83.
Deus, quis similis?

HOLD not thy tongue, O God, keep not still silence : refrain not thyself, O God.

2 For lo, thine enemies make a murmuring : and they that hate thee have lift up their head.

3 They have imagined craftily against thy people : and taken counsel against thy secret ones.

4 They have said, Come, and let us root them out, that they be no more a people : and that the name of Israel may be no more in remembrance.

5 For they have cast their heads together with one consent : and are confederate against thee :

6 The tabernacles of the Edomites, and the Ishmaelites : the Moabites, and Hagarenes ;

7 Gebal, and Ammon, and Amalek : the Philistines, with them that dwell at Tyre.

8 Assur also is joined with them : and have holpen the children of Lot.

9 But do thou to them as unto the Madianites : unto Sisera, and unto Jabin at the brook of Kison :

10 Who perished at Endor : and became as the dung of the earth.

11 Make them and their princes like Oreb and Zeb : yea, make all their princes like as Zeba and Salmana ;

12 Who say, Let us take to ourselves : the houses of God in possession.

13 O my God, make them like unto a wheel : and as the stubble before the wind ;

14 Like as the fire that burneth up the wood : and as the flame that consumeth the mountains.

15 Persecute them even so with thy tempest : and make them afraid with thy storm.

16 Make their faces ashamed, O Lord : that they may seek thy Name.

17 Let them be confounded and vexed ever more and more : let them be put to shame, and perish.

18 And they shall know that thou, whose Name is JEHOVAH : art only the Most Highest over all the earth.

Psalm 84.
Quam dilecta!

O HOW amiable are thy dwellings : thou Lord of hosts !

2 My soul hath a desire and longing to enter into the courts of the Lord : my heart and my flesh rejoice in the living God.

3 Yea, the sparrow hath found her an house, and the swallow a nest, where she may lay her young : even thy altars, O Lord of hosts, my King and my God.

4 Blessed are they that

dwell in thy house : they will be alway praising thee.

5 Blessed is the man whose strength is in thee : in whose heart are thy ways.

6 Who going through the vale of misery use it for a well : and the pools are filled with water.

7 They will go from strength to strength : and unto the God of gods appeareth every one of them in Sion.

8 O Lord God of hosts, hear my prayer : hearken, O God of Jacob.

9 Behold, O God our defender : and look upon the face of thine anointed.

10 For one day in thy courts : is better than a thousand.

11 I had rather be a door-keeper in the house of my God : than to dwell in the tents of ungodliness.

12 For the Lord God is a light and defence : the Lord will give grace and worship, and no good thing shall he withhold from them that live a godly life.

13 O Lord God of hosts : blessed is the man that putteth his trust in thee.

Psalm 85.

Benedixisti, Domine.

LORD, thou art become gracious unto thy land : thou hast turned away the captivity of Jacob.

2 Thou hast forgiven the offence of thy people : and covered all their sins.

3 Thou hast taken away all thy displeasure : and turned thyself from thy wrathful indignation.

4 Turn us then, O God our Saviour : and let thine anger cease from us.

5 Wilt thou be displeased at us for ever : and wilt thou stretch out thy wrath from one generation to another?

6 Wilt thou not turn again, and quicken us : that thy people may rejoice in thee ?

7 Show us thy mercy, O Lord : and grant us thy salvation.

8 I will hearken what the Lord God will say concerning me : for he shall speak peace unto his people, and to his saints, that they turn not again.

9 For his salvation is nigh them that fear him : that glory may dwell in our land.

10 Mercy and truth are met together : righteousness and peace have kissed each other.

11 Truth shall flourish out of the earth : and righteousness hath looked down from heaven.

12 Yea, the Lord shall show loving-kindness : and our land shall give her increase.

13 Righteousness shall go before him : and he shall direct his going in the way.

THE SEVENTEENTH DAY.

Morning Prayer.

PSALM 86.

Inclina, Domine.

BOW down thine ear, O Lord, and hear me : for I am poor, and in misery.

2 Preserve thou my soul, for I am holy : my God, save thy servant that putteth his trust in thee.

3 Be merciful unto me, O Lord : for I will call daily upon thee.

4 Comfort the soul of thy servant : for unto thee, O Lord, do I lift up my soul.

5 For thou, Lord, art good and gracious : and of great mercy unto all them that call upon thee.

6 Give ear, Lord, unto my prayer : and ponder the voice of my humble desires.

7 In the time of my trouble I will call upon thee : for thou hearest me.

8 Among the gods there is none like unto thee, O Lord : there is not one that can do as thou doest.

9 All nations whom thou hast made shall come and worship thee, O Lord : and shall glorify thy Name.

10 For thou art great, and doest wondrous things : thou art God alone.

11 Teach me thy way, O Lord, and I will walk in thy truth : O knit my heart unto thee, that I may fear thy Name.

12 I will thank thee, O Lord my God, with all my heart : and will praise thy Name for evermore.

13 For great is thy mercy toward me : and thou hast delivered my soul from the nethermost hell.

14 O God, the proud are risen against me : and the congregations of naughty men have sought after my soul, and have not set thee before their eyes.

15 But thou, O Lord God, art full of compassion and mercy : long-suffering, plenteous in goodness and truth.

16 O turn thee then unto me, and have mercy upon me : give my strength unto thy servant, and help the son of thine handmaid.

17 Show some token upon me for good ; that they who hate me may see it, and be ashamed : because thou, Lord, hast holpen me, and comforted me.

PSALM 87.

Fundamenta ejus.

HER foundations are upon the holy hills : the Lord loveth the gates of Sion more than all the dwellings of Jacob.

2 Very excellent things are spoken of thee : thou city of God.

3 I will think upon Rahab and Babylon : with them that know me.

4 Behold, yea the Philistines also : and they of Tyre, with the Morians ; lo, there was he born.

5 And of Sion it shall be reported that he was born in her : and the Most High shall stablish her.

6 The Lord shall rehearse it, when he writeth up the people : that he was born there.

7 The singers also and trumpeters shall he rehearse : All my fresh springs shall be in thee.

PSALM 88.

Domine, Deus.

O LORD God of my salvation, I have cried day and night before thee : O let my prayer enter into thy presence, incline thine ear unto my calling ;

2 For my soul is full of trouble : and my life draweth nigh unto hell.

3 I am counted as one of them that go down into the pit : and I have been even as a man that hath no strength.

4 Free among the dead, like unto them that are wounded, and lie in the grave : who are out of remembrance, and are cut away from thy hand.

5 Thou hast laid me in the lowest pit : *in a place* of darkness, and in the deep.

6 Thine indignation lieth hard upon me : and thou hast vexed me with all thy storms.

7 Thou hast put away mine acquaintance far

from me : and made me to be abhorred of them.

8 I am so fast in prison : that I cannot get forth.

9 My sight faileth for very trouble : LORD, I have called daily upon thee, I have stretched forth my hands unto thee.

10 Dost thou show wonders among the dead : or shall the dead rise up again, and praise thee ?

11 Shall thy loving-kindness be showed in the grave : or thy faithfulness in destruction ?

12 Shall thy wondrous works be known in the dark : and thy righteousness in the land where all things are forgotten ?

13 Unto thee have I cried, O LORD : and early shall my prayer come before thee.

14 LORD, why abhorrest thou my soul : and hidest thou thy face from me ?

15 I am in misery, and like unto him that is at the point to die : even from my youth up, thy terrors have I suffered with a troubled mind.

16 Thy wrathful displeasure goeth over me : and the fear of thee hath undone me.

17 They came round about me daily like water : and compassed me together on every side.

18 My lovers and friends hast thou put away from me : and hid mine acquaintance out of my sight.

❖

Evening Prayer.

PSALM 89.

Misericordias Domini.

MY song shall be alway of the loving-kindness of the LORD : with my mouth will I ever be showing thy truth from one generation to another.

2 For I have said, Mercy shall be set up for ever : thy truth shalt thou stablish in the heavens.

3 I have made a covenant with my chosen : I have sworn unto David my servant :

4 Thy seed will I stablish for ever : and set up thy throne from one generation to another.

5 O LORD, the very heavens shall praise thy wondrous works : and thy truth in the congregation of the saints.

6 For who is he among the clouds : that shall be compared unto the LORD ?

7 And what is he among the gods : that shall be like unto the LORD?

8 God is very greatly to be feared in the council of the saints : and to be had in reverence of all them that are round about him.

9 O LORD God of hosts, who is like unto thee : thy truth, most mighty LORD, is on every side.

10 Thou rulest the raging of the sea : thou stillest the waves thereof when they arise.

11 Thou hast subdued Egypt, and destroyed it : thou hast scattered thine enemies abroad with thy mighty arm.

12 The heavens are thine, the earth also is thine : thou hast laid the foundation of the round world, and all that therein is.

13 Thou hast made the north and the south : Tabor and Hermon shall rejoice in thy Name.

14 Thou hast a mighty arm : strong is thy hand, and high is thy right hand.

15 Righteousness and equity are the habitation of thy seat : mercy and truth shall go before thy face.

16 Blessed is the people,

O LORD, that can rejoice in thee : they shall walk in the light of thy countenance.

17 Their delight shall be daily in thy Name : and in thy righteousness shall they make their boast.

18 For thou art the glory of their strength : and in thy loving-kindness thou shalt lift up our horns.

19 For the LORD is our defence : the Holy One of Israel is our King.

20 Thou spakest sometime in visions unto thy saints, and saidst : I have laid help upon one that is mighty, I have exalted one chosen out of the people.

21 I have found David my servant : with my holy oil have I anointed him.

22 My hand shall hold him fast : and my arm shall strengthen him.

23 The enemy shall not be able to do him violence : the son of wickedness shall not hurt him.

24 I will smite down his foes before his face : and plague them that hate him.

25 My truth also and my mercy shall be with

him : and in my Name shall his horn be exalted.

26 I will set his dominion also in the sea : and his right hand in the floods.

27 He shall call me, Thou art my Father : my God, and my strong salvation.

28 And I will make him my firstborn : higher than the kings of the earth.

29 My mercy will I keep for him for evermore : and my covenant shall stand fast with him.

30 His seed also will I make to endure for ever : and his throne as the days of heaven.

31 But if *his children* forsake my law : and walk not in my judgments ;

32 If they break my statutes, and keep not my commandments : I will visit their offences with the rod, and their sin with scourges.

33 Nevertheless, my loving-kindness will I not utterly take from him : nor suffer my truth to fail.

34 My covenant will I not break, nor alter the thing that is gone out of my lips : I have sworn once by my holiness, that I will not fail David.

35 His seed shall endure for ever : and his seat is like as the sun before me.

36 He shall stand fast for evermore as the moon : and as the faithful witness in heaven.

37 But thou hast abhorred and forsaken thine anointed : and art displeased at him.

38 Thou hast broken the covenant of thy servant : and cast his crown to the ground.

39 Thou hast overthrown all his hedges : and broken down his strongholds.

40 All they that go by spoil him : and he is become a reproach to his neighbours.

41 Thou hast set up the right hand of his enemies : and made all his adversaries to rejoice.

42 Thou hast taken away the edge of his sword : and givest him not victory in the battle.

43 Thou hast put out his glory : and cast his throne down to the ground.

44 The days of his youth hast thou shortened : and covered him with dishonour.

45 Lord, how long wilt thou hide thyself, for ever :

and shall thy wrath burn like fire?

46 O remember how short my time is: wherefore hast thou made all men for nought?

47 What man is he that liveth, and shall not see death: and shall he deliver his soul from the hand of hell?

48 Lord, where are thy old loving-kindnesses: which thou swarest unto David in thy truth?

49 Remember, Lord, the rebuke that thy servants have: and how I do bear in my bosom the rebukes of many people;

50 Wherewith thine enemies have blasphemed thee, and slandered the footsteps of thine anointed: Praised be the LORD for evermore. Amen, and Amen.

THE EIGHTEENTH DAY.

Morning Prayer.

PSALM 90.

Domine, refugium.

LORD, thou hast been our refuge: from one generation to another.

2 Before the mountains were brought forth, or ever the earth and the world were made: thou art God from everlasting, and world without end.

3 Thou turnest man to destruction: again thou sayest, Come again, ye children of men.

4 For a thousand years in thy sight are but as yesterday: seeing that is past as a watch in the night.

5 As soon as thou scatterest them they are even as a sleep: and fade away suddenly like the grass.

6 In the morning it is green, and groweth up: but in the evening it is cut down, dried up, and withered.

7 For we consume away in thy displeasure: and are afraid at thy wrathful indignation.

8 Thou hast set our misdeeds before thee: and our secret sins in the light of thy countenance.

9 For when thou art angry all our days are gone: we *bring our years to an end*, as it were a tale that is told.

10 The days of our age are threescore years and ten; and though men be so strong that they come to fourscore years: yet is their strength then but

labour and sorrow; so soon passeth it away, and we are gone.

11 But who regardeth the power of thy wrath: for even thereafter as a man feareth, so is thy displeasure.

12 O teach us to number our days: that we may apply our hearts unto wisdom.

13 Turn thee again, O Lord, at the last: and be gracious unto thy servants.

14 O satisfy us with thy mercy, and that soon: so shall we rejoice and be glad all the days of our life.

15 Comfort us again now after the time that thou hast plagued us: and for the years wherein we have suffered adversity.

16 Show thy servants thy work: and their children thy glory.

17 And the glorious majesty of the Lord our God be upon us: prosper thou the work of our hands upon us; O prosper thou our handy-work.

Psalm 91.

Qui habitat.

WHOSO dwelleth under the defence of the Most High: shall abide under the shadow of the Almighty.

2 I will say unto the Lord, Thou art my hope, and my stronghold: my God, in him will I trust.

3 For he shall deliver thee from the snare of the hunter: and from the noisome pestilence.

4 He shall defend thee under his wings, and thou shalt be safe under his feathers: his faithfulness and truth shall be thy shield and buckler.

5 Thou shalt not be afraid for any terror by night: nor for the arrow that flieth by day;

6 For the pestilence that walketh in darkness: nor for the sickness that destroyeth in the noon-day.

7 A thousand shall fall beside thee, and ten thousand at thy right hand: but it shall not come nigh thee.

8 Yea, with thine eyes shalt thou behold: and see the reward of the ungodly.

9 For thou, Lord, art my hope: thou hast set thine house of defence very high.

10 There shall no evil happen unto thee: nei-

ther shall any plague come nigh thy dwelling.

11 For he shall give his angels charge over thee : to keep thee in all thy ways.

12 They shall bear thee in their hands : that thou hurt not thy foot against a stone.

13 Thou shalt go upon the lion and adder : the young lion and the dragon shalt thou tread under thy feet.

14 Because he hath set his love upon me, therefore will I deliver him : I will set him up, because he hath known my Name.

15 He shall call upon me, and I will hear him : yea, I am with him in trouble ; I will deliver him, and bring him to honour.

16 With long life will I satisfy him : and show him my salvation.

PSALM 92.

Bonum est confiteri.

IT is a good thing to give thanks unto the LORD : and to sing praises unto thy Name, O Most Highest ;

2 To tell of thy loving-kindness early in the morning : and of thy truth in the night season ;

3 Upon an instrument of ten strings, and upon the lute : upon a loud instrument, and upon the harp.

4 For thou, LORD, hast made me glad through thy works : and I will rejoice in giving praise for the operations of thy hands.

5 O LORD, how glorious are thy works : thy thoughts are very deep.

6 An unwise man doth not well consider this : and a fool doth not understand it.

7 When the ungodly are green as the grass, and when all the workers of wickedness do flourish : then shall they be destroyed for ever ; but thou, LORD, art the most Highest for evermore.

8 For lo, thine enemies, O LORD, lo, thine enemies shall perish : and all the workers of wickedness shall be destroyed.

9 But my horn shall be exalted like the horn of an unicorn : for I am anointed with fresh oil.

10 Mine eye also shall see his lust of mine enemies : and mine ear shall hear his desire of the wicked that arise up against me.

11 The righteous shall

flourish like a palm-tree : and shall spread abroad like a cedar in Libanus.

12 Such as are planted in the house of the LORD : shall flourish in the courts of the house of our God.

13 They also shall bring forth more fruit in their age : and shall be fat and well-liking ;

14 That they may show how true the LORD my strength is : and that there is no unrighteousness in him.

Evening Prayer.

PSALM 93.
Dominus regnavit.

THE LORD is King, and hath put on glorious apparel : the LORD hath put on his apparel, and girded himself with strength.

2 He hath made the round world so sure : that it cannot be moved.

3 Ever since the world began, hath thy seat been prepared : thou art from everlasting.

4 The floods are risen, O LORD, the floods have lift up their voice : the floods lift up their waves.

5 The waves of the sea are mighty, and rage horribly : but yet the LORD,

who dwelleth on high, is mightier.

6 Thy testimonies, O LORD, are very sure : holiness becometh thine house for ever.

PSALM 94.
Deus ultionum.

O LORD God, to whom vengeance belongeth : thou God, to whom vengeance belongeth, show thyself.

2 Arise, thou Judge of the world : and reward the proud after their deserving.

3 LORD, how long shall the ungodly : how long shall the ungodly triumph ?

4 How long shall all wicked doers speak so disdainfully : and make such proud boasting ?

5 They smite down thy people, O LORD : and trouble thine heritage.

6 They murder the widow and the stranger : and put the fatherless to death.

7 And yet they say, Tush, the LORD shall not see : neither shall the God of Jacob regard it.

8 Take heed, ye unwise among the people : O ye fools, when will ye understand ?

9 He that planted the ear, shall he not hear : or he that made the eye, shall he not see?

10 Or he that nurtureth the heathen : it is he that teacheth man knowledge ; shall not he punish?

11 The LORD knoweth the thoughts of man : that they are but vain.

12 Blessed is the man whom thou chastenest, O LORD : and teachest him in thy law ;

13 That thou mayest give him patience in time of adversity : until the pit be digged up for the ungodly.

14 For the LORD will not fail his people : neither will he forsake his inheritance.

15 Until righteousness turn again unto judgment: all such as are true in heart shall follow it.

16 Who will rise up with me against the wicked : or who will take my part against the evil doers ?

17 If the LORD had not helped me : it had not failed, but my soul had been put to silence.

18 But when I said, My foot hath slipt : thy mercy, O LORD, held me up.

19 In the multitude of the sorrows that I had in my heart : thy comforts have refreshed my soul.

20 Wilt thou have any thing to do with the stool of wickedness : which imagineth mischief as a law ?

21 They gather themselves together against the soul of the righteous : and condemn the innocent blood.

22 But the LORD is my refuge : and my God is the strength of my confidence.

23 He shall recompense them their wickedness, and destroy them in their own malice : yea, the LORD our God shall destroy them.

❧

THE NINETEENTH DAY.

Morning Prayer.

PSALM 95.

Venite, exultemus.

O COME, let us sing unto the LORD : let us heartily rejoice in the strength of our salvation.

2 Let us come before his presence with thanksgiving: and show ourselves glad in him with psalms.

3 For the LORD is a great God : and a great King above all gods.

4 In his hand are all

the corners of the earth : and the strength of the hills is his also.

5 The sea is his, and he made it : and his hands prepared the dry land.

6 O come, let us worship and fall down : and kneel before the LORD our Maker.

7 For he is the Lord our God : and we are the people of his pasture, and the sheep of his hand.

8 To-day if ye will hear his voice, harden not your hearts : as in the provocation, and as in the day of temptation in the wilderness :

9 When your fathers tempted me : proved me, and saw my works.

10 Forty years long was I grieved with this generation, and said : It is a people that do err in their hearts, for they have not known my ways :

11 Unto whom I sware in my wrath : that they should not enter into my rest.

Psalm 96.

Cantate Domino.

O SING unto the LORD a new song : sing unto the LORD, all the whole earth.

2 Sing unto the LORD, and praise his Name : be telling of his salvation from day to day.

3 Declare his honour unto the heathen : and his wonders unto all people.

4 For the LORD is great, and cannot worthily be praised : he is more to be feared than all gods.

5 As for all the gods of the heathen, they are but idols : but it is the LORD that made the heavens.

6 Glory and worship are before him : power and honour are in his sanctuary.

7 Ascribe unto the LORD, O ye kindreds of the people : ascribe unto the LORD worship and power.

8 Ascribe unto the LORD the honour due unto his Name : bring presents, and come into his courts.

9 O worship the LORD in the beauty of holiness : let the whole earth stand in awe of him.

10 Tell it out among the heathen, that the LORD is King : and that it is he who hath made the round world so fast that it cannot be moved ; and how that he shall judge the people righteously.

11 Let the heavens rejoice, and let the earth be

glad : let the sea make a noise, and all that therein is.

12 Let the field be joyful, and all that is in it : then shall all the trees of the wood rejoice before the LORD.

13 For he cometh, for he cometh to judge the earth : and with righteousness to judge the world, and the people with his truth.

PSALM 97.
Dominus regnavit.

THE LORD is King, the earth may be glad thereof : yea, the multitude of the isles may be glad thereof.

2 Clouds and darkness are round about him : righteousness and judgment are the habitation of his seat.

3 There shall go a fire before him : and burn up his enemies on every side.

4 His lightnings gave shine unto the world : the earth saw it, and was afraid.

5 The hills melted like wax at the presence of the LORD : at the presence of the Lord of the whole earth.

6 The heavens have de-clared his righteousness : and all the people have seen his glory.

7 Confounded be all they that worship carved images, and that delight in vain gods : worship him, all ye gods.

8 Sion heard of it, and rejoiced : and the daughters of Judah were glad, because of thy judgments, O LORD.

9 For thou, LORD, art higher than all that are in the earth : thou art exalted far above all gods.

10 O ye that love the LORD, see that ye hate the thing which is evil : the Lord preserveth the souls of his saints; he shall deliver them from the hand of the ungodly.

11 There is sprung up a light for the righteous : and joyful gladness for such as are true-hearted.

12 Rejoice in the LORD, ye righteous : and give thanks for a remembrance of his holiness.

❖

Evening Prayer.

PSALM 98.
Cantate Domino.

O SING unto the LORD a new song : for he

hath done marvellous things.

2 With his own right hand, and with his holy arm : hath he gotten himself the victory.

3 The LORD declared his salvation : his righteousness hath he openly showed in the sight of the heathen.

4 He hath remembered his mercy and truth toward the house of Israel : and all the ends of the world have seen the salvation of our God.

5 Show yourselves joyful unto the LORD, all ye lands : sing, rejoice, and give thanks.

6 *Praise the LORD upon the harp* : sing to the harp with a psalm of thanksgiving.

7 With trumpets also and shawms : O show yourselves joyful before the LORD, the King.

8 Let the sea make a noise, and all that therein is : the round world, and they that dwell therein.

9 Let the floods clap their hands, and let the hills be joyful together before the LORD : for he is come to judge the earth.

10 With righteousness shall he judge the world :

and the people with equity.

PSALM 99.

Dominus regnavit.

THE LORD is King, be the people never so impatient : he sitteth between the Cherubim, be the earth never so unquiet.

2 The LORD is great in Sion : and high above all people.

3 They shall give thanks unto thy Name : which is great, wonderful, and holy.

4 The King's power loveth judgment ; thou hast prepared equity : thou hast executed judgment and righteousness in Jacob.

5 O magnify the LORD our God : and fall down before his footstool ; for he is holy.

6 Moses and Aaron among his priests, and Samuel among such as call upon his Name : these called upon the LORD, and he heard them.

7 He spake unto them out of the cloudy pillar : for, they kept his testimonies, and the law that he gave them.

8 Thou heardest them, O LORD our God : thou forgavest them, O God,

and punishedst their own inventions.

9 O magnify the LORD our God, and worship him upon his holy hill : for the LORD our God is holy.

PSALM 100.

Jubilate Deo.

O BE joyful in the LORD, all ye lands : serve the LORD with gladness, and come before his presence with a song.

2 Be ye sure that the LORD he is God ; it is he that hath made us, and not we ourselves : we are his people, and the sheep of his pasture.

3 O go your way into his gates with thanksgiving, and into his courts with praise : be thankful unto him, and speak good of his Name.

4 For the LORD is gracious, his mercy is everlasting : and his truth endureth from generation to generation.

PSALM 101.

Misericordiam et judicium.

M Y song shall be of mercy and judgment : unto thee, O LORD, will I sing.

2 O let me have understanding : in the way of godliness !

3 When wilt thou come unto me : I will walk in my house with a perfect heart.

4 I will take no wicked thing in hand ; I hate the sins of unfaithfulness : there shall no such cleave unto me.

5 A froward heart shall depart from me : I will not know a wicked person.

6 Whoso privily slandereth his neighbour : him will I destroy.

7 Whoso hath also a proud look and high stomach : I will not suffer him.

8 Mine eyes look upon such as are faithful in the land : that they may dwell with me.

9 Whoso leadeth a godly life : he shall be my servant.

10 There shall no deceitful person dwell in my house : he that telleth lies shall not tarry in my sight.

11 I shall soon destroy all the ungodly that are in the land : that I may root out all wicked doers from the city of the LORD.

THE TWENTIETH DAY.

𝔐orning 𝔓rayer.

PSALM 102.

Domine, exaudi.

HEAR my prayer, O
LORD : and let my
crying come unto thee.

2 Hide not thy face
from me in the time of
my trouble : incline thine
ear unto me when I call ;
O hear me, and that right
soon.

3 For my days are con-
sumed away like smoke :
and my bones are burnt
up as it were a firebrand.

4 My heart is smitten
down, and withered like
grass : so that I forget to
eat my bread.

5 For the voice of my
groaning : my bones will
scarce cleave to my flesh.

6 I am become like a
pelican in the wilderness :
and like an owl that is
in the desert.

7 I have watched, and
am even as it were a sparrow : that sitteth alone
upon the housetop.

8 Mine enemies revile
me all the day long : and
they that are mad upon
me are sworn together
against me.

9 For I have eaten ashes
as it were bread : and mingled my drink with weep-
ing ;

10 And that, because of
thine indignation and
wrath : for thou hast
taken me up, and cast
me down.

11 My days are gone
like a shadow : and I am
withered like grass.

12 But thou, O LORD,
shalt endure for ever :
and thy remembrance
throughout all genera-
tions.

13 Thou shalt arise, and
have mercy upon Sion :
for it is time that thou
have mercy upon her, yea,
the time is come.

14 And why? thy ser-
vants think upon her
stones : and it pitieth
them to see her in the
dust.

15 The heathen shall
fear thy Name, O LORD :
and all the kings of the
earth thy majesty ;

16 When the LORD shall
build up Sion : and when
his glory shall appear ;

17 When he turneth
him unto the prayer of
the poor destitute : and
despiseth not their desire.

18 This shall be written
for those that come after :
and the people which shall

be born shall praise the LORD.

19 For he hath looked down from his sanctuary : out of the heaven did the LORD behold the earth ;

20 That he might hear the mournings of such as are in captivity : and deliver the children appointed unto death ;

21 That they may declare the Name of the LORD in Sion : and his worship at Jerusalem ;

22 When the people are gathered together : and the kingdoms also, to serve the LORD.

23 He brought down my strength in my journey : and shortened my days.

24 But I said, O my God, take me not away in the midst of mine age : as for thy years, they endure throughout all generations.

25 Thou, Lord, in the beginning hast laid the foundation of the earth : and the heavens are the work of thy hands.

26 They shall perish, but thou shalt endure : they all wax old as doth a garment ;

27 And as a vesture shalt thou change them, and they shall be chang-

ed : but thou art the same, and thy years shall not fail.

28 The children of thy servants shall continue : and their seed shall stand fast in thy sight.

Psalm 103.

Benedic, anima mea.

PRAISE the LORD, O my soul : and all that is within me, praise his holy Name.

2 Praise the LORD, O my soul : and forget not all his benefits ;

3 Who forgiveth all thy sin : and healeth all thine infirmities ;

4 Who saveth thy life from destruction : and crowneth thee with mercy and loving-kindness ;

5 Who satisfieth thy mouth with good things : making thee young and lusty as an eagle.

6 The LORD executeth righteousness and judgment : for all them that are oppressed with wrong.

7 He showed his ways unto Moses : his works unto the children of Israel.

8 The LORD is full of compassion and mercy : long-suffering, and of great goodness.

9 He will not alway be

chiding : neither keepeth he his anger for ever.

10 He hath not dealt with us after our sins : nor rewarded us according to our wickednesses.

11 For look how high the heaven is in comparison of the earth : so great is his mercy also toward them that fear him.

12 Look how wide also the east is from the west : so far hath he set our sins from us.

13 Yea, like as a father pitieth his own children : even so is the Lord merciful unto them that fear him.

14 For he knoweth whereof we are made : he remembereth that we are but dust.

15 The days of man are but as grass : for he flourisheth as a flower of the field.

16 For as soon as the wind goeth over it, it is gone : and the place thereof shall know it no more.

17 But the merciful goodness of the Lord endureth for ever and ever upon them that fear him : and his righteousness upon children's children ;

18 Even upon such as keep his covenant : and think upon his commandments to do them.

19 The Lord hath prepared his seat in heaven : and his kingdom ruleth over all.

20 O praise the Lord, ye angels of his, ye that excel in strength : ye that fulfil his commandment, and hearken unto the voice of his words.

21 O praise the Lord, all ye his hosts : ye servants of his that do his pleasure.

22 O speak good of the Lord, all ye works of his, in all places of his dominion : praise thou the Lord, O my soul.

❧

Evening Prayer.

Psalm 104.

Benedic, anima mea.

PRAISE the Lord, O my soul : O Lord my God, thou art become exceeding glorious ; thou art clothed with majesty and honour.

2 Thou deckest thyself with light as it were with a garment : and spreadest out the heavens like a curtain.

3 Who layeth the beams of his chambers in the

waters : and maketh the clouds his chariot, and walketh upon the wings of the wind.

4 He maketh his angels spirits : and his ministers a flaming fire.

5 He laid the foundations of the earth : that it never should move at any time.

6 Thou coveredst it with the deep like as with a garment : the waters stand in the hills.

7 At thy rebuke they flee : at the voice of thy thunder they are afraid.

8 They go up as high as the hills, and down to the valleys beneath : even unto the place which thou hast appointed for them.

9 Thou hast set them their bounds, which they shall not pass : neither turn again to cover the earth.

10 He sendeth the springs into the rivers : which run among the hills.

11 All beasts of the field drink thereof : and the wild asses quench their thirst.

12 Beside them shall the fowls of the air have their habitation : and sing among the branches.

13 He watereth the hills from above : the earth is filled with the fruit of thy works.

14 He bringeth forth grass for the cattle : and green herb for the service of men ;

15 That he may bring food out of the earth, and wine that maketh glad the heart of man : and oil to make him a cheerful countenance, and bread to strengthen man's heart.

16 The trees of the Lord also are full of sap : even the cedars of Libanus which he hath planted ;

17 Wherein the birds make their nests : and the fir-trees are a dwelling for the stork.

18 The high hills are a refuge for the wild goats : and so are the stony rocks for the conies.

19 He appointed the moon for certain seasons : and the sun knoweth his going down.

20 Thou makest darkness that it may be night : wherein all the beasts of the forest do move.

21 The lions, roaring after their prey : do seek their meat from God.

22 The sun ariseth, and they get them away to-

gether : and lay them down in their dens.

23 Man goeth forth to his work, and to his labour : until the evening.

24 O Lord, how manifold are thy works : in wisdom hast thou made them all ; the earth is full of thy riches.

25 So is the great and wide sea also : wherein are things creeping innumerable, both small and great beasts.

26 There go the ships, and there is that leviathan : whom thou hast made to take his pastime therein.

27 These wait all upon thee : that thou mayest give them meat in due season.

28 When thou givest it them, they gather it : and when thou openest thy hand, they are filled with good.

29 When thou hidest thy face, they are troubled : when thou takest away their breath, they die, and are turned again to their dust.

30 When thou lettest thy breath go forth, they shall be made : and thou shalt renew the face of the earth.

31 The glorious majesty of the Lord shall endure for ever : the Lord shall rejoice in his works.

32 The earth shall tremble at the look of him : if he do but touch the hills, they shall smoke.

33 I will sing unto the Lord as long as I live : I will praise my God while I have my being.

34 And so shall my words please him : my joy shall be in the Lord.

35 As for sinners, they shall be consumed out of the earth, and the ungodly shall come to an end : Praise thou the Lord, O my soul. Praise the Lord.

THE TWENTY-FIRST DAY.

Morning Prayer.

PSALM 105.

Confitemini Domino.

O GIVE thanks unto the Lord, and call upon his Name : tell the people what things he hath done.

2 O let your songs be of him, and praise him : and let your talking be of all his wondrous works.

3 Rejoice in his holy Name : let the heart of them rejoice that seek the Lord.

4 Seek the LORD and his strength : seek his face evermore.

5 Remember the marvellous works that he hath done : his wonders, and the judgments of his mouth ;

6 O ye seed of Abraham his servant : ye children of Jacob his chosen.

7 He is the LORD our God : his judgments are in all the world.

8 He hath been alway mindful of his covenant and promise : that he made to a thousand generations ;

9 Even the covenant that he made with Abraham : and the oath that he sware unto Isaac ;

10 And appointed the same unto Jacob for a law : and to Israel for an everlasting testament ;

11 Saying, Unto thee will I give the land of Canaan : the lot of your inheritance ;

12 When there were yet but a few of them : and they strangers in the land ;

13 What time as they went from one nation to another : from one kingdom to another people ;

14 He suffered no man to do them wrong : but reproved even kings for their sakes ;

15 Touch not mine anointed : and do my prophets no harm.

16 Moreover, he called for a dearth upon the land : and destroyed all the provision of bread.

17 But he had sent a man before them : even Joseph, who was sold to be a bond-servant ;

18 Whose feet they hurt in the stocks : the iron entered into his soul ;

19 Until the time came that his cause was known : the word of the LORD tried him.

20 The king sent, and delivered him : the prince of the people let him go free.

21 He made him lord also of his house : and ruler of all his substance ;

22 That he might inform his princes after his will : and teach his senators wisdom.

23 Israel also came into Egypt : and Jacob was a stranger in the land of Ham.

24 And he increased his people exceedingly : and made them stronger than their enemies ;

25 Whose heart turned so, that they hated his people : and dealt untruly with his servants.

26 Then sent he Moses his servant : and Aaron whom he had chosen.

27 And these showed his tokens among them : and wonders in the land of Ham.

28 He sent darkness, and it was dark : and they were not obedient unto his word.

29 He turned their waters into blood : and slew their fish.

30 Their land brought forth frogs : yea, even in their kings' chambers.

31 He spake the word, and there came all manner of flies : and lice in all their quarters.

32 He gave them hailstones for rain : and flames of fire in their land.

33 He smote their vines also and fig-trees : and destroyed the trees that were in their coasts.

34 He spake the word, and the grasshoppers came, and caterpillars innumerable : and did eat up all the grass in their land, and devoured the fruit of their ground.

35 He smote all the firstborn in their land : even the chief of all their strength.

36 He brought them forth also with silver and gold : there was not one feeble person among their tribes.

37 Egypt was glad at their departing : for they were afraid of them.

38 He spread out a cloud to be a covering : and fire to give light in the night season.

39 At their desire he brought quails : and he filled them with the bread of heaven.

40 He opened the rock of stone, and the waters flowed out : so that rivers ran in the dry places.

41 For why? he remembered his holy promise : and Abraham his servant.

42 And he brought forth his people with joy : and his chosen with gladness;

43 And gave them the lands of the heathen : and they took the labours of the people in possession;

44 That they might keep his statutes : and observe his laws.

Evening Prayer.

PSALM 106.

Confitemini Domino.

O GIVE thanks unto the LORD, for he is gracious : and his mercy endureth for ever.

2 Who can express the noble acts of the LORD : or show forth all his praise ?

3 Blessed are they that alway keep judgment : and do righteousness.

4 Remember me, O LORD, according to the favour that thou bearest unto thy people : O visit me with thy salvation ;

5 That I may see the felicity of thy chosen : and rejoice in the gladness of thy people, and give thanks with thine inheritance.

6 We have sinned with our fathers : we have done amiss, and dealt wickedly.

7 Our fathers regarded not thy wonders in Egypt, neither kept they thy great goodness in remembrance : but were disobedient at the sea, even at the Red Sea.

8 Nevertheless, he helped them for his Name's sake : that he might make his power to be known.

9 He rebuked the Red Sea also, and it was dried up : so he led them through the deep, as through a wilderness.

10 And he saved them from the adversary's hand : and delivered them from the hand of the enemy.

11 As for those that troubled them, the waters overwhelmed them : there was not one of them left.

12 Then believed they his words : and sang praise unto him.

13 But within a while they forgat his works : and would not abide his counsel.

14 But lust came upon them in the wilderness : and they tempted God in the desert.

15 And he gave them their desire : and sent leanness withal into their soul.

16 They angered Moses also in the tents : and Aaron the saint of the LORD.

17 So the earth opened, and swallowed up Dathan : and covered the congregation of Abiram.

18 And the fire was kindled in their company : the flame burnt up the ungodly.

19 They made a calf in Horeb : and worshipped the molten image.

20 Thus they turned their glory : into the similitude of a calf that eateth hay.

21 And they forgat God their Saviour : who had done so great things in Egypt :

22 Wondrous works in the land of Ham : and fearful things by the Red Sea.

23 So he said he would have destroyed them, had not Moses his chosen stood before him in the gap : to turn away his wrathful indignation, lest he should destroy them.

24 Yea, they thought scorn of that pleasant land : and gave no credence unto his word ;

25 But murmured in their tents : and hearkened not unto the voice of the Lord.

26 Then lift he up his hand against them : to overthrow them in the wilderness ;

27 To cast out their seed among the nations : and to scatter them in the lands.

28 They joined themselves unto Baal-peor : and ate the offerings of the dead.

29 Thus they provoked him to anger with their own inventions : and the plague was great among them.

30 Then stood up Phinees, and prayed : and so the plague ceased.

31 And that was counted unto him for righteousness : among all posterities for evermore.

32 They angered him also at the waters of strife : so that he punished Moses for their sakes ;

33 Because they provoked his spirit : so that he spake unadvisedly with his lips.

34 Neither destroyed they the heathen : as the Lord commanded them ;

35 But were mingled among the heathen : and learned their works.

36 Insomuch that they worshipped their idols, which turned to their own decay : yea, they offered their sons and their daughters unto devils ;

37 And shed innocent blood, even the blood of their sons and of their daughters : whom they offered unto the idols of Canaan ; and the land was defiled with blood.

38 Thus were they stained with their own works :

and went a whoring with their own inventions.

39 Therefore was the wrath of the LORD kindled against his people : insomuch that he abhorred his own inheritance.

40 And he gave them over into the hand of the heathen : and they that hated them were lords over them.

41 Their enemies oppressed them : and had them in subjection.

42 Many a time did he deliver them : but they rebelled against him with their own inventions, and were brought down in their wickedness.

43 Nevertheless, when he saw their adversity : he heard their complaint.

44 He thought upon his covenant, and pitied them, according unto the multitude of his mercies : yea, he made all those that led them away captive to pity them.

45 Deliver us, O LORD our God, and gather us from among the heathen : that we may give thanks unto thy holy Name, and make our boast of thy praise.

46 Blessed be the LORD God of Israel, from ever-lasting, and world without end : And let all the people say, Amen.

THE TWENTY-SECOND DAY.

Morning Prayer.

PSALM 107.

Confitemini Domino.

O GIVE thanks unto the LORD, for he is gracious : and his mercy endureth for ever.

2 Let them give thanks whom the LORD hath redeemed : and delivered from the hand of the enemy;

3 And gathered them out of the lands, from the east, and from the west : from the north, and from the south.

4 They went astray in the wilderness out of the way : and found no city to dwell in.

5 Hungry and thirsty : their soul fainted in them.

6 So they cried unto the LORD in their trouble : and he delivered them from their distress.

7 He led them forth by the right way : that they might go to the city where they dwelt.

8 O that men would therefore praise the LORD

for his goodness : and declare the wonders that he doeth for the children of men!

9 For he satisfieth the empty soul : and filleth the hungry soul with goodness.

10 Such as sit in darkness, and in the shadow of death : being fast bound in misery and iron ;

11 Because they rebelled against the words of the Lord : and lightly regarded the counsel of the Most Highest ;

12 He also brought down their heart through heaviness : they fell down, and there was none to help them.

13 So when they cried unto the Lord in their trouble : he delivered them out of their distress.

14 For he brought them out of darkness, and out of the shadow of death : and brake their bonds in sunder.

15 O that men would therefore praise the Lord for his goodness : and declare the wonders that he doeth for the children of men!

16 For he hath broken the gates of brass : and smitten the bars of iron in sunder.

17 Foolish men are plagued for their offence : and because of their wickedness.

18 Their soul abhorred all manner of meat : and they were even hard at death's door.

19 So when they cried unto the Lord in their trouble : he delivered them out of their distress.

20 He sent his word, and healed them : and they were saved from their destruction.

21 O that men would therefore praise the Lord for his goodness : and declare the wonders that he doeth for the children of men!

22 That they would offer unto him the sacrifice of thanksgiving : and tell out his works with gladness!

23 They that go down to the sea in ships : and occupy their business in great waters ;

24 These men see the works of the Lord : and his wonders in the deep.

25 For at his word the stormy wind ariseth : which lifteth up the waves thereof.

26 They are carried up to the heaven, and down again to the deep : their

soul melteth away because of the trouble.

27 They reel to and fro, and stagger like a drunken man : and are at their wit's end.

28 So when they cry unto the LORD in their trouble : he delivereth them out of their distress.

29 For he maketh the storm to cease : so that the waves thereof are still.

30 Then are they glad, because they are at rest : and so he bringeth them unto the haven where they would be.

31 O that men would therefore praise the LORD for his goodness : and declare the wonders that he doeth for the children of men !

32 That they would exalt him also in the congregation of the people : and praise him in the seat of the elders !

33 Who turneth the floods into a wilderness : and drieth up the watersprings.

34 A fruitful land maketh he barren : for the wickedness of them that dwell therein.

35 Again, he maketh the wilderness a standing water : and water-springs of a dry ground.

36 And there he setteth the hungry : that they may build them a city to dwell in ;

37 That they may sow their land, and plant vineyards : to yield them fruits of increase.

38 He blesseth them, so that they multiply exceedingly : and suffereth not their cattle to decrease.

39 And again, when they are minished and brought low : through oppression, through any plague or trouble ;

40 Though he suffer them to be evil entreated through tyrants : and let them wander out of the way in the wilderness ;

41 Yet helpeth he the poor out of misery : and maketh him households like a flock of sheep.

42 The righteous will consider this, and rejoice : and the mouth of all wickedness shall be stopped.

43 Whoso is wise, will ponder these things : and they shall understand the loving-kindness of the LORD.

Evening Prayer.

PSALM 108.

Paratum cor meum.

O God, my heart is ready, my heart is ready : I will sing, and give praise with the best member that I have.

2 Awake, thou lute and harp : I myself will awake right early.

3 I will give thanks unto thee, O LORD, among the people : I will sing praises unto thee among the nations.

4 For thy mercy is greater than the heavens : and thy truth reacheth unto the clouds.

5 Set up thyself, O God, above the heavens : and thy glory above all the earth ;

6 That thy beloved may be delivered : let thy right hand save them, and hear thou me.

7 God hath spoken in his holiness : I will rejoice therefore, and divide Sichem, and mete out the valley of Succoth.

8 Gilead is mine, and Manasses is mine : Ephraim also is the strength of my head ;

9 Judah is my lawgiver ; Moab is my wash-pot : over Edom will I cast out my shoe ; upon Philistia will I triumph.

10 Who will lead me into the strong city : and who will bring me into Edom ?

11 Hast not thou forsaken us, O God : and wilt not thou, O God, go forth with our hosts ?

12 O help us against the enemy : for vain is the help of man.

13 Through God we shall do great acts : and it is he that shall tread down our enemies.

PSALM 109.

Deus, laudem.

HOLD not thy tongue, O God of my praise : for the mouth of the ungodly, yea, the mouth of the deceitful is opened upon me.

2 And they have spoken against me with false tongues : they compassed me about also with words of hatred, and fought against me without a cause.

3 For the love that I had unto them, lo, they take now my contrary part : but I give myself unto prayer.

4 Thus have they rewarded me evil for good :

and hatred for my good-will.

5 Set thou an ungodly man to be ruler over him : and let Satan stand at his right hand.

6 When sentence is given upon him, let him be condemned : and let his prayer be turned into sin.

7 Let his days be few : and let another take his office.

8 Let his children be fatherless : and his wife a widow.

9 Let his children be vagabonds, and beg their bread : let them seek it also out of desolate places.

10 Let the extortioner consume all that he hath : and let the stranger spoil his labour.

11 Let there be no man to pity him : nor to have compassion upon his fatherless children.

12 Let his posterity be destroyed : and in the next generation let his name be clean put out.

13 Let the wickedness of his fathers be had in remembrance in the sight of the Lord : and let not the sin of his mother be done away.

14 Let them alway be before the Lord : that he may root out the memorial of them from off the earth ;

15 And that, because his mind was not to do good : but persecuted the poor helpless man, that he might slay him that was vexed at the heart.

16 His delight was in cursing, and it shall happen unto him : he loved not blessing, therefore shall it be far from him.

17 He clothed himself with cursing like as with a raiment : and it shall come into his bowels like water, and like oil into his bones.

18 Let it be unto him as the cloak that he hath upon him : and as the girdle that he is alway girded withal.

19 Let it thus happen from the Lord unto mine enemies : and to those that speak evil against my soul.

20 But deal thou with me, O Lord God, according unto thy Name : for sweet is thy mercy.

21 O deliver me, for I am helpless and poor : and my heart is wounded within me.

22 I go hence like the shadow that departeth : and am driven away as the grasshopper.

23 My knees are weak through fasting : my flesh is dried up for want of fatness.

24 I became also a reproach unto them : they that looked upon me shaked their heads.

25 Help me, O Lord my God : O save me according to thy mercy ;

26 And they shall know how that this is thy hand : and that thou, Lord, hast done it.

27 Though they curse, yet bless thou : and let them be confounded that rise up against me ; but let thy servant rejoice.

28 Let mine adversaries be clothed with shame : and let them cover themselves with their own confusion, as with a cloak.

29 As for me, I will give great thanks unto the Lord with my mouth : and praise him among the multitude ;

30 For he shall stand at the right hand of the poor : to save his soul from unrighteous judges.

THE TWENTY-THIRD DAY.

Morning Prayer.

PSALM 110.

Dixit Dominus.

THE Lord said unto my Lord : Sit thou on my right hand, until I make thine enemies thy footstool.

2 The Lord shall send the rod of thy power out of Sion : be thou ruler, even in the midst among thine enemies.

3 In the day of thy power shall thy people offer thee free-will offerings with an holy worship : the dew of thy birth is of the womb of the morning.

4 The Lord sware, and will not repent : Thou art a Priest for ever after the order of Melchizedech.

5 The Lord upon thy right hand : shall wound even kings in the day of his wrath.

6 He shall judge among the heathen ; he shall fill the places with the dead bodies : and smite in sunder the heads over divers countries.

7 He shall drink of the brook in the way : therefore shall he lift up his head.

PSALM 111.

Confitebor tibi.

I WILL give thanks unto the LORD with my whole heart : secretly among the faithful, and in the congregation.

2 The works of the LORD are great : sought out of all them that have pleasure therein.

3 His work is worthy to be praised and had in honour : and his righteousness endureth for ever.

4 The merciful and gracious LORD hath so done his marvellous works : that they ought to be had in remembrance.

5 He hath given meat unto them that fear him : he shall ever be mindful of his covenant.

6 He hath showed his people the power of his works : that he may give them the heritage of the heathen.

7 The works of his hands are verity and judgment : all his commandments are true.

8 They stand fast for ever and ever : and are done in truth and equity.

9 He sent redemption unto his people : he hath commanded his covenant for ever ; holy and reverend is his Name.

10 The fear of the LORD is the beginning of wisdom : a good understanding have all they that do thereafter ; the praise of it endureth for ever.

PSALM 112.

Beatus vir.

BLESSED is the man that feareth the LORD : he hath great delight in his commandments.

2 His seed shall be mighty upon earth : the generation of the faithful shall be blessed.

3 Riches and plenteousness shall be in his house : and his righteousness endureth for ever.

4 Unto the godly there ariseth up light in the darkness : he is merciful, loving, and righteous.

5 A good man is merciful, and lendeth : and will guide his words with discretion.

6 For he shall never be moved : and the righteous shall be had in everlasting remembrance.

7 He will not be afraid of any evil tidings : for his heart standeth fast, and believeth in the LORD.

8 His heart is stablished, and will not shrink : until he see his desire upon his enemies.

9 He hath dispersed abroad, and given to the poor : and his righteousness remaineth for ever ; his horn shall be exalted with honour.

10 The ungodly shall see it, and it shall grieve him : he shall gnash with his teeth, and consume away ; the desire of the ungodly shall perish.

Psalm 113.

Laudate, pueri.

PRAISE the Lord, ye servants : O praise the Name of the Lord.

2 Blessed be the Name of the Lord : from this time forth for evermore.

3 The Lord's Name is praised : from the rising up of the sun unto the going down of the same.

4 The Lord is high above all heathen : and his glory above the heavens.

5 Who is like unto the Lord our God, that hath his dwelling so high : and yet humbleth himself to behold the things that are in heaven and earth !

6 He taketh up the simple out of the dust : and lifteth the poor out of the mire ;

7 That he may set him with the princes : even with the princes of his people.

8 He maketh the barren woman to keep house : and to be a joyful mother of children.

❖

Evening Prayer.

Psalm 114.

In exitu Israel.

WHEN Israel came out of Egypt : and the house of Jacob from among the strange people,

2 Judah was his sanctuary : and Israel his dominion.

3 The sea saw that, and fled : Jordan was driven back.

4 The mountains skipped like rams : and the little hills like young sheep.

5 What aileth thee, O thou sea, that thou fleddest : and thou Jordan, that thou wast driven back ?

6 Ye mountains, that ye skipped like rams : and ye little hills, like young sheep ?

7 Tremble, thou earth,

at the presence of the Lord : at the presence of the God of Jacob;

8 Who turned the hard rock into a standing water : and the flint-stone into a springing well.

Psalm 115.

Non nobis, Domine.

NOT unto us, O Lord, not unto us, but unto thy Name give the praise : for thy loving mercy, and for thy truth's sake.

2 Wherefore shall the heathen say : Where is now their God?

3 As for our God, he is in heaven : he hath done whatsoever pleased him.

4 Their idols are silver and gold : even the work of men's hands.

5 They have mouths, and speak not : eyes have they, and see not.

6 They have ears, and hear not : noses have they, and smell not.

7 They have hands, and handle not ; feet have they, and walk not : neither speak they through their throat.

8 They that make them are like unto them : and so are all such as put their trust in them.

9 But thou, house of Israel, trust thou in the Lord : he is their succour and defence.

10 Ye house of Aaron, put your trust in the Lord : he is their helper and defender.

11 Ye that fear the Lord, put your trust in the Lord : he is their helper and defender.

12 The Lord hath been mindful of us, and he shall bless us : even he shall bless the house of Israel, and he shall bless the house of Aaron.

13 He shall bless them that fear the Lord : both small and great.

14 The Lord shall increase you more and more : you and your children.

15 Ye are the blessed of the Lord : who made heaven and earth.

16 All the whole heavens are the Lord's : the earth hath he given to the children of men.

17 The dead praise not thee, O Lord : neither all they that go down into silence.

18 But we will praise the Lord : from this time forth for evermore. Praise the Lord.

THE TWENTY-FOURTH DAY.

Morning Prayer.

PSALM 116.

Dilexi, quoniam.

I AM well pleased : that the LORD hath heard the voice of my prayer ;

2 That he hath inclined his ear unto me : therefore will I call upon him as long as I live.

3 The snares of death compassed me round about : and the pains of hell gat hold upon me.

4 I shall find trouble and heaviness, and I will call upon the Name of the LORD : O LORD, I beseech thee, deliver my soul.

5 Gracious is the LORD, and righteous : yea, our God is merciful.

6 The LORD preserveth the simple : I was in misery, and he helped me.

7 Turn again then unto thy rest, O my soul : for the LORD hath rewarded thee.

8 And why? thou hast delivered my soul from death : mine eyes from tears, and my feet from falling.

9 I will walk before the LORD : in the land of the living.

10 I believed, and therefore will I speak ; but I was sore troubled : I said in my haste, All men are liars.

11 What reward shall I give unto the LORD : for all the benefits that he hath done unto me?

12 I will receive the cup of salvation : and call upon the Name of the LORD.

13 I will pay my vows now in the presence of all his people : right dear in the sight of the LORD is the death of his saints.

14 Behold, O LORD, how that I am thy servant : I am thy servant, and the son of thine handmaid ; thou hast broken my bonds in sunder.

15 I will offer to thee the sacrifice of thanksgiving : and will call upon the Name of the LORD.

16 I will pay my vows unto the LORD, in the sight of all his people : in the courts of the LORD's house, even in the midst of thee, O Jerusalem. Praise the LORD.

PSALM 117.

Laudate Dominum.

O PRAISE the LORD, all ye heathen : praise him, all ye nations.

2 For his merciful kindness is ever more and more toward us : and the truth of the LORD endureth for ever. Praise the LORD.

Psalm 118.

Confitemini Domino.

O GIVE thanks unto the LORD, for he is gracious : because his mercy endureth for ever.

2 Let Israel now confess that he is gracious : and that his mercy endureth for ever.

3 Let the house of Aaron now confess : that his mercy endureth for ever.

4 Yea, let them now that fear the LORD confess : that his mercy endureth for ever.

5 I called upon the LORD in trouble : and the LORD heard me at large.

6 The LORD is on my side : I will not fear what man doeth unto me.

7 The LORD taketh my part with them that help me : therefore shall I see my desire upon mine enemies.

8 It is better to trust in the LORD : than to put any confidence in man.

9 It is better to trust in the LORD : than to put any confidence in princes.

10 All nations compassed me round about : but in the Name of the LORD will I destroy them.

11 They kept me in on every side, they kept me in, I say, on every side : but in the Name of the LORD will I destroy them.

12 They came about me like bees, and are extinct even as the fire among the thorns : for in the Name of the LORD I will destroy them.

13 Thou hast thrust sore at me, that I might fall : but the LORD was my help.

14 The LORD is my strength, and my song : and is become my salvation.

15 The voice of joy and health is in the dwellings of the righteous : the right hand of the LORD bringeth mighty things to pass.

16 *The right hand of the LORD hath the preeminence : the right hand of the LORD bringeth mighty things to pass.*

17 I shall not die, but live : and declare the works of the LORD.

18 The LORD hath chastened and corrected me :

but he hath not given me over unto death.

19 Open me the gates of righteousness: that I may go into them, and give thanks unto the LORD.

20 This is the gate of the LORD: the righteous shall enter into it.

21 I will thank thee, for thou hast heard me: and art become my salvation.

22 The same stone which the builders refused: is become the head-stone in the corner.

23 This is the LORD's doing: and it is marvellous in our eyes.

24 This is the day which the LORD hath made: we will *rejoice and be glad* in it.

25 Help me now, O LORD: O LORD, send us now prosperity.

26 Blessed be he that cometh in the Name of the LORD: we have wished you good luck, ye that are of the house of the LORD.

27 God is the LORD, who hath showed us light: bind the sacrifice with cords, yea, even unto the horns of the altar.

28 Thou art my God, and I will thank thee: thou art my God, and I will praise thee.

29 O give thanks unto the LORD, for he is gracious: and his mercy endureth for ever.

Evening Prayer.

PSALM 119.

Beati immaculati.

BLESSED are those that are undefiled in the way: and walk in the law of the LORD.

2 Blessed are they that keep his testimonies: and seek him with their whole heart.

3 For they who do no wickedness: walk in his ways.

4 Thou hast charged: that we shall diligently keep thy commandments.

5 O that my ways were made so direct: that I might keep thy statutes!

6 So shall I not be confounded: while I have respect unto all thy commandments.

7 I will thank thee with an unfeigned heart: when I shall have learned the judgments of thy righteousness.

8 I will keep thy ceremonies: O forsake me not utterly.

In quo corrigit?

WHEREWITHAL shall a young man cleanse his way : even by ruling himself after thy word.

10 With my whole heart have I sought thee : O let me not go wrong out of thy commandments.

11 Thy words have I hid within my heart : that I should not sin against thee.

12 Blessed art thou, O LORD : O teach me thy statutes.

13 With my lips have I been telling : of all the judgments of thy mouth.

14 I have had as great delight in the way of thy testimonies : as in all manner of riches.

15 I will talk of thy commandments : and have respect unto thy ways.

16 My delight shall be in thy statutes : and I will not forget thy word.

Retribue servo tuo.

O DO well unto thy servant : that I may live, and keep thy word.

18 Open thou mine eyes : that I may see the wondrous things of thy law.

19 I am a stranger upon earth : O hide not thy commandments from me.

20 My soul breaketh out for the very fervent desire : that it hath alway unto thy judgments.

21 Thou hast rebuked the proud : and cursed are they that do err from thy commandments.

22 O turn from me shame and rebuke : for I have kept thy testimonies.

23 Princes also did sit and speak against me : but thy servant is occupied in thy statutes.

24 For thy testimonies are my delight : and my counsellors.

Adhæsit pavimento.

MY soul cleaveth to the dust : O quicken thou me, according to thy word.

26 I have acknowledged my ways, and thou heardest me : O teach me thy statutes.

27 Make me to understand the way of thy commandments : and so shall I talk of thy wondrous works.

28 My soul melteth away for very heaviness : comfort thou me according unto thy word.

29 Take from me the

way of lying : and cause thou me to make much of thy law.

30 I have chosen the way of truth : and thy judgments have I laid before me.

31 I have stuck unto thy testimonies : O LORD, confound me not.

32 I will run the way of thy commandments : when thou hast set my heart at liberty.

THE TWENTY-FIFTH DAY.

Morning Prayer.

Legem pone.

TEACH me, O LORD, the way of thy statutes : and I shall keep it unto the end.

34 Give me understanding, and I shall keep thy law : yea, I shall keep it with my whole heart.

35 Make me to go in the path of thy commandments : for therein is my desire.

36 Incline my heart unto thy testimonies : and not to covetousness.

37 O turn away mine eyes, lest they behold vanity : and quicken thou me in thy way.

38 O stablish thy word

in thy servant : that I may fear thee.

39 Take away the rebuke that I am afraid of : for thy judgments are good.

40 Behold, my delight is in thy commandments : O quicken me in thy righteousness.

Et veniat super me.

LET thy loving mercy come also unto me, O LORD : even thy salvation, according unto thy word.

42 So shall I make answer unto my blasphemers : for my trust is in thy word.

43 O take not the word of thy truth utterly out of my mouth : for my hope is in thy judgments.

44 So shall I alway keep thy law : yea, for ever and ever.

45 And I will walk at liberty : for I seek thy commandments.

46 I will speak of thy testimonies also, even before kings : and will not be ashamed.

47 And my delight shall be in thy commandments : which I have loved.

48 My hands also will I lift up unto thy command-

ments, which I have loved : and my study shall be in thy statutes.

Memor esto verbi tui.

O THINK upon thy servant, as concerning thy word : wherein thou hast caused me to put my trust.

50 The same is my comfort in my trouble : for thy word hath quickened me.

51 The proud have had me exceedingly in derision : yet have I not shrinked from thy law.

52 For I remembered thine everlasting judgments, O LORD : and received comfort.

53 I am horribly afraid : for the ungodly that forsake thy law.

54 Thy statutes have been my songs : in the house of my pilgrimage.

55 I have thought upon thy Name, O LORD, in the night season : and have kept thy law.

56 This I had : because I kept thy commandments.

Portio mea, Domine.

THOU art my portion, O LORD : I have promised to keep thy law.

58 I made my humble petition in thy presence with my whole heart : O be merciful unto me, according to thy word.

59 I called mine own ways to remembrance : and turned my feet unto thy testimonies.

60 I made haste, and prolonged not the time : to keep thy commandments.

61 The congregations of the ungodly have robbed me : but I have not forgotten thy law.

62 At midnight I will rise to give thanks unto thee : because of thy righteous judgments.

63 I am a companion of all them that fear thee : and keep thy commandments.

64 The earth, O LORD, is full of thy mercy : O teach me thy statutes.

Bonitatem fecisti.

O LORD, thou hast dealt graciously with thy servant : according unto thy word.

66 O learn me true understanding and knowledge : for I have believed thy commandments.

67 Before I was troubled, I went wrong : but

now have I kept thy word.

68 Thou art good and gracious : O teach me thy statutes.

69 The proud have imagined a lie against me : but I will keep thy commandments with my whole heart.

70 Their heart is as fat as brawn : but my delight hath been in thy law.

71 It is good for me that I have been in trouble : that I may learn thy statutes.

72 The law of thy mouth is dearer unto me : than thousands of gold and silver.

❀

Evening Prayer.

Manus tuæ fecerunt me.

THY hands have made me and fashioned me : O give me understanding, that I may learn thy commandments.

74 They that fear thee will be glad when they see me : because I have put my trust in thy word.

75 I know, O LORD, that thy judgments are right : and that thou of very faithfulness hast caused me to be troubled.

76 O let thy merciful kindness be my comfort : according to thy word unto thy servant.

77 O let thy loving mercies come unto me, that I may live : for thy law is my delight.

78 Let the proud be confounded, for they go wickedly about to destroy me : but I will be occupied in thy commandments.

79 Let such as fear thee, and have known thy testimonies : be turned unto me.

80 O let my heart be sound in thy statutes : that I be not ashamed.

Deficit anima mea.

MY soul hath longed for thy salvation : and I have a good hope because of thy word.

82 Mine eyes long sore for thy word : saying, O when wilt thou comfort me?

83 For I am become like a bottle in the smoke : yet do I not forget thy statutes.

84 How many are the days of thy servant : when wilt thou be avenged of them that persecute me?

85 The proud have dig-

ged pits for me : which are not after thy law.

86 All thy commandments are true : they persecute me falsely ; O be thou my help.

87 They had almost made an end of me upon earth : but I forsook not thy commandments.

88 O quicken me after thy loving-kindness : and so shall I keep the testimonies of thy mouth.

In æternum, Domine.

O LORD, thy word : endureth for ever in heaven.

90 Thy truth also remaineth from one generation to another : thou hast laid the foundation of the earth, and it abideth.

91 They continue this day according to thine ordinance : for all things serve thee.

92 If my delight had not been in thy law : I should have perished in my trouble.

93 I will never forget thy commandments : for with them thou hast quickened me.

94 I am thine, O save me : for I have sought thy commandments.

95 The ungodly laid wait for me, to destroy me : but I will consider thy testimonies.

96 I see that all things come to an end : but thy commandment is exceeding broad.

Quomodo dilexi !

LORD, what love have I unto thy law : all the day long is my study in it.

98 Thou, through thy commandments, hast made me wiser than mine enemies : for they are ever with me.

99 I have more understanding than my teachers : for thy testimonies are my study.

100 I am wiser than the aged : because I keep thy commandments.

101 I have refrained my feet from every evil way : that I may keep thy word.

102 I have not shrunk from thy judgments : for thou teachest me.

103 O how sweet are thy words unto my throat : yea, sweeter than honey unto my mouth !

104 Through thy commandments I get understanding : therefore I hate all evil ways.

THE TWENTY-SIXTH DAY.

Morning Prayer.

Lucerna pedibus meis.

THY word is a lantern unto my feet : and a light unto my paths.

106 I have sworn, and am stedfastly purposed : to keep thy righteous judgments.

107 I am troubled above measure : quicken me, O LORD, according to thy word.

108 Let the free-will offerings of my mouth please thee, O LORD : and teach me thy judgments.

109 My soul is alway in my hand : yet do I not forget thy law.

110 The ungodly have laid a snare for me : but yet I swerved not from thy commandments.

111 Thy testimonies have I claimed as mine heritage for ever : and why ? they are the very joy of my heart.

112 I have applied my heart to fulfil thy statutes alway : even unto the end.

Iniquos odio habui.

I HATE them that imagine evil things : but thy law do I love.

114 Thou art my defence and shield : and my trust is in thy word.

115 Away from me, ye wicked : I will keep the commandments of my God.

116 O stablish me according to thy word, that I may live : and let me not be disappointed of my hope.

117 Hold thou me up, and I shall be safe : yea, my delight shall be ever in thy statutes.

118 Thou hast trodden down all them that depart from thy statutes : for they imagine but deceit.

119 Thou puttest away all the ungodly of the earth like dross : therefore I love thy testimonies.

120 My flesh trembleth for fear of thee : and I am afraid of thy judgments.

Feci judicium.

I DEAL with the thing that is lawful and right : O give me not over unto mine oppressors.

122 Make thou thy servant to delight in that which is good : that the proud do me no wrong.

123 Mine eyes are wasted away with looking for thy health : and for the word of thy righteousness.

124 O deal with thy servant according unto thy loving mercy : and teach me thy statutes.

125 I am thy servant ; O grant me understanding : that I may know thy testimonies.

126 It is time for thee, LORD, to lay to thine hand : for they have destroyed thy law.

127 For I love thy commandments : above gold and precious stones.

128 Therefore hold I straight all thy commandments : and all false ways I utterly abhor.

Mirabilia.

THY testimonies are wonderful : therefore doth my soul keep them.

130 When thy word goeth forth : it giveth light and understanding unto the simple.

131 I opened my mouth, and drew in my breath : for my delight was in thy commandments.

132 O look thou upon me, and be merciful unto me : as thou usest to do unto those that love thy Name.

133 Order my steps in thy word : and so shall no wickedness have dominion over me.

134 O deliver me from the wrongful dealings of men : and so shall I keep thy commandments.

135 Show the light of thy countenance upon thy servant : and teach me thy statutes.

136 Mine eyes gush out with water : because men keep not thy law.

Justus es, Domine.

RIGHTEOUS art thou, O LORD : and true is thy judgment.

138 The testimonies that thou hast commanded : are exceeding righteous and true.

139 My zeal hath even consumed me : because mine enemies have forgotten thy words.

140 Thy word is tried to the uttermost : and thy servant loveth it.

141 I am small and of no reputation : yet do I not forget thy commandments.

142 Thy righteousness is an everlasting righteousness : and thy law is the truth.

143 Trouble and heaviness have taken hold upon me : yet is my delight in thy commandments.

144 The righteousness of thy testimonies is ever-

lasting : O grant me understanding, and I shall live.

✤

Evening Prayer.

Clamavi in toto corde meo.

I CALL with my whole heart : hear me, O LORD, I will keep thy statutes.

146 Yea, even unto thee do I call : help me, and I shall keep thy testimonies.

147 Early in the morning do I cry unto thee : for in thy word is my trust.

148 Mine eyes prevent the night watches : that I might be occupied in thy words.

149 Hear my voice, O LORD, according unto thy loving-kindness : quicken me, according as thou art wont.

150 They draw nigh that of malice persecute me : and are far from thy law.

151 Be thou nigh at hand, O LORD : for all thy commandments are true.

152 As concerning thy testimonies, I have known long since : that thou hast grounded them for ever.

Vide humilitatem.

O CONSIDER mine adversity, and deliver me : for I do not forget thy law.

154 Avenge thou my cause, and deliver me : quicken me according to thy word.

155 Health is far from the ungodly : for they regard not thy statutes.

156 Great is thy mercy, O LORD : quicken me, as thou art wont.

157 Many there are that trouble me, and persecute me : yet do I not swerve from thy testimonies.

158 It grieveth me when I see the transgressors : because they keep not thy law.

159 Consider, O LORD, how I love thy commandments : O quicken me, according to thy loving-kindness.

160 Thy word is true from everlasting : all the judgments of thy righteousness endure for evermore.

Principes persecuti sunt.

P RINCES have persecuted me without a cause : but my heart standeth in awe of thy word.

162 I am as glad of thy word : as one that findeth great spoils.

163 As for lies, I hate and abhor them : but thy law do I love.

164 Seven times a day do

I praise thee : because of thy righteous judgments.

165 Great is the peace that they have who love thy law : and they are not offended at it.

166 LORD, I have looked for thy saving health : and done after thy commandments.

167 My soul hath kept thy testimonies : and loved them exceedingly.

168 I have kept thy commandments and testimonies : for all my ways are before thee.

Appropinquet deprecatio.

LET my complaint come before thee, O LORD : give me understanding according to thy word.

169 Let my supplication come before thee : deliver me according to thy word.

171 My lips shall speak of thy praise : when thou hast taught me thy statutes.

172 Yea, my tongue shall sing of thy word : for all thy commandments are righteous.

173 Let thine hand help me : for I have chosen thy commandments.

174 I have longed for thy saving health, O LORD : and in thy law is my delight.

175 O let my soul live, and it shall praise thee : and thy judgments shall help me.

176 I have gone astray like a sheep that is lost : O seek thy servant, for I do not forget thy commandments.

✿

THE TWENTY-SEVENTH DAY.

𝕸orning 𝕻rayer.

PSALM 120.

Ad Dominum.

WHEN I was in trouble, I called upon the LORD : and he heard me.

2 Deliver my soul, O LORD, from lying lips : and from a deceitful tongue.

3 What reward shall be given or done unto thee, thou false tongue : even mighty and sharp arrows, with hot burning coals.

4 Woe is me, that I am constrained to dwell with Mesech : and to have my habitation among the tents of Kedar !

5 My soul hath long dwelt among them : that are enemies unto peace.

6 I labour for peace ; but when I speak unto them thereof : they make them ready to battle.

PSALM 121.

Levavi oculos.

I WILL lift up mine eyes unto the hills : from whence cometh my help.

2 My help cometh even from the LORD : who hath made heaven and earth.

3 He will not suffer thy foot to be moved : and he that keepeth thee will not sleep.

4 Behold, he that keepeth Israel : shall neither slumber nor sleep.

5 The LORD himself is thy keeper : the LORD is thy defence upon thy right hand ;

6 So that the sun shall not burn thee by day : neither the moon by night.

7 The LORD shall preserve thee from all evil : yea, it is even he that shall keep thy soul.

8 The LORD shall preserve thy going out, and thy coming in : from this time forth for evermore.

PSALM 122.

Lætatus sum.

I WAS glad when they said unto me : We will go into the house of the LORD.

2 Our feet shall stand in thy gates : O Jerusalem.

3 Jerusalem is built as a city : that is at unity in itself.

4 For thither the tribes go up, even the tribes of the LORD : to testify unto Israel, to give thanks unto the Name of the LORD.

5 For there is the seat of judgment : even the seat of the house of David.

6 O pray for the peace of Jerusalem : they shall prosper that love thee.

7 Peace be within thy walls : and plenteousness within thy palaces.

8 For my brethren and companions' sakes : I will wish thee prosperity.

9 Yea, because of the house of the LORD our God : I will seek to do thee good.

PSALM 123.

Ad te levavi oculos meos.

UNTO thee lift I up mine eyes : O thou that dwellest in the heavens.

2 Behold, even as the eyes of servants look unto the hand of their masters, and as the eyes of a maiden unto the hand of her mistress : even so our eyes wait upon the LORD our God, until he have mercy upon us.

3 Have mercy upon us, O LORD, have mercy upon us : for we are utterly despised.

4 Our soul is filled with the scornful reproof of the wealthy : and with

the despitefulness of the proud.

PSALM 124.
Nisi quia Dominus.

IF the Lord himself had not been on our side, now may Israel say : if the Lord himself had not been on our side, when men rose up against us ;

2 They had swallowed us up quick: when they were so wrathfully displeased at us.

3 Yea, the waters had drowned us : and the stream had gone over our soul.

4 The deep waters of the proud : had gone even over our soul.

5 But praised be the Lord : who hath not given us over for a prey unto their teeth.

6 Our soul is escaped even as a bird out of the snare of the fowler : the snare is broken, and we are delivered.

7 Our help standeth in the Name of the Lord : who hath made heaven and earth.

PSALM 125.
Qui confidunt.

THEY that put their trust in the Lord shall be even as the mount Sion: which may not be removed, but standeth fast for ever.

2 The hills stand about Jerusalem : even so standeth the Lord round about his people, from this time forth for evermore.

3 For the rod of the ungodly cometh not into the lot of the righteous : lest the righteous put their hand unto wickedness.

4 Do well, O Lord : unto those that are good and true of heart.

5 As for such as turn back unto their own wickedness : the Lord shall lead them forth with the evil doers ; but peace shall be upon Israel.

✠

Evening Prayer.
PSALM 126.
In convertendo.

WHEN the Lord turned again the captivity of Sion : then were we like unto them that dream.

2 Then was our mouth filled with laughter : and our tongue with joy.

3 Then said they among the heathen : The Lord hath done great things for them.

4 Yea, the Lord hath done great things for us already : whereof we rejoice.

5 Turn our captivity, O Lord : as the rivers in the south.

6 They that sow in tears : shall reap in joy.

7 He that now goeth on his way weeping, and beareth forth good seed : shall doubtless come again with joy, and bring his sheaves with him.

Psalm 127.
Nisi Dominus.

EXCEPT the Lord build the house : their labour is but lost that build it.

2 Except the Lord keep the city : the watchman waketh but in vain.

3 It is but lost labour that ye haste to rise up early, and so late take rest, and eat the bread of carefulness : for so he giveth his beloved sleep.

4 Lo, children, and the fruit of the womb : are an heritage and gift that cometh of the Lord.

5 Like as the arrows in the hand of the giant : even so are the young children.

6 Happy is the man that hath his quiver full of them : they shall not be ashamed when they speak with their enemies in the gate.

Psalm 128.
Beati omnes.

BLESSED are all they that fear the Lord : and walk in his ways.

2 For thou shalt eat the labours of thine hands : O well is thee, and happy shalt thou be.

3 Thy wife shall be as the fruitful vine : upon the walls of thine house.

4 Thy children like the olive-branches : round about thy table.

5 Lo, thus shall the man be blessed : that feareth the Lord.

6 The Lord from out of Sion shall so bless thee : that thou shalt see Jerusalem in prosperity all thy life long ;

7 Yea, that thou shalt see thy children's children : and peace upon Israel.

Psalm 129.
Sæpe expugnaverunt.

MANY a time have they fought against me from my youth up : may Israel now say ;

2 Yea, many a time have they vexed me from my youth up : but they have not prevailed against me.

3 The plowers plowed upon my back : and made long furrows.

4 But the righteous Lord : hath hewn the snares of the ungodly in pieces.

5 Let them be confounded and turned backward :

as many as have evil will
at Sion.

6 Let them be even as
the grass growing upon the
housetops : which wither-
eth afore it be plucked up;

7 Whereof the mower
filleth not his hand : neither he that bindeth up
the sheaves his bosom.

8 So that they who go
by say not so much as,
The LORD prosper you :
we wish you good luck in
the Name of the LORD.

Psalm 130.

De profundis.

OUT of the deep have I
called unto thee, O
LORD : Lord, hear my voice.

2 O let thine ears con-
sider well : the voice of
my complaint.

3 If thou, LORD, wilt be
extreme to mark what is
done amiss : O Lord, who
may abide it?

4 For there is mercy
with thee : therefore shalt
thou be feared.

5 I look for the LORD ;
my soul doth wait for him :
in his word is my trust.

6 My soul fleeth unto
the Lord : before the
morning watch, I say, be-
fore the morning watch.

7 O Israel, trust in the
LORD, for with the LORD

there is mercy : and with
him is plenteous redemp-
tion.

8 And he shall redeem
Israel : from all his sins.

Psalm 131.

Domine, non est.

LORD, I am not high-
minded : I have no
proud looks.

2 I do not exercise my-
self in great matters :
which are too high for me.

3 But I refrain my soul,
and keep it low, like as a
child that is weaned from
his mother : yea, my soul
is even as a weaned child.

4 O Israel, trust in the
LORD : from this time
forth for evermore.

❂

THE TWENTY-EIGHTH DAY.

Morning Prayer.

Psalm 132.

Memento, Domine.

LORD, remember David :
and all his trouble ;

2 How he sware unto
the LORD : and vowed a
vow unto the Almighty
God of Jacob ;

3 I will not come within the
tabernacle of mine house :
nor climb up into my bed ;

4 I will not suffer mine
eyes to sleep, nor mine

eyelids to slumber : neither the temples of my head to take any rest ;

5 Until I find out a place for the temple of the LORD : an habitation for the Mighty God of Jacob.

6 Lo, we heard of the same at Ephrata : and found it in the wood.

7 We will go into his tabernacle : and fall low on our knees before his footstool.

8 Arise, O LORD, into thy resting-place : thou, and the ark of thy strength.

9 Let thy priests be clothed with righteousness : and let thy saints sing with joyfulness.

10 For thy servant David's sake : turn not away the presence of thine anointed.

11 The LORD hath made a faithful oath unto David : and he shall not shrink from it :

12 Of the fruit of thy body : shall I set upon thy seat.

13 If thy children will keep my covenant, and my testimonies that I shall learn them : their children also shall sit upon thy seat for evermore.

14 For the LORD hath chosen Sion to be an habitation for himself : he hath longed for her.

15 This shall be my rest for ever : here will I dwell, for I have a delight therein.

16 I will bless her victuals with increase : and will satisfy her poor with bread.

17 I will deck her priests with health : and her saints shall rejoice and sing.

18 There shall I make the horn of David to flourish : I have ordained a lantern for mine anointed.

19 As for his enemies, I shall clothe them with shame : but upon himself shall his crown flourish.

PSALM 133.
Ecce, quam bonum!

BEHOLD, how good and joyful a thing it is : brethren to dwell together in unity!

2 It is like the precious ointment upon the head, that ran down unto the beard : even unto Aaron's beard, and went down to the skirts of his clothing.

3 Like as the dew of Hermon : which fell upon the hill of Sion.

4 For there the LORD promised his blessing : and life for evermore.

PSALM 134.
Ecce nunc.

BEHOLD now, praise the LORD : all ye servants of the LORD ;

2 Ye that by night stand in the house of the LORD : even in the courts of the house of our God.

3 Lift up your hands in the sanctuary : and praise the LORD.

4 The LORD that made heaven and earth : give thee blessing out of Sion.

PSALM 135.

Laudate Nomen.

O PRAISE the LORD, laud ye the Name of the LORD : praise it, O ye servants of the LORD ;

2 Ye that stand in the house of the LORD : in the courts of the house of our God.

3 O praise the LORD, for the LORD is gracious : O sing praises unto his Name, for it is lovely.

4 For why? the LORD hath chosen Jacob unto himself : and Israel for his own possession.

5 For I know that the LORD is great : and that our Lord is above all gods.

6 Whatsoever the LORD pleased, that did he in heaven, and in earth : and in the sea, and in all deep places.

7 He bringeth forth the clouds from the ends of the world : and sendeth forth lightnings with the rain, bringing the winds out of his treasures.

8 He smote the first-born of Egypt : both of man and beast.

9 He hath sent tokens and wonders into the midst of thee, O thou land of E-gypt : upon Pharaoh, and all his servants.

10 He smote divers nations : and slew mighty kings :

11 Sehon, king of the Amorites, and Og, the king of Basan : and all the kingdoms of Canaan ;

12 And gave their land to be an heritage : even an heritage unto Israel his people.

13 Thy Name, O LORD, endureth for ever : so doth thy memorial, O LORD, from one generation to another.

14 For the LORD will avenge his people : and be gracious unto his servants.

15 As for the images of the heathen, they are but silver and gold : the work of men's hands.

16 They have mouths, and speak not : eyes have they, but they see not.

17 They have ears, and yet they hear not : neither is there any breath in their mouths.

18 They that make them

are like unto them : and so are all they that put their trust in them.

19 Praise the LORD, ye house of Israel : praise the LORD, ye house of Aaron.

20 Praise the LORD, ye house of Levi : ye that fear the LORD, praise the LORD.

21 Praised be the LORD out of Sion : who dwelleth at Jerusalem.

☙

Ebening Prayer.

PSALM 136.

Confitemini.

O GIVE thanks unto the LORD, for he is gracious : and his mercy endureth for ever.

2 O give thanks unto the God of all gods : for his mercy endureth for ever.

3 O thank the Lord of all lords : for his mercy endureth for ever.

4 Who only doeth great wonders : for his mercy endureth for ever.

5 Who by his excellent wisdom made the heavens : for his mercy endureth for ever.

6 Who laid out the earth above the waters : for his mercy endureth for ever.

7 Who hath made great lights : for his mercy endureth for ever :

8 The sun to rule the day : for his mercy endureth for ever ;

9 The moon and the stars to govern the night : for his mercy endureth for ever.

10 Who smote Egypt, with their firstborn : for his mercy endureth for ever ;

11 And brought out Israel from among them : for his mercy endureth for ever ;

12 With a mighty hand and stretched-out arm : for his mercy endureth for ever.

13 Who divided the Red Sea in two parts : for his mercy endureth for ever ;

14 And made Israel to go through the midst of it : for his mercy endureth for ever.

15 But as for Pharaoh and his host, he overthrew them in the Red Sea : for his mercy endureth for ever.

16 Who led his people through the wilderness : for his mercy endureth for ever.

17 Who smote great kings : for his mercy endureth for ever ;

18 Yea, and slew mighty kings : for his mercy endureth for ever ;

19 Sehon, king of the Amorites : for his mercy endureth for ever ;

20 And Og, the king of

Basan : for his mercy endureth for ever ;

21 And gave away their land for an heritage : for his mercy endureth for ever ;

22 Even for an heritage unto Israel his servant : for his mercy endureth for ever.

23 Who remembered us when we were in trouble : for his mercy endureth for ever ;

24 And hath delivered us from our enemies : for his mercy endureth for ever.

25 Who giveth food to all flesh : for his mercy endureth for ever.

26 O give thanks unto the God of heaven : for his mercy endureth for ever.

27 O give thanks unto the Lord of lords : for his mercy endureth for ever.

Psalm 137.
Super flumina.

BY the waters of Babylon we sat down and wept : when we remembered thee, O Sion.

2 As for our harps, we hanged them up : upon the trees that are therein.

3 For they that led us away captive, required of us then a song, and melody in our heaviness : Sing us one of the songs of Sion.

4 How shall we sing the Lord's song : in a strange land ?

5 If I forget thee, O Jerusalem : let my right hand forget her cunning.

6 If I do not remember thee, let my tongue cleave to the roof of my mouth : yea, if I prefer not Jerusalem in my mirth.

7 Remember the children of Edom, O Lord, in the day of Jerusalem : how they said, Down with it, down with it, even to the ground.

8 O daughter of Babylon, wasted with misery : yea, happy shall he be that rewardeth thee as thou hast served us.

9 Blessed shall he be that taketh thy children : and throweth them against the stones.

Psalm 138.
Confitebor tibi.

I WILL give thanks unto thee, O Lord, with my whole heart : even before the gods will I sing praise unto thee.

2 I will worship toward thy holy temple, and praise thy Name, because of thy loving-kindness and truth : for thou hast magnified thy Name, and thy word, above all things.

3 When I called upon thee, thou heardest me :

and enduedst my soul with much strength.

4 All the kings of the earth shall praise thee, O Lord : for they have heard the words of thy mouth.

5 Yea, they shall sing in the ways of the Lord : that great is the glory of the Lord.

6 For though the Lord be high, yet hath he respect unto the lowly : as for the proud, he beholdeth them afar off.

7 Though I walk in the midst of trouble, yet shalt thou refresh me : thou shalt stretch forth thy hand upon the furiousness of mine enemies, and thy right hand shall save me.

8 The Lord shall make good his loving-kindness toward me : yea, thy mercy, O Lord, endureth for ever ; despise not then the works of thine own hands.

❖

THE TWENTY-NINTH DAY.

Morning Prayer.

Psalm 139.
Domine, probasti.

O LORD, thou hast searched me out, and known me : thou knowest my down-sitting, and mine uprising ; thou understandest my thoughts long before.

2 Thou art about my path, and about my bed : and spiest out all my ways.

3 For lo, there is not a word in my tongue : but thou, O Lord, knowest it altogether.

4 Thou hast fashioned me behind and before : and laid thine hand upon me.

5 Such knowledge is too wonderful and excellent for me : I cannot attain unto it.

6 Whither shall I go then from thy Spirit : or whither shall I go then from thy presence ?

7 If I climb up into heaven, thou art there : if I go down to hell, thou art there also.

8 If I take the wings of the morning : and remain in the uttermost parts of the sea ;

9 Even there also shall thy hand lead me : and thy right hand shall hold me.

10 If I say, Peradventure the darkness shall cover me : then shall my night be turned to day.

11 Yea, the darkness is no darkness with thee, but the night is as clear as the day : the darkness and light to thee are both alike.

12 For my reins are thine : thou hast covered me in my mother's womb.

13 I will give thanks unto thee, for I am fearfully and

wonderfully made : marvellous are thy works, and that my soul knoweth right well.

14 My bones are not hid from thee : though I be made secretly, and fashioned beneath in the earth.

15 Thine eyes did see my substance, yet being imperfect : and in thy book were all my members written ;

16 Which day by day were fashioned : when as yet there was none of them.

17 How dear are thy counsels unto me, O God : O how great is the sum of them !

18 If I tell them, they are more in number than the sand : when I wake up, I am present with thee.

19 Wilt thou not slay the wicked, O God : Depart from me, ye bloodthirsty men.

20 For they speak unrighteously against thee : and thine enemies take thy Name in vain.

21 Do not I hate them, O LORD, that hate thee : and am not I grieved with those that rise up against thee ?

22 Yea, I hate them right sore : even as though they were mine enemies.

23 Try me, O God, and seek the ground of my heart : prove me, and examine my thoughts.

24 Look well if there be any way of wickedness in me : and lead me in the way everlasting.

PSALM 140.
Eripe me, Domine.

DELIVER me, O LORD, from the evil man : and preserve me from the wicked man ;

2 Who imagine mischief in their hearts : and stir up strife all the day long.

3 They have sharpened their tongues like a serpent : adder's poison is under their lips.

4 Keep me, O LORD, from the hands of the ungodly : preserve me from the wicked men, who are purposed to overthrow my goings.

5 The proud have laid a snare for me, and spread a net abroad with cords : yea, and set traps in my way.

6 I said unto the LORD, Thou art my God : hear the voice of my prayers, O LORD.

7 O LORD God, thou strength of my health : thou hast covered my head in the day of battle.

8 Let not the ungodly have his desire, O LORD : let not his mischievous

imagination prosper, lest they be too proud.

9 Let the mischief of their own lips fall upon the head of them : that compass me about.

10 Let hot burning coals fall upon them : let them be cast into the fire, and into the pit, that they never rise up again.

11 A man full of words shall not prosper upon the earth : evil shall hunt the wicked person to overthrow him.

12 Sure I am that the LORD will avenge the poor : and maintain the cause of the helpless.

13 The righteous also shall give thanks unto thy Name : and the just shall continue in thy sight.

✿

Evening Prayer.

PSALM 141.
Domine, clamavi.

LORD, I call upon thee, haste thee unto me : and consider my voice, when I cry unto thee.

2 Let my prayer be set forth in thy sight as the incense : and let the lifting up of my hands be an evening sacrifice.

3 Set a watch, O LORD,

before my mouth : and keep the door of my lips.

4 O let not mine heart be inclined to any evil thing : let me not be occupied in ungodly works with the men that work wickedness, lest I eat of such things as please them.

5 Let the righteous rather smite me friendly : and reprove me.

6 But let not their precious balms break my head : yea, I will pray yet against their wickedness.

7 Let their judges be overthrown in stony places : that they may hear my words ; for they are sweet.

8 Our bones lie scattered before the pit : like as when one breaketh and heweth wood upon the earth.

9 But mine eyes look unto thee, O LORD God : in thee is my trust ; O cast not out my soul.

10 Keep me from the snare that they have laid for me : and from the traps of the wicked doers.

11 Let the ungodly fall into their own nets together : and let me ever escape them.

PSALM 142.
Voce mea ad Dominum.

I CRIED unto the LORD with my voice : yea,

even unto the LORD did I make my supplication.

2 I poured out my complaints before him : and showed him of my trouble.

3 When my spirit was in heaviness, thou knewest my path : in the way wherein I walked, have they privily laid a snare for me.

4 I looked also upon my right hand : and saw there was no man that would know me.

5 I had no place to flee unto : and no man cared for my soul.

6 I cried unto thee, O LORD, and said : Thou art my hope, and my portion in the land of the living.

7 Consider my complaint : for I am brought very low.

8 O deliver me from my persecutors : for they are too strong for me.

9 Bring my soul out of prison, that I may give thanks unto thy Name : which thing if thou wilt grant me, then shall the righteous resort unto my company.

Psalm 143.
Domine, exaudi.

HEAR my prayer, O LORD, and consider my desire : hearken unto me for thy truth and righteousness' sake.

2 And enter not into judgment with thy servant : for in thy sight shall no man living be justified.

3 For the enemy hath persecuted my soul ; he hath smitten my life down to the ground : he hath laid me in the darkness, as the men that have been long dead.

4 Therefore is my spirit vexed within me : and my heart within me is desolate.

5 Yet do I remember the time past ; I muse upon all thy works : yea, I exercise myself in the works of thy hands.

6 I stretch forth my hands unto thee : my soul gaspeth unto thee as a thirsty land.

7 Hear me, O LORD, and that soon, for my spirit waxeth faint : hide not thy face from me, lest I be like unto them that go down into the pit.

8 O let me hear thy loving-kindness betimes in the morning, for in thee is my trust : show thou me the way that I should walk in, for I lift up my soul unto thee.

9 Deliver me, O LORD, from mine enemies : for I flee unto thee to hide me.

10 Teach me to do the thing that pleaseth thee ; for thou art my God : let

thy loving Spirit lead me forth into the land of righteousness.

11 Quicken me, O Lord, for thy Name's sake : and for thy righteousness' sake bring my soul out of trouble.

12 And of thy goodness slay mine enemies : and destroy all them that vex my soul ; for I am thy servant.

THE THIRTIETH DAY.

Morning Prayer.

PSALM 144.

Benedictus Dominus.

BLESSED be the Lord my strength : who teacheth my hands to war, and my fingers to fight ;

2 My hope and my fortress, my castle and deliverer, my defender in whom I trust : who subdueth my people that is under me.

3 Lord, what is man, that thou hast such respect unto him : or the son of man, that thou so regardest him ?

4 Man is like a thing of nought : his time passeth away like a shadow.

5 Bow thy heavens, O Lord, and come down : touch the mountains, and they shall smoke.

6 Cast forth thy light-

ning, and tear them : shoot out thine arrows, and consume them.

7 Send down thine hand from above : deliver me, and take me out of the great waters, from the hand of strange children ;

8 Whose mouth talketh of vanity : and their right hand is a right hand of wickedness.

9 I will sing a new song unto thee, O God : and sing praises unto thee upon a ten-stringed lute.

10 Thou hast given victory unto kings : and hast delivered David thy servant from the peril of the sword.

11 Save me, and deliver me from the hand of strange children : whose mouth talketh of vanity, and their right hand is a right hand of iniquity :

12 That our sons may grow up as the young plants : and that our daughters may be as the polished corners of the temple ;

13 That our garners may be full and plenteous with all manner of store : that our sheep may bring forth thousands, and ten thousands in our streets ;

14 That our oxen may be strong to labour, that there be no decay : no lead-

ing into captivity, and no complaining in our streets.

15 Happy are the people that are in such a case : yea, blessed are the people who have the LORD for their God.

PSALM 145.

Exaltabo te, Deus.

I WILL magnify thee, O God, my King : and I will praise thy Name for ever and ever.

2 Every day will I give thanks unto thee : and praise thy Name for ever and ever.

3 Great is the LORD, and marvellous worthy to be praised : there is no end of his greatness.

4 One generation shall praise thy works unto another : and declare thy power.

5 As for me, I will be talking of thy worship : thy glory, thy praise, and wondrous works ;

6 So that men shall speak of the might of thy marvellous acts: and I will also tell of thy greatness.

7 The memorial of thine abundant kindness shall be showed : and men shall sing of thy righteousness.

8 The LORD is gracious and merciful : long-suffering, and of great goodness.

9 The LORD is loving unto every man : and his mercy is over all his works.

10 All thy works praise thee, O LORD: and thy saints give thanks unto thee.

11 They show the glory of thy kingdom : and talk of thy power ;

12 That thy power, thy glory, and mightiness of thy kingdom : might be known unto men.

13 Thy kingdom is an everlasting kingdom : and thy dominion endureth throughout all ages.

14 The LORD upholdeth all such as fall : and lifteth up all those that are down.

15 The eyes of all wait upon thee, O Lord : and thou givest them their meat in due season.

16 Thou openest thine hand : and fillest all things living with plenteousness.

17 The LORD is righteous in all his ways : and holy in all his works.

18 The LORD is nigh unto all them that call upon him : yea, all such as call upon him faithfully.

19 He will fulfil the desire of them that fear him : he also will hear their cry, and will help them.

20 The LORD preserveth all them that love him :

but scattereth abroad all the ungodly.

21 My mouth shall speak the praise of the LORD : and let all flesh give thanks unto his holy Name for ever and ever.

Psalm 146.

Lauda, anima mea.

PRAISE the LORD, O my soul; while I live, will I praise the LORD : yea, as long as I have any being, I will sing praises unto my God.

2 O put not your trust in princes, nor in any child of man : for there is no help in them.

3 For when the breath of man goeth forth, he shall turn again to his earth : and then all his thoughts perish.

4 Blessed is he that hath the God of Jacob for his help : and whose hope is in the LORD his God :

5 Who made heaven and earth, the sea, and all that therein is : who keepeth his promise for ever ;

6 Who helpeth them to right that suffer wrong : who feedeth the hungry.

7 The LORD looseth men out of prison : the LORD giveth sight to the blind.

8 The LORD helpeth them that are fallen : the LORD careth for the righteous.

9 The LORD careth for the strangers; he defendeth the fatherless and widow : as for the way of the ungodly, he turneth it upside down.

10 The LORD thy God, O Sion, shall be King for evermore : and throughout all generations.

❂

Evening Prayer.

Psalm 147.

Laudate Dominum.

O PRAISE the LORD, for it is a good thing to sing praises unto our God : yea, a joyful and pleasant thing it is to be thankful.

2 The LORD doth build up Jerusalem : and gather together the outcasts of Israel.

3 He healeth those that are broken in heart : and giveth medicine to heal their sickness.

4 He telleth the number of the stars : and calleth them all by their names.

5 Great is our Lord, and great is his power : yea, and his wisdom is infinite.

6 The LORD setteth up the meek : and bringeth the ungodly down to the ground.

7 O sing unto the LORD with thanksgiving : sing

praises upon the harp unto our God :

8 Who covereth the heaven with clouds, and prepareth rain for the earth : and maketh the grass to grow upon the mountains, and herb for the use of men;

9 Who giveth fodder unto the cattle : and feedeth the young ravens that call upon him.

10 He hath no pleasure in the strength of an horse : neither delighteth he in any man's legs.

11 But the Lord's delight is in them that fear him : and put their trust in his mercy.

12 Praise the Lord, O Jerusalem : praise thy God, O Sion.

13 For he hath made fast the bars of thy gates : and hath blessed thy children within thee.

14 He maketh peace in thy borders : and filleth thee with the flour of wheat.

15 He sendeth forth his commandment upon earth : and his word runneth very swiftly.

16 He giveth snow like wool : and scattereth the hoar-frost like ashes.

17 He casteth forth his ice like morsels : who is able to abide his frost ?

18 He sendeth out his word, and melteth them : he bloweth with his wind, and the waters flow.

19 He showeth his word unto Jacob : his statutes and ordinances unto Israel.

20 He hath not dealt so with any nation : neither have the heathen knowledge of his laws.

PSALM 148.

Laudate Dominum.

O PRAISE the Lord of heaven : praise him in the height.

2 Praise him, all ye angels of his : praise him, all his host.

3 Praise him, sun and moon : praise him, all ye stars and light.

4 Praise him, all ye heavens : and ye waters that are above the heavens.

5 Let them praise the Name of the Lord : for he spake the word, and they were made ; he commanded, and they were created.

6 He hath made them fast for ever and ever : he hath given them a law which shall not be broken.

7 Praise the Lord upon earth : ye dragons and all deeps :

8 Fire and hail, snow and vapours : wind and storm, fulfilling his word ;

9 Mountains and all hills : fruitful trees and all cedars ;

10 Beasts and all cattle : worms and feathered fowls;

11 Kings of the earth, and all people : princes, and all judges of the world ;

12 Young men and maidens, old men and children, praise the Name of the LORD : for his Name only is excellent, and his praise above heaven and earth.

13 He shall exalt the horn of his people : all his saints shall praise him: even the children of Israel, even the people that serveth him.

PSALM 149.

Cantate Domino.

O SING unto the LORD a new song : let the congregation of saints praise him.

2 Let Israel rejoice in him that made him : and let the children of Sion be joyful in their King.

3 Let them praise his Name in the dance : let them sing praises unto him with tabret and harp.

4 For the LORD hath pleasure in his people : and helpeth the meek-hearted.

5 Let the saints be joyful with glory : let them rejoice in their beds.

6 Let the praises of God be in their mouth : and a two-edged sword in their hands ;

7 To be avenged of the heathen : and to rebuke the people ;

8 To bind their kings in chains : and their nobles with links of iron ;

9 That they may be avenged of them, as it is written : Such honour have all his saints.

PSALM 150.

Laudate Dominum.

O PRAISE God in his holiness : praise him in the firmament of his power.

2 Praise him in his noble acts : praise him according to his excellent greatness.

3 Praise him in the sound of the trumpet : praise him upon the lute and harp.

4 Praise him in the cymbals and dances : praise him upon the strings and pipe.

5 Praise him upon the well-tuned cymbals : praise him upon the loud cymbals.

6 Let every thing that hath breath : praise the LORD.

THE END OF THE PSALTER.

THE FORM AND MANNER OF

MAKING, ORDAINING, AND CONSECRATING

BISHOPS, PRIESTS, AND DEACONS;

ACCORDING TO THE ORDER OF THE PROTESTANT EPISCOPAL CHURCH IN THE UNITED STATES OF AMERICA, AS ESTABLISHED BY THE BISHOPS, THE CLERGY, AND LAITY OF SAID CHURCH, IN GENERAL CONVENTION, IN THE MONTH OF SEPTEMBER, A. D. 1792.

❊

THE PREFACE.

*I*T *is evident unto all men, diligently reading Holy Scripture and ancient Authors, that from the Apostles' time there have been these Orders of Ministers in Christ's Church,—Bishops, Priests, and Deacons. Which Offices were evermore had in such reverend estimation, that no man might presume to execute any of them, except he were first called, tried, examined, and known to have such qualities as are requisite for the same ; and also by public Prayer, with Imposition of Hands, were approved and admitted thereunto by lawful Authority. And therefore, to the intent that these Orders may be continued, and reverently used and esteemed in this Church, no man shall be accounted or taken to be a lawful Bishop, Priest, or Deacon, in this Church, or suffered to execute any of the said Functions, except he be called, tried, examined, and admitted thereunto, according to the Form hereafter following, or hath had Episcopal Consecration or Ordination.*

And none shall be admitted a Deacon, Priest, or Bishop, except he be of the age which the Canon in that case provided may require.

And the Bishop, knowing either by himself, or by sufficient testimony, any Person to be a man of virtuous conversation, and without crime ; and, after examination and trial, finding him sufficiently instructed in the Holy Scripture, and otherwise learned as the Canons require, may, at the times appointed, or else, on urgent occasion, upon some other day, in the face of the Church, admit him a Deacon, in such manner and form as followeth.

THE FORM AND MANNER OF

MAKING DEACONS.

¶ *When the day appointed by the Bishop is come, after Morning Prayer is ended, there shall be a Sermon, or Exhortation, declaring the Duty and Office of such as come to be admitted Deacons; how necessary that Order is in the Church of Christ, and also, how the People ought to esteem them in their Office.*

¶ *A Priest shall present unto the Bishop, sitting in his chair near to the Holy Table, such as desire to be ordained Deacons, each of them being decently habited, saying these words,*

REVEREND Father in God, I present unto you these persons present, to be admitted Deacons.

The Bishop.

TAKE heed that the persons, whom ye present unto us, be apt and meet, for their learning and godly conversation, to exercise their Ministry duly, to the honour of God, and the edifying of his Church.

¶ *The Priest shall answer,*

I HAVE inquired concerning them, and also examined them, and think them so to be.

¶ *Then the Bishop shall say unto the People,*

BRETHREN, if there be any of you who knoweth any Impediment, or notable Crime, in any of these persons presented to be ordered Deacons, for the which he ought not to be admitted to that Office, let him come forth in the Name of God, and show what the Crime or Impediment is.

¶ *And if any great Crime or Impediment be objected, the Bishop shall cease from Ordering that person, until such time as the party accused shall be found clear of that Crime.*

¶ *Then the Bishop (commending such as shall be found meet to be Ordered, to the Prayers of the congregation) shall, with the Clergy and People present, say the Litany.*

¶ *Then shall be said the Service for the Communion, with the Collect, Epistle, and Gospel, as followeth.*

The Collect.

ALMIGHTY God, who by thy divine providence hast appointed divers Orders of Ministers in thy Church, and didst inspire thine Apostles to choose into the Order of Deacons the first Martyr Saint Stephen, with others; Mercifully behold these thy servants now called to the like Office and Administration: so replenish them with the truth of thy Doctrine, and adorn them with innocency of life, that, both by word and good example, they may faithfully serve thee in this Office, to the glory of thy Name, and the edification of thy Church; through the merits of our Saviour Jesus Christ, who liveth and reigneth with thee and the

Holy Ghost, now and for ever. *Amen.*

The Epistle. 1 Tim. iii. 8.

LIKEWISE must the deacons be grave, not doubletongued, not given to much wine, not greedy of filthy lucre; holding the mystery of the faith in a pure conscience. And let these also first be proved; then let them use the office of a deacon, being found blameless. Even so must their wives be grave, not slanderers, sober, faithful in all things. Let the deacons be the husbands of one wife, ruling their children and their own houses well. For they that have used the office of a deacon well purchase to themselves a good degree, and great boldness in the faith which is in Christ Jesus.

¶ *Or else this, out of the sixth Chapter of the Acts of the Apostles.*

Acts vi. 2.

THEN the twelve called the multitude of the disciples unto them, and said, It is not reason that we should leave the word of God, and serve tables. Wherefore, brethren, look ye out among you seven men of honest report, full of the Holy Ghost and wisdom, whom we may appoint over this business. But we will give ourselves continually to prayer, and to the ministry of the word. *And the saying pleased the whole multitude: and they chose Stephen, a man full of faith and of the Holy Ghost, and Philip, and Prochorus, and Nicanor, and Timon, and Parmenas, and Nicolas a proselyte of Antioch: whom they set before the apostles: and when they had prayed, they laid their hands on them. And the word of God increased;* and the number of the disciples multiplied in Jerusalem greatly; and a great company of the priests were obedient to the faith.

¶ *Then shall the Bishop examine every one of those who are to be Ordered, in the presence of the People, after this manner following.*

DO you trust that you are inwardly moved by the Holy Ghost to take upon you this Office and Ministration, to serve God for the promoting of his glory, and the edifying of his people?

Answer. I trust so.

The Bishop.

DO you think that you are truly called, according to the will of our Lord Jesus Christ, and according to the Canons of this Church, to the Ministry of the same?

Answer. I think so.

The Bishop.

DO you unfeignedly believe all the Canonical Scriptures of the Old and New Testament?

Answer. I do believe them.

The Bishop.

WILL you diligently read the same unto the people assembled in the Church where you shall be appointed to serve?

Answer. I will.

The Bishop.

IT appertaineth to the Office of a Deacon, in the Church where he shall be appointed to serve, to assist the Priest in Divine Service, and specially when he ministereth the Holy Communion, and to help him in the distribution thereof; and to read Holy Scriptures and Homilies in the Church; and to instruct the youth in the Catechism; in the absence of the Priest to baptize infants; and to preach, if he be admitted thereto by the Bishop. And furthermore, it is his Office, where provision is so made, to search for the sick, poor, and impotent people of the Parish, to intimate their estates, names, and places where they dwell, unto the Curate, that by his exhortation they may be relieved with the alms of the Parishioners, or others. Will you do this gladly and willingly?

Answer. I will so do, by the help of God.

The Bishop.

WILL you apply all your diligence to frame and fashion your own lives, and the lives of your families, according to the Doctrine of Christ; and to make both yourselves and them, as much as in you lieth, wholesome examples of the flock of Christ?

Answer. I will so do, the Lord being my helper.

The Bishop.

WILL you reverently obey your Bishop, and other chief Ministers, who, according to the Canons of the Church, may have the charge and government over you; following with a glad mind and will their godly admonitions?

Answer. I will endeavour so to do, the Lord being my helper.

¶ *Then the Bishop, laying his Hands severally upon the Head of every one of them, humbly kneeling before him, shall say,*

TAKE thou Authority to execute the Office of a Deacon in the Church of God committed unto thee; In the Name of the Father, and of the Son, and of the Holy Ghost. Amen.

¶ *Then shall the Bishop deliver to every one of them the New Testament, saying,*

TAKE thou Authority to read the Gospel in the Church of God, and to preach the same, if thou be thereto licensed by the Bishop himself.

¶ *Then one of them, appointed by the Bishop, shall read the Gospel.*

St. Luke xii. 35.

LET your loins be girded about, and your lights burning; and ye yourselves like unto men that wait for their lord, when he will return from the wedding; that when he cometh and knocketh, they may open unto him immediately. Blessed are those servants, whom the lord when he cometh shall find watching: verily I say unto you, that he shall gird himself, and make them to sit down to meat, and will come forth and serve them. And if he shall come in the second watch, or come in the third watch, and find them so, blessed are those servants.

¶ *Then shall the Bishop proceed in the Communion; and all who are Ordered shall tarry, and receive the Holy Communion the same day, with the Bishop.*

¶ *The Communion ended, after the last Collect, and immediately before the Benediction, shall be said this Collect following.*

ALMIGHTY God, giver of all good things, who of thy great goodness hast vouchsafed to accept and take these thy servants unto the Office of Deacons in thy Church; Make them, we beseech thee, O Lord, to be modest, humble, and constant in their Ministration, to have a ready will to observe all spiritual Discipline; that they, having always the testimony of a good conscience, and continuing ever stable and strong in thy Son Christ, may so well behave themselves in this inferior Office, that they may be found worthy to be called unto the higher Ministries in thy Church; through the same thy Son our Saviour Jesus Christ, to whom be glory and honour, world without end. *Amen.*

THE Peace of God, which passeth all understanding, keep your hearts and minds in the knowledge and love of God, and of his Son Jesus Christ our Lord: And the Blessing of God Almighty, the Father, the Son, and the Holy Ghost, be amongst you, and remain with you always. *Amen.*

¶ And here it must be declared unto the Deacon, that he must continue in that Office of a Deacon the space of a whole year, (except for reasonable causes it shall otherwise seem good unto the Bishop,) to the intent he may be perfect and well expert in the things appertaining to the Ecclesiastical Administration. In executing whereof if he be found faithful and diligent, he may be admitted by his Diocesan to the Order of Priesthood, at the times appointed in the Canon; or else, on urgent occasion, upon some other day, in the face of the Church, in such manner and form as hereafter followeth.

THE FORM AND MANNER OF
ORDERING PRIESTS.

¶ When the day appointed by the Bishop is come, after Morning Prayer is ended, there shall be a Sermon, or Exhortation, declaring the Duty and Office of such as come to be admitted Priests; how necessary that Order is in the Church of Christ, and also, how the People ought to esteem them in their Office.

¶ A Priest shall present unto the Bishop, sitting in his chair near to the Holy Table, all those who are to receive the Order of Priesthood that day, each of them being decently habited, and shall say,

REVEREND Father in God, I present unto you these persons present, to be admitted to the Order of Priesthood.

The Bishop.

TAKE heed that the persons, whom ye present unto us, be apt and meet, for their learning and godly conversation, to exercise their Ministry duly, to the honour of God, and the edifying of his Church.

¶ The Priest shall answer,

I HAVE inquired concerning them, and also examined them, and think them so to be.

¶ Then the Bishop shall say unto the People,

GOOD People, these are they whom we purpose, God

willing, to receive this day unto the holy Office of Priesthood; for, after due examination, we find not to the contrary, but that they are lawfully called to their Function and Ministry, and that they are persons meet for the same. But yet, if there be any of you who knoweth any Impediment, or notable Crime, in any of them, for the which he ought not to be received into this holy Ministry, let him come forth in the Name of God, and show what the Crime or Impediment is.

¶ *And if any great Crime or Impediment be objected, the Bishop shall cease from Ordering that person, until such time as the party accused shall be found clear of that Crime.*

¶ *Then the Bishop (commending such as shall be found meet to be Ordered, to the Prayer of the congregation) shall, with the Clergy and People present, say the Litany, with the Prayers, as before appointed in the Form of Ordering Deacons : save only, that in the proper Suffrage there added, the word Deacons shall be omitted, and the word Priests inserted instead of it.*

¶ *Then shall be said the Service for the Communion, with the Collect, Epistle, and Gospel, as followeth.*

The Collect.

ALMIGHTY God, giver of all good things, who by thy Holy Spirit hast appointed divers Orders of Ministers in the Church; Mercifully behold these thy servants now called to the Office of Priesthood ; and so replenish them with the truth of thy doctrine, and adorn them with innocency of life, that, both by word and good example, they may faithfully serve thee in this Office, to the glory of thy Name, and the edification of thy Church ; through the merits of our Saviour Jesus Christ, who liveth and reigneth with thee and the Holy Ghost, world without end. *Amen.*

The Epistle. Ephes. iv. 7.

UNTO every one of us is given grace according to the measure of the gift of Christ. Wherefore he saith, When he ascended up on high, he led captivity captive, and gave gifts unto men. (Now that he ascended, what is it but that he also descended first into the lower parts of the earth? He that descended is the same also that ascended up far above all heavens, that he might fill all things.) And he gave some, apostles ; and some, prophets ; and some, evangelists ; and some, pastors and teachers ; for the perfecting of the saints, for the work of the ministry, for the edifying of the body of Christ : till we all come in the unity of the faith, and of the knowledge of the Son of God, unto a perfect man, unto the measure of the stature of the fulness of Christ.

¶ *After this shall be read for the Gospel part of the ninth Chapter of Saint Matthew, as followeth.*

St. Matt. ix. 36.

WHEN Jesus saw the multitudes, he was moved with compassion on them, because they fainted, and were scattered abroad as sheep having no shepherd. Then saith he unto his disciples, The harvest truly is plenteous, but the labourers are few ; pray ye therefore the Lord of the harvest, that he will send forth labourers into his harvest.

¶ *Or else that followeth, out of the tenth Chapter of* Saint John.

St. John x. 1.

VERILY, verily, I say unto you, He that entereth not by the door into the sheepfold, but climbeth up some other way, the same is a thief and a robber. But he that entereth in by the door is the shepherd of the sheep. To him the porter openeth : and the sheep hear his voice : and he calleth his own sheep by name, and leadeth them out. And when he putteth forth his own sheep, he goeth before them, and the sheep follow him : for they know his voice. And a stranger will they not follow, but will flee from him : for they know not the voice of strangers. This parable spake Jesus unto them : but they understood not what things they were which he spake unto them. Then said Jesus unto them again, Verily, verily, I say unto you, I am the door of the sheep. All that ever came before me are thieves and robbers : but the sheep did not hear them. I am the door : by me if any man enter in, he shall be saved, and shall go in and out, and find pasture. The thief cometh not, but for to steal, and to kill, and to destroy : I am come that they might have life, and that they might have it more abundantly. I am the good shepherd : the good shepherd giveth his life for the sheep. But he that is an hireling, and not the shepherd, whose own the sheep are not, seeth the wolf coming, and leaveth the sheep, and fleeth : and the wolf catcheth them, and scattereth the sheep. The hireling fleeth, because he is an hireling, and careth not for the sheep. I am the good shepherd, and know my sheep, and am known of mine. As the Father knoweth me, even so know I the Father : and I lay down my life for the sheep. And other sheep I have, which are not of this fold : them also I must bring, and they shall hear my voice ; and there shall be one fold, and one shepherd.

¶ *Then the Bishop shall say unto them as followeth.*

YE have heard, Brethren, as well in your private examination, as in the exhortation which was now made to you, and in the holy Lessons taken out of the Gospel, and the writings of the Apostles, of what dignity, and of how great importance this Office is, whereunto ye are called. And now again we exhort you, in the Name of our Lord Jesus Christ, that ye have in remembrance, into how high a Dignity, and to how weighty an Office and Charge ye are called : that is to say, to be Messengers, Watchmen, and Stewards of the Lord ; to teach, and to premonish, to feed and provide for the Lord's family : to seek for Christ's sheep that are dispersed abroad, and for his children who are in the midst of this naughty world, that they may be saved through Christ for ever.

Have always therefore printed in your remembrance, how great a *treasure* is committed to your charge. For they are *the sheep* of Christ, which he bought with his death, and for whom he shed his blood. The Church and Congregation whom you must serve, is his Spouse, and his Body. And if it shall happen that the same Church, or any Member thereof, do take any hurt or hindrance by reason of your negligence, ye know the greatness of the fault, and also the horrible punishment that will ensue. Wherefore consider with yourselves the end of the Ministry towards the children of God, towards the Spouse and Body of Christ; and see that ye never cease your labour, your care and diligence, until ye have done all that lieth in you, according to your bounden duty, to bring all such as are or shall be committed to your charge, unto that agreement in the faith and knowledge of God, and to that ripeness and perfectness of age in Christ, that there be no place left among you, either for error in religion, or for viciousness in life.

Forasmuch then as your Office is both of so great excellency, and of so great difficulty, ye see with how great care and study ye ought to apply yourselves, as well to show yourselves dutiful and thankful unto that Lord, who hath placed *you* in so high *a dignity*; as also to beware that neither you yourselves offend, nor be occasion that others offend. Howbeit, ye cannot have a mind and will thereto of yourselves; for that will and ability is given of God alone: therefore ye ought, and have need, to pray earnestly for his Holy Spirit. And seeing that ye cannot by any other means compass the doing of so weighty a work, pertaining to the salvation of man, but with doctrine and exhortation taken out of the Holy Scriptures, and with a life agreeable to the same; consider how studious ye ought to be in reading and learning the Scriptures, and in framing the manners both of yourselves, and of them that specially pertain unto you, according to the rule of the same Scriptures; and for this

self-same cause, how ye ought to forsake and set aside, as much as ye may, all worldly cares and studies.

We have good hope that ye have well weighed these things with yourselves, long before this time; and that ye have clearly determined, by God's grace, to give yourselves wholly to this Office, whereunto it hath pleased God to call you: so that, as much as lieth in you, ye will apply yourselves wholly to this one thing, and draw all your cares and studies this way; and that ye will continually pray to God the Father, by the mediation of our only Saviour Jesus Christ, for the heavenly assistance of the Holy Ghost; that, by daily reading and weighing the Scriptures, ye may wax riper and stronger in your Ministry; and that ye may so endeavour yourselves, from time to time, to sanctify the lives of you and yours, and to fashion them after the Rule and Doctrine of Christ, that ye may be wholesome and godly examples and patterns for the people to follow.

And now, that this present Congregation of Christ may also understand your minds and wills in these things, and that this your promise may the more move you to do your duties; ye shall answer plainly to these things, which we, in the Name of God, and of his Church, shall demand of you touching the same.

Do you think in your heart, that you are truly called, according to the will of our Lord Jesus Christ, and according to the Canons of this Church, to the Order and Ministry of Priesthood?

Answer. I think it.

The Bishop.

ARE you persuaded that the Holy Scriptures contain all Doctrine required as necessary for eternal salvation through faith in Jesus Christ? And are you determined, out of the said Scriptures to instruct the people committed to your charge; and to teach nothing, as necessary to eternal salvation, but that which you shall be persuaded may be concluded and proved by the Scripture?

Answer. I am so persuaded, and have so determined, by God's grace.

The Bishop.

WILL you then give your faithful diligence always so to minister the Doctrine and Sacraments, and the Discipline of Christ, as the Lord hath commanded, and as this Church hath received the same, according to the Commandments of God; so that you may teach the people committed to your Cure and Charge with all diligence to keep and observe the same?

Answer. I will so do, by the help of the Lord.

The Bishop.

WILL you be ready, with all faithful diligence, to banish and drive away from the Church all erroneous and strange doctrines contrary to God's Word; and to use both public and private monitions and exhortations, as well to the sick as to the whole, within your Cures, as need shall require, and occasion shall be given?

Answer. I will, the Lord being my helper.

The Bishop.

WILL you be diligent in Prayers, and in reading the Holy Scriptures, and in such studies as help to the knowledge of the same, laying aside the study of the world and the flesh?

Answer. I will endeavour so to do, the Lord being my helper.

The Bishop.

WILL you be diligent to frame and fashion your own selves, and your families, according to the Doctrine of Christ; and to make both yourselves and them, as much as in you lieth, wholesome examples and patterns to the flock of Christ?

Answer. I will apply myself thereto, the Lord being my helper.

The Bishop.

WILL you maintain and set forwards, as much as lieth in you, quietness, peace, and love, among all Christian people, and especially among them that are or shall be committed to your charge?

Answer. I will so do, the Lord being my helper.

The Bishop.

WILL you reverently obey your Bishop, and other chief Ministers, who, according to the Canons of the Church, may have the charge and government over you; following with a glad mind and will their godly admonitions, and submitting yourselves to their godly judgments?

Answer. I will so do, the Lord being my helper.

¶ *Then shall the Bishop, standing up, say,*

ALMIGHTY God, who hath given you this will to do all these things; Grant also unto you strength and power to perform the same, that he may accomplish his work which he hath begun in you: through Jesus Christ our Lord. *Amen.*

¶ *After this, the Congregation shall be desired, secretly in their Prayers, to make their humble supplications to God for all these things; for the which Prayers there shall be silence kept for a space.*

¶ *After which, shall be sung or said by the Bishop, the persons to be ordained Priests all kneeling, Veni, Creator Spiritus; the Bishop beginning, and the Priests, and others that are present, answering by verses, as followeth.*

COME, Holy Ghost, our souls inspire,
And lighten with celestial fire.
Thou the anointing Spirit art,
Who dost thy sevenfold gifts impart.

Thy blessed unction from above,
Is comfort, life, and fire of love.
Enable with perpetual light
The dulness of our blinded sight.

Anoint and cheer our soiled face
With the abundance of thy grace.
Keep far our foes, give peace at home;
Where thou art guide, no ill can come.

Teach us to know the Father, Son,
And thee, of both, to be but One;
That, through the ages all along,
This may be our endless song:
Praise to thy eternal merit,
Father, Son, and Holy Spirit.

¶ *Or this.*

COME, Holy Ghost, eternal God,
Proceeding from above,
Both from the Father and the Son,
The God of peace and love;

Visit our minds, into our hearts
Thy heavenly grace inspire;
That truth and godliness we may
Pursue with full desire.

Thou art the very Comforter
In grief and all distress:
The heavenly gift of God most
High;
No tongue can it express;

The fountain and the living spring
Of joy celestial;
The fire so bright, the love so
sweet,
The unction spiritual.

Thou in thy gifts art manifold,
By them Christ's Church doth stand:
In faithful hearts thou writ'st
thy law,
The finger of God's hand.

According to thy promise, Lord,
Thou givest speech with grace:
That, through thy help, God's
praises may
Resound in every place.

O Holy Ghost, into our minds
Send down thy heavenly light:
Kindle our hearts with fervent
zeal,
To serve God day and night.

Our weakness strengthen and confirm,
(For, Lord, thou know'st us frail;)
That neither devil, world, nor
flesh,
Against us may prevail.

Put back our enemy far from us,
And help us to obtain
Peace in our hearts with God
and man,
(The best, the truest gain;)

And grant that thou being, O Lord,
Our leader and our guide,
We may escape the snares of sin,
And never from thee slide.

Such measures of thy powerful
grace
Grant, Lord, to us, we pray;
That thou may'st be our Comfort
er
At the last dreadful day.

Of strife and of dissension
Dissolve, O Lord, the bands,
And knit the knots of peace and
love
Throughout all Christian
lands.

Grant us the grace that we may
know
The Father of all might,
That we of his beloved Son
May gain the blissful sight;

And that we may with perfect
faith
Ever acknowledge thee,
The Spirit of Father, and of
Son,
One God in Persons Three.

To God the Father laud and
praise,
And to his blessed Son,
And to the Holy Spirit of grace,
Co-equal Three in One.

And pray we, that our only Lord
Would please his Spirit to
send
On all that shall profess his
Name,
From hence to the world's
end. Amen.

¶ *That done, the Bishop shall pray*
in this wise, and say,

Let us pray.

ALMIGHTY God, and heavenly Father, who, of thine
infinite love and goodness towards us, hast given to thy
only and most dearly beloved
Son Jesus Christ, to be our Redeemer, and the Author of everlasting life; who, after he had
made perfect our redemption by
his death, and was ascended into
heaven, sent abroad into the
world his Apostles, Prophets,
Evangelists, Doctors, and Pastors; by whose labour and ministry he gathered together a great
flock in all the parts of the world,
to set forth the eternal praise
of thy holy Name: For these so
great benefits of thy eternal
goodness, and for that thou hast
vouchsafed to call these thy servants here present to the same
Office and Ministry, appointed
for the salvation of mankind,
we render unto thee most hearty
thanks, we praise and worship
thee; and we humbly beseech
thee, by the same thy blessed
Son, to grant unto all, which
either here or elsewhere call upon thy holy Name, that we may
continue to show ourselves
thankful unto thee for these and
all thy other benefits; and that
we may daily increase and go
forwards in the knowledge and
faith of thee and thy Son, by the
Holy Spirit. So that as well by
these thy Ministers, as by them
over whom they shall be appointed thy Ministers, thy holy
Name may be for ever glorified,
and thy blessed kingdom enlarged; through the same thy
Son Jesus Christ our Lord, who
liveth and reigneth with thee
in the unity of the same Holy
Spirit, world without end. Amen.

¶ *When this Prayer is done, the*
Bishop with the Priests present,
shall lay their Hands severally
upon the Head of every one that
receiveth the Order of Priesthood;
the Receivers humbly kneeling, and
the Bishop saying,

RECEIVE the Holy Ghost for
the Office and Work of a
Priest in the Church of God, now
committed unto thee by the
Imposition of our hands. Whose

sins thou dost forgive, they are forgiven ; and whose sins thou dost retain, they are retained. And be thou a faithful Dispenser of the Word of God, and of his holy Sacraments ; In the Name of the Father, and of the Son, and of the Holy Ghost. Amen.

¶ *Or this.*

TAKE thou Authority to execute the Office of a Priest in the Church of God, now committed to thee by the Imposition of our hands. And be thou a faithful Dispenser of the Word of God, and of his holy Sacraments ; In the Name of the Father, and of the Son, and of the Holy Ghost. Amen.

¶ *Then the Bishop shall deliver to every one of them kneeling, the Bible into his hand, saying,*

TAKE thou Authority to preach the Word of God, and to minister the holy Sacraments in the Congregation, where thou shalt be lawfully appointed thereunto.

¶ *When this is done, the Nicene Creed shall be said, and the Bishop shall go on in the Service of the Communion, which all they who receive Orders shall take together and remain in the same*

¶ *And if, on the same day, the Order of Deacons be given to some, and the Order of Priesthood to others ; the Deacons shall be first presented, and then the Priests ; and it shall suffice that the Litany be once said for both. The Collects shall both be used ; first that for Deacons, then that for Priests. The Epistle shall be Ephesians iv. 7 to 13, as before in this Office. Immediately after which, they that are to be made Deacons, shall be examined and Ordained, as is above prescribed. Then one of them having read the Gospel, (which shall be either out of Saint Matthew ix. 36, as before in this Office ; or else Saint Luke xii. 35 to 38, as before in the Form for the Ordering of Deacons,) they that are to be made Priests shall likewise be examined and Ordained, as is in this Office before appointed.*

place where Hands were laid upon them, until such time as they have received the Communion.

¶ *The Communion being done, after the last Collect, and immediately before the Benediction, shall be said this Collect.*

MOST merciful Father, we beseech thee to send upon these thy servants thy heavenly blessing; that they may be clothed with righteousness, and that thy Word spoken by their mouths may have such success, that it may never be spoken in vain. Grant also, that we may have grace to hear and receive what they shall deliver out of thy most holy Word, or agreeable to the same, as the means of our salvation ; that in all our words and deeds we may seek thy glory, and the increase of thy kingdom ; through Jesus Christ our Lord. *Amen.*

THE Peace of God, which passeth all understanding, keep your hearts and minds in the knowledge and love of God, and of his Son Jesus Christ our Lord: And the Blessing of God Almighty, the Father, the Son, and the Holy Ghost, be amongst you, and remain with you always. *Amen.*

THE FORM OF
ORDAINING OR CONSECRATING
A BISHOP.

❦

¶ *When all things are duly prepared in the Church, and set in order, after Morning Prayer is ended, the Presiding Bishop, or some other Bishop appointed by the Bishops present, shall begin the Communion Service, in which this shall be*

The Collect.

ALMIGHTY God, who by thy Son Jesus Christ didst give to thy holy Apostles many excellent gifts, and didst charge them to feed thy flock; Give grace, we beseech thee, to all Bishops, the Pastors of thy Church, that they may diligently preach thy Word, and duly administer the godly Discipline thereof; and grant to the people, that they may obediently follow the same; that all may receive the crown of everlasting glory; through Jesus Christ our Lord. Amen.

¶ *And another Bishop shall read the Epistle.*

1 Tim. iii. 1.

THIS is a true saying, If a man desire the office of a bishop, he desireth a good work. A bishop then must be blameless, the husband of one wife, vigilant, sober, of good behaviour, given to hospitality, apt to teach; not given to wine, no striker, not greedy of filthy lucre; but patient, not a brawler, not covetous; one that ruleth well his own house, having his children in subjection with all gravity; (for if a man know not how to rule his own house, how shall he take care of the church of God?) not a novice, lest being lifted up with pride he fall into the condemnation of the devil. Moreover he must have a good report of them which are without; lest he fall into reproach and the snare of the devil.

¶ *Or this.*

For the Epistle. Acts xx. 17.

FROM Miletus Paul sent to Ephesus, and called the elders of the church. And when they were come to him, he said unto them, Ye know, from the first day that I came into Asia, after what manner I have been with you at all seasons, serving the Lord with all humility of mind, and with many tears, and temptations, which befell me by the lying in wait of the Jews: and how I kept back nothing that was profitable unto you, but have shewed you, and have taught you publickly, and from house to house, testifying both to the Jews, and also to the Greeks, repentance toward God, and faith toward our Lord Jesus Christ. And now, behold, I go bound in the spirit unto Jerusalem, not knowing the things that shall befall me there: save that the Holy Ghost witnesseth in every city, saying that bonds and afflictions abide me. But none of these things move me, neither count I my life dear unto myself, so that I might finish my course with joy, and the ministry, which I have received of the Lord Jesus, to testify the gospel of the grace of God. And now, behold, I know that ye all, among whom I have gone preaching the kingdom of God, shall see my face no more, Wherefore I take you to record this day, that I am pure from the blood of all men. For I have not shunned to declare unto you all the counsel of God. Take heed therefore unto yourselves, and to all the flock, over the which the Holy Ghost hath made you overseers, to feed the church of God, which he hath purchased with his own blood. For I know this, that after my departing shall grievous wolves enter in among you, not sparing the flock. Also of your own selves shall men arise, speaking perverse things, to draw away disciples after them. Therefore watch, and remember, that by the space of three years I ceased not to warn every one night and day with tears. And now, brethren, I commend you to God, and to the word of his grace, which is able to build you up, and to give you an inheritance among all them which are sanctified. I have coveted no man's silver, or gold, or apparel. Yea, ye yourselves know, that these hands have ministered unto my necessities, and to them that were with me, I have shewed you all things, how that so labouring ye ought to support the weak, and to remember the words of the Lord Jesus, how he said, It is more blessed to give than to receive.

¶ *Then another Bishop shall read the Gospel.*

St. John xxi. 15.

JESUS saith to Simon Peter, Simon, son of Jonas, lovest thou me more than these? He saith unto him, Yea, Lord; thou knowest that I love thee. He saith unto him, Feed my lambs. He saith to him again the second time, Simon, son of Jonas, lovest thou me? He saith unto him, Yea, Lord; thou knowest that I love thee. He saith unto him, Feed my sheep. He saith unto him the third time, Simon, son of Jonas, lovest thou me? Peter was grieved because he said unto him the third time, Lovest thou me? And he said unto him, Lord, thou knowest all things; thou knowest that I love thee. Jesus saith unto him, Feed my sheep.

¶ *Or this.*

St. John xx. 19.

THE same day at evening, being the first day of the week, when the doors were shut where the disciples were assembled for fear of the Jews, came Jesus, and stood in the midst, and saith unto them, Peace be unto you. And when he had so said, he shewed unto them his hands and his side. Then were the disciples glad, when they saw the Lord. Then said Jesus to them again, Peace be unto you: as my Father hath sent me, even so send I you. And when he had said this, he breathed on them, and saith unto them, Receive ye the Holy Ghost: whose soever sins ye remit, they are remitted unto them; and whose soever sins ye retain, they are retained.

St. Matt. xxviii. 18.

JESUS came and spake unto them, saying, All power is given unto me in heaven and in earth. Go ye therefore, and teach all nations, baptizing them in the name of the Father, and of the Son, and of the Holy Ghost: teaching them to observe all things whatsoever I have commanded you: and, lo, I am with you alway, even unto the end of the world.

¶ *Then shall follow the Nicene Creed, and after that the Sermon ; which being ended, the Elected Bishop, vested with his Rochet, shall be presented by two Bishops of this Church unto the Presiding Bishop, or to the Bishop appointed, sitting in his chair, near the Holy Table ; the Bishops who present him saying,*

REVEREND Father in God, we present unto you this godly and well-learned man, to be Ordained and Consecrated Bishop.

¶ *Then shall the Presiding Bishop demand Testimonials of the person presented for Consecration, and shall cause them to be read.*

¶ *He shall then require of him the following Promise of Conformity to the Doctrine, Discipline, and Worship of the Protestant Episcopal Church.*

IN the Name of God, Amen. I, *N.*, chosen Bishop of the Protestant Episcopal Church in *N.*, do promise conformity and obedience to the Doctrine, Discipline, and Worship of the Protestant Episcopal Church in the United States of America. So help me God, through Jesus Christ.

¶ *Then the Presiding Bishop shall move the Congregation present to pray, saying thus to them :*

¶ *Or this.*

BRETHREN, it is written in the Gospel of Saint Luke, that our Saviour Christ continued the whole night in prayer, before he chose and sent forth his twelve Apostles. It is written also, that the holy Apostles prayed before they ordained Matthias to be of the number of the Twelve. Let us, therefore, following the example of our Saviour Christ, and his Apostles, offer up our prayers to Almighty God, before we admit and send forth this person presented unto us, to the work whereunto we trust the Holy Ghost hath called him.

¶ *And then shall be said the Litany; save only, that after this place, That* it may please thee to illuminate all Bishops, *etc., the proper Suffrage shall be,*

THAT it may please thee to bless this our Brother elected, and to send thy grace upon him, that he may duly execute the office whereunto he is called, to the edifying of thy Church, and to the honour, praise, and glory of thy Name ;

Answer. *We beseech thee to hear us, good Lord.*

¶ *Then shall be said this Prayer following.*

ALMIGHTY God, giver of all good things, who by thy Holy Spirit hast appointed divers Orders of Ministers in thy Church ; Mercifully behold this thy servant, now called to the Work and Ministry of a Bishop ; and so replenish him with the truth of thy Doctrine, and adorn him with innocency of life, that, both by word and deed, he may faithfully serve thee in this Office, to the glory of thy Name, and the edifying and well-governing of thy Church ; through the merits of our Saviour Jesus Christ, who liveth and reigneth with thee and the Holy Ghost, world without end. *Amen.*

¶ *Then the Presiding Bishop, sitting in his chair, shall say to him that is to be Consecrated,*

BROTHER, forasmuch as the Holy Scripture and the ancient Canons command, that we should not be hasty in laying on hands, and admitting any person to Government in the Church of Christ, which he hath purchased with no less price than the effusion of his own blood; before we admit you to this Administration, we will examine you in certain Articles, to the end that the Congregation present may have a trial, and bear witness, how you are minded to behave yourself in the Church of God.

ARE you persuaded that you are truly called to this Ministration, according to the will of our Lord Jesus Christ, and the order of this Church?

Answer. I am so persuaded.

The Presiding Bishop.

ARE you persuaded that the Holy Scriptures contain all Doctrine required as necessary for eternal salvation through faith in Jesus Christ? And are you determined out of the same Holy Scriptures to instruct the people committed to your charge; and to teach or maintain nothing, as necessary to eternal salvation, but that which you shall be persuaded may be concluded and proved by the same?

Answer. I am so persuaded, and determined, by God's grace.

The Presiding Bishop.

WILL you then faithfully exercise yourself in the Holy Scriptures, and call upon God by prayer for the true understanding of the same: so that you may be able by them to teach and exhort with wholesome Doctrine, and to withstand and convince the gainsayers?

Answer. I will so do, by the help of God.

The Presiding Bishop.

ARE you ready, with all faithful diligence, to banish and drive away from the Church all erroneous and strange Doctrine contrary to God's Word; and both privately and openly to call upon and encourage others to the same?

Answer. I am ready, the Lord being my helper.

The Presiding Bishop.

WILL you deny all ungodliness and worldly lusts, and live soberly, righteously, and godly in this present world; that you may show yourself in all things an example of good works unto others, that the adversary may be ashamed, having nothing to say against you?

Answer. I will so do, the Lord being my helper.

The Presiding Bishop.

WILL you maintain and set forward, as much as shall lie in you, quietness, love, and peace among all men; and diligently exercise such discipline as by the authority of God's Word, and by the order of this Church, is committed to you?

Answer. I will so do, by the help of God.

The Presiding Bishop.

WILL you be faithful in Ordaining, sending, or laying hands upon others?

Answer. I will so be, by the help of God.

The Presiding Bishop.

WILL you show yourself gentle, and be merciful for Christ's sake to poor and needy people, and to all strangers destitute of help?

Answer. I will so show myself, by God's help.

¶ *Then the Presiding Bishop, standing up, shall say,*

ALMIGHTY God, our heavenly Father, who hath given you a good will to do all these things; Grant also unto you strength and power to perform the same; that, he accomplishing in you the good work which he hath begun, you may be found perfect and irreprehensible at the latter day; through Jesus Christ our Lord. *Amen.*

¶ *Then shall the Bishop elect put on the rest of the Episcopal habit; and, kneeling down, Veni, Creator Spiritus shall be sung or said over him; the Presiding Bishop beginning, and the Bishops, with others that are present, answering by verses, as followeth.*

COME, Holy Ghost, our souls inspire,
And lighten with celestial fire.
Thou the anointing Spirit art,
Who dost thy sevenfold gifts impart.

Thy blessed unction from above,
Is comfort, life, and fire of love.
Enable with perpetual light
The dulness of our blinded sight.

Anoint and cheer our soiled face
With the abundance of thy grace.
Keep far our foes, give peace at home;
Where thou art guide, no ill can come.

Teach us to know the Father, Son,
And thee, of both, to be but One;
That, through the ages all along,
This may be our endless song:
Praise to thy eternal merit,
Father, Son, and Holy Spirit.

¶ *Or else the longer paraphrase of the same Hymn, as in the Ordering of Priests.*

¶ *That ended, the Presiding Bishop shall say,*

Lord, hear our prayer.
Answer. And let our cry come unto thee.

Let us pray.

ALMIGHTY God, and most merciful Father, who, of thine infinite goodness, hast given thy only and dearly beloved Son Jesus Christ, to be our Redeemer, and the Author of everlasting life; who, after that he had made perfect our redemption by his death, and was ascended into heaven, poured down his gifts abundantly upon men, making some Apostles, some Prophets, some Evangelists, some Pastors and Doctors, to the edifying and making perfect his Church; Grant, we beseech thee, to this thy servant, such grace, that he may evermore be ready to spread abroad thy Gospel, the glad tidings of reconciliation with thee; and use the authority given him, not to destruction, but to salvation; not to hurt, but to help: so that, as a wise and faithful servant, giving to thy family their portion in due season, he may at last be received unto everlasting joy; through Jesus Christ our Lord; who, with thee and the Holy Ghost, liveth and reigneth, one God, world without end. *Amen.*

¶ *Then the Presiding Bishop and Bishops present shall lay their Hands upon the Head of the Elected Bishop, kneeling before him, the Presiding Bishop saying,*

RECEIVE the Holy Ghost for the Office and Work of a Bishop in the Church of God, now committed unto thee by the Imposition of our hands: In the Name of the Father, and of the Son, and of the Holy Ghost. Amen. And remember that thou stir up the grace of God, which is given thee by this Imposition of our hands; for God hath not given us the spirit of fear, but of power, and love, and soberness.

¶ *Then the Presiding Bishop shall deliver him the Bible, saying,*

GIVE heed unto reading, exhortation, and doctrine. Think upon the things contained in this Book. Be diligent in them, that the increase coming thereby may be manifest unto all men; for by so doing thou shalt both save thyself and them that hear thee. Be to the flock of Christ a shepherd, not a wolf; feed them, devour them not. Hold up the weak, heal the sick, bind up the broken, bring again the outcasts, seek the lost. Be so merciful, that you be not too remiss; so minister discipline, that you forget not mercy; that when the Chief Shepherd shall appear, you may receive the never-fading crown of glory; through Jesus Christ our Lord. *Amen.*

¶ *Then the Presiding Bishop shall proceed in the Communion Service; with whom the new Consecrated Bishop, with others, shall also communicate.*

¶ *And for the last Collect, immediately before the Benediction, shall be said this Prayer.*

MOST merciful Father, we beseech thee so to send down upon this thy servant thy heavenly blessing; and so endue him with thy Holy Spirit, that he, preaching thy Word, may not only be earnest to reprove, beseech, and rebuke, with all patience and doctrine; but also may be, to such as believe, a wholesome example in word, in conversation, in love, in faith, in chastity, and in purity; that, faithfully fulfilling his course, at the latter day he may receive the crown of righteousness, laid up by the Lord, the righteous Judge, who liveth and reigneth one God with the Father and the Holy Ghost, world without end. *Amen.*

THE Peace of God, which passeth all understanding, keep your hearts and minds in the knowledge and love of God, and of his Son Jesus Christ our Lord: And the Blessing of God Almighty, the Father, the Son, and the Holy Ghost, be amongst you, and remain with you always. *Amen.*

THE LITANY AND SUFFRAGES.

O GOD the Father of heaven; have mercy upon us miserable sinners.

O God the Father of heaven; have mercy upon us miserable sinners.

O God the Son, Redeemer of the world; have mercy upon us miserable sinners.

O God the Son, Redeemer of the world; have mercy upon us miserable sinners.

O God the Holy Ghost, proceeding from the Father and the Son; have mercy upon us miserable sinners.

O God the Holy Ghost, proceeding from the Father and the Son; have mercy upon us miserable sinners.

O holy, blessed, and glorious Trinity, three Persons and one God; have mercy upon us miserable sinners.

O holy, blessed, and glorious Trinity, three Persons and one God: have mercy upon us miserable sinners.

Remember not, Lord, our offences, nor the offences of our forefathers; neither take thou vengeance of our sins: Spare us, good Lord, spare thy people, whom thou hast redeemed with thy most precious blood, and be not angry with us for ever.

Spare us, good Lord.

From all evil and mischief; from sin; from the crafts and assaults of the devil; from thy wrath, and from everlasting damnation,

Good Lord, deliver us.

From all blindness of heart; from pride, vain-glory, and hypocrisy; from envy, hatred, and malice, and all uncharitableness,

Good Lord, deliver us.

From all inordinate and sinful affections; and from all the deceits of the world, the flesh, and the devil,

Good Lord, deliver us.

From lightning and tempest; from plague, pestilence, and famine; from battle and murder, and from sudden death,

Good Lord, deliver us.

From all sedition, privy conspiracy, and rebellion; from all false doctrine, heresy, and schism; from hardness of heart, and contempt of thy Word and Commandment,

Good Lord, deliver us.

By the mystery of thy holy Incarnation; by thy holy Nativity and Circumcision; by thy Baptism, Fasting, and Temptation,

Good Lord, deliver us.

By thine Agony and Bloody Sweat; by thy Cross and Passion; by thy precious Death and Burial; by thy glorious Resurrection and Ascension; and by the Coming of the Holy Ghost,

Good Lord, deliver us.

In all time of our tribulation; in all time of our prosperity; in the hour of death, and in the day of judgment,

Good Lord, deliver us.

We sinners do beseech thee to hear us, O Lord God; and that it may please thee to rule and govern thy holy Church universal in the right way;

We beseech thee to hear us, good Lord.

That it may please thee to bless and preserve all Christian Rulers and Magistrates, giving them grace to execute justice, and to maintain truth;

We beseech thee to hear us, good Lord.

That it may please thee to illuminate all Bishops, Priests, and Deacons, with true knowledge and understanding of thy Word; and that both by their preaching and living they may set it forth, and show it accordingly;

We beseech thee to hear us, good Lord.

That it may please thee to bless these thy servants, now to be admitted to the Order of Deacons, [or Priests,] and to pour thy grace upon them; that they may duly execute their office, to the edifying of thy

Church, and the glory of thy holy Name;

We beseech thee to hear us, good Lord.

That it may please thee to send forth labourers into thy harvest;

We beseech thee to hear us, good Lord.

That it may please thee to bless and keep all thy people;

We beseech thee to hear us, good Lord.

That it may please thee to give to all nations unity, peace, and concord;

We beseech thee to hear us, good Lord.

That it may please thee to give us an heart to love and fear thee, and diligently to live after thy commandments;

We beseech thee to hear us, good Lord.

That it may please thee to give to all thy people increase of grace to hear meekly thy Word, and to receive it with pure affection, and to bring forth the fruits of the Spirit;

We beseech thee to hear us, good Lord.

That it may please thee to bring into the way of truth all such as have erred, and are deceived;

We beseech thee to hear us, good Lord.

That it may please thee to strengthen such as do stand; and to comfort and help the weak-hearted; and to raise up those who fall; and finally to beat down Satan under our feet;

We beseech thee to hear us, good Lord.

That it may please thee to succour, help, and comfort, all who are in danger, necessity, and tribulation;

We beseech thee to hear us, good Lord.

That it may please thee to preserve all who travel by land or by water, all women in the perils of child-birth, all sick persons, and young children; and to show thy pity upon all prisoners and captives;

We beseech thee to hear us, good Lord.

That it may please thee to defend, and provide for, the fatherless children, and widows, and all who are desolate and oppressed;

We beseech thee to hear us, good Lord.

That it may please thee to have mercy upon all men;

We beseech thee to hear us, good Lord.

That it may please thee to forgive our enemies, persecutors, and slanderers, and to turn their hearts;

We beseech thee to hear us, good Lord.

That it may please thee to give and preserve to our use the kindly fruits of the earth, so that in due time we may enjoy them;

We beseech thee to hear us, good Lord.

That it may please thee to give us true repentance; to forgive us all our sins, negligences, and ignorances; and to endue us with the grace of thy Holy Spirit to amend our lives according to thy holy Word;

We beseech thee to hear us, good Lord.

Son of God, we beseech thee to hear us.

Son of God, we beseech thee to hear us.

O Lamb of God, who takest away the sins of the world;

Grant us thy peace.

O Lamb of God, who takest away the sins of the world;

Have mercy upon us.

¶ *The Bishop may, at his discretion, omit all that followeth to the Prayer,* We humbly beseech thee, O Father, *etc.*

O Christ, hear us.

O Christ, hear us.

Lord, have mercy upon us.

Lord, have mercy upon us.

Christ, have mercy upon us.

Christ, have mercy upon us.

Lord, have mercy upon us.

Lord, have mercy upon us.

¶ *Then shall the Bishop, and the People with him, say the Lord's Prayer.*

OUR Father, who art in heaven, Hallowed be thy Name. Thy kingdom come. Thy will be done on earth, As it is in heaven. Give us this day our daily bread. And forgive us our trespasses, As we forgive those who trespass against us. And lead us not into temptation; But deliver us from evil. Amen.

Bishop. O Lord, deal not with us according to our sins.

Answer. Neither reward us according to our iniquities.

Let us pray.

O GOD, merciful Father, who despisest not the sighing of a contrite heart, nor the desire of such as are sorrowful: Mercifully assist our prayers which we make before thee in all our troubles and adversities, whensoever they oppress us; and graciously hear us, that those evils which the craft and subtilty of the devil or man worketh against us, may, by thy good providence, be brought to nought; that we thy servants, being hurt by no persecutions, may evermore give thanks unto thee in thy holy Church; through Jesus Christ our Lord.

O Lord, arise, help us, and deliver us for thy Name's sake.

O GOD, we have heard with our ears, and our fathers have declared unto us, the noble works that thou didst in their days, and in the old time before them.

O Lord, arise, help us, and deliver us for thine honour.

Glory be to the Father, and to the Son, and to the Holy Ghost;

Answer. As it was in the beginning, is now, and ever shall be, world without end. Amen.

From our enemies defend us, O Christ.

Graciously look upon our afflictions.

With pity behold the sorrows of our hearts.

Mercifully forgive the sins of thy people.

Favourably with mercy hear our prayers.

O Son of David, have mercy upon us.

Both now and ever vouchsafe to hear us, O Christ.

Graciously hear us, O Christ; graciously hear us, O Lord Christ.

Bishop. O Lord, let thy mercy be showed upon us;

Answer. As we do put our trust in thee.

Let us pray.

WE humbly beseech thee, O Father, mercifully to look upon our infirmities; and, for the glory of thy Name, turn from us all those evils that we most justly have deserved; and grant, that in all our troubles we may put our whole trust and confidence in thy mercy, and evermore serve thee in holiness and pureness of living, to thy honour and glory; through our only Mediator and Advocate, Jesus Christ our Lord. Amen.

THE ORDER FOR
THE ADMINISTRATION OF THE LORD'S SUPPER,
OR
HOLY COMMUNION.

Our Father, who art in heaven, Hallowed be thy Name. Thy kingdom come. Thy will be done on earth, As it is in heaven. Give us this day our daily bread. And forgive us our trespasses, As we forgive those who trespass against us. And lead us not into temptation; But deliver us from evil. Amen.

The Collect.

Almighty God, unto whom all hearts are open, all desires known, and from whom no secrets are hid; Cleanse the thoughts of our hearts by the inspiration of thy Holy Spirit, that we may perfectly love thee, and worthily magnify thy holy Name; through Christ our Lord. Amen.

¶ *Then shall the Bishop, turning to the People, rehearse distinctly The Ten Commandments; and the People, still kneeling, shall, after every Commandment, ask God mercy for their transgressions for the time past, and grace to keep the law for the time to come.*

¶ *The Decalogue may be omitted, provided it be said once on each Sunday. But Note, That whenever it is omitted, the Bishop shall say the Summary of the Law, beginning, Hear what our Lord Jesus Christ saith.*

Bishop.

God spake these words, and said: I am the Lord thy God; Thou shalt have none other gods but me.

People. Lord, have mercy upon us, and incline our hearts to keep this law.

Bishop. Thou shalt not make to thyself any graven image, nor the likeness of any thing that is in heaven above, or in the earth beneath, or in the water under the earth; thou shalt not bow down to them, nor worship them; for I the Lord thy God am a jealous God, and visit the sins of the fathers upon the children, unto the third and fourth generation of them that hate me; and show mercy unto thousands in them that love me and keep my commandments.

People. Lord, have mercy upon us, and incline our hearts to keep this law.

Bishop. Thou shalt not take the Name of the Lord thy God in vain; for the Lord will not hold him guiltless, that taketh his Name in vain.

People. Lord, have mercy upon us, and incline our hearts to keep this law.

Bishop. Remember that thou keep holy the Sabbath-day. Six

days shalt thou labour, and do all that thou hast to do: but the seventh day is the Sabbath of the LORD thy God. In it thou shalt do no manner of work; thou, and thy son, and thy daughter, thy man-servant, and thy maid-servant, thy cattle, and the stranger that is within thy gates. For in six days the LORD made heaven and earth, the sea, and all that in them is, and rested the seventh day: wherefore the LORD blessed the seventh day, and hallowed it.

People. Lord, have mercy upon us, and incline our hearts to keep this law.

Bishop. Honour thy father and thy mother; that thy days may be long in the land which the LORD thy God giveth thee.

People. Lord, have mercy upon us, and incline our hearts to keep this law.

Bishop. Thou shalt do no murder.

People. Lord, have mercy upon us, and incline our hearts to keep this law.

Bishop. Thou shalt not commit adultery.

People. Lord, have mercy upon us, and incline our hearts to keep this law.

Bishop. Thou shalt not steal.

People. Lord, have mercy upon us, and incline our hearts to keep this law.

Bishop. Thou shalt not bear false witness against the neighbour.

People. Lord, have mercy upon us, and incline our hearts to keep this law.

Bishop. Thou shalt not covet thy neighbour's house, thou shalt not covet thy neighbour's wife, nor his servant, nor his maid, nor his ox, nor his ass, nor any thing that is his.

People. Lord, have mercy upon us, and write all these thy laws in our hearts, we beseech thee.

¶ *Then the Bishop may said,*

Hear also what our Lord Jesus Christ saith.

THOU shalt love the Lord thy God with all thy heart, and with all thy soul, and with all thy mind. This is the first and great commandment. And the second is like unto it; Thou shalt love thy neighbour as thyself. On these two commandments hang all the Law and the Prophets.

¶ *Here, if the Decalogue hath been omitted, shall be said,*

Lord, have mercy upon us.
Christ, have mercy upon us.
Lord, have mercy upon us.

¶ *Then the Bishop may say,*

Let us pray.

O ALMIGHTY Lord, and everlasting God, vouchsafe, we beseech thee, to direct, sanctify, and govern, both our hearts and bodies, in the ways of thy laws, and in the works of thy commandments; that, through thy most mighty protection, both here and ever, we may be preserved in body and soul; through our Lord and Saviour Jesus Christ. Amen.

¶ *Then shall be read the Collect, Epistle, and Gospel, as they are appointed.*

¶ *Then shall be said the Creed commonly called the Nicene, or else the Apostles' Creed; but the Creed may be omitted, if it hath been said immediately before in Morning Prayer; Provided, that the Nicene Creed shall be said on Christmas-day, Easter-day, Ascension-day, Whitsunday, and Trinity-Sunday.*

I BELIEVE in one God the Father Almighty, Maker of heaven and earth, And of all things visible and invisible:

And in one Lord Jesus Christ, the only-begotten Son of God; Begotten of his Father before all worlds, God of God, Light of Light, Very God of very God; Begotten, not made; Being of one substance with the Father; By whom all things were made: Who for us men and for our salvation came down from heaven, And was incarnate by the Holy Ghost of the Virgin Mary, And was made man: And was crucified also for us under Pontius Pilate: He suffered and was buried: And the third day he rose again according to the Scriptures: And ascended into heaven, And sitteth on the right hand of the Father: And he shall come again, with glory, to judge both the quick and the dead; Whose kingdom shall have no end.

And I believe in the Holy Ghost, The Lord, and Giver of Life, Who proceedeth from the Father and the Son; Who with the Father and the Son together is worshipped and glorified; Who spake by the Prophets: And I believe one Catholic and Apostolic Church: I acknowledge one Baptism for the remission of sins: And I look for the Resurrection of the dead: And the Life of the World to come. Amen.

¶ *Then shall the Bishop begin the Offertory, saying one or more of these Sentences following, as he thinketh most convenient.*

REMEMBER the words of the Lord Jesus, how he said, It is more blessed to give than to receive. *Acts* xx. 35.

Let your light so shine before men, that they may see your good works, and glorify your Father which is in heaven. *St. Matt.* v. 16.

Lay not up for yourselves treasures upon earth, where moth and rust doth corrupt, and where thieves break through and steal: but lay up for yourselves treasures in heaven, where neither moth nor rust doth corrupt, and where thieves do not break through nor steal. *St. Matt.* vi. 19, 20.

Whatsoever ye would that men should do to you, even so do to them: for this is the Law and the Prophets. *St. Matt.* vii. 12.

Not every one that saith unto me, Lord, Lord, shall enter into the kingdom of heaven; but he that doeth the will of my Father which is in heaven. *St. Matt.* vii. 21.

Zacchæus stood forth, and said unto the Lord, Behold, Lord, the half of my goods I give to the poor; and if I have done any wrong to any man, I restore fourfold. *St. Luke* xix. 8.

Who goeth a warfare at any time of his own cost? Who planteth a vineyard, and eateth not of the fruit thereof? Or who feedeth a flock, and eateth not of the milk of the flock? 1 *Cor.* ix. 7.

If we have sown unto you spiritual things, is it a great matter if we shall reap your worldly things? 1 *Cor.* ix. 11.

Do ye not know, that they who minister about holy things live of the sacrifice; and they who wait at the altar are partakers with the altar? Even so hath the Lord also ordained, that they who preach the Gospel should live of the Gospel. 1 *Cor.* ix. 13, 14.

He that soweth little shall

reap little; and he that soweth plenteously shall reap plenteously. Let every man do according as he is disposed in his heart, not grudgingly, or of necessity; for God loveth a cheerful giver. *2 Cor.* ix. 6, 7.

Let him that is taught in the Word minister unto him that teacheth, in all good things. Be not deceived, God is not mocked: for whatsoever a man soweth that shall he reap. *Gal.* vi. 6, 7.

While we have time, let us do good unto all men; and especially unto them that are of the household of faith. *Gal.* vi. 10.

Godliness is great riches, if a man be content with that he hath: for we brought nothing into this world, neither may we carry any thing out. *1 Tim.* vi. 6, 7.

Charge them who are rich in this world, that they be ready to give, and glad to distribute; laying up in store for themselves a good foundation against the time to come, that they may attain eternal life. *1 Tim.* vi. 17, 18, 19.

God is not unrighteous, that he will forget your works, and labour that proceedeth of love; which love ye have showed for his Name's sake, who have ministered unto the saints, and yet do minister. *Heb.* vi. 10.

To do good, and to distribute, forget not; for with such sacrifices God is well pleased. *Heb.* xiii. 16.

Whoso hath this world's good, and seeth his brother have need, and shutteth up his compassion from him, how dwelleth the love of God in him? *1 St. John* iii. 17.

Give alms of thy goods, and never turn thy face from any poor man; and then the face of the Lord shall not be turned away from thee. *Tobit* iv. 7.

Be merciful after thy power. If thou hast much, give plenteously; if thou hast little, do thy diligence gladly to give of that little: for so gatherest thou thyself a good reward in the day of necessity. *Tobit* iv. 8, 9.

He that hath pity upon the poor lendeth unto the LORD: and look, what he layeth out, it shall be paid him again. *Prov.* xix. 17.

Blessed be the man that provideth for the sick and needy: the LORD shall deliver him in the time of trouble. *Psalm* xli. 1.

Speak unto the children of Israel, that they bring me an offering; of every man that giveth it willingly with his heart ye shall take my offering. *Exod.* xxv. 2.

Ye shall not appear before the LORD empty; every man shall give as he is able, according to the blessing of the LORD thy God which he hath given thee. *Deut.* xvi. 16, 17.

Thine, O LORD, is the greatness, and the power, and the glory, and the victory, and the majesty: for all that is in the heaven and in the earth is thine; thine is the kingdom, O LORD, and thou art exalted as head above all. *1 Chron.* xxix. 11.

All things come of thee, O LORD, and of thine own have we given thee. *1 Chron.* xxix. 14.

¶ *Whilst these Sentences are in reading, the Deacons, Church-wardens, or other fit persons appointed for that purpose, shall receive the Alms for the Poor, and other Devotions of the People, in a decent Basin to be provided by the Parish for that purpose; and reverently bring it to the Bishop, who shall humbly present and place it upon the Holy Table*

¶ *And the Bishop shall then place upon the Table so much Bread and* Wine *as he shall think sufficient.*

¶ *And when the Alms and Oblations are presented, there may be sung a Hymn, or an Offertory Anthem in the words of Holy Scripture or of the Book of Common Prayer, under the direction of the Bishop.*

¶ *Then shall the Bishop say,*

Let us pray for the whole state of Christ's Church militant.

ALMIGHTY and everliving God, who by thy holy Apostle hast taught us to make prayers, and supplications, and to give thanks for all men; We humbly beseech thee most mercifully [*to accept our alms and oblations, and] to receive these* prayers, which we offer unto thy Divine Majesty; beseeching thee to inspire continually the universal Church with the spirit of truth, unity, and concord: And grant that all those who do confess thy holy Name may agree in the truth of thy holy Word, and live in unity and godly love. We beseech thee also, so to direct and dispose the hearts of all Christian Rulers, that they may truly and impartially administer justice, to the punishment of wickedness and vice, and to the maintenance of thy true religion, and virtue. Give grace, O heavenly Father, to all Bishops and other Ministers, that they may, both by their life and doctrine, set forth thy true and lively Word, and rightly and duly administer thy holy Sacraments. And to all thy People give thy heavenly grace; and especially to this congregation here present; that, with meek

* *If there be no alms or oblations, then shall the words [*to accept our alms and oblations, and] be left unsaid.*

heart and due reverence, they may hear, and receive thy holy Word; truly serving thee in holiness and righteousness all the days of their life. And we most humbly beseech thee, of thy goodness, O Lord, to comfort and succour all those who, in this transitory life, are in trouble, sorrow, need, sickness, or any other adversity. And we also bless thy holy Name for all thy servants departed this life in thy faith and fear; beseeching thee to give us grace so to follow their good examples, that with them we may be partakers of thy heavenly kingdom. Grant this, O Father, for Jesus Christ's sake, our only Mediator and Advocate. *Amen.*

¶ *The Bishop shall then say this Exhortation. But Note, That the Exhortation may be omitted if it hath been already said on one Lord's Day in that same month.*

DEARLY beloved in the Lord, ye who mind to come to the holy Communion of the Body and Blood of our Saviour Christ, must consider how Saint Paul exhorteth all persons diligently to try and examine themselves, before they presume to eat of that Bread, and drink of that Cup. For as the benefit is great, if with a true penitent heart and lively faith we receive that holy Sacrament; so is the danger great, if we receive the same unworthily. Judge therefore yourselves, brethren, that ye be not judged of the Lord; repent you truly for your sins past; have a lively and stedfast faith in Christ our Saviour; amend your lives, and be in perfect charity with all men; so shall ye be meet partakers of those holy mysteries. And above all things ye must give most humble and hearty thanks to God, the Father, the Son, and the Holy Ghost, for the redemption of the world by the death and passion of our Saviour Christ, both God and man : who did humble himself, even to the death upon the Cross, for us, miserable sinners, who lay in darkness and the shadow of death ; that he might make us the children of God, and exalt us to everlasting life. And to the end that we should always remember the exceeding great love of our Master, and only Saviour, Jesus Christ, thus dying for us, and the innumerable benefits which by his precious blood-shedding he hath obtained for us ; he hath instituted and ordained holy mysteries, as pledges of his love, and for a continual remembrance of his death, to our great and endless comfort. To him therefore, with the Father and the Holy Ghost, let us give (as we are most bounden) continual thanks, submitting ourselves wholly to his holy will and pleasure, and studying to serve him in true holiness and righteousness all the days of our life. *Amen.*

¶ *Then shall the Bishop say to those who come to receive the Holy Communion,*

YE who do truly and earnestly repent you of your sins, and are in love and charity with your neighbours, and intend to lead a new life, following the commandments of God, and walking from henceforth in his holy ways ; Draw near with faith, and take this holy Sacrament to your comfort ; and make your humble confession to Almighty God, devoutly kneeling.

¶ *Then shall this General Confession be made, by the Bishop and all those who are minded to receive the Holy Communion, humbly kneeling.*

ALMIGHTY God, Father of our Lord Jesus Christ, Maker of all things, Judge of all men ; We acknowledge and bewail our manifold sins and wickedness, Which we, from time to time, most grievously have committed, By thought, word, and deed, Against thy Divine Majesty, Provoking most justly thy wrath and indignation against us. We do earnestly repent, And are heartily sorry for these our misdoings ; The remembrance of them is grievous unto us ; The burden of them is intolerable. Have mercy upon us, Have mercy upon us, most merciful Father ; For thy Son our Lord Jesus Christ's sake, Forgive us all that is past ; And grant that we may ever hereafter Serve and please thee In newness of life, To the honour and glory of thy Name ; Through Jesus Christ our Lord. *Amen.*

¶ *Then shall the Bishop stand up, and turning to the People, say,*

ALMIGHTY God, our heavenly Father, who of his great mercy hath promised forgiveness of sins to all those who with hearty repentance and true faith turn unto him ; Have mercy upon you ; pardon and deliver you from all your sins : confirm and strengthen you in all goodness : and bring you to everlasting life ; through Jesus Christ our Lord. *Amen.*

¶ *Then shall the Bishop say,*

Hear what comfortable words our Saviour Christ saith unto all who truly turn to him.

COME unto me, all ye that travail and are heavy laden, and I will refresh you. *St. Matt.* xi. 28.

So God loved the world, that he gave his only-begotten Son, to the end that all that believe in him should not perish, but have everlasting life. *St. John* iii. 16.

Hear also what Saint Paul saith.

This is a true saying, and worthy of all men to be received, That Christ Jesus came into the world to save sinners. 1 *Tim.* i. 15.

Hear also what Saint John saith.

If any man sin, we have an Advocate with the Father, Jesus Christ the righteous; and he is the Propitiation for our sins. 1 *St. John* ii. 1, 2.

¶ *After which the Bishop shall proceed, saying,*

Lift up your hearts.

Answer. We lift them up unto the Lord.

Bishop. Let us give thanks unto our Lord God.

Answer. It is meet and right so to do.

¶ *Then shall the Bishop turn to the Lord's Table, and say,*

IT is very meet, right, and our bounden duty, that we should at all times, *[* These in all places, give words* (Holy thanks unto thee, Father] *must* O Lord, [* Holy *be omitted in* Father,] Almighty, *Trinity-Sun-* Everlasting God. *day.*

¶ *Here shall follow the Proper Preface, according to the time, if there be any specially appointed; or else immediately shall be said or sung by the Bishop,*

THEREFORE with Angels and Archangels, and with all the company of heaven, we laud and magnify thy glorious Name; evermore praising thee, and saying,

HOLY, HOLY, ¶ *Bishop* HOLY, Lord God *and People.* of hosts, Heaven and earth are full of thy glory: Glory be to thee, O Lord Most High. Amen.

PROPER PREFACES.

Upon Christmas-day, *and seven days after.*

BECAUSE thou didst give Jesus Christ, thine only Son, to be born as at this time for us; who, by the operation of the Holy Ghost, was made very man, of the substance of the Virgin Mary his mother; and that without spot of sin, to make us clean from all sin. Therefore with Angels *etc.*

Upon Easter-day, *and seven days after.*

BUT chiefly are we bound to praise thee for the glorious Resurrection of thy Son Jesus Christ our Lord: for he is the very Paschal Lamb, which was offered for us, and hath taken away the sin of the world; who by his death hath destroyed death, and by his rising to life again hath restored to us everlasting life. Therefore with Angels, *etc.*

Upon Ascension-day, *and seven days after.*

THROUGH thy most dearly beloved Son Jesus Christ our Lord; who, after his most glorious Resurrection, manifestly appeared to all his Apostles, and in their sight ascended up into heaven, to prepare a place for us; that where he is, thither we might also ascend, and reign with him in glory. Therefore with Angels, etc.

Upon Whitsunday, and six days after.

THROUGH Jesus Christ our Lord; according to whose most true promise, the Holy Ghost came down as at this time from heaven, with a sudden great sound, as it had been a mighty wind, in the likeness of fiery tongues, lighting upon the Apostles, to teach them, and to lead them to all truth; giving them both the gift of divers languages, and also boldness with fervent zeal constantly to preach the Gospel unto all nations: whereby we have been brought out of darkness and error into the clear light and true knowledge of thee, and of thy Son Jesus Christ. Therefore with Angels, etc.

Upon the Feast of Trinity only, may be said,

WHO art one God, one Lord; not one only Person, but three Persons in one Substance. For that which we believe of the glory of the Father, the same we believe of the Son, and of the Holy Ghost, without any difference or inequality. Therefore with Angels, etc.

¶ *Or else this may be said, the words* [Holy Father] *being retained in the introductory Address.*

FOR the precious death and merits of thy Son Jesus Christ our Lord, and for the sending to us of the Holy Ghost, the Comforter; who are one with thee in thy Eternal Godhead. Therefore with Angels, etc.

¶ *Then shall the Bishop, kneeling down at the Lord's Table, say in the name of all those who shall receive the Communion, this Prayer following.*

WE do not presume to come to this thy Table, O merciful Lord, trusting in our own righteousness, but in thy manifold and great mercies. We are not worthy so much as to gather up the crumbs under thy Table. But thou art the same Lord, whose property is always to have mercy: Grant us therefore, gracious Lord, so to eat the flesh of thy dear Son Jesus Christ, and to drink his blood, that our sinful bodies may be made clean by his body, and our souls washed through his most precious blood, and that we may evermore dwell in him and he in us. *Amen.*

¶ *When the Bishop, standing before the Table, hath so ordered the Bread and Wine, that he may with the more readiness and decency break the Bread before the People, and take the Cup into his hands, he shall say the Prayer of Consecration, as followeth.*

ALL glory be to thee, Almighty God, our heavenly Father, for that thou, of thy tender mercy, didst give thine only Son Jesus Christ to suffer death upon the Cross for our redemption; who made there (by his one oblation of himself once offered) a full, perfect, and sufficient sacrifice, oblation, and satisfaction, for the sins of the whole world; and did institute, and in his holy Gospel command us to continue, a perpetual memory of that his precious death and sacrifice, until his coming again: For in the night in which he was betrayed, (*a*) he took Bread; and when he had given

(a) Here the Bishop is to take the Paten into his hands.

thanks,(b) he brake it, and gave it to his disciples, saying, Take, eat, (c) this is my Body, which is given for you; Do this in remembrance of me. Likewise, after supper, (d) he took the Cup; and when he had given thanks, he gave it to them, saying, Drink ye all of this; for (e) this is my Blood of the New Testament, which is shed for you, and for many, for the remission of sins: Do this, as oft as ye shall drink it, in remembrance of me.

(b) And here he is to break the Bread.

(c) And here to lay his hand upon all the Bread.

(d) Here he is to take the Cup into his hands.

(e) And here he is to lay his hand upon every vessel in which there is any Wine to be consecrated.

WHEREFORE, O Lord and heavenly Father, according to the institution of *thy dearly beloved* Son our Saviour Jesus Christ, we, thy humble servants, do celebrate and make here before thy Divine Majesty, with these thy holy gifts, which we now offer unto thee, the memorial thy Son hath commanded us to make; having in remembrance his blessed passion and precious death, his mighty resurrection and glorious ascension; rendering unto thee most hearty thanks for the innumerable benefits procured unto us by the same.

The Oblation.

AND we most humbly beseech thee, O merciful Father, to hear us; and, of thy almighty goodness, vouchsafe to bless and sanctify, with thy Word and Holy Spirit, these thy gifts and creatures of bread and wine; that we, receiving

The Invocation.

them according to thy Son our Saviour Jesus Christ's holy institution, in remembrance of his death and passion, may be partakers of his most blessed Body and Blood.

AND we earnestly desire thy fatherly goodness, mercifully to accept this our sacrifice of praise and thanksgiving; most humbly beseeching thee to grant that, by the merits and death of thy Son Jesus Christ, and through faith in his blood, we, and all thy whole Church, may obtain remission of our sins, and all other benefits of his passion. And here we offer and present unto thee, O Lord, our selves, our souls and bodies, to be a reasonable, holy, and living sacrifice unto thee; humbly beseeching thee, that we, and all others who shall be partakers of this Holy Communion, may worthily receive the most precious Body and Blood of thy Son Jesus Christ, be filled with thy grace and heavenly benediction, and made one body with him, that he may dwell in us, and we in him. And although we are unworthy, through our manifold sins, to offer unto thee any sacrifice; yet we beseech thee to accept this our bounden duty and service; not weighing our merits, but pardoning our offences, through Jesus Christ our Lord; by whom, and with whom, in the unity of the Holy Ghost, all honour and glory be unto thee, O Father Almighty, world without end. *Amen.*

¶ *Here may be sung a Hymn.*

¶ *Then shall the Bishop first receive the Holy Communion in both kinds himself, and proceed to deliver the same to the Bishops, Priests, and Deacons, in like manner, and after that, to the People also in order, into their hands, all devoutly kneeling. And sufficient opportunity shall be given to those present to communicate. And when he delivereth the Bread, he shall say,*

THE Body of our Lord Jesus Christ, which was given for thee, preserve thy body and soul unto everlasting life. Take and eat this in remembrance that Christ died for thee, and feed on him in thy heart by faith, with thanksgiving.

¶ *And the Bishop, delivering the Cup, shall say,*

THE Blood of our Lord Jesus Christ, which was shed for thee, preserve thy body and soul unto everlasting life. Drink this in remembrance that Christ's Blood was shed for thee, and be thankful.

¶ *If the consecrated Bread or Wine be spent before all have communicated, the Bishop is to consecrate more, according to the Form before prescribed; beginning at, All glory be to thee, Almighty God, and ending with these words, partakers of his most blessed Body and Blood.*

¶ *When all have communicated, the Bishop shall return to the Lord's Table, and reverently place upon it what remaineth of the consecrated Elements, covering the same with a fair linen cloth.*

¶ *Then shall the Bishop say the Lord's Prayer, the People repeating after him every Petition.*

OUR Father, who art in heaven, Hallowed be thy Name. Thy kingdom come. Thy will be done on earth, As it is in heaven. Give us this day our daily bread. And forgive us our trespasses, As we forgive those who trespass against us. And lead us not into temptation; But deliver us from evil: For thine is the kingdom, and the power, and the glory, for ever and ever. Amen.

¶ *After shall be said as followeth.*

ALMIGHTY and everliving God, we most heartily thank thee, for that thou dost vouchsafe to feed us who have duly received these holy mysteries, with the spiritual food of the most precious Body and Blood of thy Son our Saviour Jesus Christ; and dost assure us thereby of thy favour and goodness towards us; and that we are very members incorporate in the mystical body of thy Son, which is the blessed company of all faithful people; and are also heirs through hope of thy everlasting kingdom, by the merits of the most precious death and passion of thy dear Son. And we most humbly beseech thee, O heavenly Father, so to assist us with thy grace, that we may continue in that holy fellowship, and do all such good works as thou hast prepared for us to walk in; through Jesus Christ our Lord, to whom, with thee and the Holy Ghost, be all honour and glory, world without end. *Amen.*

¶ *Then shall be said or sung, all standing, Gloria in excelsis; or some proper Hymn from the Selection.*

GLORY be to God on high, and on earth peace, good will towards men. We praise thee, we bless thee, we worship thee, we glorify thee, we give thanks to thee for thy great glory, O Lord God, heavenly King, God the Father Almighty. O Lord, the only-begotten Son, Jesus Christ; O Lord God, Lamb of God, Son of the Father, that takest away the sins of the world, have mercy upon us. Thou that takest away the sins of the world, have mercy upon us. Thou that takest away the sins of the world, receive our prayer. Thou that sittest at the right hand of God the Father, have mercy upon us.

For thou only art holy; thou only art the Lord; thou only, O Christ, with the Holy Ghost, art most high in the glory of God the Father. Amen.

¶ *Then the Bishop shall let them depart with this Blessing.*

THE Peace of God, which passeth all understanding,

keep your hearts and minds in the knowledge and love of God, and of his Son Jesus Christ our Lord: And the Blessing of God Almighty, the Father, the Son, and the Holy Ghost, be amongst you, and remain with you always. *Amen.*

¶ *If any of the consecrated Bread and Wine remain after the Communion, it shall not be carried out of the Church; but the Bishop and other Communicants shall, immediately after the Blessing, reverently eat and drink the same.*

Here endeth the Order for the Administration of the Holy Communion.

THE FORM OF
CONSECRATION OF A CHURCH OR CHAPEL.

¶ *The Bishop is to be received at the entrance of the Church, or Chapel, by the Church-wardens and Vestrymen, or some other persons appointed for that purpose. The Bishop and the Clergy who are present shall go up the aisle of the Church, or Chapel, to the Communion Table, repeating the twenty-fourth Psalm alternately, the Bishop one verse and the Clergy another.*

Psalm xxiv.

THE earth is the LORD'S, and all that therein is : the compass of the world, and they that dwell therein.

2 For he hath founded it upon the seas : and prepared it upon the floods.

3 Who shall ascend into the hill of the LORD : or who shall rise up in his holy place?

4 Even he that hath clean

hands, and a pure heart : and that hath not lift up his mind unto vanity, nor sworn to deceive his neighbour.

5 He shall receive the blessing from the LORD : and righteousness from the God of his salvation.

6 This is the generation of them that seek him : even of them that seek thy face, O Jacob.

7 Lift up your heads, O ye

gates; and be ye lift up, ye everlasting doors; and the King of glory shall come in.

8 Who is this King of glory: It is the LORD strong and mighty, even the LORD mighty in battle.

9 Lift up your heads, O ye gates; and be ye lift up, ye everlasting doors; and the King of glory shall come in.

10 Who is this King of glory: Even the LORD of hosts, he is the King of glory.

Glory be to the Father, and to the Son: and to the Holy Ghost;

As it was in the beginning, is now, and ever shall be: world without end. Amen.

¶ *The Bishop shall go within the rails, with such of the Clergy as can be there accommodated. The Bishop, sitting in his chair, shall have the instruments of Donation and Endowment, if there be any, presented to him; and then standing up, and turning to the Congregation, shall say,*

DEARLY beloved in the Lord; forasmuch as devout and holy men, as well under the Law as under the Gospel, moved either by the express command of God, or by the secret inspiration of the blessed Spirit, and acting agreeably to their own reason and sense of the natural decency of things, have erected houses for the public worship of God, and separated them from all unhallowed, worldly, and common uses, in order to fill men's minds with greater reverence for his glorious Majesty, and affect their hearts with more devotion and humility in his service; which pious works have been approved of and graciously accepted by our heavenly Father: Let us not doubt but that he will also favourably approve our godly purpose of setting a-

part this place in solemn manner, for the performance of the several offices of religious worship, and let us faithfully and devoutly beg his blessing on this our undertaking.

¶ *Then the Bishop, kneeling, shall say the following Prayer.*

O ETERNAL God, mighty in power, and of majesty incomprehensible, whom the heaven of heavens cannot contain, much less the walls of temples made with hands, and who yet hast been graciously pleased to promise thy especial presence, wherever two or three of thy faithful servants shall assemble in thy Name, to offer up their praises and supplications unto thee; Vouchsafe, O Lord, to be present with us, who are here gathered together with all humility and readiness of heart, to consecrate this place to the honour of thy great Name: separating it henceforth from all unhallowed, ordinary, and common uses; and dedicating it to thy service, for reading thy holy Word, for celebrating thy holy Sacraments, for offering to thy glorious Majesty the sacrifices of prayer and thanksgiving, for blessing thy people in thy Name, and for all other holy offices: accept, O Lord, this service at our hands, and bless it with such success as may tend most to thy glory, and the furtherance of our happiness both temporal and spiritual; through Jesus Christ our blessed Lord and Saviour. *Amen.*

¶ *After this the Bishop shall stand up, and turning his face towards the Congregation, shall say,*

REGARD, O Lord, the supplications of thy servants, and grant that whosoever shall be dedicated to thee in this house by Baptism, may be sanctified by the Holy Ghost, delivered from thy wrath and eternal death, and received as a living member of Christ's Church, and may ever remain in the number of thy faithful children. *Amen.*

Grant, O Lord, that they who at this place shall in their own persons renew the promises and vows of their Baptism, and be Confirmed by the Bishop, may receive such a measure of thy Holy Spirit, that they may be enabled faithfully to fulfil the same, and grow in grace unto their lives' end. *Amen.*

Grant, O Lord, that whosoever shall receive in this place the blessed Sacrament of the Body and Blood of Christ, may come to that holy ordinance with faith, charity, and true repentance; and being filled with thy grace and heavenly benediction, may, to their great and endless comfort, obtain remission of their sins, and *all other benefits* of this passion. *Amen.*

Grant, O Lord, that by thy holy Word which shall be read and preached in this place, and by thy Holy Spirit grafting it inwardly in the heart, the hearers thereof may both perceive and know what things they ought to do, and may have power and strength to fulfil the same. *Amen.*

Grant, O Lord, that whosoever shall be joined together in this place in the holy estate of Matrimony, may faithfully perform and keep the vow and covenant between them made, and may remain in perfect love together unto their lives' end. *Amen.*

Grant, we beseech thee, blessed Lord, that whosoever shall draw near to thee in this place, to give thee thanks for the benefits which they have received at thy hands, to set forth thy most worthy praise, to confess their sins unto thee, and to ask such things as are requisite and necessary, as well for the body as for the soul, may do it with such steadiness of faith, and with such seriousness, affection, and devotion of mind, that thou mayest accept their bounden duty and service, and vouchsafe to give whatever in thy infinite wisdom thou shalt see to be most expedient for them. All which we beg for Jesus Christ's sake, our most blessed Lord and Saviour. *Amen.*

¶ *Then, the Bishop sitting in his chair, the Sentence of Consecration is to be read by some person appointed by him, and then laid by him upon the Communion Table; after which, the Bishop shall say,*

BLESSED be thy Name, O Lord, that it hath pleased thee to put it into the hearts of thy servants to appropriate and devote this house to thy honour and worship; and grant that all who shall enjoy the benefit of this pious work, may show forth their thankfulness, by making a right use of it, to the glory of thy blessed Name; through Jesus Christ our Lord. *Amen.*

¶ *After this, the Minister appointed is to read the Service for the day.*

PROPER PSALMS.

Psalm lxxxiv. *Psalm* cxxii.
Psalm cxxxii.

PROPER LESSONS.

FIRST. 1 Kings 8, v. 22 to v. 63; *or* Genesis 28, at v. 10.
SECOND. Hebrews 10, v. 19 to v. 26; *or* Revelation 21, at v. 10.

¶ *The Bishop shall then proceed to the Communion Service. The following shall be the Collect, Epistle, and Gospel, for the occasion.*

The Collect.

O MOST glorious Lord, we acknowledge that we are not worthy to offer unto thee any thing belonging unto us; yet we beseech thee, in thy great goodness, graciously to accept the Dedication of this place to thy service, and to prosper this our undertaking; receive the prayers and intercessions of all those thy servants who shall call upon thee in this house; and give them grace to prepare their hearts to serve thee with reverence and godly fear; affect them with an awful apprehension of thy Divine Majesty, and a deep sense of their own unworthiness; that so, approaching thy sanctuary with lowliness and devotion, and coming before thee with clean thoughts and pure hearts, with bodies undefiled and minds sanctified, they may always perform a service acceptable to thee; through Jesus Christ our Lord. *Amen.*

The Epistle. 2 Cor. vi. 14.

BE ye not unequally yoked together with unbelievers: for what fellowship hath righteousness with unrighteousness? and what communion hath light with darkness? and what concord hath Christ with Belial? or, what part hath he that believeth with an infidel? and what agreement hath the temple of God with idols? for ye are the temple of the living God; as God hath said, I will dwell in them, and walk in them; and

I will be their God, and they shall be my people.

The Gospel. St. John ii. 13.

AND the Jews' passover was at hand, and Jesus went up to Jerusalem, and found in the temple those that sold oxen and sheep and doves, and the changers of money sitting: and when he had made a scourge of small cords, he drove them all out of the temple, and the sheep, and the oxen; and poured out the changers' money, and overthrew the tables; and said unto them that sold doves, Take these things hence; make not my Father's house an house of merchandise. And his disciples remembered that it was written, The zeal of thine house hath eaten me up.

¶ *For the last Collect, immediately before the final Blessing, the Bishop shall say this Prayer.*

BLESSED be thy Name, O Lord God, for that it hath pleased thee to have thy habitation among the sons of men, and to dwell in the midst of the assembly of the saints upon the earth; Grant, we beseech thee, that in this place now set apart to thy service, thy holy Name may be worshipped in truth and purity through all generations; through Jesus Christ our Lord. *Amen.*

THE Peace of God, which passeth all understanding, keep your hearts and minds in the knowledge and love of God, and of his Son Jesus Christ our Lord: and the Blessing of God Almighty, the Father, the Son, and the Holy Ghost, be amongst you, and remain with you always. *Amen*

AN OFFICE OF

INSTITUTION OF MINISTERS

INTO PARISHES OR CHURCHES.

¶ *The Bishop having received due Notice of the Election of a Minister into a Parish or Church, as prescribed by the Canon, concerning "the Election and Institution of Ministers," and being satisfied that the "person chosen is a qualified Minister of this Church," may proceed to institute him into the Parish.*

¶ *In any Diocese, the concluding Paragraph in the Letter of Institution may be omitted, where it interferes with the Usages, Laws, or Charters of the Church in the same.*

To our well-beloved in Christ,
A. B., Presbyter, Greeting.

WE do by these Presents give and grant unto you, in whose Learning, Diligence, sound Doctrine, and Prudence, we do fully confide, our License and Authority to perform the Office of a Priest, in the Parish [or Church] of *E.* And also hereby do institute you into said Parish, [or Church, possessed of full power to perform every Act of sacerdotal Function among the People of the same; you continuing in communion with us, and complying with the rubrics and canons of the Church, and with such lawful directions as you shall at any time receive from us.

And as a canonically instituted Priest into the Office of Rector of —— Parish, [or Church,] you are faithfully to feed that portion of the flock of Christ which is now intrusted to you; not as a man-pleaser, but as continually bearing in mind that you are accountable to us here, and to the Chief Bishop and Sovereign Judge of all, hereafter.

And as the Lord hath ordained that they who serve at the altar should live of the things belonging to the altar; so we authorize you to claim and enjoy all the accustomed temporalities appertaining to your cure, until some urgent reason or reasons occasion a wish in you, or in the congregation committed to your charge, to bring about a separation, and dissolution of all sacerdotal relation, between you and them; of all which you will give us due notice; and in case of any difference between you and your congregation, as to a separation and dissolution of all sacerdotal connection between you and them, we, your Bishop, with the advice of our Presbyters, are to be the ultimate arbiter and judge.

In witness whereof, we have hereunto affixed our episcopal seal and signature, at this —— day of ——, A.D. ——, and in the —— year of our consecration.

Sigillum.

Signat.

✠

¶ On the day designated for the new Incumbent's Institution, at the usual hour of Morning Prayer, the Bishop, or the Institutor appointed by him, attended by the new Incumbent, and by the other Clergy present, shall enter the Chancel. Then all the Clergy present standing in the Chancel or Choir, except the Bishop, or the Priest who acts as Institutor, who shall go within the rails of the Altar; the Wardens (or, in case of their necessary absence, two members of the Vestry) standing on the right and left of the Altar, without the rails; the Senior Warden (or the member of the Vestry supplying his place) holding the keys of the Church in his hand, in open view, the officiating Priest shall read Morning Prayer.

PROPER PSALMS.

Psalm cxxii.   *Psalm* cxxxii.
Psalm cxxxiii.

PROPER LESSONS.

FIRST.   Ezekiel 33, to v. 10.
SECOND.   St. John 10, to v. 19.

¶ *Morning Prayer ended, the Bishop, or the Priest who acts as the Institutor, standing within the rails of the Altar, shall say,*

DEARLY beloved in the Lord, we have assembled for the purpose of instituting the Rev. *A. B.* into this Parish, [or Church,] as Priest and Rector of the same; and we are possessed of your Vote that he has been so elected; as also of the prescribed Letter of Institution. But if any of you can show just cause why he may not be instituted, we proceed no further, because we would not that an unworthy person should minister among you.

¶ *If any objection be offered, the Bishop, or the Priest who acts as the Institutor, shall judge whether it afford just cause to suspend the Service.*

¶ *No objection being offered, or the Institutor choosing to go on with the Service, then shall be read the Letter of Institution.*

¶ *And then shall the Senior Warden (or the member of the Vestry supplying his place) present the keys of the Church to the new Incumbent, saying,*

IN the name and behalf of —— Parish [or Church] I do receive and acknowledge you, the Rev. *A. B.,* as Priest and Rector of the same; and in token thereof, give into your hands the keys of this Church.

¶ *Then the new Incumbent shall say,*

I, *A. B.,* receive these keys of the House of God at your hands, as the pledges of my Institution, and of your parochial recognition, and promise to be a faithful shepherd over you: In the Name of the Father, and of the Son, and of the Holy Ghost.

¶ *Here the Institutor shall begin the Office.*

Minister. The Lord be with you.

Answer. And with thy spirit.
Let us pray.

DIRECT us, O Lord, in all our doings, with thy most gracious favour, and further us with thy continual help; that in all our works begun, continued, and ended in thee, we may glorify thy holy Name, and finally, by thy mercy, obtain everlasting life; through Jesus Christ our Lord, who hath taught us to pray unto thee, O Almighty Father, in his prevailing Name and words,

OUR Father, who art in heaven, Hallowed be thy Name. Thy kingdom come. Thy will be done on earth, As it is in heaven. Give us this day our daily bread. And forgive us our trespasses, As we forgive those who trespass against us. And lead us not into temptation; But deliver us from evil: For thine is the kingdom, and the power, and the glory, for ever and ever. Amen.

¶ *Then shall the Institutor receive the Incumbent within the rails of the Altar, and present him the Bible, Book of Common Prayer, and Books of Canons of the General and Diocesan Convention, saying as follows.*

RECEIVE these Books; and let them be the rule of thy conduct in dispensing the divine Word, in leading the Devotions of the People, and in exercising the Discipline of the Church; *and be thou in all things a pattern to the flock committed to thy care.*

¶ *Then shall be said or sung Psalm lxviii. Exsurgat Deus, or Psalm xxvi. Judica me, Domine.*

Minister. The Law was given by Moses:

People. But Grace and Truth came by Jesus Christ:

Minister and People. Who is God over all, blessed for evermore. Amen.

Let us pray.

MOST gracious God, the giver of all good and perfect gifts, who of thy wise providence hast appointed others Orders in thy Church: Give thy grace, we beseech thee, to thy servant, to whom the charge of this Congregation is now committed; and so replenish him

with the truth of thy doctrine, and endue him with innocency of life, that he may faithfully serve before thee, to the glory of thy great Name, and the benefit of thy holy Church; through Jesus Christ, our only Mediator and Redeemer. Amen.

O HOLY Jesus, who hast purchased to thyself an universal Church, and hast promised to be with the Ministers of Apostolic Succession to the end of the world; Be graciously pleased to bless the ministry and service of him who is now appointed to offer the sacrifices of prayer and praise to thee in this house, which is called by thy Name. May the words of his mouth, and the meditation of his heart, be alway acceptable in thy sight, O Lord, our strength and our Redeemer. Amen.

O GOD, Holy Ghost, Sanctifier of the faithful, visit, we pray thee, this Congregation with thy love and favour; enlighten their minds more and more with the light of the everlasting Gospel; graft in their hearts a love of the truth; increase in them true religion; nourish them with all goodness; and of thy great mercy keep them in the same, O blessed Spirit, whom, with the Father and the Son together, we worship and glorify as one God, world without end. Amen.

Benediction.

THE God of peace, who brought again from the dead our Lord Jesus Christ, the great Shepherd of the sheep, through the blood of the everlasting covenant; Make you perfect in every good work to do his will, working in you that which is well pleasing in his sight; through Jesus Christ, to whom be glory for ever and ever. *Amen.*

¶ *Then shall the Instituted Minister kneel at the Altar, to present his supplication for himself, in this form.*

O LORD my God, I am not worthy that thou shouldest come under my roof; yet thou hast honoured thy servant with appointing him to stand in thy House, and to serve at thy holy Altar. To thee and to thy service I devote myself, soul, body, and spirit, with all their powers and faculties. Fill my memory with the words of thy Law; enlighten my understanding with the illumination of the Holy Ghost; and may all the wishes and desires of my will centre in what thou hast commanded. And, to make me instrumental in promoting the salvation of the people now committed to my charge, grant that I may faithfully administer thy holy Sacraments, and by my life and doctrine set forth thy true and lively Word. Be ever with me in the performance of all the duties of my ministry: in prayer, to quicken my devotion; in praises, to heighten my love and gratitude; and in preaching, to give a readiness of thought and expression suitable to the clearness and excellency of thy holy Word. Grant this for the sake of Jesus Christ thy Son our Saviour.

¶ *Then shall follow the Sermon; and, after that, the Instituted Minister shall proceed to the Communion Service, and to administer the holy Eucharist to his Congregation; and after the Benediction, (which he shall always pronounce,) the Wardens, Vestry, and others, shall salute and welcome him, bidding him God speed.*

¶ *When the Bishop of the Diocese is present at the Institution of a Minister, he shall make to him the address prescribed in this Office in the form of a letter.*

¶ *The Instituted Minister, standing up, shall say,*

The Lord be with you.
Answer. And with thy spirit.

Let us pray.

O ALMIGHTY God, who hast built thy Church upon the foundation of the Apostles and Prophets, Jesus Christ himself being the chief corner-stone; Grant that, by the operation of the Holy Ghost, all Christians may be so joined together in unity of spirit, and in the bond of peace, that they may be an holy temple acceptable unto thee. And especially to this Congregation present, give the abundance of thy grace; that with one heart they may desire the prosperity of thy holy Apostolic Church, and with one mouth may profess the faith once delivered to the Saints. Defend them from the sins of heresy and schism; let not the foot of pride come nigh to hurt them, nor the hand of the ungodly to cast them down. And grant that the course of this world may be so peaceably ordered by thy governance, that thy Church may joyfully serve thee in all godly quietness; that so they may walk in the ways of truth and peace, and at last be numbered with thy saints in glory everlasting; through thy merits, O blessed Jesus, thou gracious Bishop and Shepherd of our souls, who art with the Father and the Holy Ghost one God, world without end. *Amen.*

ARTICLES OF RELIGION;

AS ESTABLISHED BY

The Bishops, the Clergy, and the Laity

OF

THE PROTESTANT EPISCOPAL CHURCH

IN THE UNITED STATES OF AMERICA,

In Convention,

ON THE TWELFTH DAY OF SEPTEMBER,

IN THE YEAR OF OUR LORD

1801.

ARTICLES OF RELIGION.

ARTICLE I. *Of Faith in the Holy Trinity.*

THERE is but one living and true God, everlasting, without body, parts, or passions; of infinite power, wisdom, and goodness; the Maker, and Preserver of all things both visible and invisible. And in unity of this Godhead there be three Persons, of one substance, power, and eternity; the Father, the Son, and the Holy Ghost.

ART. II. *Of the Word or Son of God, which was made very Man.*

THE Son, which is the Word of the Father, begotten from everlasting of the Father, the very and eternal God, and of one substance with the Father, took Man's nature in the womb of the blessed Virgin, of her substance: so that two whole and perfect Natures, that is to say, the Godhead and Manhood, were joined together in one Person, never to be divided, whereof is one Christ, very God, and very Man: who truly suffered, was crucified, dead, and buried, to reconcile his Father to us, and to be a sacrifice, not only for original guilt, but also for actual sins of men.

ART. III. *Of the going down of Christ into Hell.*

AS Christ died for us, and was buried; so also is it to be believed, that he went down into Hell.

ART. IV. *Of the Resurrection of Christ.*

CHRIST did truly rise again from death, and took again his body, with flesh, bones, and all things appertaining to the perfection of Man's nature: wherewith he ascended into Heaven, and there sitteth, until he return to judge all Men at the last day.

ART. V. *Of the Holy Ghost.*

THE Holy Ghost, proceeding from the Father and the Son, is of one substance, majesty, and glory, with the Father and the Son, very and eternal God.

ART. VI. *Of the Sufficiency of the Holy Scriptures for Salvation.*

HOLY Scripture containeth all things necessary to salvation: so that whatsoever is not read therein, nor may be proved thereby, is not to be required of any man, that it should be believed as an article of the Faith, or be thought requisite or necessary to salvation. In the name of the Holy Scripture we do understand those canonical Books of the Old and New Testament, of whose authority was never any doubt in the Church.

OF THE NAMES AND NUMBER OF THE CANONICAL BOOKS.

Genesis,
Exodus,
Leviticus,
Numbers,
Deuteronomy,
Joshua,
Judges,
Ruth,
The First Book of Samuel,
The Second Book of Samuel,
The First Book of Kings,
The Second Book of Kings,
The First Book of Chronicles,
The Second Book of Chronicles,
The First Book of Esdras,
The Second Book of Esdras,
The Book of Esther,
The Book of Job,
The Psalms,
The Proverbs,
Ecclesiastes or Preacher,
Cantica, or Songs of Solomon,
Four Prophets the greater,
Twelve Prophets the less.

And the other Books (as *Hierome* saith) the Church doth read for example of life and instruction of manners; but yet doth it not apply them to establish any doctrine; such are these following:

The Third Book of Esdras,
The Fourth Book of Esdras,
The Book of Tobias,
The Book of Judith,
The rest of the Book of Esther,
The Book of Wisdom,
Jesus the Son of Sirach,
Baruch the Prophet,
The Song of the Three Children,
The Story of Susanna,
Of Bel and the Dragon,
The Prayer of Manasses,
The First Book of Maccabees,
The Second Book of Maccabees.

All the Books of the New Testament, as they are commonly received, we do receive, and account them Canonical.

Art. VII. *Of the Old Testament.*

THE Old Testament is not contrary to the New: for both in the Old and New Testament everlasting life is offered to Mankind by Christ, who is the only Mediator between God and Man, being both God and Man. Wherefore they are not to be heard, which feign that the old Fathers did look only for transitory promises. Although the Law given from God by Moses, as touching Ceremonies and Rites, do not bind Christian men, nor the Civil precepts thereof ought of necessity to be received in any commonwealth; yet notwithstanding, no Christian man whatsoever is free from the obedience of the Commandments which are called Moral.

Art. VIII. *Of the Creeds.*

THE *Nicene* Creed, and that which is commonly called the *Apostles'* Creed, ought thoroughly to be received and believed; for they may be proved by most certain warrants of Holy Scripture.

Art. IX. *Of Original or Birth-Sin.*

ORIGINAL sin standeth not in the following of *Adam*, (as the *Pelagians* do vainly talk;) but it is the fault and corruption of the Nature of every man, that naturally is engendered of the offspring of *Adam*; whereby man is very far gone from original righteousness, and is of his own nature inclined to evil, so that the flesh lusteth always contrary to the Spirit; and therefore in every person born into this world, it deserveth God's wrath and damnation. And this infection of nature doth remain, yea in them that are regenerated; whereby the lust of the flesh, called in Greek, φρόνημα σαρκὸς, (which some do expound the wisdom, some sensuality, some the affection, some the desire, of the flesh,) is not subject to the Law of God. And although there is no condemnation for them that believe and are baptized; yet the Apostle doth confess, that concupiscence and lust hath of itself the nature of sin.

Art. X. *Of Free-Will.*

THE condition of Man after the fall of *Adam* is such, that he cannot turn and prepare himself, by his own natural strength and good works, to faith, and calling upon God. Wherefore we have no power to do good works pleasant and acceptable to God, without the grace of God by Christ preventing us, that we may have a good will, and working with us, when we have that good will.

ART. XI. *Of the Justification of Man.*

WE are accounted righteous before God, only for the merit of our Lord and Saviour Jesus Christ by Faith, and not for our own works or deservings. Wherefore, that we are justified by Faith only, is a most wholesome Doctrine, and very full of comfort, as more largely is expressed in the Homily of Justification.

ART. XII. *Of Good Works.*

ALBEIT that Good Works, which are the fruits of Faith, and follow after Justification, cannot put away our sins, and endure the severity of God's judgment; yet are they pleasing and acceptable to God in Christ, and do spring out necessarily of a true and lively Faith; insomuch that by them a lively Faith may be as evidently known as a tree discerned by the fruit.

ART. XIII. *Of Works before Justification.*

WORKS done before the grace of Christ, and the Inspiration of his Spirit, are not pleasant to God, forasmuch as they spring not of faith in Jesus Christ; neither do they make men meet to receive grace, or (as the School-authors say) deserve grace of congruity: yea rather, for that they are not done as God hath willed and commanded them to be done, we doubt not but they have the nature of sin.

ART. XIV. *Of Works of Supererogation.*

VOLUNTARY Works besides, over and above, God's Commandments, which they call Works of Supererogation, cannot be taught without arrogancy and impiety: for by them men do declare, that they do not only render unto God as much as they are bound to do, but that they do more for his sake, than of bounden duty is required: whereas Christ saith plainly, When ye have done all that are commanded to you, say, We are unprofitable servants.

ART. XV. *Of Christ alone without Sin.*

CHRIST in the truth of our nature was made like unto us in all things, sin only except, from which he was clearly void, both in his flesh, and in his spirit. He came to be the Lamb without spot, who, by sacrifice of himself once made, should take away the sins of the world; and sin (as Saint *John* saith) was not in him. But all we the rest, although baptized, and born again in Christ, yet offend in many things; and if we say we have no sin, we deceive ourselves, and the truth is not in us.

ART. XVI. *Of Sin after Baptism.*

NOT every deadly sin willingly committed after Baptism is sin against the Holy Ghost, and unpardonable. Wherefore the grant of repentance is not to be denied to such as fall into sin after Baptism. After we have received the Holy Ghost, we may depart from grace given, and fall into sin, and by the grace of God we may arise again, and amend our lives. And therefore they are to be condemned, which say, they can no more sin as long as they live here, or deny the place of forgiveness to such as truly repent.

ART. XVII. *Of Predestination and Election.*

PREDESTINATION to Life is the everlasting purpose of

God, whereby (before the foundations of the world were laid) he hath constantly decreed by his counsel secret to us, to deliver from curse and damnation those whom: he hath chosen in Christ out of mankind, and to bring them by Christ to everlasting salvation, as vessels made to honour. Wherefore, they which be endued with so excellent a benefit of God, be called according to God's purpose by his Spirit working in due season: they through Grace obey the calling: they be justified freely: they be made sons of God by adoption: they be made like the image of his only-begotten Son Jesus Christ: they walk religiously in good works, and at length, by God's mercy, they attain to everlasting felicity.

As the godly consideration of Predestination, and our Election in Christ, is full of sweet, pleasant, and unspeakable comfort to godly persons, and such as feel in themselves the working of the Spirit of Christ, mortifying the works of the flesh, and their earthly members, and drawing up their mind to high and heavenly things, as well because it doth greatly establish and confirm their faith of eternal Salvation to be enjoyed through Christ, as because it doth fervently kindle their love towards God: So, for curious and carnal persons, lacking the Spirit of Christ, to have continually before their eyes the sentence of God's Predestination, is a most dangerous downfall, whereby the Devil doth thrust them either into desperation, or into wretchlessness of most unclean living, no less perilous than desperation.

Furthermore, we must receive God's promises in such wise, as they be generally set forth to us in Holy Scripture: and, in our doings, that Will of God is to be followed, which we have expressly declared unto us in the Word of God.

ART. XVIII. Of obtaining eternal Salvation only by the Name of Christ.

THEY also are to be had accursed that presume to say, That every man shall be saved by the Law or Sect which he professeth, so that he be diligent to frame his life according to that Law, and the light of Nature. For Holy Scripture doth set out unto us only the Name of Jesus Christ, whereby men must be saved.

ART. XIX. Of the Church.

THE visible Church of Christ is a congregation of faithful men, in the which the pure Word of God is preached, and the Sacraments be duly ministered according to Christ's ordinance, in all those things that of necessity are requisite to the same.

As the Church of *Jerusalem, Alexandria*, and *Antioch*, have erred; so also the Church of *Rome* hath erred, not only in their living and manner of Ceremonies, but also in matters of Faith.

ART. XX. Of the Authority of the Church.

THE Church hath power to decree Rites or Ceremonies, and authority in Controversies of Faith: and yet it is not lawful for the Church to ordain any thing that is contrary to God's Word written, neither may it so expound one place of Scripture, that it be repugnant to another. Wherefore, although the Church be a witness and a keeper of Holy Writ, yet, as it ought not to decree any thing against the same, so besides the same ought it not to enforce any thing to be believed for necessity of Salvation.

ART. XXI. Of the Authority of General Councils.*

ART. XXII. Of Purgatory.

THE Romish Doctrine concerning Purgatory, Pardons, Worshipping and Adoration, as well of Images as of Relics, and also Invocation of Saints, is a fond thing, vainly invented, and grounded upon no warranty of Scripture, but rather repugnant to the Word of God.

ART. XXIII. Of Ministering in the Congregation.

IT is not lawful for any man to take upon him the office of public preaching, or ministering the Sacraments in the Congregation, before he be lawfully called, and sent to execute the same. And those we ought to judge lawfully called and sent, which be chosen and called to this work by men who have public authority given unto them in the Congregation, to call and send Ministers into the Lord's vineyard.

ART. XXIV. Of Speaking in the Congregation in such a Tongue as the people understandeth.

IT is a thing plainly repugnant to the Word of God, and the custom of the Primitive Church, to have public Prayer in the Church, or to minister the Sacraments, in a tongue not understanded of the people.

* The Twenty-first of the former Articles is omitted; because it is partly of a local and civil nature, and is provided for, as to the remaining parts of it, in other Articles.

ART. XXV. Of the Sacraments.

SACRAMENTS ordained of Christ be not only badges or tokens of Christian men's profession, but rather they be certain sure witnesses, and effectual signs of grace, and God's good will towards us, by the which he doth work invisibly in us, and doth not only quicken, but also strengthen and confirm our Faith in him.

There are two Sacraments ordained of Christ our Lord in the Gospel, that is to say, Baptism, and the Supper of the Lord.

Those five commonly called Sacraments, that is to say, Confirmation, Penance, Orders, Matrimony, and Extreme Unction, are not to be counted for Sacraments of the Gospel, being such as have grown partly of the corrupt following of the Apostles, partly are states of life allowed in the Scriptures; but yet have not like nature of Sacraments with Baptism, and the Lord's Supper, for that they have not any visible sign or ceremony ordained of God.

The Sacraments were not ordained of Christ to be gazed upon, or to be carried about, but that we should duly use them. And in such only as worthily receive the same, they have a wholesome effect or operation: but they that receive them unworthily, purchase to themselves damnation, as Saint *Paul* saith.

ART. XXVI. Of the Unworthiness of the Ministers, which hinders not the effect of the Sacraments.

ALTHOUGH in the visible Church the evil be ever mingled with the good, and sometimes the evil have chief authority in the Ministration of the Word and Sacraments, yet forasmuch as they do not the same in their own name, but in Christ's, and do minister by his commission and authority, we may use their Ministry, both in hearing the Word of God, and in receiving the Sacraments. Neither is the effect of Christ's ordinance taken away by their wickedness, nor the grace of God's gifts diminished from such as by faith, and rightly, do receive the Sacraments ministered unto them; which be effectual, because of Christ's institution and promise, although they be ministered by evil men.

Nevertheless, it appertaineth to the discipline of the Church, that inquiry be made of evil Ministers, and that they be accused by those that have knowledge of their offences; and finally, being found guilty, by just judgment be deposed.

ART. XXVII. *Of Baptism.*

BAPTISM is not only a sign of profession, and mark of difference, whereby Christian men are discerned from others that be not christened, but it is also a sign of Regeneration or New-Birth, whereby, as by an instrument, they that receive Baptism rightly are grafted into the Church; the promises of the forgiveness of sin, and of our adoption to be the sons of God by the Holy Ghost, are visibly signed and sealed; Faith is confirmed, and Grace increased by virtue of prayer unto God.

The Baptism of young Children is in any wise to be retained in the Church, as most agreeable with the institution of Christ.

ART. XXVIII. *Of the Lord's Supper.*

THE Supper of the Lord is not only a sign of the love that Christians ought to have among themselves one to another: but rather it is a Sacrament of our Redemption by Christ's death: insomuch that to such as rightly, worthily, and with faith, receive the same, the Bread which we break is a partaking of the Body of Christ; and likewise the Cup of Blessing is a partaking of the Blood of Christ.

Transubstantiation (or the change of the substance of Bread and Wine) in the Supper of the Lord, cannot be proved by Holy Writ: but is repugnant to the plain words of Scripture, overthroweth the nature of a Sacrament, and hath given occasion to many superstitions.

The Body of Christ is given, taken, and eaten, in the Supper, only after an heavenly and spiritual manner. And the mean whereby the Body of Christ is received and eaten in the Supper, is Faith.

The Sacrament of the Lord's Supper was not by Christ's ordinance reserved, carried about, lifted up, or worshipped.

ART. XXIX. *Of the Wicked, which eat not the Body of Christ in the use of the Lord's Supper.*

THE Wicked, and such as be void of a lively faith, although they do carnally and visibly press with their teeth (as Saint *Augustine* saith) the Sacrament of the Body and Blood of Christ; yet in no wise are they partakers of Christ: but rather, to their condemnation, do eat and drink the sign or Sacrament of so great a thing.

ART. XXX. *Of both Kinds.*

THE Cup of the Lord is not to be denied to the Lay-people: for both the parts of the Lord's Sacrament, by Christ's ordinance and commandment, ought to be ministered to all Christian men alike.

ART. XXXI. *Of the one Oblation of Christ finished upon the Cross.*

THE Offering of Christ once made is that perfect redemption, propitiation, and satisfaction, for all the sins of the whole world, both original and actual; and there is none other satisfaction for sin, but that alone. Wherefore the sacrifices of Masses, in the which it was commonly said, that the Priest did offer Christ for the quick and the dead, to have remission of pain or guilt, were blasphemous fables, and dangerous deceits.

ART. XXXII. *Of the Marriage of Priests.*

BISHOPS, Priests, and Deacons, are not commanded by God's Law, either to vow the estate of single life, or to abstain from marriage: therefore it is lawful for them, as for all other Christian men, to marry at their own discretion, as they shall judge the same to serve better to godliness.

ART. XXXIII. *Of excommunicate Persons, how they are to be avoided.*

THAT person which by open denunciation of the Church is rightly cut off from the unity of the Church, and excommunicated, ought to be taken of the whole multitude of the faithful, as an Heathen and Publican, until he be openly reconciled by penance, and received into the Church by a Judge that hath authority thereunto.

ART. XXXIV. *Of the Traditions of the Church.*

IT is not necessary that Traditions and Ceremonies be in all places one, or utterly like; for at all times they have been divers, and may be changed ac-

cording to the diversity of countries, times, and men's manners, so that nothing be ordained against God's Word. Whosoever, through his private judgment, willingly and purposely, doth openly break the Traditions and Ceremonies of the Church, which be not repugnant to the Word of God, and be ordained and approved by common authority, ought to be rebuked openly, (that others may fear to do the like,) as he that offendeth against the common order of the Church, and hurteth the authority of the Magistrate, and woundeth the consciences of the weak brethren.

Every particular or national Church hath authority to ordain, change, and abolish, Ceremonies or Rites of the Church ordained only by man's authority, so that all things be done to edifying.

ART. XXXV. *Of the Homilies.*

THE Second Book of Homilies, the several titles whereof we have joined under this Article, doth contain a godly and wholesome Doctrine, and necessary for these times, as doth the former Book of Homilies, which were set forth in the time of *Edward the Sixth*; and therefore we judge them to be read in Churches by the Ministers, diligently and distinctly, that they may be understanded of the people.

OF THE NAMES OF THE HOMILIES.

1 *Of the right Use of the Church.*
2 *Against Peril of Idolatry.*
3 *Of repairing and keeping clean of Churches.*
4 *Of good Works: first of Fasting.*
5 *Against Gluttony and Drunkenness.*
6 *Against Excess of Apparel.*

7 Of Prayer.
8 Of the Place and Time of Prayer.
9 That Common Prayers and Sacraments ought to be ministered in a known tongue.
10 Of the reverend Estimation of God's Word.
11 Of Alms-doing.
12 Of the Nativity of Christ.
13 Of the Passion of Christ.
14 Of the Resurrection of Christ.
15 Of the worthy receiving of the Sacrament of the Body and Blood of Christ.
16 Of the Gifts of the Holy Ghost.
17 For the Rogation-days.
18 Of the State of Matrimony.
19 Of Repentance.
20 Against Idleness.
21 Against Rebellion.

[This Article is received in this Church, so far as it declares the Books of Homilies to be an explication of Christian doctrine, and instructive in piety and morals. But all references to the constitution and laws of England are considered as inapplicable to the circumstances of this Church; which also suspends the order for the reading of said Homilies in churches, until a revision of them may be conveniently made, for the clearing of them, as well from obsolete words and phrases, as from the local references.]

ART. XXXVI. Of Consecration of Bishops and Ministers.

THE Book of Consecration of Bishops, and Ordering of Priests and Deacons, as set forth by the General Convention of this Church in 1792, doth contain all things necessary to such Consecration and

Ordering; neither hath it any thing that, of itself, is superstitious and ungodly. And, therefore, whosoever are consecrated or ordered according to said Form, we decree all such to be rightly, orderly, and lawfully consecrated and ordered.

ART. XXXVII. Of the Power of the Civil Magistrates.

THE Power of the Civil Magistrate extendeth to all men, as well Clergy as Laity, in all things temporal; but hath no authority in things purely spiritual. And we hold it to be the duty of all men who are professors of the Gospel, to pay respectful obedience to the Civil Authority, regularly and legitimately constituted.

ART. XXXVIII. Of Christian Men's Goods, which are not common.

THE Riches and Goods of Christians are not common, as touching the right, title, and possession of the same; as certain Anabaptists do falsely boast. Notwithstanding, every man ought, of such things as he possesseth, liberally to give alms to the poor, according to his ability.

ART. XXXIX. Of a Christian Man's Oath.

AS we confess that vain and rash Swearing is forbidden Christian men by our Lord Jesus Christ, and James his Apostle, so we judge, that Christian Religion doth not prohibit, but that a man may swear, when the Magistrate requireth, in a cause of faith and charity, so it be done according to the prophet's teaching, in justice, judgment, and truth.